"While many North American Catholics today play down their tradition's historic devotion to Mary, pronouncements about her exalted status remain official Catholic dogma and prove highly influential on most other continents. Svendsen painstakingly examines every biblical reference to Mary, in dialogue with major apologists for traditional Catholicism, and convincingly demonstrates how little biblical support there is for treating Mary differently from any other believer. No other work available today surveys this landscape in quite this way."

—Dr. Craig L. Blomberg
Professor of New Testament, Denver Seminary

"No single subject better illustrates the differences between Protestants and Roman Catholics on the interpretation and sufficiency of Scripture than does the role and status of Mary, the mother of our Lord. For the Roman Catholic, Mary is an essential part of the Gospel message and Christian discipleship. For the Protestant, she is a highly regarded but fallible disciple of the Lord. Rome says that she is an impeccable co-mediatrix. Geneva says that she is a sinner saved by grace, but called to an extraordinary task in the kind providence of God. Who is right? What saith the Lord? What does the Bible say? Eric Svendsen graciously but rigorously surveys the New Testament material, in constant interaction with Rome's best scholarly representatives. When he is done, no doubt is left on the matter. Roman Marian devotion is without a shred of legitimacy based on the New Testament witness. I challenge any impartial reader to read Scott Hahn's treatment of Mariology and then read Eric Svendsen, and then answer a question: 'Does the Roman Catholic teaching on Mary square with the Bible's teaching on Mary?' I can already give you the answer!"

—J. Ligon Duncan III, Ph.D.
Senior Minister, First Presbyterian Church, Jackson, Mississippi
Adjunct Professor of Systematic Theology,
Reformed Theological Seminary
Council Member, Alliance of Confessing Evangelicals

"Today, as much as ever, Christians need to understand the difference between Roman Catholicism and Biblical Christianity, and in this discussion the Biblical teaching regarding the person and role of Mary looms large. Indeed, I have found that in the minds of many sincere Roman Catholics, this is the issue that divides them from the Evangelical faith of their friends. For this discussion, Svendsen has given us more information than is available in any other single book and has provided a reliable reference on the subject. His exegetical work is thorough, his conclusions are objective, and his writing is clear, helpful, and non-offensive. It is a pleasure to commend this most timely book."

—FRED G. ZASPEL
Pastor, Word of Life Baptist Church, Pottsville, PA
Emanuel Church, Minersville, PA
Adjunct Lecturer in New Testament, Pennsylvania State University
Author of *The Theology of Fulfillment*

"Dr. Svendsen is to be warmly commended for this winsome study of New Testament Mariology. His detailed analysis of the biblical evidence about Mary gives Evangelicals the resources to appreciate and understand a subject they have often tended to ignore due to their opposition of the Roman Catholic exaltation of Mary. Right-minded though this opposition is, they do need to know what Scripture teaches on this subject. Svendsen's solid biblical exegesis also shows, however, that there are absolutely no Scriptural foundations for the distinctive aspects of Roman Catholic teaching on Mary. Roman Catholic theology and piety have deeply erred in this regard and have no God-given mandate for what they teach about the mother of Jesus. I highly recommended this as must reading in a day when the lines between Roman Catholic and Evangelical are being blurred."

—MICHAEL A. G. HAYKIN
Professor of Church History,
Heritage Theological Seminary, Cambridge, Ontario

"*Who Is My Mother?* by Eric D. Svendsen incorporates the best sort of holistic argument for a controversial theological topic. Dealing with the question of the exaltation of Mary in Roman Catholic theology and her elevation to mediatorial status, Svendsen makes biblical exposition the key contributor to his argument. His exposition, however, brims with pertinency for he allows history to inform the texts and the particular questions he asks about the texts. Every key text used for the development of Mariology, or even Mariolatry, is subjected to careful scrutiny. Bibliographical knowledge, theological reasoning, logical examination, historical awareness, and clear biblical interpretation form the substance of each chapter. I give my humble but heart-convicted endorsement of this book. I know of no other such clear and thorough treatment of one of the central dividing points between Roman Catholics and Evangelical Protestants."

—TOM J. NETTLES
Professor of Historical theology,
The Southern Baptist Theological Seminary, Louisville, KY

"Eric Svendsen has given us a capable treatment of the Protestant view of Mary, the mother of Our Lord. Avoiding the extremes of adoration and hostility, he articulates a careful biblical Mariology, and yes, there is such a thing."

—DOUGLAS WILSON
Author, Editor of *Credenda Agenda* Magazine,
Senior Fellow at New St. Andrews College,
Pastor of Christ Church, Moscow, Idaho

"Dr. Svendsen's study of Mary illustrates a basic theorem of Christian theology, namely, that any addition to the truth is always a subtraction from it. Is Jesus Christ the church's only, sufficient Savior and Mediator, yes or no? And was Mary fully like us, sin included, yes or no? There's a lot at stake in our answer to these questions. *Who is My Mother?* helps both Roman Catholics and Protestants respond with a biblical yes to both. What better way to honor both Jesus and Mary?"

—NELSON D. KLOOSTERMAN
Professor of Ethics and New Testament,
Mid-America Reformed Seminary, Dyer, Indiana

Who Is My Mother?

Who Is My Mother?

THE ROLE AND STATUS OF THE
MOTHER OF JESUS IN THE
NEW TESTAMENT AND
ROMAN CATHOLICISM

Eric D. Svendsen

2001
CALVARY PRESS · AMITYVILLE, NEW YORK

Calvary Press Publishing
Post Office Box 805
Amityville, NY 11701
1-800-789-8175
www.calvarypress.com

Book design and typography by Studio E Books
Santa Barbara, CA www.studio-e-books.com

Cover photo: Donatello (c. 1386–1466). Madonna Pazzi.
Copyright Vanni/Art Resource, NY. Staatliche Museen, Berlin, Germany.

Svendsen, Eric D., 1960–
    Who Is My Mother? : The Role and Status of the Mother of Jesus in the New Testament and Roman Catholicism / by Eric D. Svendsen.
    ISBN 1-879737-45-0
Suggested subject headings:
    1. Christianity—doctrines.
    2. Religion
    I. Title

10 9 8 7 6 5 4 3 2 1

*To the unsung few in Christ's church
who fearlessly advance the truth*

ACKNOWLEDGEMENTS

There are many who were instrumental in the development of this book, and to whom I owe a debt of gratitude: Dr. Carl Judson Davis, who offered invaluable suggestions in the early stages of this work; Dr. James White, who greatly aided my research of Matthew 1:25 by graciously allowing me use of his Thesaurus Linguae Graecae program; Dr. F. N. Sutherland (Greenwich School of Theology, U.K.) and Prof. Francois Viljoen (Potchefstroom University), who promoted my work at GST and provided helpful suggestions; and Dr. D. A. Carson (Trinity Evangelical Divinity School), my former mentor, whose excellence in scholarship and style of writing continue to inspire me. To these, and to the others who in various ways inspired me to press on in this work, many thanks.

Contents

Foreword

On October 17, 1904, Pope Pius X, calling Mary the Spouse of the Holy Ghost, announced that "already Adam saw her in the distance as the destroyer of the serpent's head, and at the sight of her dried up his tears over the curse which had struck him"; the Pope goes on to assert that Noah recalled her while he was preparing the Ark; Abraham was actually stopped from sacrificing Isaac by thinking of Mary; Jacob saw Mary in the ladder on which angels were ascending and descending; and even Moses looked up to Mary when he gazed at the burning bush.

This kind of exaltation and worship of Mary fills the piety and religious experience of the majority of the Popes of the last few centuries. As a result, Marian piety has exploded, becoming the central religious experience of many who wear the scapular, pray the Rosary, and bow before statues of the Virgin, seeking her intercession and aid.

It is an act of kindness and love to identify this kind of religious activity truthfully and honestly in the light of God's Word: it is idolatry, plain and simple. The person who truly desires to call the historical Mary of Nazareth "blessed" will oppose the false Mariolatry of Rome and instead do as Mary did: direct others away from herself, and solely to her divine Son, the Lord Jesus Christ.

Dr. Eric Svendsen has provided the evangelical community at large a great service in this day of compromise and apathy in writing *Who Is My Mother?* With the resurgence of Roman Catholic apologetics in our day, such a work is a welcome addition to the arsenal of truth already available to the person who wishes to refute the rampant falsehoods that fill the slick magazines and polished books of Rome's ardent defenders. The evangelist seeking to communicate the gospel message to the zealous follower of Mary will reap a rich harvest in the pages of Dr. Svendsen's work. I especially appreciate the ground-breaking study of the phrase ἕως οὗ and its relevance to Matthew 1:25 and the doctrine of "perpetual virginity." And surely the honest reader will be struck by the vast exegetical difference that separates a sober, serious work such as this, and that found in the most popular of Rome's apologists.

But one would be remiss to pass over the great value of the positive inquiry into the truly *biblical* Mary, the Mary lost to many a Protestant due to an understandably negative reaction to the Roman exaltation of the faithful servant of the Lord. The Christian reader cannot help but be blessed by the in-depth study of the Word's testimony to Mary as given by the inspired authors of Scripture.

JAMES WHITE
Director, Alpha and Omega Ministries

Preface

The place of Mary in the church has long been a topic of debate between Roman Catholics and Evangelicals. The former camp tends to portray Mary as the most exalted of God's creatures, something of a demigod between the rest of mankind and the Trinity; while the latter camp, in contrast, not only denies this place for Mary, but tends to downplay any significance of Mary at all. My own interest in this issue can be traced to my active involvement in dialoguing with Roman Catholic apologists and scholars on many distinctively Roman Catholic issues (including this one), culminating in the present work—which is in essence my Ph.D. dissertation, submitted to the faculty of theology at Greenwich School of Theology, U.K.

I find the issue of Mary fascinating because of the *prima facie* disparity between the Roman Catholic view of Mary and that of the New Testament. Through focused reading on this topic I have arrived at a much greater understanding of the theological rationale for the Roman Catholic position, and I have as a result learned to appreciate the contributions toward a biblical Mariology made by both sides. Still, as a survey of the existing literature will reveal, the contributions from each side, at least so far as an Evangelical perspective is concerned, have been less than satisfying. In spite of the progress that has been made since Vatican II, the tendency on the Roman Catholic side to read the Marian texts in far too favorable a light is still highly prevalent. Somewhat surprisingly, this tendency also exists among some on the Protestant side. Many Protestants, either in the interest of ecumenism (particularly among those who have spearheaded the dialogue between Roman Catholics and Lutherans), or for lack of sufficiently close examination of the relevant texts, have conceded ground that exegetically they should have upheld. A sound, even-handed treatment of the issues from a thoroughgoing Evangelical perspective has been thus far lacking from the discussion.

This treatment of the mother of Jesus seeks to fill that void. It reexamines the New Testament Marian texts from an Evangelical perspective and seeks to show how the New Testament writers viewed the mother of Jesus in her person, role and status. The intent of such an endeavor is to call attention to the fact that, in the development of a *biblical* Mariology, we must allow our thoughts to be guided entirely by the New Testament writers themselves, apart from any preconceived notions we may hold about Mary. It is with that firm foundation in place that we proceed.

Eric Svendsen

Who Is My Mother?

An Overview of Mariology

The literature on Mary is voluminous. Treatment of Marian issues range from historical development of her role in the church, to the theology behind her various titles, to devotional studies. Obviously, with such a wide range of issues one must limit any inquiry to one aspect of Mariology. This study will therefore focus only on the direct NT evidence for the role of Mary in the Church. This will address most of the teachings of Roman Catholic Mariology, but unfortunately will not go into detail concerning the two sole infallibly proclaimed Marian dogmas—the Immaculate Conception and the Assumption of Mary. Such articles of faith, while important to any study of current views on Mary, are issues of theological inquiry—based on *a priori* theological constructs and symbolic readings of the Bible, and not on any direct NT evidence; they are therefore outside the scope of this study, except where an examination of the specific biblical texts that are adduced in support of these beliefs necessitates a brief comment.

Moreover, we will not enter into discussion on the virgin birth. While such a discussion has its place in Marian studies, it is usually an issue only for those works that either deny its historicity or that engage in polemic against such a denial. Since this work is neither, and since its targeted audience is the conservative wing of Catholicism and Protestantism—both of which affirm the historicity of the virgin birth—we will not attempt to prove what is already common ground. There will therefore be no need to examine potential Marian references in the Pauline writings.[1]

Purpose of the Undertaking

Recent attempts among conservative Roman Catholic scholars and apologists to define a biblical Mariology have resulted in an uneasy "Romanizing" of the biblical data that has yet to be balanced by an even-handed Evangelical treatment. One scholar puts the issue this way:

> Everything suggests that Protestantism is being challenged to deal more intensively with these questions [of Mariology], and to reply to them more in detail than it has done up to date. Protestant theology also will in the immediate future find itself no longer able to dispense with the theme of Mary in the customary fashion.... It would [not] be Protestant...if the Protestant contribution were not *biblical*. This is the place where contributions on the Protestant side have been inadequate, and the real exegetical treatment of the theme is only now beginning.... *Mary must be defended from becoming the product of our pious imagination*.... The most important fruit of a Protestant contribution might then well be, that behind the rank foliage of a mystical and uncontrolled "Mariology," the real picture of our Lord's mother would be revealed in new astringency, simplicity, and beauty.[2]

That is what this work attempts to do. By examining current Roman Catholic belief regarding Mary, and comparing that belief to the biblical evidence, it is the hope of this author that the dialogue surrounding Marian issues might be tempered by sound exegesis that is at once scholarly and thoroughly Evangelical. We shall begin our inquiry in this chapter by first noting the background for this study; including the influence of Vatican II for Rome's current understanding of Marian issues. We will then spend time defining terms, including those involving current Marian titles and roles. Finally, we shall conclude this chapter with a brief history of Mariology so as to set the stage for the current Marian climate, as well as for the exegesis of the relevant biblical passages that follows in subsequent chapters.

Background of the Issues

It is acknowledged by the majority of Roman Catholic scholars that the Bible offers little support for the full-blown Mariology that is prevalent among the Roman Catholic masses. It must ever be kept in mind while reading through the biblical record that the NT writers, for the most part, wrote toward the latter part of their lives, and that whatever beliefs they held about Mary would have been fully or nearly fully developed by that time. It is revealing that the things they write not only do not give special significance to Mary, but actually portray her at times in an unflattering light. Objections from conservative Roman Catholic apologists, that this agreement by the majority of Catholic scholars with the general Protestant view is based upon historical criticism and does not therefore represent the official Roman Catholic position, are without warrant. For while it is true that these scholars, using the same historical-critical methods, reject the historicity of a good portion of the gospels as well, it is equally true that many of them point out quite apart from historical-critical considerations that even the *prima facie* reading of the Marian texts yields no support for the inflated Roman Catholic position on Mary. Moreover, the assumption of conservative Roman Catholic apologists that theirs is the official Roman Catholic position (over against the majority of Roman Catholic scholars, who take a decidedly more moderate position) is based on a misreading of the encyclical "Pascendi" in the Syllabus of Pius X (1907) in which he condemns liberalism ("modernism") in general terms, but makes no specific application to the moderate segment of Roman Catholicism.

Consequently, moderate Roman Catholic scholars such as R. Brown, J. A. Fitzmyer and J. L. McKenzie are considered to be well within the pale of official Roman Catholic teaching, and indeed are more representative of this teaching than are conservatives who make up the minority position. Indeed, these same scholars have insisted that the historical-critical method implies no denial of divine inspiration and is in accord with Pope Pius XII's 1943 encyclical, *Divino Afflante Spiritu*, in which he advocates the principle of acknowledging the differences of literary forms in the Bible.[3] Pope John Paul II's recent statements concerning his acceptance of the legitimacy of evolutionary theory, with its attendant ramifications for the literal reading of

Genesis 1–2, does not help the cause of the conservative wing of Roman Catholicism. Most conservative Roman Catholics would uphold the special creation of Adam and Eve as fully developed human beings and reject the mythical reading of Genesis held by the majority of Roman Catholic scholars; but the pope's statements suggest that he is coming down on the side of the historical-critical and mythical reading of the Bible.

Hans Küng, relating the events at Vatican II (1962–1965), informs us that the proposal to draw up a separate document on Mary was rejected by a slim majority of the council (1,114 votes to 1,074), and Marian doctrine was instead incorporated within the larger Constitution on the Church (*Lumen Gentium*). The council further "explicitly warned against Marian exaggerations."[4] Since that time Marian emphasis has waned considerably from the excesses found in the period just prior to the council. McKenzie witnesses to this same phenomenon when he says: "When I studied theology nearly fifty years ago, my professor said that this belief [Mary as Mediatrix of all grace] was ripe for dogmatic definition [by the pope]; now it has fallen into the Marian silence."[5]

Nevertheless, the issue of Mary is still an Achilles' heel to many Roman Catholic scholars who would rather downplay the current Marian emphasis among Roman Catholics: "The more the Marian superstructure has been developed, the more it has estranged Christians from Jews, the Church from the New Testament, Evangelical from Catholic Christians, and Christians in general from modern man."[6] Tambasco indicates that Vatican II acted as a corrective to an inflated view of Mary when he notes that the council was a "watershed" that opened the door to new biblical and theological insights concerning Mary,[7] particularly in regard to a redirection of emphasis on just how to view Mary. Pre-Vatican II Mariology was marked by a view of Mary "from above,"[8] according to which Mary paralleled Christ and was seen to be "joined with Christ facing the Church in the work of redemption"[9]; that is to say, Mary was more a part of the divine order dispensing graces than a part of the church which needed redemption. This was based primarily on philosophical reasoning, and Scripture was used merely "to yield one or two lines of prooftext, often divorced from context."[10] Vatican II's *Lumen Gentium*, on the other hand, portrays an ecclesiotypical view of Mary "from below"; that is to say, a Mary who is "joined to the Church facing Christ and being redeemed by Christ."[11] Tambasco also sees significance in the fact that although almost half of the bishops at the council (following the pre-council emphasis on a "Mary from above") vied for a separate document on Mary (an issue which was "hotly debated"), they were voted down, and it was decided instead that a small section on Mary would be placed as chapter eight in the document on the Church[12] (which itself was merely one of sixteen documents composed at Vatican II): "It said by its very location that theology of Mary needs to be inserted into the context of other theology and that Mary needs to be seen…within the Church as fully redeemed herself."[13]

The primary reason that the majority of Roman Catholic scholars can so freely embrace the Protestant view of the biblical texts regarding Mary is that these scholars make a distinction between the historicity of the biblical texts and the biblical texts themselves. If Mary is portrayed in a less than flattering light by the NT writers, it is of no consequence for Roman Catholic belief. The latter is to be held as a matter of faith in spite of the often very real contradictions with the former. Tambasco rejects the objection by conservative Roman Catholic scholars (including Unger) that the historical accuracy of the Marian accounts in the gospels is assumed by Pope Paul VI (the presiding pope at the conclusion of Vatican II), since, as he argues, this does not properly distinguish the pope's use of biblical texts to exhort the faithful from his "authoritative *judgment* on the historicity of the texts themselves."[14] Indeed, in light of the council's bold closing messages to "men of thought and science," that they should continue their search "without tiring and without ever despairing of the truth,"[15] it seems odd that any Catholic scholar could deny, except perhaps by appealing to his own conservative interpretation of the words of the council, that biblical and historical criticism have been officially legitimized by the Roman Catholic Magisterium. In fact, most moderate Roman Catholic scholars simply assume its legitimacy: "The Mary of Christian legend, art, poetry, hymnody, and even theology is a fictitious character.… *Faith in the Mary of traditional Christian devotion is faith in something which is not true.*"[16]

Marian Roles

Roman Catholicism has in many ways attributed the unique role and activity of the Holy Spirit to Mary, in that she guides, inspires and acts as the link between the believer and Christ.[17] Tambasco points out that prior to Vatican II Roman Catholic Theology manuals had no section on the Holy Spirit, and that this "lack of an explicit treatment in the theology books [indicated] a lack of explicit awareness of the role of the Spirit, with some consequent lack of insight."[18] He further notes that the period between Trent and Vatican II was concurrently a time of great development in Mariology and a time of depreciation in Pneumatology. As a result:

> Roman Catholics tended to assign to Mary roles that could also be assign to the Spirit. Notable examples are found in the mottos or titles used frequently in Marian tradition: 'To Jesus through Mary'; 'Mary forms Christ in us'; Mary is the 'Mother of Good Counsel, the Source of grace, the Consoler.'[19]

The Eastern Orthodox also seem to be guilty of displacing the role of the Holy Spirit with that of Mary. For instance, Nissiotis writes:

> [Mary's] motherhood in the Church is a direct appeal for the unity of the Church on a charismatic basis by way of inviting our mutual repentance in the face of God and in obedience to him. We have to grow into 'the mature stature of a man' in faith (Eph. 4:13) by appreciating the charismata of the 'woman' as *Theotókos*, who as the Mother unites all members of the Body of Christ in one undivided family in unbroken continuity.[20]

It is not difficult to see in the above citation how Mary has replaced the Holy Spirit. Mary is the "charismatic" agent of "unity," "repentance," and spiritual "growth" in the body that unites all members into one undivided family—activities and terms that, so far as the NT is concerned, are reserved for the Holy Spirit. One wonders, if this is Mary's role, just what the Holy Spirit does in Eastern Orthodox theology.

On the other hand, Mary is often paralleled with Jesus. Jesus is born without the stain of original sin; and, in Roman Catholicism, so is Mary. Jesus lives a sinless life; as does Mary. Jesus remains a virgin all his life; Mary is Ever-Virgin. Jesus is the Redeemer; Mary is Co-Redemptress. Jesus is the one Mediator between man and God; Mary, too, is Mediatrix. Jesus is bodily assumed into heaven at the end of his earthly ministry; Mary is bodily assumed into heaven at the end of her earthly life. Børresen suggests a solution to this tendency among Roman Catholic interpreters to place Mary and Jesus in parallel:

> The main problem with Catholic discourse about Mary is *the disparity between the biblical data and the doctrinal interpretation put on it.…* The resulting gap between the Mary of Scripture and the Mary of Doctrine can easily be done away with by a Christological approach, in which it is only in Christ that the divine is made concretely manifest in the human. *Mary will thus be stripped of her Christological attributes.*[21] [emphasis in original]

Børresen's advice is sound, but not likely to be accepted by the majority of Roman Catholic exegetes who address Marian issues. To many of these exegetes, Mariology is not something that one adduces primarily from the biblical texts, but rather from the teaching of the Roman Catholic magisterium:

> In his endeavor to plumb the profound meaning of Sacred Scripture, the Catholic exegete enjoys a unique privilege. He is not left solely to the resources of patient scholarship. He is directed in his study and guided by the divinely appointed custodian and the authentic interpreter of the inspired word, the Magisterium. The Holy Spirit, whom the glorified Jesus sent upon his Church, teaches her all things.[22]

Obviously, no amount of exhortation to limit one's inquiry about Mary to the teachings of Scripture is likely to persuade those who follow Kugelman's approach above. Hence, we have an *a prior* impasse to hurdle if we are to arrive at a common Mariology.

Mary's Immaculate Conception

The Roman Catholic teaching regarding Mary's sinlessness finds its apex in the dogma of her Immaculate Conception. In his Constitution *Ineffabilis Deus* (1854), Pius IX defined the Marian dogma this way: "in the first instance of her conception, by a singular privilege and grace granted by God, in view of the merits of Jesus Christ, the Saviour of the human race, [she] was preserved exempt from all stain of original sin." This statement represents the final stage of development of the teaching about Mary's sinlessness, which had its inception several centuries after the Nicene period: "From the eighth century (John Damascene), it was considered fitting that, as Christ's mother, Mary should be purified of original sin."[23] It was originally thought, up to at least the time of Aquinas, that Mary was conceived in the normal way (i.e., with original sin), and that the first stage of her sanctification did not occur until sometime while still in the womb, the second and final stage in which she was totally purified of original sin not occurring until she conceived Christ.[24]

Roman Catholic belief in this Marian tenet differs somewhat from the Eastern church's sentiment. In the view of the Eastern Orthodox:

> The immaculate conception can only be praised, but it cannot be made the subject of dogma. The sinfulness becomes inactive, while original sin remains with Mary as a human being…. The Eastern Orthodox praise the *Theotókos* as an immaculate (*aspilos*) virgin and mother but without making a dogma of her exemption from original sin. The 'immaculate conception' taken literally is another rationalisation of the mystery from the human point of view, introducing as it does a gap between Mary and humankind in the most crucial and delicate issue of salvation.[25]

As we shall see, this view of Mary introduces an even more pronounced "gap" between Roman Catholic Mariology and NT Mariology, and consequently between Roman Catholic Mariology and Evangelical Mariology.

The Assumption of Mary

The Assumption of Mary represents yet another gap between Roman Catholic Mariology and Evangelical Mariology. According to this teaching, Mary was bodily assumed into heaven.[26] Although speculation abounds among Roman Catholic theologians whether this implies that Mary actually died,[27] most are of the opinion that we cannot know with certainty one way or the other. It is at this point that the Roman Catholic view of this issue differs from that of Eastern Orthodoxy:

> Though in its hymns the Eastern Tradition seems to adopt the idea of the 'bodily assumption' of the *Theotókos*, because one cannot admit that the body which held the divine Logos could ever perish, the teaching of the Church confessed unanimously that the *Theotókos* fully shared in the death of all human beings.[28]

Biblical support for this teaching is often adduced from the "woman clothed with the sun" in Revelation 12, although this interpretation of the Revelation was held by no one of standing for the first eight centuries of church history.[29] Moreover, the idea of Mary's assumption into heaven is found nowhere in the patristic literature of the second and third centuries.[30] The *MNT* taskforce (relying on the work of M. Jurgie whom the taskforce regards as the "foremost authority on this question"[31]), has shown that there is no witness to the notion of Mary's assumption in the patristic tradition prior to the Council of Nicaea.[32] Hence, the Assumption of Mary introduces yet another gap between the Roman Catholic view of Mary and the Evangelical view. As with the other distinctively Roman Catholic Marian beliefs, there is a disparity between the evidence we find in the Bible and in church history, and that which we find in Roman Catholic theology. We will examine this disparity in depth throughout this work.

Marian Titles

Equally important as the various roles and functions of Mary within Roman Catholicism are the Marian titles. She is the Ever-Virgin, the Co-Redemptress, and the Mediatrix of graces. Arguably, all of these titles have as their center yet another Marian title, Mother of God.

Mother of God

Mary is first and foremost in Roman Catholic theology the Mother of God:

> Traditional mariology has concentrated on Mary's identity as mother of God. This privileged link to Jesus Christ is the foundation on which the various attributes of Mary have been based and the fuel for most popular devotion to Mary though the ages. Mary's role as mother of Jesus is the fundamental datum of the New Testament and, ultimately, is the lynch pin for all other scriptural assertions about her.[33]

Tambasco points out that the title Mother of God came about through a logical syllogism: "the Bible says Mary is the mother of Jesus; it also says Jesus is God; therefore, it says equivalently that Mary is mother of God."[34] The nomenclature "Mother of God" finds its basis in the term *theotokos*, which was used by the framers of the councils of Ephesus (430) and Chalcedon (451). Yet, neither the title "Mother of God," nor any of its implied privileges, is consonant with the original intent of the term *theotokos*:

> The title *Theotokos*, is used not so much to say something about Mary as to say something about Jesus.... Recent Christology, emphasizing an approach 'from below,' finds the formula of Chalcedon in need of reformulation. The language has little meaning for contemporary society, and the formulation does not seem to allow enough room for a full treatment of the humanity of Jesus.[35]

Indeed, even at the time of the councils that used the term *theotokos* (literally, "God bearer"), another, more precise term, *mater theou* ("Mother of God") was in use as a supplemental term by Cyril of Alexandria, who spearheaded the council of Ephesus. Significantly, Cyril's supplemental term did not gain acceptance by the framers of either council. This title will be given detailed consideration later in this work.

Co-Redemptress/Mediatrix

In what way can Mary be considered Co-Redemptress or Mediatrix?

Tambasco explains that traditional Mariology distinguished between objective redemption (the work of Christ in salvation) and subjective redemption (the appropriation of that salvation to the individual). The ecclesiotypical Mariology "from below" tends toward associating Mary with the latter (although elements of the former are still present). She is not so much Co-Redemptrix as she is an associate of the Redeemer, insofar as she invites others to join in Christ's redemption—which, it must be stressed, is not to be seen as *qualitatively* different from the role of all other Christians who share that same role, even if to a lesser degree. And she is not so much Mediatrix (in the sense of playing a role between Christ and man) with a mediation of a different kind than all other Christians, as she is mediator like all other Christians, only perhaps to a greater degree.[36]

Yet even those who historically have held to the Christotypical Mariology "from above" have disagreed as to the exact relationship of Mary to these two options. Even today, the conservative wing of Catholicism stresses a unique role for Mary and insists that she be seen as playing a part in objective redemption. Yet even here there is disagreement as to whether her involvement is direct (i.e., through her dispensing of grace to individuals), or indirect (i.e., through her consent to bear the one who would eventually dispense grace).

A Brief History of Mariology

The majority of Roman Catholic scholars candidly admit with Perkins that most of the Marian dogmas in Roman Catholicism have little or no basis in Scripture: "Dogmas of this sort are not directly derived from New Testament evidence."[37] McKenzie puts it even more bluntly: "The New Testament affords *no historical basis for the beliefs in the immaculate conception or the assumption* of Mary."[38] But if these dogmas have no biblical support, then how did they originate? It will be helpful briefly to survey the history of Mariology and to trace the lines of developing thought around this issue.[39]

Mary in the Early Church

The first theological considerations about Mary after the NT era occur in Justin Martyr (*Dialogue with Trypho* 100) and Irenaeus (*Against Heresies* 3,22,4; 5,19,1). Both writers see a parallelism between Mary and Eve, in which Mary's obedience reverses the disobedience of Eve.[40] While the church of this period does refer to Mary as "the Virgin," she is never called "ever-virgin." Instead, the title "the Virgin" is always used with reference to what Mary was when Christ was conceived. In other words, it speaks not of her life's vocation (as some Roman Catholic interpreters understand it), but rather her calling in bringing forth the Christ in a virginal way. Aside from this, "the stories of Mary linked to the ministry of Jesus are of no interest to second and third century authors."[41] Indeed, "their primary interest lies in the 'virgin birth' of Jesus"[42]; and "one tradition even spoke of the Holy Spirit as 'mother' of Jesus."[43] Such a view of Mary is decidedly free of excesses.[44]

The Beginnings of a Developed Mariology

By the fourth century we begin to find traces of a Mariology that is decidedly at odds with the NT evidence. One of the earliest prayers to Mary occurs in either the late third or early fourth century, although we do not know who the author is and cannot be certain that it is a mainstream sentiment: "We fly to thy patronage, O holy mother of God. Despise not our petitions in our necessities; deliver us from all dangers, O glorious and blessed Virgin" (*Sub Tuum Praesidium*).

It is during this period that we also find the first instance of the title "Ever Virgin" (*aeiparthenos, semper virgo*), found in a dubious passage by Peter of Alexandria.[45] This idea of Mary's ever-virgin status propelled itself into the next century and subsequent patristic thought. However, the rationale for such an idea comes not from Christian sources, but rather Gnostic. Tambasco notes that the perceived need for Mary's perpetual virginity seems to have been based on the antiquated notion that sexuality is somehow associated with sin.[46] McKenzie concurs:

> At this point the student begins to sense the possible influence of some form of *gnosticism*; and he does not have to appeal to *ratio theologicae convenientiae* [arguments of theological priority] to know that in early Christianity there were forms of gnosticism which identified sexuality with sin and radical sinfulness. One knows that the belief that Mary conceived Jesus without what was for centuries called 'the stain of carnal commerce' suits gnostic ideals.[47]

As much as the fourth century was key in the development of Mario-logical innovations, the fifth century was even more so. It is not until the fifth century that hymns and prayers to Mary occur in the West,[48] and that devotion to Mary really arose in the Eastern church.[49] Christian art also began to emerge with more and more emphasis on Marian imagery:

> Scholars of early Christian history who have studied the origins of the links between the figure of Mary and imagery of the divine have found morphological similarities between the post-Constantinian ecclesial cult of Mary and the pervasive cults of the great mother in the Mediterranean world into which Christianity was moving…such similarities at least in superficially observable matters are simply a matter of historical fact.[50]

Johnson notes that the development of Marian imagery parallels the development of Mariology itself:

> The iconography of Mary seated with her child facing outward on her lap was arguably patterned on the prose of Isis with Horus, the mother herself an upright royal throne on which the god-king was presented to the world. In hymns reminiscent of the aretalogies of Isis she was praised with titles and attributes of female deities, as all-holy, merciful, wise, the universal mother…protector of…all who called on her in need. In prayers patterned on petitions to the great mother, Mary was directly invoked as protector and asked to deliver simple people from danger.[51]

Shinners explains that during this period Marian champions, such as Cyril of Alexandria (who spearheaded the condemnation of Nestorius for rejecting the title of *Theotokos* in favor of the more balanced *Christotokos*), began to take on the cause of Mary:

> The real impetus for the cult [of Mary] begins at the council of Ephesus in 431, when—partly by virtue of the shrewd political maneuvering of Cyril of Alexandria—the dogmatic definition of Mary as theotokos…was declared. Cyril's victory

over his Nestorian opponents ensured the success of the cult of Mary because it underscored her unique role as the bearer of God. While church fathers and later theologians preferred the ambiguous term—in either Greek or Latin—'God-bearer' to 'mother of God' (a title first officially used of Mary at the Second Vatican Council) it is easy to see how this fine distinction would be lost on ordinary people.[52]

Still, as Børresen has noted, even here Mary is referred to only in Christological contexts, and the title *Theotokos* referred to "the act of giving birth, not to motherhood in general,"[53] which would have been the case had the framers of the councils used *mater theou* instead of *theotokos*. "The first council to use *mater Dei* [*mater theou*] was Vatican II" in its *lumen gentium*.[54] It is not until later, then, that we see evidence for a full-blown Roman Catholic Mariology.

The Apex of Mariology

By the eleventh and twelfth centuries, devotion to Mary became widespread. The pervasive view of Jesus as King in a feudal society carried with it certain negative connotations, which had a distancing effect on the rank and file. Johnson notes that it is at this time that the parallelism between Jesus and Mary as Redeemer/Co-Redemptress became prominent: "While Jesus Christ was acknowledged as gracious Savior, his function of judging frequently overshadowed the quality of his mercy, which in turn was attributed abundantly to Mary."[55] Shinners explains that Jesus:

> along with the awesome figure of his Father, was king and judge. Like the distant feudal kings whom ordinary people seldom encountered but whose justice was all too sure…Christ was much too powerful, much too threatening to be approached directly. It made much more sense to cultivate the attentions of his mother, who, like a kind-hearted feudal noblewoman, could bend her son's ear in one's favor.[56]

Shinners notes, moreover, that the names commonly associated with Mary, including Our Lady, Notre Dame, and Madonna, were respectful titles given to feudal aristocrats. It is not difficult to see how this devotion to Mary gave rise to modern Marian veneration. Although, as McKenzie notes, "the New Testament affords *no basis for belief in Mary as the mediatrix of all grace*,"[57] by the eleventh and twelfth centuries no one was asking what the NT said regarding Mary. Shinners notes that during this period Mary's role as mediatrix "became enormously popular…[and by this time, her] maternal mediation with Jesus is commonplace."[58] Shinners points to one example of this excessive mariology in an English monk by the name Eadmer, a student of Anselm, who writes: "Sometimes salvation is quicker if we remember Mary's name than if we invoke the name of the Lord Jesus."[59] In another example, a French historian and theologian of that era expresses his sentiments in this way: "Christ…cannot, I am sure, refuse [Mary] anything; and what she demands, not by asking but by *commanding*, will surely come to pass."[60]

As bold as Mariology was in the eleventh and twelfth centuries, it was bolder still in the sixteenth century, which century marked not only the true beginning of the apex of Mariology, but the Reformation and Counter Reformation as well. Even in Christian art, Mary's figure "had taken on divinized attributes and functions borrowed not from the ancient goddess but from the Christian Trinity itself."[61] In short, Mariology " was at its worst from the time of the counter-reformation until the early twentieth century, the heyday of 'mariolatry'."[62] Indeed, by this time, Erasmus, annoyed by the excesses that had become rampant in devotion to Mary, writes: "No veneration of Mary is more beautiful than the imitation of her humility."[63]

Shinners traces numerous examples of this type of "mariolatry" from the period following the Reformation down to the present day; beliefs which include Mary's ability to save *even if God is bent on judgment*, and salvation through devotion to Mary alone.[64] Post-Tridentine Catholic theology "went so far as to develop arguments from 'fittingness,' holding that it was impossible to say too much about Mary. In her regard, if God could have done it, God should have done it, and therefore God did it!"[65] Excesses such as this lent credibility to the Protestant charge that Catholics "divinized" Mary in an idolatrous way. Johnson puts it this way:

> Mary at first paralleled and then occasionally outshone God the Father and especially God the Son. The power and

creativity of God the Father was mirrored in Mary who by virtue of her role at the incarnation which gave the world the Savior was in some way creative of all that was renewed.... Veneration directed to her in light of her recreative power included such acts as rewriting the psalms in order to substitute Mary for God as the acting subject of divine deeds and consequently as recipient of praise.[66]

One such instance in which a Psalm had been rewritten in honor—indeed, in adoration—of Mary reads as follows:

We praise thee, O Mother of God; we confess thee, Mary ever Virgin.... Thee all angels and archangels, thrones and principalities serve. Thee all powers and virtues of heaven and all dominations obey. Before thee all the angelic choirs, the cherubim and seraphim, exulting, stand. With unceasing voice every angelic creature proclaims thee: Holy, holy, holy, Mary Virgin Mother of God![67]

Johnson characterizes the situation accurately when she notes that Marian devotion during this time was based on the notion that by so honoring Mary, Jesus himself was honored since, as her son, he had in this way honored Mary as well. In effect, however, "this kind of devotion to the mother of God was actually devotion to God the Mother."[68] This same devotion, with its attendant explanation that it gives glory to God, has changed little in modern Roman Catholic piety, even if it *has* changed in Roman Catholicism's official documents: "Vatican II reversed a several hundred years' trajectory toward defining more and more Marian privileges. It presented Mary not as apart from us, but ahead of us."[69] While it is true that the new Catholic theology downplays the role and status of Mary in comparison to the way medieval theology portrayed her; still, to speak of Mary as "ahead" of all other Christians once again raises the question, "What saith the Scriptures?" It is to that source that we now turn.

CHAPTER I

Marian Issues in Matthew 1:18–25

Matthew 1:18–25 is a key text in any discussion about Mary's person and role in the church, as well as a major support for the orthodox view of the virgin birth of Christ. Conservative Roman Catholics and Evangelicals are in agreement on the latter, and so no attempt will be made here to enter into that discussion.[1] It is the former issue that concerns us here. The passage reads:

> This is how the birth of Jesus Christ[2] came about: His mother Mary was pledged to be married to Joseph, but before they came together, she was found to be with child through the Holy Spirit. Because Joseph her husband was a righteous man and did not want to expose her to public disgrace, he had in mind to divorce her quietly. But after he had considered this, an angel of the Lord appeared to him in a dream and said, "Joseph son of David, do not be afraid to take Mary home as your wife, because what is conceived in her is from the Holy Spirit. She will give birth to a son, and you are to give him the name Jesus, because he will save his people from their sins." All this took place to fulfill what the Lord had said through the prophet[3]: "The virgin will be with child and will give birth to a son, and they will call him Immanuel"—which means, "God with us." When Joseph woke up, he did what the angel of the Lord had commanded him and took Mary home as his wife. But he had no union with

her until she gave birth to a son.[4] And he gave him the name Jesus.[5]

The Meaning of the Phrase "before they came together"

What is meant by the phrase "before they came together" (πρὶν ἢ συνελθεῖν αὐτούς); sexual relations or living together?[6] John McHugh allows that the verb συνελθεῖν does in some instances have the meaning "to have sexual intercourse,"[7] but rejects that specific meaning here.[8] He concludes that the meaning "living together" is the proper exegesis here, but also that the virginity of Mary is implied since, although in Judaea sexual relations between a betrothed couple may have been allowed,[9] it was certainly frowned upon in Galilee where the custom was for the girl to remain a virgin until the marriage ceremony.[10]

No doubt McHugh is correct about the implications he draws for Mary's prenuptial virginity. Yet *this* implication from the verb συνελθεῖν cannot be maintained while the implication for sexual relations after marriage is denied—for this too was the normal custom for a betrothed Jewish couple, regardless of region.[11] Moreover, if we take this simply as a reference to Joseph and Mary taking up residence together without thought of ensuing sexual relations, Matthew's point regarding the virgin birth is then quite lost. If he is attempting to show (as he surely is in this passage) that the birth of Christ was a *virginal* birth, then the phrase "before they came together" must mean "before they engaged in sexual relations," and cannot mean "before they began to reside together platonically"; for if the latter is true then it would be no more remarkable—nor significant for that matter—that Mary became pregnant *before* they came together, than it would be if she became pregnant *after* they came together.

If, then, we are to adopt McHugh's interpretation, the passage offers no direct support for the virgin birth of Jesus. McHugh cannot have it both ways. Either Matthew intends for us to understand a virginal conception in this phrase, in which case πρὶν ἢ συνελθεῖν αὐτούς must also entail sexual relations after marriage; or Matthew, intending to preserve the perpetual virginity of Mary, wants us to understand the phrase πρὶν ἢ συνελθεῖν αὐτούς as nothing more than a platonic living arrangement, in which case support for the virgin birth of Jesus must be sought elsewhere.[12]

The Righteousness of Joseph

Matthew continues his narrative by relating to us Joseph's response to the news of Mary's pregnancy: "Because Joseph her husband was a righteous man and did not want to expose her to public disgrace, he had in mind to divorce her quietly." There are three main options for what is meant by the "righteousness" of Joseph: they are (1) Joseph's obedience to the law in refusing to be married to an adulteress, (2) Joseph's compassion and mercy in not exposing Mary's apparent infidelity, and (3) a double entendre of (1) and (2) above.

Senior[13] prefers the second option, while the *MNT* taskforce opts for the first and sees the specific law as Deut 22:20–21 which commands the stoning of a newly married woman who upon presentation to her husband is found not to be a virgin.[14] The obvious weakness with the latter position is that "obedience" to this law (and therefore the status of being "righteous") is bound up in the stoning of the woman; something Joseph did not contemplate doing. The *MNT* taskforce recognizes this and gives an alternative rendering: Joseph, as an observer of the spirit of the law in general (not specifically Deut 22:20–21), is "righteous" in refusing to consummate marriage with someone whom he suspects to be a violator of the law.[15]

McHugh finds fault with the first two options given above (and by extension, the third option as well) and proposes his own view. He argues that the views of Joseph's righteousness in terms of upholding the law of Moses or of showing compassion both *assume*, without warrant, that Joseph did not know *how* the child had been conceived.[16] The "righteous by law" view, argues McHugh, is weakened by the fact that it implies a conflict in Joseph's mind between obeying the law by divorcing and exposing Mary, and sparing Mary the disrepute associated with being an adulteress. This, he contends, cannot be reconciled with the text which states *not* that Joseph was a righteous man "but" (ἀλλά) did not wish to expose Mary; but rather that Joseph was a righteous man "and" (καί) did not wish to expose Mary. The two ideas are complimentary, not contradictory.[17]

Another weakness that McHugh sees in this view is that there was no moral obligation to divorce an unfaithful wife, and that examples from Hos 2:18–3:2 indicate that pardoning her was an option under the law.[18] Moreover, Joseph's plan to keep the divorce secret would have been "singularly inept" since (presumably due to the increasing obviousness of Mary's pregnancy) the story was bound to become public at some point.[19] McHugh notes that while the second view ("righteous by compassion") escapes the first two objections, it is still liable to the third.[20] He rejects both views on the grounds that they assume Joseph's ignorance about Mary's virginal conception until the point at which the angel announces it to him (1:20), and sees it as an odd contention that Mary would not have made mention to Joseph of such an astounding event as a visitation by an angel who proclaims to her that she will conceive as a virgin.[21] McHugh's alternative is to assume that Joseph knew about the angelic visit and the virginal conception, and that he believed Mary's report. His "righteousness" would then be defined in terms of his *humility* in withdrawing from marriage to a woman as divinely favored as Mary. He would have seen himself as unworthy to proceed with the marriage now that he knew of Mary's status as future mother of the Messiah. Joseph therefore desired to release his betrothed from her obligation to such a mundane thing as marriage to him.[22]

At this point McHugh launches into a long discussion about the proper way of taking the word δειγματίζω.[23] He takes pains to show that none of the meanings found in the major translations is required and that the "neutral" meaning is simply "to expose what is hidden."[24] The purpose for McHugh's distinction here is to show that there is no assumption on the part of Joseph that Mary had "failed in her duty of faithfulness."[25]

McHugh adduces final support for his view from Matt 1:20–21 where the angel appears to Joseph:

> But after he had considered this, an angel of the Lord appeared to him in a dream and said, "Joseph son of David,[26] do not be afraid to take Mary home as your wife, because what is conceived in her is from the Holy Spirit. She will give birth to a son, and you are to give him the name Jesus, because he will save his people from their sins."

McHugh admits that the *prima facie* reading of this passage seems to indicate that Joseph first learned of the virginal conception through the angel, not through Mary. He points out, however, that v. 18 *implies* Joseph's knowledge of the virginal conception in the words, "before they

came together, she was found to be with child *through the Holy Spirit.*"
If Joseph had not known about the virginal conception, McHugh argues, the final prepositional phrase would be meaningless. Moreover, the angel's words, "do not be afraid (μὴ φοβηθῇς) to take Mary home as your wife," indicate that Joseph's unwillingness to take Mary as his wife was not motivated by confusion over whether or not Mary had been faithful, but rather by a "fear" that he was unworthy to be associated with such a privileged woman as Mary. McHugh takes γὰρ as explaining Joseph's fear, so that we are to understand the verse this way: "Do not be afraid to take Mary as your wife. *I say this because* her child has been conceived by the Holy Ghost," by which McHugh means: "Do not be afraid to take Mary as your wife. I say this because *you are fearful over the fact that* her child has been conceived by the Holy Ghost."[27] McHugh assigns to δε; (v. 21) "its full adversative force": "*But,* she will give birth to a son, and you are to give him the name Jesus," hence reaffirming to Joseph what he already knew about Mary, and that he had a part to play in the plan.[28]

While McHugh raises some interesting observations about the text, he falls short of adequately explaining many of the questions that must be raised about his own position. McHugh's insistence that there is no warrant for the assumption that Joseph had no knowledge of Mary's visitation by the angel (his first objection to the other two views) may very well be valid (although nothing in the text can rule it out—perhaps Mary simply did not expect Joseph to believe her); but it does not negate the possibility that Joseph may have known about it but found it too incredible to believe. It could very well be that a confused Joseph may not have known what to believe. Wanting to believe his wife, but at the same time not wanting to take a chance that she was both unfaithful *and* untruthful, it would not be difficult to understand the action he chose under the circumstances.

McHugh's second objection to the "righteous by law" view (viz., that there was no moral obligation to divorce an unfaithful wife) oversimplifies the issue. The OT specifically commands, not divorce, but the *death* of the offender:

> If a man commits adultery with another man's wife—with the wife of his neighbor—both the adulterer and the adulteress must be put to death (Lev 20:10).… If, however, the charge

is true and no proof of the girl's virginity can be found, she shall be brought to the door of her father's house and there the men of her town shall stone her to death. She has done a disgraceful thing in Israel by being promiscuous while still in her father's house (Deut 22:20–21).… If a man is found sleeping with another man's wife, both the man who slept with her and the woman must die. You must purge the evil from Israel. If a man happens to meet in a town a virgin pledged to be married and he sleeps with her, you shall take both of them to the gate of that town and stone them to death—the girl because she was in a town and did not scream for help, and the man because he violated another man's wife. You must purge the evil from among you (Deut 22:24).

While it is true that first-century Israel had relaxed its rule in regard to putting the offenders to death, the reason was a political one—they were not allowed to carry out a death penalty under Roman rule.[29] So, while Joseph could not lawfully (under Roman rule) carry out the strict mandates of the law in putting Mary to death, he was no less obligated to do all that he could in removing himself from an alleged adulteress—divorce was his only viable option. McHugh's citation of Hos 2–3 is selective and does not overturn the general law concerning adultery. God used Hosea's marriage to a prostitute as an object lesson to illustrate how he has continued to love Israel in spite of her spiritual adultery. Indeed, the shock value of the object lesson is diminished if we assume that this was a normal and acceptable, alternative practice in Israel. We should no more see this as an acceptable alternative than God's command to Hosea at the beginning of this book: "Go, take to yourself an adulterous wife and children of unfaithfulness, because the land is guilty of the vilest adultery in departing from the LORD" (Hos 1:2). Hosea was to take back his wife after her adultery for the same reason that he was to marry her in the first place— merely as an illustrative device.

Joseph's "righteousness" makes better sense if we view it in terms of double entendre (a combination of righteousness according to the standards of the law and righteousness according to compassion). Although Joseph knew the child wasn't his, he could not be *absolutely* certain that Mary's story about the angel was a farce. There was always the chance that it happened just as she told it. The Mosaic law made provision for such cases of uncertainty about so important a matter: "If a man marries a woman who becomes displeasing to him because he finds something indecent about her, and he writes her a certificate of divorce, gives it to her and sends her from his house, and if after she leaves his house she becomes the wife of another man" (Deut 24:1–2). Although this part of the passage is only incidental to the thrust of the main instruction,[30] it does qualify as a provision for those who find "something indecent" about their wives, and the passage *assumes* divorce in such a case.[31] Joseph may also have connected this to Jer 3:8 where God divorces Israel for this same reason: "I gave faithless Israel her certificate of divorce and sent her away because of all her adulteries." McHugh's second objection to the "righteous according to law" view—namely, that there was no moral obligation to divorce an unfaithful wife—is thereby rendered baseless.

McHugh's third objection, which he applies to both the "righteous according to law" view as well as the "righteous according to compassion" view (viz., that Joseph's plan to keep the divorce secret would have been "singularly inept" since, presumably due to the increasing obviousness of Mary's pregnancy, the story was bound to become public at some point), may be leveled with equal force against his own view. It matters not that *Joseph* believed Mary's story; his plan to divorce her would still have resulted in scandal. As Mary's pregnancy became more and more obvious, so too would the fact that Joseph was conspicuously no longer on the scene. No matter what Joseph's motives for his decision, Mary would have suffered the same fate at the hands of the surrounding townspeople who would no doubt find her story too fantastic to be believed.

McHugh's alternative view, that Joseph's "righteousness" is wrapped up in his *humility* in withdrawing from marriage to a woman as divinely favored as Mary, and that he would have seen himself as unworthy to proceed with the marriage now that he knew of Mary's high calling, is plagued by much more serious difficulties. First, it is not the natural reading of the text and seems to be based more on romantic and pious notions of Joseph's personal worthiness to be the husband of Mary than on sound exegesis of the passage. McHugh as much as admits to this motivation when, in justifying his choice of options, he states that his view "satisfies that Christian piety which has ever regarded Joseph as a worthy partner of the Blessed Virgin."[32] Such a statement reveals polemic intent rather than exegetical soundness.

At the end of the day, McHugh's long discussion over the precise meaning of the word δειγματίζω seems open to several objections. The word occurs only here and in Col 2:15 in the NT, and both contexts demand the meaning "an exposure of something negative." BAGD cites several instances of the word in Hellenistic and Jewish literature, and all of them suggest the same negative connotation.[33] Moreover, if McHugh's view that Joseph knew about and believed Mary's virginal conception were correct, what need would there then be for Joseph to divorce Mary "quietly" (λάθρα)?[34] Why not instead boldly proclaim the situation? The inclusion of λάθρα here seems inexplicable if we are to assume that Joseph's intent was something other than to avoid exposing Mary to public shame. Indeed, his quiet bowing out of the situation could only have raised suspicion in the minds of onlookers and would have left Mary at the merciless hands of over-zealous enforcers of the law.

Perhaps the most obvious difficulty for McHugh's view is the angel's announcement in Matt 1:20. McHugh agrees that the *prima facie* reading lends strong support to the view that this is either the first Joseph heard the report, or the first he believed it.[35] Moreover, his appeal to the final phrase in Matt 1:18 ("before they came together, she was found to be with child *through the Holy Spirit*") offers little help for his view. There can be no serious objection to the possibility that Matthew included it as his own polemic to clarify the cause of Mary's pregnancy for his readers before recording the announcement of the angel to Joseph: "The audience is assured that Mary's pregnancy is without scandal, although Joseph is not privy to this crucial information."[36] In any event, McHugh's observation here would have little impact on the view that Joseph knew about the virginal conception but simply did not believe it.

McHugh's contention, that the angel's words, "do not be afraid," indicate that Joseph's unwillingness to take Mary as his wife was motivated by "fear" of unworthiness to be counted in such a grandiose plan, is not impossible. It seems precarious, however, to conclude that Joseph could not have experienced fear about the situation apart from McHugh's explanation. Joseph may have been afraid that Mary's unfaithfulness might continue even into the marriage; or he may have feared taking a wife who suffered from both promiscuity *and* delusions of grandeur in her claim to have been impregnated by God[37]—or, indeed, he may have feared the consequences that awaited both him and Mary if her seemingly blasphemous claim ever became public! Moreover, even if her claim to a virginal conception remained concealed, the increasing obviousness of the advanced stages of her pregnancy in an unmarried (or newly married) state would have caused problems of its own for Joseph, and would have given him ample reason to "fear" taking Mary as his wife. As Carson aptly puts it, "such a marriage would have been a tacit admission of his own guilt."[38] Moreover, McHugh's understanding of γὰρ as "I say this because you are fearful over the fact that [Mary's child has been conceived by the Holy Spirit]" is highly doubtful. He offers no support from parallel uses of γὰρ elsewhere.

His thought-provoking discussion notwithstanding, McHugh falls short of establishing his case. On its face, the text makes better sense if we view Joseph's righteousness in terms of the balance he strikes between following the law of Moses and following the law of compassion.[39] His fear is explained by his deep concern for taking Mary as his wife after such a fantastic story. This serves as a backdrop for the angel's visit to convince Joseph to take Mary home as his wife.

The Meaning of "until" in Matthew 1:25

Matthew next tells us that Joseph "did what the angel of the Lord had commanded him and took Mary home as his wife. But he had no union with her until she gave birth to a son. And he gave him the name Jesus" (1:24–25). At issue in this passage is just what impact it has (if any) on Mary's perpetual virginity. There are at least two points in the phrase οὐκ ἐγίνωσκεν αὐτὴν ἕως οὗ ἔτεκεν υἱόν on which Evangelicals and Catholics can agree. Both sides agree (1) that ἐγίνωσκεν refers to sexual union,[40] and (2) that Mary remained a virgin until she gave birth. Many Evangelical scholars, pressing the implications of the passage further, argue that the passage not only demonstrates Mary's prenatal virginity, but also directly conflicts with any notion of ongoing, postnatal virginity.[41] Matthew tells us that Joseph abstained from sexual union with Mary *until* she gave birth, implying that normal marital relations ensued after the birth of Jesus.

Roman Catholic scholars and apologists counter this point by appealing to the use of "until" (ἕως) elsewhere in Scripture. Karl

Keating, for instance, argues that this word means only that "some action did not happen up to a certain point, but does not imply that the action did happen later."[42] He appeals to several OT passages where ἕως has this meaning, including 2 Sam 6:23 ("Michal daughter of Saul had no children to [ἕως] the day of her death"), Gen 8:7 ("and sent out a raven, and it kept flying back and forth until [ἕως] the water had dried up from the earth"), and Deut 34:6 ("He buried him in Moab, in the valley opposite Beth Peor, but to [ἕως] this day no one knows where his grave is"),[43] and concludes from this that "nothing at all can be proved from the use of the word 'till' in Matthew 1:25."[44]

In most of the passages cited above, ἕως does indeed have the meaning Keating assigns to it.[45] Michal certainly did not have children *after* her death, and it is doubtful that the writer of Deut 34:6 meant to imply that the whereabouts of Moses' body would be revealed after the day he wrote this passage. Nor is there any doubt that passages with this meaning of ἕως could be multiplied. Yet Keating does not take into account the differences of the Greek phrases used in the passages he cites, and in Matt 1:25. In each of the passages cited above ἕως alone is used. Yet in Matt 1:25, the construction ἕως οὗ is used.[46] The difference of meaning between these two phrases can be appreciated only through a comparative study of the semantic range of each phrase within the NT itself.

A Comparison of the Various Uses of ἕως in the New Testament

Ἕως occurs in its various forms some 146 times in the NT.[47] There are several Greek constructions of ἕως with the particle in the NT, including ἕως ἄν, ἕως οὗ, and ἕως ὅτου.[48] Each of these will be considered in turn, beginning with the use of ἕως by itself.

The Meaning of ἕως in the New Testament

When used alone ἕως occurs 104 times in the NT.[49] The breakdown of occurrences by author is Matthew (43x), Luke-Acts (34x), Pauline corpus (12x), Johannine corpus (11x), Hebrews (2x), and James (2x). Clearly Matthew's use is most significant for our purposes since not only does it constitute the bulk of occurrences of ἕως in the entire NT (41%),[50] but it is also the book in which the passage in question is found. When it occurs in this form (i.e., without ἄν, οὗ, or ὅτου), ἕως can take the prepositional (spatial or logical) meaning "to"; i.e., from point A to point B (Matt 1:17; "from Abraham *to* David"[51]; Mark 14:54, "Peter followed him at a distance, right *up to* the courtyard of the high priest"); or the conjunctive meaning "until" [an event, point, degree] (Luke 12:59, "you will not get out *until* you have paid the last penny"), or the conjunctive "while" (Luke 17:8, "wait on me while I eat and drink; after that you may eat").[52]

Within the two broader categories of the prepositional and conjunctive usages, we may divide ἕως into the sub-categories of *space*, *time*, and *extent*. Spatial ἕως occurs thirty-three times in the NT and is almost always prepositional.[53] However, there are eight occurrences of this form of ἕως that may carry a secondary connotation of *extent* (e.g., Matt 11:23, "will you be lifted up *as far as*[54] the skies?"; Matt 24:31, "from one end of the heavens *to* the other"), and four that may carry a secondary connotation of *time* (e.g., Matt 1:17, "fourteen generations in all from Abraham *to* David"). Of those occurrences that have the spatial meaning, over half (eighteen) are found in Luke/Acts, eleven are in Matthew, two are in Mark, one is in John, and one is in Paul.

Ἕως is used also where the idea of *extent* is primary. Included here are the extent of Jesus' sufferings (Matt 26:38, "My soul is overwhelmed with sorrow *to the point* of [ἕως] death"), the extent to which Christians are to forgive others (Matt 18:22, "*up to* seventy-seven times"), the extent to which Herod was prepared to reward the daughter of Herodias (Mark 6:23, "*up to* half my kingdom"), and the extent to which we are to understand Paul's message (2 Cor 1:13, "And I hope that, as you have understood us in part, you will come *to understand fully*" [ἕως τέλους ἐπιγνώσεσθε]). There are thirteen examples of this usage in the NT, two of which may have a secondary spatial connotation (Matt 24:27, "lightning that comes from the east is visible even *until* the west"; and Mark 13:27, "from the ends of the earth *to* the ends of the heavens"). Of those occurrences that have extent as the meaning, five are found in Matthew, three are in Mark, two are in Luke/Acts, two are in Paul, and one is in Hebrews.

A third and final way that ἕως is used by itself is the *temporal* usage denoting a period of time. This category, consisting of fifty-eight instances of ἕως (well over half of all instances where ἕως occurs by itself in the NT), is by far the largest. Of these, as many as thirty mean "until a specified time (but not after)"[55] (e.g., 2 Thess 2:7, "will continue to do so *until* he is taken out of the way"; Matt 2:15; "[and left for Egypt] where he stayed *until* the death of Herod"). In such instances of ἕως the time frame of the action of the main clause (the protasis) is clearly limited by the subordinate clause (the apodosis) (i.e., "up to this time but no further"). Five within this last set have secondary connotations of extent (two in Matt 17:17, two in Mark 9:19, and one in Luke 9:41—all of which record the same saying of Jesus), and one has a secondary meaning of "while" (Luke 17:8). At least twelve[56] in this category mean "up to a specified time (with no reference to cessation or continuance of the action of the main clause)" (Matt 11:12, "from the days of John the Baptist *until* now"). Thirteen mean "to a certain point (*and continuing*)" (Mark 13:19, "unequaled from the beginning, when God created the world, *until* now—*and never to be equaled again*"). In such instances the action of the main clause continues into the subordinate clause (i.e., "up to this time and beyond"). Only three instances of temporal ἕως are certainly to be translated "while" (or, "during the period in which")[57] (e.g., John 9:4, "*while* [ἕως] it is day, we must do the work of him who sent me"). Of those occurrences that have the temporal meaning, fifteen are found in Matthew, fourteen are in Luke/Acts, ten are in the Johannine literature, nine are in Paul, seven are in Mark, two are in James, and one is in Hebrews.

When used alone, then, ἕως sometimes takes on a spatial connotation (roughly a third of all occurrences), is sometimes used to show extent (roughly ten percent of all occurrences), and sometimes carries a temporal meaning (roughly fifty-six percent of all occurrences). Within this last category, a mere handful mean "while" (less than one percent of all instances of ἕως occurring by itself); twenty-two percent mean "until a specified time (but not after)"; and forty-three percent mean "up to a specified time" with either no reference to cessation or continuance of the action of the main clause, or where the writer wants to show that the action of the main clause continues even after the action of the subordinate clause has occurred.

The Meaning of ἕως ἄν in the New Testament

When used with ἄν, ἕως occurs twenty times in the NT,[58] almost all of which occur with direct reference to the *eschaton*.[59] Moreover, all instances of ἕως ἄν are temporal, and may be translated "up to a specified time" (e.g., Matt 10:23, "you will not finish going through the cities of Israel *until* the Son of Man comes"). The overwhelming majority of occurrences (fourteen) imply neither continuance nor cessation of the action of the main clause by the initiation of the action of the subordinate clause. In such cases, the phrase may be translated as "up to a specified time [with no reference to cessation or continuance]" (Matt 12:20, "a smoldering wick he will not snuff out, *until* he leads justice to victory"). On the other hand, fewer than a third of all occurrences imply cessation or modification of the action of the main clause by the action of the subordinate clause, giving the meaning "up to a specified time [but not beyond]" (Matt 10:11, "stay at his house *until* you leave").[60] There seems to be no instance of ἕως ἄν where continuance of the action of the main verb is certainly implied. Moreover, there seems to be no favored usage of ἕως ἄν with the negative—it is used both in passages that indicate cessation of the action of the main clause (e.g., Matt 5:26, "you will not get out *until* you have paid the last penny"), as well as in passages where neither cessation nor continuance is implied (e.g., Matt 16:28, "some who are standing here will not taste death *until* they see the Son of Man coming in his kingdom").

The construction ἕως ἄν, then, seems to occur mostly in eschatological contexts (though not always), or where the connotation is primarily (or even strictly) temporal, or where the writer wants to imply no necessary cessation, modification, or continuance of the action of the main clause due to the action of the subordinate clause. It is found eleven times in Matthew, four times in Luke/Acts, three times in Mark, once in Paul, and once in Hebrews.

The Meaning of ἕως ὅτου in the New Testament

The construction ἕως ὅτου occurs only five times in the NT, all of which are in the Gospels.[61] Moreover, all occurrences are temporal; two have the temporal meaning "while" (Matt 5:25 and Luke 13:8), while the other three mean "until" (Luke 12:50; 22:16; and John 9:18). All three of the latter are instances in which the action of the main clause is modified by the action of the subordinate clause ("until [but not after]"). There are three occurrences in Luke, two in Matthew, and one in John. Most grammars treat this construction as a variant form of ἕως οὗ, and so its meaning holds significance for the passage under consideration.[62]

The Meaning of ἕως οὗ in the New Testament

This construction is used in Matt 1:25 and so is of special interest here. It occurs only seventeen times in the NT,[63] and all are temporal. Two of these have the meaning "while" (Matt 14:22; 26:36),[64] whereas the other fifteen occurrences are instances in which the action of the main clause is limited by the action of the subordinate clause and require the meaning "until a specified time (but not after)." Hence, the disciples were not to tell anyone what they had seen "*until* the Son of Man has been raised from the dead" (Matt 17:9), but they surely were not to keep silent afterwards. The wicked servant was to be tortured "*until* he should pay back all he owed" (Matt 18:34), but that torture (it is implied) would cease after payment had been rendered. The woman who loses the coin sweeps the house and searches carefully *until* she finds it (Luke 15:8), but ceases the search once it is found. Similarly Jesus' promise to abstain from eating and drinking at table will be kept only "*until* the kingdom of God comes" (Luke 22:18), after which he will inaugurate the Messianic Banquet.[65]

Other instances carry this same meaning. The disciples were to stay in Jerusalem after Christ's ascension "*until* [they had] been clothed with power from on high" (Luke 24:49), but then were expected to leave Jerusalem and take the gospel into all the world. The rooster would not crow *until* Peter disowned Christ three times (John 13:38); but then it is clear that the rooster did crow. The days of the purification rite which Paul observed (Acts 21:26) lasted only *until* a sacrifice was offered. Paul's Jewish adversaries vowed not to eat or drink anything *until* they had killed Paul (Acts 23:12; 23:14; 23:21); clearly they intended to eat afterwards. Likewise, Festus ordered Paul to be "kept" (τηρεῖσθαι, i.e., in Caesarea, as opposed to Jerusalem where the Jews wanted him tried, and in anticipation of his imminent journey to Rome where Paul wished to be tried) *until* he could send him to Rome (Acts 25:21); once he left for Rome he was no longer kept in Caesarea. Finally, Peter entreats us to pay attention to the word of the prophets "as to a light shining in a dark place, *until* the day dawns and the morning star rises" (2 Pet 1:19)—doubtless a reference to the *parousia*, after which it will no longer be necessary to turn to the word of the prophets as a guide which navigates us through a dark place; Christ himself will supersede any such need.

There are two instances of ἕως οὗ (parallel passages of each other) that, although having primarily a temporal meaning, have a secondary connotation of extent: Matt 13:33 ("The kingdom of heaven is like yeast that a woman took and mixed into a large amount of flour *until* it worked all through the dough"), and Luke 13:21 ("It is like yeast that a woman took and mixed into a large amount of flour *until* it worked all through the dough"). Both *could* mean "*to the extent that* the flour and yeast were thoroughly mixed." However, even here a primarily temporal meaning is not thereby excluded, for it is doubtful that the woman intends to continue mixing the ingredients after she has thoroughly mixed them.

The constructions in this category that come closest to Matt 1:25 are, perhaps, those instances of ἕως οὗ where the main clause is negated (οὐκ, Matt 1:25; cf. μηδενί, Matt 17:9; οὐ μή, Luke 22:18; μή, John 13:38; μήτε, Acts 23:12, 14, 21).[66] In each case where the negative is used with the main clause, it means that the action of the main clause will be in effect *only until* the action of the subordinate clause has been accomplished; that is to say, there are no instances of *extent* or the temporal "while" in this category. Hence, the disciples *will* witness to the transfiguration after the resurrection (Matt 17:9); Jesus *will* eat and drink again in the kingdom (Luke 22:18); the rooster *will* crow after Peter's denials (John 13:38); and the Jews *do* intend to eat and drink after they kill Paul (Acts 23:12, 14, 21).

The Meaning of Matthew 1:25

We may now apply this understanding of ἕως οὗ to the passage under consideration: "But he did not know her until she gave birth to a son." We may safely eliminate several of the meanings we have established for these constructions. It cannot here mean "while" or "to the extent that," as this construction may mean elsewhere; such meanings would render the present passage nonsensical. Nor can it have a prepositional/spatial connotation (from point A to point B) as ἕως sometimes has when used alone; the usage here is clearly conjunctive/temporal. The meaning "until (and continuing)" is not impossible, and many Roman Catholic scholars (including those on the *MNT* taskforce) appeal to this meaning for Matt 1:25: "Thus, *in itself* the verse tells us nothing about what happened by way of marital relations after Jesus was born."[67] The taskforce goes on to assert that ἕως οὗ with a negative "often has no implication at all about what happened after the limit of the 'until' was reached."[68]

However true this assertion may be for LXX usage of ἕως οὗ,[69] this meaning for this construction is unattested elsewhere in the NT. Had Matthew wanted to convey the notion that Joseph refrained from having sexual relations with Mary even *post partum*, he might have used ἕως alone, since as many as one fifth of all instances of the temporal use of ἕως in this form has this meaning. Better still, he could have used ἕως ἄν since, as has already been pointed out, all instances of this form are temporal, and most imply no limitation of the action of the main clause by the action of the subordinate clause, even when used with the negative.

Whatever meaning we finally adopt for ἕως οὗ in Matt 1:25 must be tempered by the fact that this phrase never elsewhere has the meaning "until (and continuing)" in the NT.[70] Moreover, when used with the negative, this phrase (at least so far as the NT is concerned) *always* means "*not* [main clause] *until* [subordinate clause], after which [main clause] ensues."[71] In light of this evidence, the most probable meaning for Matt 1:25 is, "Joseph did not have sexual relations with Mary *until* she gave birth to a firstborn son; after which sexual relations ensued."[72] If Matthew means to communicate to us that Mary remained a virgin after the birth of Jesus, we might expect him to use either ἕως alone or ἕως ἄν to show no necessary change in the action of the main clause—both are used with the negative where this meaning is intended (Matt 24:21, "unequaled from the beginning of the world *until* [ἕως] now"; Matt 5:18, "not the least stroke of a pen will by any means disappear from the Law *until* [ἕως ἄν] everything is accomplished").[73]

So far from remaining silent on this issue, the Scriptures here provide us with positive evidence of Mary's normal marital relations after the birth of Jesus. [74] Matthew's use of ἕως, both in the shear number of occurrences as well as in the extent of varying constructions, is unmatched by any other NT writer. Yet even he will not use ἕως οὗ in a way that violates the meaning found everywhere else in the NT. When he wants to convey that the action of the main clause continues *into* or *after* the action of the subordinate clause, he prefers ἕως or ἕως ἄν. When he wants to convey no such continuation (or discontinuation) of the action of the main clause, he prefers ἕως ἄν. Yet, both of these constructions are used by Matthew to give other senses as well. The ratio of usages between the meaning "until (but not after)" and "until (and continuing or no reference to continuation/discontinuation) in Matthew is, in the case of temporal ἕως alone, ten to five,[75] and in the case of ἕως ἄν, four to seven.[76] Not so in the case of ἕως οὗ and ἕως ὅτου. Both constructions are used solely—not only by Matthew but also by all NT writers who use this construction—to convey that the action of the main clause is discontinued by the action of the subordinate clause.[77] Matt 1:25 is just such a case, and there seems to be no justification for assigning to ἕως οὗ here any other meaning than that demanded by normal usage elsewhere in the New Testament.

CHAPTER II

Use of the Phrases ἕως οὗ and ἕως ὅτου in Literature Outside the New Testament

As we have already noted in the previous chapter, an examination of the NT usage of the phrase ἕως οὗ (ἕως ὅτου) has yielded little support for the understanding of this phrase in Matt 1:25 as it relates to the perpetual virginity of Mary. This in itself does not thereby exclude the interpretation in question, for if evidence in support of this understanding can be found in the literature outside of the NT, we may be able to preserve that meaning here as well. It will therefore be helpful to examine the various nuances of these phrases found both in the LXX and in the non-biblical literature closest to the time of the writing of Matthew to see whether this is the case.

The Phrases ἕως οὗ and ἕως ὅτου in the LXX

There are eighty-five occurrences of ἕως οὗ in seventy-eight verses of the LXX, and fourteen occurrences of ἕως ὅτου in fourteen verses. The nuances of each phrase range more broadly here than in the NT, although the major categories are left intact. The following is a summary of each.

A Summary of the Phrase ἕως οὗ

We may subdivide the occurrences of the phrase ἕως οὗ found in the LXX into three major categories: the spatial/prepositional category (a rare usage, occurring only once in the LXX); the telic category (which accounts for twenty occurrence); and the temporal (which accounts for the remaining sixty-four occurrences). The latter two of these categories have subdivisions of their own which we will detail below.

The phrase ἕως οὗ occurs only once with a spatial meaning, and that occurrence is found in the book of Judith: "And those in Galaad and those in Galilee chased them in a great slaughter *until* they had passed Damascus and her borders" (Jdt 15:5).[1] In this case the phrase carries the meaning *until a spatial point is reached*, and is therefore almost prepositional in meaning.[2]

Within the telic category there are as many as eleven instances that have the meaning *to the extent that*. Hence, the rich man's wealth continued to grow "until" (*to the extent that*) he became very rich (Gen 26:13); Moses ground the golden calf "until" (*to the extent that*) it became dust (Deut 9:21); Eleazar struck down the Philistines "until" (*to the extent that*) his hand grew tired and froze to the sword; and Manasseh shed much blood, "until" (*to the extent that*) he had filled Jerusalem from one end to another. One variation on this meaning occurs in Dan 8:11 where we are told that the little horn "magnified himself *until* the Prince of hosts." In this case, while extent is still in mind, ἕως οὗ means something like *to the extent of*, or (more colloquially) *to be as great as*.

Another sub-category of the telic usage is that of *result*. There are only two unambiguous instances that fit this category. The first (Eccl 2:3) is Solomon's explanation of his experimentation with hedonism: "I sought in my heart to give myself to wine…and to lay hold of folly, until I might see what was good for the sons of men to do under heaven all the days of their life." The meaning of ἕως οὗ in this case is *so that*. Similarly, in Isa 33:23 the instability of the various parts of the ship (riggings, mast, and sail) are contributing to the overall failure of the voyage, "*until* [i.e., *with the result that*] an abundance of spoils will be divided and even the lame will carry off plunder."

There are seven remaining passages in the telic category for which a decision between extent and result is less certain. Both Judg 4:24 ("the hand of the Israelites grew stronger and stronger against Jabin…*until*[3] they destroyed him") and Ps 57:8 [58:7] ("They will amount to nothing as water that flows away. He will stretch his bow *until* they will be weak") probably have extent as the primary idea suggested by the *increasing nature* of both the strength of the Israelites and the stretching of the bow, but with a possible secondary connotation of result. The remaining five have result as their primary idea and extent as a possible secondary connotation. Hence, 1 Kgs 17:17 tells us that the woman's son "grew worse and worse, *until* [i.e., *with the result that*] he finally stopped breathing." As with the first two passages above, extent is suggested by the increasing nature of the sickness. Nevertheless, result seems to be the primary idea here since the apodosis is the natural consequent of the protasis. Similarly with 2 Kgs 17:23, "[the Israelites persisted in their sins] *until* [*with the result that*] the Lord removed them from his presence"; 2 Chron 21:15, "you yourself will be very ill with a lingering disease of the bowels, *until* [*with the result that*] the disease causes your bowels to come out"; and 2 Chron 24:10, "All the officials and all the people brought their contributions gladly, dropping them into the chest *until* [*with the result that*] it was full." One final instance of this usage is found in Deut 2:15, where we read that "the Lord's hand was against them *until* he had completely eliminated them from the camp." It is unclear whether the meaning here is *to the extent that*, or *with the result that*. Either option, however, is preferred over the temporal "until" since the passage is constructed in such a way as to suggest that the apodosis ("he eliminated them") is either the goal or the result of the protasis ("his hand was against them"); hence, the verse as a whole is telic. In each of the seven cases above it is difficult to separate result and extent, and it is very likely that both ideas are present.

The largest category by far is that of the temporal usage, comprising fifty-eight occurrences of this phrase. Within this category there are several smaller divisions, the largest of which carries the meaning *until a specified time, but not after*, denoting a discontinuation of the action of the main clause (or, the protasis) at the onset of the action of the subordinate clause (or, the apodosis).[4] Examples of this usage are replete in the LXX: "And the time that passed between the time we departed from Kadesh Barnea, *until* we arrived over the brook Zered, was thirty and eight years; *until* all the generation of the men of war had passed away from among the host, as the Lord swore to them" (Deut 2:14). Here the conjunction occurs twice, and in both instances there is a discontinuation of the action of the main clause (in this case, the counting of years). Similarly, Ruth 2:23, "So Ruth stayed close to the servant girls of Boaz to glean *until* the barley and wheat harvests were finished"; and 2 Chron 9:6, "But I did not believe what they said *until* I came and saw with my own eyes."

Every instance of this phrase in Judges is disputed. Judg 3:30 of the LXX, for instance, includes an addition not found in the Hebrew (nor in most translations). A comparison of the Greek and Hebrew texts reads as follows:

> καὶ ἡσύχασεν ἡ γῆ ὀγδοήκοντα ἔτη, [καὶ ἔκρινεν αὐτοὺς
>   Αωδ ἕως οὗ ἀπέθανεν]
> And the land had rest eighty years. [And Ehud judged them
>   *until* he died]

> וַתִּשְׁקֹט הָאָרֶץ שְׁמוֹנִים שָׁנָה
> And the land had peace eighty years.

The bracketed phrase in the LXX reading occurs in both A and B. In yet another passage the question is not whether the phrase ἕως οὗ is used but whether it is repeated: "Village life in Israel ceased, ceased *until* Deborah arose[5], [*until*] she arose a mother in Israel" (Judg 5:7). The MT has a single occurrence of עַד here, which the LXX family A follows with a single instance of ἕως οὗ (B repeats the phrase). Finally, Judg 19:26 may or may not include this phrase: "At daybreak the woman went back to the house where her master was staying, fell down at the door and lay there *until* daylight." Both families have ἕως, but family B omits οὗ.

None of the questions surrounding these passages affects the nuance, however, since in each case the meaning is still *until* [*but not after*]. In the case of Judg 3:30, Ehud could not have judged Israel *after* he died. Likewise, Judg 5:7 implies that village life once again thrived under Deborah. Even in Judg 19:26 the dead corpse of the concubine lay at the door only until morning; then the man placed her on his donkey (v. 28).

Other occurrences where the phrase has this meaning include Ruth 3:3 where Naomi gives instructions to Ruth concerning Boaz: "Then go down to the threshing floor, but don't let him know you are there *until* he has finished eating and drinking." This prohibition by Naomi is discontinued in v. 4: "Then go and uncover his feet and lie down. He will tell you what to do." Similarly, Jeroboam fled to Egypt *only until*

Solomon's death (1 Kgs 11:40; cf. 12:2); the prophets of Baal continued to prophesy *only until* the time of the evening sacrifice, at which point they were slaughtered (1 Kgs 18:29; cf. vv. 36–40); the men in charge of music performed their musical ministry before the "Tent of Meeting" *only until* Solomon finished building the temple in Jerusalem (1 Chron 6:17 [6:32])—at which point a necessary change of venue made the Tent of Meeting obsolete. The commission to build the temple itself is also said to have been "carried out" in full and lasted only from the day it started "*until* its completion," at which point Solomon's work was "finished" (2 Chron 8:16). In the same way, the Levites assisted the priests in the burnt offerings *only until* the task was finished and other priests had been consecrated (2 Chron 29:34); Jeremiah will continue his weeping only until (it is implied) he captures the Lord's attention (Lam 3:50)[6]; God's "binding" of Israel would be in effect *only until* she has finished the days of her siege (Ezek 4:8); and Jerusalem would remain in ruins only "*until* he comes to whom it rightfully belongs" (Ezek 21:32).

There are several instances of this meaning for ἕως οὗ in Daniel, but in each case the text is disputed. In most cases, Theodotion (q v) has the construction ἕως οὗ while (O)G[7] is missing the entire sentence where ἕως οὗ should occur (4:8, 4:23, 4:25, and 5:21). In one case ἕως alone occurs in (O)G (7:22), and in another case the differences between q v and (O)G are so great that they do not even follow the same story line (4:32), much less use similar words and phrases. Yet, again, in each case where ἕως οὗ occurs it has the same meaning as above. None of the magicians could interpret Nebuchadnezzar's dream until Daniel interpreted it (Dan 4:8). Here Daniel is considered to be within the category of magicians, not distinct from them (cf. v. 9), and so the impotence of the "magicians" discontinues after Daniel's interpretation. Similarly, Nebuchadnezzar would lose his sanity *until* seven years had passed, but no longer (4:23, 25, 32, 5:21; cf. vv. 34–36). Likewise, the "little horn" of Daniel's vision persisted in defeating the saints *only until* the Ancient of Days came and pronounced judgment in their favor (7:22).

There are only two remaining occurrences in the OT where the phrase ἕως οὗ carries the meaning *until* [*but not after*] (all other occurrences with this meaning in the LXX are found in the Apocrypha). One of these is followed by an affirmation that the action of the main clause is temporary. In Hos 5:15 God distances himself from Israel: "Then I will go back to my place *until* they admit their guilt"; but returns after their repentance (cf. 6:1, "but *he will heal us*"). In Jonah 4:5, however, discontinuation is simply implied: "Jonah…made a shelter, and sat under it in the shade, until he might see what would become of the city." Although nothing is specifically said about Jonah's action after God's decision to spare the city, the tenor of the verse itself assumes that he sat under the shelter only until he discovered the city's fate.

In some respects the apocryphal books show this meaning even more clearly than does the OT. There are two of these in Tobit. Hence, Tob 2:4: "And before I had tasted anything, I got up and took him up into a room *until* the sun went down"[8] (cf. v. 7; "Then at sunset I went out, dug a grave, and buried him); and Tob 2:10, "Achiacharus took care of me for two years, *until* he left for Elymais."[9] Judith contains four occurrences as well: Achior would not see Holofernes' face again *until* the latter would take vengeance on the nation Israel (6:5); consequently, Achior would not die *until* Holofernes' armies returned and killed him (6:8; cf. v. 6). There is a dual occurrence in Judith 10:10: "and the men of the city kept her in view *until* she had gone down the mountain and *until* she had passed the valley and could see her no more." In both cases the ability to keep Judith in view is discontinued after she descends the mountain and crosses the valley.[10] One last occurrence of this phrase in Judith is in 14:8: "Then Judith declared to him in the midst of the people all that she had done, from the day that she left *until* she spoke to them." Clearly nothing could be included in Judith's report beyond the current moment, and so a discontinuation of the report is necessarily implied.

Three final occurrences where this phrase has this meaning may be found in Sirach (Ecclesiasticus). Wisdom, it is said, "at first" tries her child with discipline and brings "fear and dread" on him "*until* she may trust his soul" (4:17); but afterward she brings him happiness (v. 18). In 13:7, the rich man is said quite literally to "disgrace you with his food, *until* he has drained you two or three times"; afterward, however, "he will scorn you." Likewise, the man who borrows money "kisses the lender's hand, and for his neighbor's money he will speak submissively"; he does this, however, "only until he receives," after which "when payment is due, he disappoints him" (29:5).[11]

In each of the cases above ἕως οὗ appears in a context where the action of the main clause discontinues after the action of the subordinate clause. This is, with relatively few exceptions, the primary usage of this phrase. There are a few instances, however, in which this connotation is present, but is secondary to the temporal meaning *before*. The psalmist, for instance, writes: "I will allow no sleep to my eyes, no slumber to my eyelids *until* I find a place for the Lord, a dwelling for the Mighty One of Jacob (Ps 131[132]:4–5)," by which he means "I will allow no sleep to my eyes…*before* I find a place for the LORD."[12] Yet, technically, the action of the main clause still ceases after the action of the subordinate clause; for we would not expect the psalmist to continue his sleep deprivation after he has reached his goal. Perhaps a clearer example may be found in Eccl 12:1–2: "Remember your Creator in the days of your youth…*before* the sun and the light and the moon and the stars grow dark, and the clouds return after the rain." Again, while *before* is the primary meaning here, the action of the main clause (remember…*in the days of your youth*) ceases in the subordinate clause where the subject has grown old. At that point there is no longer any opportunity to remember his creator *while he is young*.

In another instance where this meaning is primary, Song of Songs warns us not to "arouse or awaken love *until* it so desires"; by which is meant, "*before* it desires." Similarly, the bride held the groom "and would not let him go" *before* she had brought him safely to the bridle chamber. At that point the threat of being separated from him was over and it was then safe to relax her grip on him. Three additional passages that fall into this category include Ezek 24:13: "Because I tried to cleanse you but you would not be cleansed from your impurity, you will not be clean again *until* (*before*) my wrath against you has subsided"; Dan 6:25[24]: "And they did not reach the floor *until* (*before*) the lions had overpowered them"; and Tob 1:21: "And not fifty days passed *until* (*before*) two of his sons killed him." In each of these cases the action of the main clause is assumed to be discontinued at the action of the subordinate clause.

Another usage of the phrase ἕως οὗ in the LXX (also present in the NT) is the temporal meaning *while* (or, *during the period in which*). There are approximately six instances where this meaning is primary. The man who undergoes discipline from the Lord is granted "relief from days of trouble, *while* a pit is dug for the wicked" (Ps 93[94]:13). In another passage, David entreats God to "let the wicked fall into their own nets, *while* I pass by in safety" (Ps 140[141]:10). The bride allowed her perfume to spread its fragrance "*while* the king was at his table" (Cant 1:12). Two instances of this usage may be found in Daniel's vision: "You were watching *while* a rock was cut out, but not by human hands" (Dan 2:34); and "I watched *while* its wings were torn off and it was lifted from the ground" (Dan 7:4).[13] This "watched while" usage resurfaces later in certain pseudepigraphical visions.[14] One final instance where this meaning is possible is Tob 10:7, where we read that Tobiah's mother, Anna, believing that her son was dead "did not cease during the nights to bewail her son Tobiah *while* [*during the time in which*] the fourteen days of the wedding were being accomplished." It is not altogether certain whether ἕως οὗ should be taken with what comes before, or with what follows.[15] If the latter, the passage would read: "*Before* the fourteen days of the wedding were accomplished, which Raguel promised to hold for his daughter, Tobiah went to him and said, 'please let me go'," and would therefore fall into the previous category (*before*).

Two additional instances where this meaning may be intended are Josh 4:10: "Now the priests who carried the ark remained standing in the middle of the Jordan *while* (*during the time in which*) everything the Lord had commanded Joshua was done by the people"; and Ruth 1:13: "would you wait *while* they grew up? Would you remain unmarried for them?" In each of these two cases, however, the simple temporal meaning *until* makes equally good sense and is in fact more probable (although the meaning *while* may be a secondary connotation).[16] Moreover, both are examples of instances in which the action of the main clause ceases after the action of the subordinate clause. In the case of Josh 4:10, the biblical writer afterward tells us: "as soon as all of them had crossed, the ark of the Lord and the priests came to the other side." Ruth 1:13 contains no similarly explicit affirmation that the action of the main clause ceases; we may, however, assume that it does cease. It would be unreasonable to suppose that Naomi's daughters-in-law would envision waiting to marry until her sons came of age, and then continue to wait after that time.

In the passages we have examined so far, we have found no clear example where the action of the main clause continues after the action of the subordinate clause. Indeed, in each case the action of the main clause is either explicitly said to have ceased in a subsequent verse, or is assumed to have ceased logically. There are, however, as many as eleven occurrences of this phrase in the LXX where the action of the main clause either continues after the action of the subordinate clause, or there is no clear reference to the continuation or discontinuation of that action (although several of the latter are doubtful). Approximately half of these instances occur in the Psalms. In Ps 71[72]:7, a psalm with messianic overtones, we are told that in the days of the great king "prosperity will abound *until* the moon is no more." Similarly, Ps 93[94]:14–15: "For the Lord will not reject his people; he will never forsake his inheritance *until* judgment returns to righteousness, and all the upright in heart will follow it." In both of these examples it seems evident that the action of the main clause continues into the action of the subordinate clause. Prosperity will abound in eternity as much as it will abound during the messianic age.[17] The meaning here is likely that prosperity will never end when the Messiah has begun to rule. In the same way, we cannot envision that the Lord will reject/forsake his people after "judgment returns to righteousness."

Nor can we detect a discontinuation of the action of the main clause in Ps 111[112]:8: "His heart is established, he will by no means be afraid, *until* he binds his enemies"; nor in Ps 141:8 [142:7]: "Set me free from my prison, that I may praise your name. The righteous will await on me *until* you return to me," although in the latter an argument may be made that the righteous are standing by only long enough to see that the psalmist receives justice. A modern paraphrase of this might read: "the righteous will hold their breath until they see evidence that you are once again with me." If this meaning is correct, then this passage would fall under the category of those passages where the action of the main clause is discontinued after the action of the subordinate clause. Nevertheless, the former passage (Ps 111[112]:8) seems clearly to be an instance where there is no discontinuation of the action of the main clause.

One other relatively clear example of this usage is found in 2 Chron 29:28: "The whole assembly bowed in worship, and the singers sang and the trumpeters played. All this continued *until* the sacrifice of the burnt offering was completed." We read later that the worship and singing continued after the sacrifices as well (v. 29). The writer of 4 Maccabees may also have intended this meaning when he writes: "[The reasoning of Eleazar] in no way turned the rudder of godliness *until* it sailed into the harbor of victory over death" (7:3). The metaphorical nature of this passage makes it exceedingly difficult to make a firm decision as to the continuation/discontinuation of the action of the main clause. Do we assume that Eleazar's reasoning did or did not "turn the rudder of godliness" *after* it "sailed into the harbor of victory over death"? Or do we assume that the question itself is moot since no reference to cessation or continuation is in mind? Even the meaning of the phrases themselves ("turn the rudder of godliness"; "sailed into the harbor of victory over death") remains uncertain. It would therefore be unwise to uphold this isolated passage as an example of one meaning or the other.

Two instances in which no reference to cessation or continuance is given are Cant 2:17 and 4:6, both of which begin with the phrase "*Until* the day breaks and the shadows flee." The former continues with the bride entreating her lover: "turn, my lover, and be like a gazelle or like a young stag on the rugged hills"; while the latter is the groom to his bride: "I will go to the mountain of myrrh and to the hill of incense." Although both main clauses *could* be viewed as discontinuing after "the day breaks and the shadows flee," it is more likely that no reference to cessation or continuation is in mind.

There are three additional passages that may have no reference to cessation or continuation, but may just as easily fall under the category of discontinuation. In Ps 56:2 [57:1] the psalmist writes: "I will take refuge in the shadow of your wings *until* the disaster has passed." It may of course be argued that the psalmist would not cease to take refuge in God even after the disaster had passed. But this assumes that the phrase "take refuge" means something like "trust in" in the sense of a continuous faith in God. More likely the psalmist is referring to a specific disastrous situation and assumes there would be no need to take this kind of "refuge" in times of peace. The same is true of Ps 122[123]:2, which states: "as the eyes of a maid look to the hand of her mistress, so our eyes look to the Lord our God, *until* he shows us his mercy." Once again, while it may be argued that the psalmist would never entertain the notion that we should *at any time* take our eyes off the Lord, this misses the point of the passage. The psalmist may again be thinking of a specific need that he is awaiting; and once that need is met, his eyes are no longer "looking" (i.e., "anticipating" that specific need). Nevertheless, a clear-cut decision cannot be made either way on either of these passages. Such a decision on one final passage may be easier. In Dan 2:9, Nebuchadnezzar is recorded as saying: "You [magicians] have conspired to tell me misleading and wicked things, *until* the situation changes."[18] Although this may be an instance in which there is no reference to cessation or continuation, it is more likely taken as an instance where the action of the main clause is discontinued after the action of the subordinate clause; for there is no reason that the magicians should lie to the king *after* "the situation changes."

A Summary of the Phrase ἕως ὅτου

The phrase ἕως ὅτου occurs only fourteen times in the LXX. The general usage for this phrase follows much of what we have seen for ἕως οὖ. It may be used to convey *extent* ("He provided food for the cities and set up arms in them *to such an extent that* his glorious name was renowned to the ends of the earth," 1 Mac 14:10), though there is only one occurrence with this meaning. It may also be used to convey the temporal meaning *before* ("[Remember your creator in the days of your youth] *before* the silver cord be loosed, or the golden bowl be broken," Eccl 12:6). The majority of the occurrence by far, however, have the temporal meaning *until* [*but not after*], in which the action of the main clause discontinues after the action of the subordinate clause. Hence: "I did not believe these things *until* I came and saw with my own eyes" (1 Kgs 10:7); "They will not know, nor see, *until* we come in the midst among them, and kill them, and cause the work to cease" (Neh 4:5[4:11]); "Joab and all the Israelites stayed there for six months, *until* they had destroyed all the men in Edom" (1 Kgs 11:16). In each of the examples above the action of the main clause discontinues after the action of the subordinate clause. The queen of Sheba certainly did not continue in her disbelief *after* she had met Solomon. Nor would Nehemiah's party remain ignorant of the presence of their enemies once their enemies had "come in their midst." In the final passage cited, we are specifically told that the Joab stayed in Edom only six months and no longer.

Other examples where this meaning is prominent include Tob 5:3, where Tobit instructs Tobiah to hire a traveling companion, "And we will pay him *until* you return"[19]; here the meaning is that the traveling companion will be under hire only until Tobiah returns. Also, Ezek 39:15: "As they go through the land and one of them sees a human bone, he will set up a marker beside it *until* the gravediggers have buried it in the Valley of Hamon Gog." There is no thought here that the markers would remain standing after each burial. Indeed, a marker left standing after the burial could only result in confusion for those looking for more bones to bury.

There are two instances in which this phrase carries a secondary telic connotation of *extent* or *result*. Hence, "David and his men wept aloud *until* they had no strength left to weep" (1 Sam 30:4); and "they persisted *until* he was too ashamed to refuse. So he said, 'Send them'," (2 Kgs 2:17). In each case the phrase may be translated *to such an extent that* or *with the result that*. Yet it is equally clear that the action of the main clause discontinues after the action of the subordinate clause, and so a temporal meaning is still in mind.

The final category of usage for this phrase is the temporal *while*, which occurs five times in the LXX. Hence, David asks the king of Moab whether he would let his father and mother stay with him *while* he figured out God's plan (1 Sam 22:3); and Solomon entreats his readers to remember their Creator while they are still young, that is, "*while* the evil days are still not here" (Eccl 12:1). There are three instances of this usage in Daniel, all of which are in vision passages, and all of which follow the apocalyptic "watch while" format found in other passages of Daniel where ἕως οὗ is used: "You were watching *while* a rock was cut out, but not by human hands" (Dan 2:34); "The first was like a lion, and it had the wings of an eagle. I watched *while* its wings were torn off and it was lifted from the ground" (Dan 7:4). In both of these passages (O)G version has ἕως ὅτου, while the same passages in θʹ has ἕως οὗ. One final occurrence of this is in Dan 7:9: "I watched *while* the thrones were cast down, and the Ancient of days sat."

Concluding Observations

We have examined every occurrence of the Greek constructions ἕως οὗ and ἕως ὅτου found in the LXX. There are several distinct usages found for the former, including a spatial connotation, the telic *extent* and *result*, the temporal *while*, the temporal *before*, the temporal *until* [*but not after*], the temporal *until* [*with no reference to cessation or continuation*], and possibly the temporal *until* [*and continuing*]. The latter two categories, however, are extremely rare, comprising only seven clear examples.[20] Similarly, the connotations for ἕως ὅτου follow most of those established for ἕως οὗ with the exception of the spatial meaning, and the meanings *until* [*with no reference to cessation or continuation*] and *until* [*and continuing*].

The Phrases ἕως οὗ and ἕως ὅτου in Non-biblical Literature from 100 B.C. to A.D. 100

The number of passages that use the constructions ἕως οὗ or ἕως ὅτου in the literature of the centuries immediately surrounding the birth of Christ is surprisingly few. The actual count in the literature currently available in a searchable format (i.e., on an electronic database) numbers fewer than fifty—roughly twice as many as are found in the comparatively scant amount of literature of the NT. The range of usage found in this literature practically mirrors that of the LXX, with the exception of perhaps one or two nuances found in the latter but not in the former. A summary of usages follows.

A Summary of the Phrase ἕως οὗ

The meaning of ἕως οὗ found to be primary in the NT and the LXX—*until [but not after]*—in which the action of the main clause discontinues after the action of the subordinate clause, is also dominant here. There are several examples of this from the writings of Dionysius of Halicarnassus. "And he continued from that time to maintain this pretense of folly from which he acquired his surname, *until* he thought the proper time had come to throw it off."[21] In this instance the action of the main clause (the protasis) discontinues after the action of the subordinate clause (the apodosis). The same is true of another instance of this phrase in Dionysius. "And from that time the two classes remained aloof from each other until the commonwealth was composed and reunited."[22] In this case the geographic separation of classes remained intact only until the commonwealth was established. Similarly, when recounting the way in which decisions were reached in the Roman military, Dionysius tells us:

> If therefore…ninety-seven [military] centuries [in the first class] were of the same opinion, the voting was at an end and the remaining ninety-six centuries were not called upon to give their votes. But if this was not the case, the second class, composed of twenty-two centuries, was called, and then the third and so on until ninety-seven centuries were of the same opinion.[23]

It is clear that votes were taken only until ninety-seven centuries were in agreement, and then the voting stopped; hence, the action of the main clause discontinues after the action of the subordinate clause.

Examples such as these abound. All five instances of ἕως οὗ in the pseudepigraphical book *The Apocalypse of Moses*[24] have this meaning. Two of these are found in Adam's instructions to Eve concerning his body:

> But when I die, leave me alone and let no one touch me *until* the angel of the Lord shall say something about me; for God will not forget me, but will seek his own vessel which he has formed. But rather rise to pray to God *until* I shall give back my spirit into the hands of the one who has given it.[25]

Here it seems reasonable to suppose that in both instances the action of the main clause would cease after the action of the subordinate clause, so that in both cases the meaning is "only until [but not after]."

Likewise with the narrative of Adam's death:

> For the earth did not receive the body [of Abel], saying, 'I shall not receive another body *until* the mound of earth which was taken from me and formed [into Adam] shall come [back] to me.' Then the angels took up the body [of Abel] and set it on the rock, *until* the time his father died, and both were buried according to the command of God in the regions of Paradise in the place from which God had found the dust.[26]

There can be no question that what is being asserted here is a reversal of the action of the main clauses by the action of the subordinate clauses. The earth would in fact receive the body of Abel, but *only after* it had received that of Adam. Consequently, the placement of Abel's body on the rock was *only until* Adam was buried—then Abel too was buried.

A final occurrence of this construction in the *Apocalypse of Moses* is found toward the end of the story. Here God sealed Adam in a temporary container "in order that no one might do anything to him for six days *until* his rib would return to him" (42.1). This also seems to be an instance where the intent of the construction is to show the discontinuation of the action of the main clause, since it is clear (based on the previous passage) that Adam was indeed touched by those who buried him after the six days had ended.

The only non-biblical Christian writer during this time frame that uses this construction is Clement of Rome, and even then it is not an original usage. In his letter to the Corinthians, Clement uses this phrase in a quote from Isa 26:20: "Enter into the closet for a very little while, *until* my anger and my wrath passes away, and I will remember a good day and will raise you from your tombs."[27] The admonition to "enter into the closet" seems designed to be temporary, lasting only until God's anger passes away. Again the construction in question follows the same usage found elsewhere in this literature.

By far the writer who makes use of this construction most extensively is Josephus. Josephus uses this phrase primarily to convey the same nuance of meaning that we have seen elsewhere (the action of the main clause discontinues after the action of the subordinate clause). In a few of these cases he directly cites the biblical record: "But the priests stood still in the midst [of the Jordan] *until* the multitude had crossed and reached the firm ground. Then, when all had crossed, the priests emerged"[28]; and again, "David departed thence and made his way to the Moabite king and besought him to receive his parents into his country and to keep them *until* he himself should know what was finally to become of him"[29]; and yet again, "As he then remained with the Killanians *until* they had secured their threshing floors and safely got in their crops, his presence there was reported to King Saul."[30]

At other times he uses the phrase in his own commentary of the biblical record: "And from the creation of Adam, the first man, *until* the time when Solomon built the temple there elapsed altogether three-thousand one-hundred and two years"[31]; "And indeed they did not weary of singing hymns or dancing *until* they reached the temple"[32]; "Jeremiah lived in Jerusalem from the thirteenth year of Josiah's reign *until* the city and the temple were demolished"[33]; "And thus they held out for eighteen months *until* they were exhausted by the famine and by the missiles which the enemy hurled at them from the towers. [Then] the city was taken."[34]

Josephus also uses this construction when commenting on extra-biblical Jewish and Greek history, such as in the following cases: "Upon learning that Bacchides had come against him, Jonathan sent his brother John, also called Gaddis, to the Nabataean Arabs to leave his equipment with them *until* they should fight against Baccides, for they were friends of the Jews"[35]; and, "They threw their spears and then drew their swords, and each, taking hold of his opponent's head and holding him fast, pierced the other's ribs and flanks with his sword *until* all were killed as though by agreement."[36] This phrase is also the one used when describing the demise of Alexander the Great: "But [King Alexander] did not cease his campaigns *until*, being exhausted from his labors, he met his death in the territory of Gerasenes while besieging Ragaba"[37]; as well as when relating the exploits of the Pharisees: "Later [the Pharisees] themselves cut down one of them, named Diogenes, and his death was followed by that of one after the other, *until* the leading citizens came to the palace…[and convinced the queen to]…entrust to them the guarding of the fortresses."[38] One last example of this nuance in Josephus is in his autobiographical *Life*: "My colleagues… decided to return home. But on my request they consented to stay until we had brought matters into order."[39] In each of the preceding cases the action of the main clause discontinues after the action of the subordinate clause.

There are few exceptions to this usage in Josephus; nevertheless he does use this phrase to show other nuances that are also found in the LXX and NT. One such usage is the temporal *while*, which occurs only twice in the literature of Josephus, both in regard to the priestly robes. The first of these describes the robe in detail:

> [The sash of the robe is] wound at first at the breast, after passing round it once again, it is tied and then hangs at length, sweeping to the ankles, *while* the priest has no task in hand.… But when it behooves him to attend to the sacrifices…he throws [the sash] back over his left shoulder.[40]

The second is more directly related to the priests themselves: "That is why wearers of the priestly robes are spotless, immaculately pure, and sober; for wine is forbidden them *while* they wear the robe."[41]

Another writer, whose use of this phrase is second only to Josephus in frequency, is Heron of Alexandria. Because of their technical and scientific subject matter Heron's writings are extremely difficult to translate with a large degree of clarity and certainty. Nevertheless, his use of ἕως οὗ seems to be in line with that of other writers of his day, using the phrase to show discontinuation of the main clause by the subordinate clause. There are several instances of this in his *Pneumatica*. In an extremely difficult passage Heron tells us about the nature of water: "Now seeing that every wet thing being held together is silent, it receives a spherical appearance, the same having a sharp point in the earth. Now it is not silent [as it flows] *until*, as it is said, it results in one spherical appearance."[42] Whatever else Heron wishes to convey here, his use of ἕως οὗ seems clear. The resulting "silence" of the sphere is a discontinuation of the previous state of "not silent."

Heron expounds upon this concept later in the same work: "Since water becomes held together, everything necessarily flows the same way to the deepest places because of its cohesion, *until* either all the water in the container truly becomes one in appearance, or the other containers become empty."[43] Hence, the "flowing" of the water discontinues after one or the other action. Similar instructions are given for further experimentation: "Then allow the excess of the water to be received in another container and let whatever can be driven off pass by, *until* the first stream no longer flows; then let it be marked upon the measuring rod and let it be written upon the cup."[44] Again, the flow of the water into another container discontinues after the action of the "first stream." At that point, the measurement is to be taken.

One final instruction in this work that uses ἕως οὗ is very similar in content to the previous one cited above, but much more technical:

> And it opened the GD stream. Then the same flowing into both the TS and the P containers, rising up the basin it will again confine the stream, until we again remove some water from the mixing bowl. And this will be the case as often as we remove water from the bowl.[45]

The complexity of this passage notwithstanding, Heron's point (so far as our construction is concerned) is that the confinement of the water discontinues after removing some water from the bowl. The same may be seen in several other works by Heron which concern the same subject matter and are no less complex. The following is a compilation of such passages in Heron:

"The H of the QK is less than four times as much, [...][46] the H, then the Q of the L, then that of the M. And allow this to occur, *until* the third from the end becomes less than K"[47]; "And allow this to occur, until [ἄχρις] the B mark appears. Allow it to occur, and allow the optical instrument to pass over the KL, *until* the B itself appears straight through the other"[48]; "Let it bend therefore, *until* the B mark appears through it"[49]; "I carry away the AZ measure standing upright before the optical instrument as I carry it to the O mark, *until* the OP measure appears through the measure in the optical instrument"[50]; "And establishing [it] in this way let it be cast from the Z ray straight toward the GD, *until* it falls together to the foundation according to the Θ"[51]; "[He turns]…not diligently measuring in any way the teeth lying beside. At the finish we turn around the first spiral [κοχλίαν=snail/spiral/screw], until one toothy instrument [ὀδοντωτὸν τύμπανον μίαν] lying beside it might receive restoration, measuring as often as he himself turns"[52]; "Make it in this way: Allow the container [κάθετος] to be filled up completely, *until* it falls together in a circle, and then divide the ropes of the step [βάσεως=step/foot] in half."[53]

Both the highly technical nature of these passages as well as their fragmentation make it next to impossible to decipher their precise meaning. Yet a fair reading of each of these passages leaves us with no clear example where the action of the main clause continues after the action of the subordinate clause. In each case the passage, while perhaps not demanding it, assumes discontinuation of the action of the main clause.

This use of the phrase ἕως οὗ is consonant with that found elsewhere in Heron's works. In *de automatis* Heron relates how through torture he was able to compel a guard to perform a certain act: "Then having pierced through against the right shoulder, I persecuted the guard well, until he might set down his hand to the small figure."[54] No thought of continuation of torture after the guard agreed to Heron's terms can be envisioned in this passage. Indeed, it must be assumed that discontinuation of torture was not only the reward for compliance, but that compliance (and therefore discontinuation) was in fact the goal of the torture to begin with.

Two additional authors of this time period whose writings, like those of Heron, focus on a technical subject matter are Discorides and Archigenes. Unlike Heron, however, the emphasis is not on scientific formulation but rather medical "recipes" of sorts. Discorides gives us several of these recipes in his *de materia medica*:

> "Boil the better one, *until* it has a sweet thickness, and then use it"[55]; "[place it] on a new earthen vessel and red-hot coals, *until* it no longer bubbles up"[56]; "Then burn the [item] that you chose beforehand by burying it in charcoal *until* it becomes translucent and bubbles up.... Then quench with wine"[57]; "Then having also a grinder made from the same wood, pour in sour wine, white and sharp, half-way into a cup, *until* it becomes sticky. Then add astringent salt."[58]

Archigenes gives instructions that appear to be similar:

> "Then, having apportioned them out, put in the dry [ingredients] and soak all day; and then boil [the mixture] again until it becomes brightened";[59] "Then, using a small, dense, and firm linen cloth add the honey and boil it again until it goes into [...],[60] and put the rest away in a good glass container."[61]

With the possible exception of the final passage cited for Archigenes,[62] each of the passages above follows the same primary nuance for ἕως οὗ as is found in all the other writers examined thus far. In no case is the action of the main clause demonstrably continued after the action of the subordinate clause.

One final example of this meaning for ἕως οὗ is found in the biography, *Vitae Aesopi*. Here the writer relates the following instructions given to the slave Aesop by his current master:

> Because the little woman is pure to me, and does not wish to be served by a shameful little body, stay on the other side of the doorway *until*, entering with your village mistress, I might say something laughable so that she does not suddenly see your corruption, demand back her money and flee.[64]

The use of the Greek phrase conforms to normal usage. It is not reasonable to suppose that Aesop was to continue standing on the other side of the doorway after his master's plan had been executed.

The biographer of *Vitae Aesopi* uses this Greek construction again, but this time with the temporal meaning "while": "A farmer spent his whole life in the field. Never having seen the city, he called for his children so that *while* he was still living he might go and see the city."[64] Two additional instances of this usage may be found in 1 Enoch, both of which use the same kind of apocalyptic "watched while" phrases found in some of Daniel's vision: "Then that sheep had his eyes opened; and he *watched* that ram which was among the sheep, *while* he abandoned his way and began to go in an illegitimate way"[65]; "The second ram fled from the presence of the first ram. Then I was *watching* the first sheep *while* he fell."[66]

Another nuance of this construction, found also in the LXX and in the NT, is that of *extent*, although it is found unambiguously only once in this literature: "They tracked them down to slaughter them *until* their swords became blunted with killing and their hands were utterly tired."[67] This may be paraphrased "they slaughtered them *to such an extent that* their swords became dull." Closely related to this usage is that of *result*, which can be confirmed for at least two of the readings in this literature. The first is found in Josephus:

> Now Herod was on his way to Fabius, who was governor of Damascus, but although he wished to rush to his brother's side, was prevented by illness; *until* [*with the result that*] Phasael by his own efforts overpowered Helix and shut him up in a tower.… When Herod recovered from his illness, he came against him.[68]

The second may be found in the literature of Appian:

> Being interested in [history], and desiring to compare the Roman prowess carefully with that of every other nation, my history has often led me from Carthage to Spain…like a wanderer, and again elsewhere, while the work was yet unfinished, *until* I have brought the parts together, showing how often the Romans sent armies or embassies into Sicily and what they did there until they brought it into its present condition.[69]

There is one other instance of ἕως οὗ in this literature that may fall under the category of *extent* or *result*. In his work on the customs of the Spartans, Plutarch notes:

> The Spartans…did not take part in any of the campaigns of…the kings of Macedonia who ruled in the following years, nor did they ever enter in the general congress or even pay tribute, *until* they ceased altogether to observe the laws of Lycurgus, and came to be ruled despotically by their own citizens…and so they became much like the rest…and were reduced to a state of subjection.[70]

There is some question here as to just what Plutarch intends by the phrase ἕως οὗ. It is possible that he wishes to express the idea of *extent*, so that the cessation of any obedience to the laws of Lycurgus is seen as the climax of the Spartans gradually increasing disregard of those laws. Or he may have in mind everything that comes after the phrase ἕως οὗ—namely, cessation of observing the laws, followed by despotic rule by Spartan citizens, followed by subjection to a foreign nation—implying result ("until all of this resulted in"), rather than extent. However, it seems likely that both ideas are in mind to varying degrees. If this is the case, then the action of the main clause ceases after the action of the subordinate clauses; for it is evident that the Spartans had no more opportunity to disregard these laws after their subjugation by Lycurgus.

A Summary of the Phrase ἕως ὅτου

The phrase ἕως ὅτου occurs only three times in all of the searchable non-biblical literature of this period, and all instances are found in Diodorus of Sicily. Moreover, only one of these occurrences takes on the meaning that we have seen to be primary in so much of the literature under consideration, both biblical and non-biblical: "Therefore, for a long time neither [the Carthaginians nor the armies of Agathocles] dared to cross the river [that separated them] in force, *until* an unexpected cause brought them into general battle."[71] The meaning of the construction here is clearly "until [but not after]," since the general battle necessarily discontinues their aloofness.

A second usage is extent: "He therefore sent in his soldiers a few at a time as if for particular needs *until* his troops far surpassed those of the city in number."[72] The meaning seems to be that the soldiers were continually sent in to such an extent that they finally outnumbered the inhabitants of the city. Nevertheless, the idea of *result* cannot be ruled out altogether, although a clearer example of result may be found in the third and final occurrence: "The dog, in the meantime, uttered neither yelp nor whimpered [at the cutting off of his leg], but continued with his teeth clamped shut [on the lion] *until* [*with the result that*], fainting with loss of blood, he died on top of the lion."[73] The action of the dog in the protasis resulted in the death of the dog in the apodosis.

Conclusion

We have examined all occurrences of the phrases ἕως οὗ and ἕως ὅτου in the LXX and in the searchable non-biblical literature spanning from the beginning of the first century BC through end of the first century AD. The purpose of this inquiry has been to see whether in fact there exists any clear example of either of these phrases that may be taken in such a way as to offer support for the meaning of ἕως οὗ in Matt 1:25 as it pertains to the perpetual virginity of Mary. The time frame for the non-biblical literature purposefully has been confined to the two centuries surrounding the birth of Christ for a number of reasons. First, there is little need to search the literature of the second century BC once we have established this usage for the phrase in the LXX (also composed in this era).[74] Our search has yielded seven such instances in the LXX where the phrase ἕως οὗ does indeed have the meaning "until [and continuing]" or "until [with no reference to continuation or discontinuation]." Second, if we can find corroborating evidence of this usage in the literature of the century just prior to the composition of Matthew's gospel, then the prospect becomes stronger that Matthew may have understood this phrase in his gospel in the same way. Third, if this usage for the phrase can also be found in the literature contemporaneous to Matthew's gospel (i.e., the first century AD), then there can be little objection to seeing this same usage in the passage in question, and Mary's perpetual virginity becomes a strong exegetical option.

While we do find support for this usage in the LXX, there are nevertheless no clear examples of this usage for at least a century and a half before Matthew wrote his Gospel; nor up to half a century afterwards.[75]

The literary evidence suggests that the Greek speaker of Matthew's time would have understood the phrase ἕως οὗ to imply cessation of the action of the main clause after the action of the subordinate clause. If Matthew had intended for us to see in his birth narrative evidence for the perpetual virginity of Mary, we might have expected him to use a phrase that would more readily lend itself to this idea.[76] In light of the lack of general attestation for this usage of ἕως οὗ during Matthew's time, we should perhaps look elsewhere for support of Mary's perpetual virginity.

CHAPTER III

The Brothers of Jesus in the New Testament

One final area of consideration in our discussion of Mary's perpetual virginity is that of the identity of those designated by the NT writers as the "brothers" of Jesus. The NT mentions several times that Jesus had brothers and sisters. A synopsis of the relevant passages follows:[1]

> While Jesus was still talking to the crowd, *his mother and brothers* stood outside, wanting to speak to him. Someone told him, "*Your mother and brothers* are standing outside, wanting to speak to you" (Matt 12:46–47=Mark 3:31–32; Luke 8:19–20). "Isn't this the carpenter's son? Isn't his mother's name Mary, and aren't *his brothers James, Joseph, Simon and Judas*? Aren't all his *sisters* with us?" (Matt 13:55–56=Mark 6:3). After this he went down to Capernaum with *his mother and brothers* and his disciples. There they stayed for a few days (John 2:12). *Jesus' brothers* said to him, "You ought to leave here and go to Judea, so that your disciples may see the miracles you do. No one who wants to become a public figure acts in secret. Since you are doing these things, show yourself to the world." For even *his own brothers* did not believe in him (John 7:3–5). [The apostles] all joined together constantly in prayer, along with the women and Mary the mother of Jesus, and with *his brothers* (Acts 1:14). Don't we have the right to take a believing wife along with us, as do the other apostles and the *Lord's brothers* and Cephas? (1 Cor 9:5). I saw none of the other apostles— only *James, the Lord's brother* (Gal 1:19).

McHugh notes that historically there are three views as to the identity of Jesus' "brothers."[2] The first of these, known as the *Helvidian* view (so-called because it was popularized by Helvidius in the late fourth century AD), posits what was eventually to become the majority Protestant view; namely, that after the birth of Jesus, Mary and Joseph consummated their marriage and had other children.[3] The second view, the *Epiphanian* view (named after its late fourth-century champion, Epiphanius), postulates that the "brothers" of Jesus were in fact his stepbrothers, children of Joseph by a previous marriage.[4] The third view, the *Hieronymian* view (advanced by Jerome in the late fourth century), sees the "brothers" of Jesus as his cousins. We will examine the merits of each of these views below.

The Helvidian View

The view that the "brothers and sisters" of Jesus are biological siblings is held by virtually all Protestant interpreters today, as well as a growing number of Roman Catholic interpreters.[5] Arguments in support of this view are as follows: First, the gospel writers would have avoided phrases such as "first-born son" (Luke 2:7), "did not know her until" (Matt 1:25), "before they came together" (Matt 1:18), and "brothers and sisters" (of Jesus) had they known of Mary's perpetual virginity. Such phrases would only have served to confuse their readers. Indeed, Luke goes out of his way to let his readers know that Joseph was only the "supposed" father of Jesus (ὧν υἱός, ὡς ἐνομίζετο, Ἰωσὴφ; Luke 3:23). Yet he gives no such qualification when speaking of the brothers and sisters of Jesus.

Second, the gospel writers customarily place these "brothers" of Jesus in attendance with Mary (Mark 3:31–35; Matt 12:46–50; Luke 8:19–21; John 2:12). The natural reading of these passages is that they were children of Mary. Third, this view was held by Tertullian, Helvidius, Bonosus, Jovinian, and others,[6] and so cannot be dismissed as a later Protestant innovation. Moreover, as Lightfoot himself pointed out, Jerome, in his polemic against the Helvidian view, could not cite even one historical proponent of his own view.[7]

McHugh cites several objections to the Helvidian view.[8] First, McHugh sees this view in conflict with his assumption that Luke 1:34 is an assertion of Mary's perpetual virginity.[9] Moreover, the phrase "first-born" (πρωτότοκος) in Luke 2:7 need not imply that other children were born afterward. This word is typically used in the LXX to denote one consecrated to God (Exod 13:12–15; 34:19–20). McHugh also objects to the Helvidian appeal to Matt 1:25 where it is asserted that Joseph "had no union with [Mary] until she gave birth to a son." He notes that the imperfect, not the aorist, is used here, which implies that Luke wanted to stress only the period of time before the birth of Jesus. He deems it likely that Matthew would have used the aorist had he wanted to convey the notion that Mary and Joseph consummated their marriage after Jesus' birth. We will critique McHugh's objections to this view after considering the evidence for the other two views.

The Hieronymian View

The Hieronymian view (Jerome's view) is the view held by the majority of Roman Catholic defenders today.[10] This view begins by pointing out the various meanings of ἀδελφός in Scripture. According to McHugh it can mean (1) blood brothers, (2) ethnic brothers (e.g., Jews), (3) distant blood relations (Gen 13:8; 29:15), (4) friends, or (5) spiritual brothers (i.e., Christians).[11] Those who hold to the Hieronymian view usually cite the third meaning as that which is to be applied in the case of Jesus and his brothers. The "brothers" of Jesus are actually his "cousins" or "relatives."

McHugh notes that the common Roman Catholic tendency to view the word ἀδελφός as "close relative" in these passages strains credulity: "Honesty compels us to admit that this 'interpretation' of the word 'brother' stretches its meaning to the breaking point, and one cannot seriously expect those unconvinced of the perpetual virginity of Mary to accept it."[12] Accordingly, McHugh argues for a revised view that is in effect a conflation of the Hieronymian view and the Epiphanian view (the view yet to be addressed). McHugh, convinced by the NT evidence that these "brothers" of Jesus must be part of his immediate family (else they would not be in constant company with Jesus' mother), contends that these "brothers" of Jesus are actually cousins who were adopted by Joseph and Mary. Hence, James and Joseph (Joses) were sons of Joseph's sister (whose name was Mary), who were reared by Mary and Joseph after the death of their biological father. Simeon is the son of Clopas' wife (also named Mary), who is distinguished from Mary the mother of Jesus by the phrase "the other Mary" (Matt 27:61; 28:1). Judas is another nephew who was adopted by Mary and Joseph perhaps after the death of his parents. The reason the boy Joseph is sometimes called the diminutive "Joses" (Mark 6:3; Matt 27:56) is precisely to distinguish him from Joseph, Mary's husband, who was living in the same household.[13] This scenario allows McHugh to affirm both that Jesus had no biological brothers (safeguarding Mary's perpetual virginity) and that those living in his household could truly be called his "brothers."[14] McHugh's scenario results in the following relationships among the Marys at the cross of Jesus:

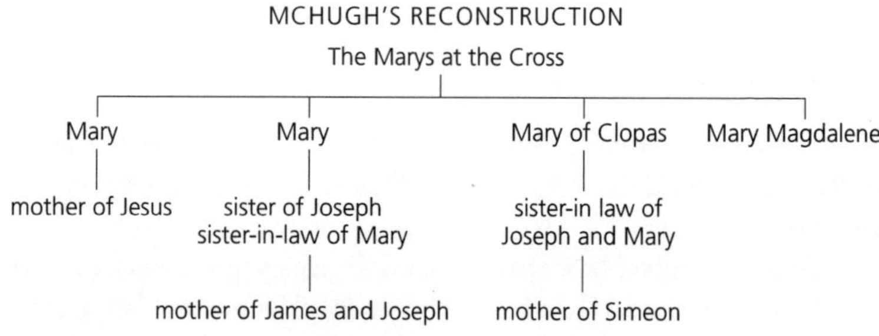

There are serious flaws in McHugh's confusing and speculative reconstruction. First, Joseph was probably dead by the time period recorded by the Gospels,[15] so there would be no reason to continue to distinguish Joses from Joseph the carpenter. Second, since Joseph was likely dead by this time, why do we find the sons of Mary of Clopas (who was still alive at this time) still living with Mary the mother of Jesus instead of their own mother? There seems to be no good reason why Mary as a widow should somehow be more capable of supporting the sons of Clopas' wife than Clopas' wife herself.

Third, that Joseph and Mary would become the foster parents of so many sets of unrelated siblings (at least three sets, and perhaps even more if we are to account for the "sisters" of Jesus using the same explanation) strains credulity.[16] There seems to be no reason to adopt this thesis other than to accommodate the gratuitous assumption that these "brothers" of Jesus cannot be biological brothers.[17] At the end of the day, McHugh's reconstruction raises more questions than it answers, and in any case seems like a farfetched solution in explaining the identity of the brothers of Jesus. In the words of Meier: "One cannot avoid the impression that every escape hatch imaginable is being pried open because a highly unlikely position has been adopted a priori on other grounds."[18]

But what of the basic tenet of the Hieronymian view that the "brothers" of Jesus are actually his cousins (or some other distant relatives)? This view, too, is fraught with difficulties. First, it seems to weaken the natural reading—and theological point—of such passages as Matt 12:46–50 (=Mark 3:31–35):

> While Jesus was still talking to the crowd, his mother and brothers stood outside, wanting to speak to him. Someone told him, "Your mother and brothers are standing outside, wanting to speak to you." He replied to him, "Who is my mother, and who are my brothers?" Pointing to his disciples, he said, "Here are my mother and my brothers. For whoever does the will of my Father in heaven is my brother and sister and mother."

Not only are "his mother and brothers" seen as a unit in this passage (as though they are of the same household), but to posit that these "brothers" are in reality "cousins" or "distant relatives" severely weakens the "punch line" that Jesus delivers at the end of this pericope.[19] His point is that a metaphysical relationship with him has priority over even the closest physical ties ("mother," "brother," and "sister"). Are we really to conclude that what Jesus is saying here is "whoever does the will of my father in heaven is my cousin/distant relative and my mother"? "The full force of the aphorism is retained only if the natural relationships mentioned are all equally close and blood-related."[20]

Another passage that would be similarly weakened is John 7:3–5:

> Jesus' brothers said to him, "You ought to leave here and go to Judea, so that your disciples may see the miracles you do. No one who wants to become a public figure acts in secret. Since you are doing these things, show yourself to the world." For even his own brothers did not believe in him.

If we are to assume that "brothers"="cousins" in this passage, what we are left with is a comparatively empty episode: "The bitter sadness of this aside loses a great deal of its rhetorical force if it means instead 'for not even his cousins believed in him'."[21] In both passages above, the meaning is all but lost if the Hieronymian view is adopted.[22]

Moreover, the Hieronymian view itself is based on the prior assumption that "cousin" is an appropriate designation for ἀδελφὸς in the NT. Defenders of this view typically appeal to the use of the word ἀδελφὸς in the LXX where this word is sometimes used of close relatives.[23] It will be helpful to examine the usage of ἀδελφὸς in the LXX and the NT to see if we can adduce support for this usage in the NT texts that speak of the brothers and sisters of Jesus.

The Use of ἀδελφὸς / ἀδελφὴ in the LXX

There are over 1,000 combined occurrences of the words ἀδελφὸς and ἀδελφὴ in the LXX. While most of these refer to biological brothers and sisters, not a few are references to other kinds of relationships. Genesis 9:5 uses ἀδελφὸς to denote "fellow man" (also 2 Kings 7:6). In Gen 14:14–16 Lot is called the "brother" of Abraham (see also 13:8), though we know from other texts (14:12; 12:5) that Lot is the son of Abraham's biological brother. Here the meaning is simply "close relative." The meaning "relative" is also found in Gen 24:27 where it refers to Abraham's immediate relatives, in Gen 24:59 where it refers to Rebekah's relationship to her mother and brother, and in Gen 29:12, 15 where it refers to the relationship between Jacob the nephew and Laban his uncle (cf. also Judg 9:18 for this sense). In each case, the relationship is a close one. In Gen 12:13 (also 12:19; 20:2, 5, 12–13) Abraham and Sarah are depicted as "brother and sister." Here however (though they are also spouses) the nomenclature is accurate (20:12).

The word ἀδελφὸς is also used of fellow citizens (Gen 19:7) or ethnic countrymen (Exod 2:11, 4:18; Lev 19:17). It is sometimes used to denote a fellow "tribesman" (distinguished from countrymen as a whole; Num 8:26, 16:10, 18:2, 6; Judg 18:8, 14; 19:23), or of the relationship between tribes (Judg 1:3, 17; 5:14; 1 Chron 9:9). On a broader scale it is used to denote the relationship between distantly related ethnic groups that share a common ancestry (e.g., the brotherhood of Israel and Edom [Num 20:14; Deut 23:7] or Israel and Esau [Deut 2:4, 8] based on common Semitic ancestry). It may also be used to denote "close friend" (as in the case of David and Jonathan, 2 Sam 1:26), "associate" (1 Chron 6:44[29]), "companion" (Prov 7:4; 18:9, 19; Job 17:14;

30:29), or simply "friend" as a term of endearment (2 Sam 20:9, where Joab calls Amasa ἀδελφὸς just before killing him; see also Jer 22:18; 1 Kings 9:13; 20:32–33; 2 Kings 9:2).[24] In a few cases the meaning is more like "colleague" (as in 1 Kings 13:30, "fellow prophet").

Both words are also used to denote spouses (such as we find in Cant 4:9, 10, 12; 5:1–2; Add Esth 5:1). The word ἀδελφὴ in particular is used figuratively for an allegorical relationship between Jerusalem and her "sisters," Samaria and Sodom (Ezek 16:45–46, 48–49, 51–52, 55–56, 61; 23:4, 11, 18, 31–33). Instances to "cousins" proper may be found in a couple of texts, including Lev 10:4 (the cousins of Nadab and Abihu) and 1 Chron 23:22 (the cousins of Eleazar's daughters).[25] Tobit 3:15, on the other hand, distinguishes between "close brother" (ἀδελφὸς ἐγγὺς)[26] and "cousin" (συγγενὴς).[27] It is probably more accurate to say then that the former instances of ἀδελφὸς and ἀδελφὴ simply mean "relative" (rather than "cousin") as they do in other texts that denote close relatives (e.g., Gen 14:14).

The Use of ἀδελφὸς / ἀδελφὴ in the New Testament

The word ἀδελφὸς, with its feminine cognate ἀδελφὴ, is used in the NT some 368 times. Ninety-one of these instances carry the meaning "sibling."[28] In some cases the siblings are named, or known from other sources: hence, Judah and his brothers (Matt 1:2); Simon Peter and Andrew his brother (Matt 4:18); James and his brother John, the sons of Zebedee (Matt 4:21); Herod and Philip (Matt 14:3; although here half-brother is in mind); Mary and Lazarus (John 11:2); Mary and Martha (Luke 10:39).

In some cases one of the siblings is named and the other is not, such as we find in Acts 23:16, "the son of Paul's sister"; and in Rom 16:15, "Greet Nereus and his sister." One such case may be John 19:25, "Near the cross of Jesus stood his mother, his mother's sister, Mary the wife of Clopas, and Mary Magdalene." The exact identity of the sister of Jesus' mother in this passage is disputed. Some, seeing three women in this passage, take the phrase, "Mary the wife of Clopas," epexegetically to "his mother's sister." Others see four different women in this passage. This is a key passage in deciphering the identity of the brothers of Jesus and so will be dealt with in greater depth later.

In other cases a specific person is in mind, but neither that person nor his sibling is named, such as with Luke 12:13, "Someone in the crowd said to him, 'Teacher, tell my brother to divide the inheritance with me' "; Luke 14:12, "When you give a dinner, do not invite your friends, your brothers, or your relatives"; Luke 15:27 (to the prodigal son), "your brother has come, and your father has killed the fattened calf"; Luke 16:28 (the rich man to Abraham), "I have five brothers." In still other cases the reference is generic, as in Matt 10:21, "brother will betray brother"; Matt 19:29, "everyone who has left houses or brothers or sisters…for my sake"; Matt 22:24, "if a man dies without having children, his brother must marry the widow."

As many as twenty-two of these instances carry the meaning "countryman/men" ("Brothers [=countrymen], I can tell you confidently that the patriarch David died and was buried," Acts 2:29); all but three of these instances are found in Acts. Up to twelve instances carry the meaning "fellow man" (Matt 5:22: "But I tell you that anyone who is angry with his brother will be subject to judgment"); all but one of these are found in Matthew and Luke.

Not surprisingly, the vast majority of instances (243) carry the meaning "spiritual sibling" (i.e., fellow Christian), and most of these (all but fifty-five) occur in the NT epistles. While the majority of those in the latter category occur either in the plural vocative ("I urge you, brothers," Rom 16:17) or with the third person plural ("the brothers who came from Macedonia supplied my needs," 2 Cor 11:9), there are many instances that occur with the plural personal pronoun ("our brother/our brothers," 2 Cor 8:22–23; "Timothy, our brother," Col 1:1), as well as with the singular personal pronoun ("my brother, Titus," 2 Cor 2:13; "Epaphroditus, my brother," Phlp 2:25). The latter is not meant to exclude the readers from being "brothers" of the men named, but rather to emphasize the close bond between these men and the writer.

There are several instances where ἀδελφὸς is used in a generic sense for any given Christian. In 1 Thess 4:6, Paul warns his readers that no one should "wrong his brother" in the matter of sexual immorality. Similarly, James issues a warning for "anyone who speaks against his brother, or judges his brother" (James 4:11); and John outlines several consequences for "anyone" who "hates his brother" (1 John 2:9, 11; 3:10, 15; 4:20), or "sees his brother in need" but does nothing to help (1 John 3:17). Such usage, where both the reader and the brother remain anonymous, operates as a rhetorical device.

Summary of Usage in the LXX and New Testament

We may now make some observations on the general usage of ἀδελφὸς and ἀδελφή. First, while the semantic range of these words is broad in the LXX, encompassing several nuances (including biological sibling, fellow man, relative, fellow citizen, countryman, tribesman, friend, colleague/associate, spouse, and distant ethnic relations based on common ancestry), the semantic range for these words in the NT seems to be limited to a few primary meanings, including biological sibling, spiritual (or metaphysical) sibling, fellow man, and countryman. The latter two meanings occur only in the masculine form, and in a few cases could carry the alternative meaning "friend," "colleague," or "associate" (Matt 5:47; Luke 6:41). The feminine ἀδελφή is used once in a figurative sense to denote a local assembly, but even here the meaning is "spiritual sibling" (collectively of a group of Christians).

Unlike its counterpart in the LXX, there are no instances of ἀδελφὸς in the NT that bear the meaning "relatives," except of course where the reference is to biological siblings.[29] Indeed, ἀδελφὸς is often found in passages where relatives, in the broad sense, are clearly distinguished from immediate siblings. In Luke 14:12 we read: "When you give a luncheon or dinner, do not invite your friends, your brothers, your relatives, or your rich neighbors." The word "relatives" (συγγενίς) here denotes a different class of people than brothers, friends, and neighbors.[30] Similarly with Luke 21:16: "You will be betrayed by parents, brothers, relatives, and friends." Here again, the word "relatives" (συγγενίς) denotes a different class than "brothers," and the two are no more interchangeable than are parents and brothers.

The NT writers have a number of special designations for relatives outside of immediate family. As we have already seen, Luke favors the word συγγενίς, and uses it again in Luke 1:36 to refer to Elizabeth as the "cousin" of Mary. It is significant that Luke recognizes a distinction between συγγενίς and ἀδελφὸς because (as we shall see later) Luke is one of the writers that makes mention of the "brothers of Jesus," once in his gospel and once in Acts. A second word, ἀνεψιὸς, occurs in Col 4:10 to refer to Mark, the "cousin" of Barnabas. Since obviously Paul knew of this word, he certainly could have used it in Gal 1:19 and 1 Cor 9:5 if he had intended to refer to the "cousins" of Jesus.

The third way that relatives are denoted in the NT is through the somewhat awkward method of identifying a person through a common relationship with another person, such as we find in Acts 23:16: ὁ υἱὸς τῆς ἀδελφῆς Παύλου, *the son of Paul's sister*," instead of "Paul's nephew," or indeed, "Paul's brother" (such as we find in the LXX to refer to the relationship between Abraham and Lot—Gen 14:14–16). It seems evident from the first two words above (συγγενίς and ἀνεψιὸς) that both Paul and Luke knew of ways to denote "cousins" when that is what they meant. In any case, "the very reason why we know that…*adelphos* [in the LXX] can mean cousin, nephew, or some other relative is that the immediate context regularly makes the exact relation clear by some sort of periphrasis…. No such clarification is given in the NT texts concerning the brothers of Jesus."[31] Indeed, even in the Greek literature contemporaneous to the NT there is no clear-cut example of ἀδελφὸς or ἀδελφὴ denoting a "cousin"[32]; so that Fitzmyer is forced to conclude: "Jerome thought that *adelphos* could mean 'cousin,' but this is almost certainly to be ruled out as the NT meaning."[33]

Moreover, ἀδελφὴ ("sister") in the NT is always used to denote a "sibling" of some sort (whether biological, spiritual, or figurative); it is never used to denote relatives generically or cousins specifically. In similar vein, everywhere ἀδελφὸς is used in contexts in which a "brother" is named it, too, always refers to a sibling. McKenzie observes that while

> There is no question that the word 'brother' is often used in the Bible to designate other members of a kinship group beyond those who are children of at least one common parent…the use of 'sister' to designate more remote kinswomen is much rarer. And there is no instance of the use of 'brothers' and 'sisters' for more remote kinsmen and kinswomen when the words accompany an enumeration of names.[34]

Both of these points are significant for our discussion because both of them are true of the passages dealing with the "brothers and sisters" of the Lord. Hence, when Matthew and Mark name the ἀδελφοὶ of Jesus—James, Joseph, Simon and Judas (Matt 13:55; Mark 6:3)—and at the same time speak of his ἀδελφαὶ (Matt 13:56; Mark 6:3), it suggests to us that the normal reading of these texts is that Jesus had biological brothers and sisters. Whereas these words do sometimes mean "spiritual sibling," or (in the case of ἀδελφὸς) are used as a term of endearment in a personal address (e.g., Acts 22:1), these meanings can hardly be applied to those who "didn't believe him" (John 7:5):

> James is hardly called 'the brother of the Lord' because he was thought to do the will of the father. Of him and of Jose, Judas and Simon (Mark 6:13) *the more probable meaning* (and of the sisters mentioned *ibid.* [*sic*]) *is children of at least one common parent*; and so it would be understood for any one else. In the same context of Mark the one parent mentioned is Mary; this does not support the explanation sometimes advanced that they are children of Joseph by a previous marriage.[35] [emphasis in original]

What is true of the Markan passage referenced above may be said of all NT passages that mention the "brothers" of Jesus. Not only are these "brothers" sharply distinguished from disciples ("spiritual siblings") in John 7:5 and elsewhere, but they are also particularized in contexts where "spiritual siblings" is assumed to include all (e.g., Acts 1:14).[36]

The Epiphanian View

The view that the "brothers of Jesus" are children of Joseph by a previous marriage remains, by and large, the least popular of the three. McHugh notes that virtually no one holds it today except some supporters in the Eastern Orthodox Church.[37] If it were not for Bauckham's recent defense of this theory, we may have safely disregarded it from further consideration. Below are Bauckham's major arguments for the Epiphanian view.

Bauchham begins his defense by agreeing with the Helvidian view that "stepbrother" is not a meaning within the semantic range of ἀδελφός, but denies the significance of that observation. He contends that this point is relevant only in societies that differentiate between full-siblings and stepsiblings, something he considers doubtful in Jewish society.[38] He cites Lev 18:11 as a possible reference to a man's stepsister who is simply called a "sister," though he acknowledges that both the LXX and the majority of scholars understand the passage to refer to a half-sister.[39] In any case, the relationship between Mary, Joseph and Jesus is "strictly unique" since Jesus had no biological father, and the relationship is "much more like an adoptive relationship than like a steprelationship."[40] Jesus was born in wedlock; and the *legal* ramification is therefore that Joseph was Jesus' father in a socially unqualified sense. So then, any children Joseph may have had before his marriage to Mary would naturally be "adoptive" siblings rather than stepsiblings.[41] Adopted children are regularly designated in the NT by the same terms that are used for natural relationships. For instance, although Moses was adopted by Pharoah's daughter he is nevertheless called her υἱός ("son," Acts 7:21; Heb 11:24). Similarly, the word ἀδελφὸς is used (without qualification) when speaking about the adoptive relationship between Christians and Jesus (Rom 8:29; cf. vv. 15–17).

Bauckham takes Meier to task for dismissing the Epiphanian view, seemingly out of hand, on the basis that the word ἀδελφὸς never means "stepbrother" in the NT:

> What is quite extraordinary is the assertion [by Meier] that the general NT usage of a word exclusively determines its meaning in particular instances in the NT, excluding meanings which are unattested in literature outside the NT.... [T]his consistency would be "amazing" only if there were occasions on which NT writers referred to stepbrothers in other ways. Since it is unusual to refer to stepbrothers at all, there is nothing amazing about the NT writers' failure to use ἀδελφὸς in this sense outside the disputed cases.... There are many Greek words which in the NT usually have one meaning but occasionally have another.... For example, τράπεζα occurs 15 times in the NT, normally with the meaning "table." Just once, in Luke 19:23, it means "bank," according to all translators and exegetes, but Meier's principle would have to disallow this.[42]

Bauckham continues his examples, citing rare usages of the word τέλος (it means "tax" in Matt 17:25 and Rom 13:7), and then concludes: "Meier's argument contradicts what nearly all translators and exegetes assume: that the range of use from which the meaning of a word in the NT must be chosen is the range of use in the language, not the range of use in the NT."[43]

Bauckham further criticizes Meier for being inconsistent with his own principle, citing Meier's conclusion that when Mark 6:17 calls Philip the "brother" of Herod, he really means "half-brother"—a usage that can be discovered only by consulting documents outside the NT! Moreover, the NT itself calls Joseph and Mary the "parents" of Jesus (Luke 2:41, 43), and Joseph is specifically designated the "father" of Jesus (Luke 2:48). We must assume a steprelationship in these cases even though:

> the use of these terms for literal family relationships elsewhere in the NT provides no example of a meaning other than biological parenthood.… If Luke can call Joseph Jesus' parent or father without implying blood relationship, then it is arbitrary to insist that reference to Jesus' brothers and sisters must imply blood relationship.[44]

Although Bauckham raises some thoughtful objections to those who would simply dismiss the Epiphanian view, much of what he argues does not hold up under close scrutiny. In the first place, although one can agree that there are rare usages of many NT words, none of the examples he cites parallels what we find in the case of ἀδελφός. In each case the reason the word under consideration (τράπεζα and τέλος) is translated contrary to normal usage is precisely because the context demands that the normal usage be abandoned. There is, on the other hand, absolutely nothing in the context of the "brothers of Jesus" passages that indicates that we should abandon the normal usage of ἀδελφός.

Second, while Bauckham is certainly right about his insistence that we take into account the usage of ἀδελφός outside the NT, he has offered no instance in which this word is unambiguously used of a stepbrother in any literature.[45] While it is true that some instances of ἀδελφός could refer to stepbrothers without our knowing it, this could be said of any word in the NT. One could just as easily argue, for instance, that τράπεζα or τέλος (to use Bauckham's examples) *could* carry other unattested meanings; but without clear-cut examples it seems rather precarious to base an entire theological construct on such meanings.

Third, his appeal to the fact that Joseph, the legal father of Jesus, is called his πατρός (cf. Luke2:48; just as Jesus is also called Joseph's υἱός, Matt 13:55) without qualification, and therefore is more of an adoptive relationship than a steprelationship, does not take into account that we are specifically told elsewhere by the same author that Joseph is the "supposed" father of Jesus (ὢν υἱός ὡς ἐνομίζετο Ἰωσὴφ, Luke 3:23)— not to mention that we are given a detailed account by both Matthew and Luke that Joseph could not have been the biological father of Jesus. We can agree with Bauckham that adoptive relationships might use these terms, but that does not thereby demonstrate an adoptive relationship between Jesus and his "brothers." In each of the cases cited by Bauckham where normal familial terms are used in adoptive families (Moses and Pharaoh's daughter; Christians and Jesus; Christians and God, etc.) we are clearly informed that the relationship in question is an adoptive relationship. Such is not the case with the brothers of Jesus, and Meier's comments regarding McHugh's view seem to apply equally to Bauckham's—"What is gratuitously asserted may be gratuitously denied."[46]

As Meier also points out: "To be honest, the so-called 'Epiphanian solution,'…strikes one from the start as arbitrary and gratuitous.… It may well be that we are dealing with a solution thought up after the fact to support the emerging idea of Mary's perpetual virginity."[47] Certainly there seems to be no other motivation to adopt this view than to uphold Mary's perpetual virginity while at the same time avoiding the charge of contradicting the NT evidence that Jesus had siblings.[48] Moreover, neither Matthew nor Luke, in their respective infancy narratives, gives us any hint that this is a subsequent marriage for Joseph.[49] It seems best, if for no other reason than the lack of any direct supporting NT evidence in its favor, to abandon the Epiphanian view from serious consideration.

A Case for the Helvidian View

Both the Hieronymian view and the Epiphanian view have been shown to be deficient on philological grounds; neither can provide evidence contemporary to that of the NT writers for their proposed usage of ἀδελφὸς. As we have already shown, the strengths of the Helvidian view are as follows:

First and foremost, the Helvidian view best explains the philological evidence of the usage of ἀδελφὸς/ἀδελφὴ, both in the NT and in the literature contemporary to the NT. Second, these siblings are presented by the NT writers as true siblings without the kinds of qualifications that we find in regard to Joseph's fatherhood of Jesus (e.g., Luke 3:23). Third, this view best accounts for the fact that Mary the mother of Jesus is regularly found in the company of these "brothers" of Jesus. Fourth, this view best preserves the force of those texts that either show Jesus distinguishing between the priority of metaphysical "brothers" over against physical "brothers" (e.g., Mark 3:31–35), or show the tragedy of disbelief even among "his own brothers" (John 7:5).

Fifth, this view has the added strength of being the simplest explanation, for it (1) affirms only what we may naturally and safely infer from the text, and (2) does not speculate about areas for which we have no information. In the case of (1), we read that Mary and Joseph are married, from which we infer that normal marital relations occurred. We further read that Jesus has "brothers" and "sisters" (in texts that place them with his "mother"), from which we infer that these are biological siblings. In the case of (2), this view does not speculate that Mary *may* have remained a virgin all through her married life, nor that these "brothers" of Jesus *may* have been cousins rather than siblings; nor that this *may* have been a second marriage for Joseph, nor that he *may* have had children from a prior marriage; nor that he and Mary *may* have adopted other children, some from what *may* have been his brother and others from what *may* have been his sister.

Moreover, all but one of the objections that McHugh raises against the Helvidian view are not objections *against* the Helvidian view *per se*, but are simply intended to aid McHugh's view. He notes, for instance, that Matt 1:25 ("he did not know her until she gave birth") does not *have* to imply that sexual relations ensued after the birth of Jesus since Matthew uses the imperfect (ἐγίνωσκεν, "was not knowing") rather than the aorist ("did not know"), stressing only the period of time before the birth of Jesus. Yet, in addition to contextual considerations,[50] other exegetes have made the opposite point; namely, that the imperfect (even more than the aorist) implies that Mary subsequently had children.[51] It is doubtful, therefore, that this point can be used as support for McHugh's view.[52]

The other objection of McHugh—namely, that the phrase "firstborn" (πρωτότοκος) in Luke 2:7 need not imply that other children were born afterward since it is typically used in the LXX to denote one consecrated to God (Exod 13:12–15; 34:19–20)—is again designed to bolster McHugh's view, and does not detract from the Helvidian view. Many scholars agree with McHugh, including the *MNT* taskforce, who does not see the term "firstborn son" (τὸν υἱὸν αὐτῆς τὸν πρωτότοκον) in Luke 2:7 as any indication of other children subsequently born of Mary since "no logically deduced answer to that question is possible from his terminology."[53] Relying on the work of R. F. Stoll[54], the taskforce appeals to a grave inscription of a Jewish woman found in Egypt and dated around 5 BC which reads: "In the pains of giving birth to a first-born child, Fate brought me to the end of my life." Clearly in this case the woman had no subsequent children.

However, this evidence may not offer the support needed by the taskforce to dismiss the possibility of seeing in this phrase an assumption of other children in the case of Mary. While it is true that the woman for whom the inscription was written did not subsequently have children, that is not to deny that the phrase *implicitly assumes* that had the woman survived the birth of the first child she would have gone on to have other children afterward. Put another way, if the author of the inscription had known that the woman had decided beforehand to bear one and only one child, it seems strange that the phrase "firstborn" would still have been used in her case. In the case of Mary, one can only assume that Luke was familiar enough with Mary's situation to know whether or not she had made such a decision. If Luke had known of any decision by Mary to remain a virgin post partum, it seems certain that he would not have used a phrase that so easily lends itself to misunderstanding. Such a phrase would make sense only if Luke knew of other children who had been born of Mary—or at least that Mary still had childbearing potential. But by the time Luke wrote his Gospel Mary was well past her natural childbearing years, and Luke would naturally have deduced that Mary was not going to have more children.

Indeed, if Luke had known of Mary's perpetual virginity it seems certain that he would have used the word μονογενής ("only born") instead of πρωτότοκος ("firstborn"), since the former is used by Luke in three other passages, all of which speak of someone's only child. In Luke 7:12 we read: "As he approached the town gate, a dead person was being carried out—the *only son* of his mother, and she was a widow." In Luke 8:41–42 we read "Then a man named Jairus, a ruler of the synagogue, came and fell at Jesus' feet, pleading with him to come to his house because his only daughter, a girl of about twelve, was dying." Finally, in Luke 9:38 we read: "A man in the crowd called out, 'Teacher, I beg you to look at my son, for he is my only child.'" In each of these passages the word μονογενὴς is used, not πρωτότοκος. In any case, as Meier notes, "since the author who writes Luke 2:7 also speaks of Jesus' mother and brothers in Luke 8:19–21 and Acts 1:14, the title "firstborn" takes on a more precise meaning in light of the larger context."[55]

One final objection that McHugh cites against the Helvidian view is his prior assumption that Luke 1:34 informs us of Mary's perpetual virginity. McHugh contends that Mary and Joseph decided on a life of virginity in order to devote their lives to Jesus: "Their motive was to put themselves entirely and exclusively at the service of Jesus, and to renounce everything that might conceivably divert or distract them from playing their full part in his mission."[56] The issue of Mary's alleged "vow of virginity" is more appropriately taken up in our discussion of Luke's portrayal of Mary, and so we shall reserve comment on McHugh's final objection until we address the issue in detail there.

The Relationship Between the "Marys" at the Cross and the Brothers of Jesus

The question of the relationship among the various "Marys" in the NT and those identified as the "brothers of Jesus" (namely, James, Jude [Judas], Joseph [Joses], and Simon) is a complex one that is fraught with difficulties. The issue is further complicated by the fact that (outside of other indicators that may tip the scales one way or the other) various relationships may be posited with equal measures of certainty; so that the *MNT* taskforce is forced to conclude: "We were not even agreed on which solution might be called the more likely."[57] Indeed, Meier may very well be correct when he says that to use Mark 15:40— or any of the "women at the cross" parallels—to attempt to explain the relationship between the various Marys and those designated the "brothers" of Jesus is to "explain the obscure by the still more obscure."[58] Nevertheless, we will examine the NT evidence for these relationships, and then propose what we believe to be the most plausible solution.

Carson gives us a helpful starting point by placing the various "women at the cross" accounts in a synoptic format:[59]

Matthew 27:56	Mark 15:40	John 19:25
Mary Magdalene	Mary Magdalene	Jesus' mother
Mary the mother of James and Joseph	Mary the mother of James the younger and Joses	Jesus' mother's sister
The Mother of Zebedee's sons	Salome	Mary wife of Clopas
		Mary Magdalene

Aside from Mary Magdalene, there is no unanimity among exegetes as to whether any of the other Marys are present in all three accounts. However, we may safely advance several certainties about the texts, and the likely scenarios that follow.

Matthew's account undoubtedly presents three women, only two of which are named. The Mary in question is identified as the mother of James and Joseph, and the unnamed woman is the mother of Zebedee's sons. Mark's account just as certainly presents three women, this time naming all of them. His mention of Mary as "the mother of James the younger and Joses" is almost certainly to be equated with Matthew's Mary "the mother of James and Joseph." So at this point it is likely that the first two women mentioned by Matthew and Mark are the same. This point is strengthened by the similarities in grammar between the prefaces of the two accounts:

> Ησαν δὲ ἐκεῖ γυναῖκες πολλαὶ ἀπὸ μακρόθεν θεωροῦσαι
> (Matt 27:55).
> Ησαν δὲ καὶ γυναῖκες ἀπὸ μακρόθεν θεωροῦσαι
> (Mark 15:40).

If we can assume that Matthew is following Mark's account (as the similarities suggest), then it becomes likely that Mark's "Salome" is to be equated with Matthew's "mother of Zebedee's sons" (i.e., Salome is the mother of the apostles James and John). If that is the case, then Matthew and Mark agree at all points in the identity of the women at the cross, and only John's Gospel must be accounted for.

John's account, however, is much more ambiguous. Carson suggests that it is possible to see in John's account two, three, or even four women.[60] The second two references may be in apposition to the first two (i.e., "his mother and his mother's sister; namely, Mary the wife of Clopas and Mary Magdalene"), hence portraying only two women. The fact that καὶ occurs only between the first and second references and the third and fourth references (being omitted between the second and third references) strengthens this view. But this view suffers from several weaknesses, including: (1) that Mary is now to be seen as remarried to Clopas after the death of Joseph; (2) that there are two sisters named Mary in the same household; and (3) that someone already identified as "his [Jesus'] mother" would need any further designation (such as "wife of Clopas") to identify her. These reasons—not to mention the fact that it is nowhere else hinted that Mary Magdalene is the sister of Jesus' mother—should suffice safely to eliminate the view that John portrays only two women at the cross.

Another possibility is that John sees three women at the cross ("his mother, his mother's sister, [namely] Mary the wife of Clopas, and Mary Magdalene"). Again, the absence of καὶ between the second and third references ("his mother's sister"/"Mary the wife of Clopas") may suggest that the third reference is in apposition to the second. But the same problem that plagues the first view (namely, the existence of two sisters named Mary in the same household) plagues this view as well, and we may reject this view on the grounds that it would be "highly improbable that two sisters should have borne the same name."[61]

The final option is that John sees four women at the cross—two named and two unnamed ("his mother and his mother's sister, [and] Mary of Clopas and Mary Magdalene").[62] The absence of καὶ between the second and third references may be explained on the grounds that John distinguishes between named and unnamed women, and perhaps sees closer ties between the first and second references and the third and fourth references than he does between either one in the first set and either one in the second set.

If we assume that of the four women he presents, John includes the three found in the accounts of Matthew and Mark, then we may conclude the following parallels:

John 19:25	Matthew 27:56	Mark 15:40
Mary Magdalene	=Mary Magdalene	=Mary Magdalene
Jesus' mother	=Mary the mother of James and Joseph	=Mary the mother of James the younger and Joses
Jesus' mother's sister	=Mother of Zebedee's sons	=Salome
Mary wife of Clopas	?	?

Carson concludes the above scenario, though only tentatively.[63] He also thinks that the identification of the mother of Zebedee's sons casts light on the understanding on Matt 20:20 where the mother of Zebedee's sons is pleading for special privileges from Jesus in behalf of her sons, perhaps on the basis of biological relations.[64] Salome reappears in Mark 16:1 (after the resurrection) where she is again in the company of Mary Magdalene and Mary the mother of James [and Joses?]. The latter Mary is also portrayed in Luke's post-resurrection account (Luke 24:10), this time in the company of not only Mary Magdalene, but also "Joanna." If James is the son of Mary, Jesus' mother, then he reappears in Gal 1:19 ("James, the Lord's brother"), as well as in Jude 1 ("Jude, a brother of James"). Both James and Jude (Judas) appear earlier in Matthew (13:55) and Mark (6:3) with two other brothers (Joseph and Simon), all of which are presented as Jesus' "brothers."

While the above scenario is the one adopted by this writer, it must be noted that it is not without its weaknesses. First, this view assumes a "cousin" relationship between Jesus and the sons of Zebedee, which relationship is never hinted at in the entire NT (except perhaps in Matt 20:20). Second, why the gospel writers should suddenly change the designation of Jesus' mother from "the mother of Jesus" (and equivalents) to "the mother of James [and Joses]" seems odd if not inexplicable.[65] One possible reason is that the gospel writers want us to see at the cross a severing of biological ties between Jesus and his family.[66] But if this is the case, then Luke (who designates Mary as the "mother of James"; Luke 24:10), reverts back to the title "mother of Jesus" in the post-resurrection community (Acts 1:14). Moreover, there is early evidence from the second century that Clopas (whose wife is one of the Marys at the cross) was actually the brother of Joseph (Jesus' step-father), and that his son was named Simon.[67] This does not seriously affect our view, however, since while this same evidence identifies Simon as the "cousin of the Lord,"[68] it also speaks of James as the "brother of the Lord."[69] Hence, our writer does not see James and Simon son of Clopas as "brothers." In any case, the name "Simon" is not exactly uncommon in the first century, and it very well could be the case that Jesus had both a brother and a cousin with this name.[70]

The Brothers of Jesus and the Perpetual Virginity of Mary in the Post-Apostolic Age

The notion that the brothers of Jesus were in fact something other than true siblings developed over time in the post-apostolic church. Ignatius, writing in the second century, clearly believed in the virginity of Mary before the birth of Christ, but there is no evidence that he believed in the virginity of Mary during birth (virginity *in partu*) or after birth (virginity *post partum*). His phrase regarding the "mysteries of renown" in his letter to the Ephesians—"the virginity of Mary was hidden from the prince of this world, as was also her offspring, and the death of the Lord"[71]—is probably to be taken in a sequential way, listing Mary's virginity first, then the birth of Christ, then his death.[72] The second-century writer, Hegesippus, on the other hand, mentions James "the brother [ἀδελφὸς] of the Lord,"[73] and Jude "who is said to have been the Lord's brother [ἀδελφὸς] according to the flesh,"[74] as well as Simeon the son of Clopas whom Hegesippus calls the "cousin [ἀνεψιὸς] of the Lord."[75] The fact that Hegesippus knows of a distinction between these two relationships indicates that when he uses ἀδελφὸς he does so with biological siblings in mind.

Tertullian, writing in the late second and early third centuries, also considered the brothers of Jesus to be biological siblings in several of his writings.[76] In *Against Marcion* he writes:

> [The Marcionites] say that He testifies Himself to His not having been born, when He asks, "Who is my mother, and who are my brethren?"…it could not possibly have been told Him that His mother and His brethren stood without, desiring to see Him, if He had had no mother and no brethren…. For tell me now, does a mother live on contemporaneously with her sons in every case? Have all sons brothers born for

> them? May a man rather not have fathers and sisters (living),
> or even no relatives at all? …[T]hey "who were standing with-
> out" were really "His mother and His brethren."…It seems as
> if [Jesus'] language amounted to a denial of His family and
> His birth; but it arose actually from the absolute nature of the
> case, and the conditional sense in which His words were to be
> explained.… He transferred the names of blood-relationship
> to others, whom He judged to be more closely related to Him
> by reason of their faith. Now no one transfers a thing except
> from him who possesses that which is transferred. If, there-
> fore, He made them "His mother and His brethren" who were
> not so, how could He deny them these relationships who really
> had them?[77]

Tertullian here offers a defense against the docetic belief that Jesus had not truly been born but rather "passed through" the woman, and therefore did not have a "true" mother and "true" siblings. In response to this belief, Tertullian shows that these relatives of Jesus are truly his mother and brothers, and not just in name. His defense presupposes both that these brothers are not merely cousins (by the rhetorical question, "Have all sons brothers born for them? May a man rather not have fathers and sisters [living]"), and that these brothers are not siblings only in an adopted sense (an "adopted" brother cannot be up-held as proof that one was born in the normal way). Both the Hiero-nymian view and the Epiphanian view are therefore precluded in Tertullian.

What was said of *Against Marcion* applies equally to another writ-ing where Tertullian uses the same argument against Apelles: "First of all, nobody would have told Him that His mother and brethren were standing outside, if he were not certain both that He had a mother and brethren, and that they were the very persons whom he was then an-nouncing."[78] Again, Tertullian must assume that these are true siblings before his argument can stand: "He assumes them to be natural chil-dren of Mary and Joseph, born after the birth of Jesus, and he is aware of no orthodox tradition to the contrary."[79]

One final writing of Tertullian, *On Monogamy*, should be considered in this regard:

[T]he two priestesses of Christian sanctity, Monogamy and Continence: one modest, in Zechariah the priest; one absolute, in John the forerunner: one appeasing God; one preaching Christ: one proclaiming a perfect priest; one exhibiting "more than a prophet,"—him, namely, who has not only preached or personally pointed out, but even baptized Christ. For who was more worthy to perform the initiatory rite on the body of the Lord, than flesh similar in kind to that which conceived and gave birth to that (body)? And indeed it was a virgin, about to marry once for all after her delivery, who gave birth to Christ, in order that each title of sanctity might be fulfilled in Christ's parentage, by means of a mother who was both virgin, and wife of one husband.[80]

Here Tertullian tells us that there are two "priestesses of Christian sanctity"—modest monogamy and absolute continence. The first, represented by the father of John the Baptist, is a life of marriage to one spouse in which marital relations are assumed (witness his son).[81] The second, represented by the Baptist himself, is a life of absolute celibacy that assumes virginity. Tertullian makes the point that Mary represents both categories at different stages of her married life: "The parallel with Zechariah naturally suggests normal intercourse and childbearing."[82]

Another writer of the second century who shows evidence of the belief that the brothers of Jesus were biological siblings is Irenaeus.

And as the protoplast himself Adam, had his substance from untilled and *as yet virgin* soil ("for God had not yet sent rain, and man had not tilled the ground"), and was formed by the hand of God, that is, by the Word of God, for "all things were made by Him," and the Lord took dust from the earth and formed man; so did He who is the Word, recapitulating Adam in Himself, rightly receive a birth, enabling Him to gather up Adam [into Himself], from Mary, who was *as yet a virgin*.[83]

The italicized phrases above ("as yet [a] virgin") are clearly intended by Irenaeus to be taken in parallel. Just as the soil of the earth was *as yet* virgin (but only until shortly thereafter when it was tilled), so also Mary was *as yet* a virgin before giving birth to Jesus. The direct implication is that she did not remain a virgin thereafter. Although this is not direct proof that Mary bore other children, it seems to be the natural inference. In any case, if this is Irenaeus' meaning, then the perpetual virginity of Mary was unknown to him.

Another passage from this same book of Irenaeus may also offer support for the Helvidian view:

> For the one and the same Spirit of God, who proclaimed by the prophets what and of what sort the advent of the Lord should be, did by these elders give a just interpretation of what had been truly prophesied; and He did Himself, by the apostles, announce that the fullness of the times of the adoption had arrived, that the kingdom of heaven had drawn nigh, and that He was dwelling within those that believe on Him who was born Emmanuel of the Virgin. To this effect they testify, [saying,] that *before Joseph had come together with Mary, while she therefore remained in virginity*, "she was found with child of the Holy Ghost."[84]

Irenaeus' allusion to Matt 1:18, as well as his words of explanation, indicate that he understands the biblical text to mean that Mary remained in a state of virginity only during that time period *before* she and Joseph "came together." It is also clear that he understands the meaning of "come together" to imply much more than mere cohabitation, both in this passage and in another one as well: "To this effect [the prophets, elders, apostles] were [saying,] that before Joseph had come together with Mary, while she therefore remained in virginity, she was found with child of the Holy Ghost."[85] It is clear from these passages that Irenaeus arrives as the same conclusion that we did in an earlier chapter concerning the phrase, "before they came together"; namely, that it means "before they engaged in marital relations." Moreover, these passages demonstrate Irenaeus' belief that this condition of Mary did not continue *after* they came together.[86]

There are writings from the second century that also offer support for the Epiphanian view (i.e., that these "brothers" of Jesus are children of Joseph by a previous marriage). The most obvious of these is the *Protevangelium of James*, which records Joseph protesting against the high priest's instructions to take Mary as his wife: "I already have sons and am old, but she is a girl."[87] Mary likewise contemplates the unique circumstances surrounding her pregnancy and wonders whether she is to conceive as other women do.[88] This is followed by an affirmation of Mary's virginity *in partu.*[89] The other two writings that may offer support for the Epiphanian view, the *Gospel of Peter* and the *Infancy Gospel of Thomas*, are purported by Bauckham to preserve a similar tradition (presumably independent from each other and from the *Protevangelium of James*) that the brothers of Jesus are children of Joseph by a previous marriage.[90]

Independent attestation for the Epiphanian view notwithstanding, the historical value of all three of these writings is suspect. Both the *Protevangelium of James* and the *Infancy Gospel of Thomas* are on Bauckham's own admission "certainly works of imagination, not of historiography"[91]; and both of these, along with the *Gospel of Peter,* are apocryphal works of dubious historical value.[92] Moreover, with the exception of the *Protevangelium of James*, the texts that Bauckham points to in support of his position may not support that position at all. In the case of the *Infancy Gospel of Thomas*, the passage in question reads:

> Joseph sent his son James to gather wood and take it into the house, and the child Jesus followed him. And while James was gathering the sticks, a viper bit the hand of James. And as he lay stretched out and about to die, Jesus came near and breathed upon the bite, and immediately the pain ceased, the creature burst, and at once James was healed.[93]

Bauckham surmises, presumably on the basis that the text calls James the "son" of Joseph and calls Jesus a "child" (and perhaps also that the text has Jesus "following" James), that the author must have known of a tradition that Joseph had sons by a previous marriage. However, it must be noted that the text simply does not tell us this. According to other passages surrounding this episode, Jesus was approximately ten years old at this time,[94] and so nothing in the text prevents James from being *younger* than Jesus. The fact that Jesus "follows" James in this episode is explained by the fact that James (and not Jesus) is told to bring in the wood; Jesus follows only to observe the unfolding events and to rescue James from death.

Moreover, Bauckham's reliance on the very brief statement given by

Origen regarding the *Gospel of Peter* is itself tenuous. Origen does not quote from the *Gospel of Peter*, but simply tells us in passing: "But some say, basing it on a tradition in the Gospel according to Peter, as it is entitled, or the 'Book of James,' that the brethren of Jesus were sons of Joseph by a former wife, whom he married before Mary."[95] The fact that the *Gospel of Peter* we currently possess contains no such information raises significant questions about Origen's reference and Bauckham's appeal to it. Has Origen mistakenly confused the information in the *Gospel of Peter* with what is the undoubted teaching of the *Protevangelium of James*? Has he interpreted ambiguous passages in the *Gospel of Peter* in the same way that Bauckham has treated the *Infancy Gospel of Thomas* above? Since we do not know what the original text said, it is impossible to take Origin's statement uncritically. It is even possible to take Origen's phrase "the Book of James" in apposition to his phrase "the Gospel according to Peter," referring to one book (viz., the *Protevangelium of James*) that is known by two titles. In any case, we obviously cannot view Origen's passing reference as being in the same category as Eusebius' citations of Hegesippus, for in the latter case direct quotations are provided to us. At the end of the day, we are left with a tradition that, so far as we know, has no independent attestation outside of the "wildly imaginative"[96] *Protevangelium of James*. In any case, the assertion that Joseph had other children by a previous marriage is not equivalent to the assertion that the "brothers of Jesus" in the NT are foster/adoptive brothers. Mary could still have had other children after the birth of Jesus, and none of the sources cited above denies that she did. While portions of the *Protevangelium of James* seem to imply that Mary was perpetually a virgin, it does not clearly express a view on it.[97]

Concluding Observations

With these patristic writers we exhaust the second-century evidence for the identity of the brothers of Jesus. We have seen that the Helvidian view (viz., that these are true biological siblings of Jesus) is supported by independent attestation from at least three writers of this time period, while the Epiphanian view (viz., that these are sons of Joseph by a previous marriage) is supported unambiguously by only one document that all are agreed is historically unreliable. Moreover, the

Helvidian view is supported by the independent witness of Josephus, and is most consistent with the first-century philological evidence for the words ἀδελφὸς and ἀδελφὴ. As Meier concludes, "if…the historian or exegete is asked to render a judgment on the NT and patristic texts we have examined, viewed simply as historical sources, the most probable opinion is that the brothers and sisters of Jesus were true siblings."[98]

In the ebb and flow of this discussion the point should not be missed that while evidence may be adduced for the Helvidian view and the Epiphanian view, there is no evidence at all in the second century that uniquely supports the Hieronymian view (viz., that these are cousins of Jesus).[99] Indeed, this view seems to have been first defended by Jerome in the post-Nicene period, and Mary's perpetual virginity did not become a widely held belief until late in the fourth century,[100] whereupon the "true siblings" view was "gradually suppressed by…a growing ascetic docetism which wished to separate Jesus as much as possible from regular family relationships."[101] Moreover, since the philological evidence of the first century seems to rule out the meaning "cousin" for ἀδελφὸς or ἀδελφὴ, it seems reasonable to conclude that if we are to find evidence for the perpetual virginity of Mary we must look beyond the NT and the early patristic writings concerning the brothers of Jesus.

CHAPTER IV

The Status of Mary in the Synoptics

We have in the past three chapters examined one Roman Catholic belief about Mary—namely, her perpetual virginity—and have found that the biblical evidence is against such a belief. But what of other uniquely Roman Catholic beliefs about Mary? Are they similarly unwarranted? Before examining these other beliefs in detail, it will be helpful to address the underlying issue that gives rise to these beliefs in the first place; namely, the issue of Mary's status in the NT. Roman Catholic exegesis often attributes a status to Mary that assumes she was the recipient of unique privileges and graces. This in turn often results in the development of a Mariology that is foreign to the biblical texts upon which it purports to be based. The general status that the NT writers attribute to Mary must guide our thinking in the development of a true biblical Mariology. We will therefore look first at how the Synoptic writers view Mary, and then (in subsequent chapters) examine the unique ways in which Luke and John portray Mary in their writings.

The Status of Mary in Mark 3:21–35 and Parallels (Matthew 12:46–50 and Luke 8:19–21)

The first episode in which Mary is mentioned in all three synoptic accounts is found in Mark 3:21–35 and parallels. Both Matthew and Luke include independent infancy narratives that involve Mary[1], as well as other passages where Mary is a significant character. But Mary is mentioned only twice in Mark, once here and once in Mark 6, and "neither time in particularly flattering circumstances."[2] Since Mark's account is the longest, we will use his as a starting point and then compare it to the accounts of Matthew and Luke. The accounts read as follows:

Then Jesus entered a house, and again a crowd gathered, so that he and his disciples were not even able to eat. When his family heard about this, they went to take charge of him, for they said, "He is out of his mind." And the teachers of the law who came down from Jerusalem said, "He is possessed by Beelzebub! By the prince of demons he is driving out demons." So Jesus called them and spoke to them in parables: "How can Satan drive out Satan? If a kingdom is divided against itself, that kingdom cannot stand. If a house is divided against itself, that house cannot stand. And if Satan opposes himself and is divided, he cannot stand; his end has come. In fact, no one can enter a strong man's house and carry off his possessions unless he first ties up the strong man. Then he can rob his house. I tell you the truth, all the sins and blasphemies of men will be forgiven them. But whoever blasphemes against the Holy Spirit will never be forgiven; he is guilty of an eternal sin." He said this because they were saying, "He has an evil spirit." Then Jesus' mother and brothers arrived. Standing outside, they sent someone in to call him. A crowd was sitting around him, and they told him, "Your mother and brothers are outside looking for you."[3] "Who are my mother and my brothers?" he asked. Then he looked at those seated in a circle around him and said, "Here are my mother and my brothers! Whoever does God's will is my brother and sister and mother." (Mark 3:20–35)

While Jesus was still talking to the crowd, his mother and brothers stood outside, wanting to speak to him. [Someone told him, "Your mother and brothers are standing outside, wanting to speak to you."][4] He replied to him, "Who is my mother, and who are my brothers?" Pointing to his disciples, he said, "Here are my mother and my brothers. For whoever does the will of my Father in heaven is my brother and sister and mother. (Matthew 12:46–50)

> Now Jesus' mother and brothers came to see him, but they were not able to get near him because of the crowd. Someone told him, "Your mother and brothers are standing outside, wanting to see you." He replied, "My mother and brothers are those who hear God's word and put it into practice." (Luke 8:19–21)

Mark's account uses a "sandwiching" technique that connects vv. 20–21 with vv. 31–35. In vv. 20–21 he notes that Jesus' family sets out to "take charge of him" because they though he was "out of his mind." His family arrives in vv. 31–35. Between the two mentions of Jesus' family Mark records that the teachers of the law charged Jesus with demon possession (analogous to the charge of insanity by his family). Neither Matthew nor Luke include a parallel for the charge of insanity in Mark 3:20–21, though Matthew does include a parallel for the "Beelzebub" episode in Mark 3:22–30 (cf. Matt 12:22–32). When Jesus' family finally reaches him (Mark 3:31–32) we discover that this family consists of Jesus' mother and brothers. The natural reading of the Markan passage is that Mary is part and parcel of the "family" that sets out to take charge of Jesus because he is out of his mind: "Not only Jesus' mother, but also other relatives are present and active. They think that Jesus has gone insane."[5] Mary is thus counted among those who are "against" Jesus rather than with him.

This view of the passage, however, has been challenged by some exegetes. There are indeed several exegetical issues in this passage that need to be weighed before a firm decision as to its meaning can be reached. Exegetical considerations include the precise meaning of the phrase οἱ παρ' αὐτοῦ (does it mean "family," or something else?), the meaning of the phrase ἐξῆλθον κρατῆσαι αὐτόν (who are "they," what is the meaning of κρατέω ["arrest," or "take control"?], and what is the referent of αὐτόν?), the referent of ἔλεγον (the crowd, the family, or something else?), and the meaning of the word ἐξέστη ("out of control," "insane," or "overworked"?).

The Meaning of οἱ παρ' αὐτοῦ (v. 21)

The traditional reading of this passage sees the phrase οἱ παρ' αὐτοῦ (literally, "those beside him") as a reference to the members of his family who then show up in v. 31.[6] Those who challenge the traditional reading posit that the phrase could mean "his friends" (i.e., his disciples), or "those in the house" (i.e., that part of "the crowd" that was able to fit inside the house).[7] There are difficulties with both of these solutions. First, as the *MNT* taskforce notes, the dialogue between Jesus and the scribes (vv. 22–30) is likely to be seen as a "filler" to account for the time it takes Jesus' family to set out on their journey in v. 21 until they arrive in v. 31.[8] Mark uses this same "sandwiching" style in Mark 5:21–43. In 5:21–24 (the "setting out") Jesus is asked by Jarius (the synagogue ruler) to go to his house and heal his daughter. In 5:25–34 (the "filler") Jesus, on his way to the house of Jarius, encounters the woman who touches his cloak hoping to be healed of her bleeding. Finally, in 5:35–43 (the "arrival") Jesus comes to the house of Jarius and heals his daughter.[9] The parallels between the sandwiching technique used in this passage and that used in 3:20–35 are too great to be ignored. This makes it all but certain that οἱ παρ᾽ αὐτοῦ must refer to the family members who arrive in v. 31.

Second, the meaning "those in the house seize the crowd" is equally unlikely since, as the *MNT* taskforce points out, in that case there is no completion of the sequence—"the 'his own' never come to the crowd."[10] Similarly, the phrase ἐξῆλθον κρατῆσαι αὐτόν ("they set out to seize him") can hardly refer to those who are already in the house with him; for what need would they have to "set out" if they were already there? If it is argued that αὐτόν refers to the crowd (as above) then it must also be pointed out that "the crowd" is said to be in the house with him as well.[11] The most likely solution is still that this phrase refers to Jesus' family members who arrive in v. 31.

The Meaning of αὐτόν (v. 21)

Another issue that bears on the interpretation of this passage is the precise referent of αὐτόν in v. 21 ("When 'those beside him' heard about this, they went to take charge of it/him [αὐτόν], for they were saying, 'He/it is out of his/its mind'"). Who is being "seized" in this verse? Is it Jesus or the crowd? Grammatically either is admissible since both Jesus and the crowd (ὄχλος) are mentioned in v. 20. Any decision on the meaning of αὐτόν must also take into account two other considerations; namely, the meaning of ἔλεγον ("they were saying") and the meaning of ἐξέστη ("he/it is out of his/its mind"). Those who hold that the crowd is the antecedent to αὐτόν also usually take ἔλεγον to refer alternatively to those in the crowd[12], or to some proverbial "they."[13] In any case the phrase is always translated "they were saying." The more pivotal issue is the meaning of—and the referent to—ἐξέστη. Those who hold that it is the crowd that is being "seized" usually postulate that the family of Jesus (or his disciples) went to take charge of the crowd to prevent it from harming Jesus, "because it was beside itself with enthusiasm" (or perhaps, "it was out of control"). Moreover, some who hold that it is Jesus who is being seized postulate that it is the crowd who accuses Jesus of being "out of his mind."

Wansbrough offers several reasons to adopt the view that it is the crowd that is "out of its mind."[14] First, ὄχλος is the closest possible antecedent of ἐξέστη. Second, ἐξέστη in the gospels is used only in contexts where awe and wonder are displayed in response to Jesus. And third, οἱ παρ' αὐτοῦ is best taken as a reference to his disciples who were next to him, not to his family. Wansbrough concedes at least one weakness to his view; namely, this view requires that the two occurrences of αὐτός, both of which occur in the same verse, have two different referents; the first to Jesus and the second to the crowd. Wansbrough's suggested translation of this verse would then read, "When they heard it, his followers went out to calm it down, for they said that it was out of control with enthusiasm."[15]

However, Best cites several observations that militate against this position.[16] First, the word ἔλεγον is accompanied by the word γὰρ. The subject of clauses which include γὰρ are always found in the immediate context in Mark.[17] In our passage above, the nearest antecedent is not ὄχλος, but rather οἱ παρ' αὐτοῦ, making it likely that it is "those beside him" who are "saying" that he is insane.

Second, and closely related to the previous point, Mark always uses a plural pronoun when referring to a crowd[18]; but here he uses the singular αὐτόν. While it is true that the nearest *possible* referent for αὐτόν is ὄχλος in the previous verse (viz., "it [the crowd] was out of its mind"]), the fact that Mark always elsewhere uses the plural pronoun when referring to "the crowd" makes it unlikely that ὄχλος could be the antecedent of αὐτόν in this instance.[19] The most natural antecedent is Jesus, since as Best notes, "Jesus as a referent is implicit throughout."[20]

Third, in Mark the "crowd" is always only astonished by Jesus—never in doubt of his sanity.[21] Moreover, while the word ἐξίστημι does sometimes mean insanity ("out of mind," 2 Cor 5:13), Wansbrough's solution ("out of control with enthusiasm") is unattested in Mark and elsewhere.[22] This seems to rule out the view that it is the crowd that needs to be seized here. Recognizing this limitation for the semantic range of ἐξίστημι, many who hold the view that ὄχλος is the antecedent of ἔλεγον further posit that the meaning here is that Jesus is "overworked" or "tired."[23] Yet this, too, suffers from the previous criticism. If the view that it is the crowd who is being seized is to be rejected on the basis that ἐξίστημι never means "out of control," then the view that Jesus is "overworked" must be rejected on similar grounds, since ἐξίστημι never means "overworked" or "tired."

Fourth, while it is true that in all other Markan usages ἐξίστημι refers to the amazement of the crowd (2:12; 5:42; 6:51), in each of these cases the cause of amazement is always supplied. That is not the case with the present passage. There seems to be no good reason why the disciples would need to "restrain" the crowd just because they were "amazed." Moreover, in other places where the disciples take the initiative to "restrain" people without express request from Jesus, they are rebuked (cf. 10:13). Best sees this as a telling point against Wansbrough's view.[24]

Fifth, the word κρατῆσαι in Mark regularly means the active "arrest" (6:17; 12:12; 14:1, 44, 46, 49, 51), "take hold of" (1:31; 5:41; 9:27), "hold fast to" (7:3, 4, 8), or "keep to oneself" (9:10), but never the passive "restrain, hinder." This meaning is found only in Luke (24:16) and Revelation (7:1).[25] Moreover, Mark does not elsewhere present the crowd as being hostile to Jesus before the crucifixion, and nothing in the narrative leads us to believe that the crowd is hostile here.[26] This renders it unlikely that "those beside him" set out to restrain the crowd.

Finally, this view makes little sense of the word ἀκούσαντες. What have the disciples heard (if the referent is to them) that causes them to restrain the crowd? Nothing in this passage prompts us to assume the crowd has gotten out of hand. If the referent is rather to Jesus' family the participle makes much better sense.

Evidence Supporting the Traditional View

In addition to the points above, the traditional view (i.e., that Jesus' family is saying that Jesus is out of his mind) is supported by the following:[27] First, the subject of "they were saying" is most easily read as the same subject of "they went out"—a change of subjects would be awkward at best.[28] Second, the parallel that this view creates between vv. 20–21 (Jesus' family accuses him of insanity) and vv. 22–30 (the teachers of the law accuse Jesus of demon possession) provides a backdrop for vv. 31–35 (Jesus rejects biological ties and inaugurates the eschatological family) that is more forceful than the other views allow:

a. there is a "group" in each pericope (family and teachers of the law)
b. each group is introduced by a participle (ἀκούσαντες, v. 21; καταβάντες, v. 22)
c. ἔλεγον is used in both (just as the teachers of the law "were saying," so those in Jesus' family "were saying")
d. the charge in v. 22 is clearly against Jesus, and this suggests that the charge in v. 21 refers to him as well
e. the statement in v. 22 has a harsh tone and this suggests that the tone in v. 21 be harsh as well (i.e., Jesus is accused of insanity rather than being overworked)

Third, this view is consistent with Mark's "sandwiching" technique that he uses elsewhere in his gospel (5:21–43).[29] Moreover, this instance of the "sandwiching" technique is strengthened by the fact that Mark places it in chiastic form:

3:20–21 The biological relatives of Jesus fail to understand his mission
22a Accusation of an evil spirit
22b Accusation that he drives out devils by the prince of devils
23–26 Saying about Satan
27 Answer to second accusation
28–29 Answer to first accusation
31–35 The true, eschatological relatives of Jesus[30]

These considerations force us back to the traditional view of this passage which, at the end of the day, is still the best option.

The Arrival of the Family of Jesus

As we have noted, in Mark 3:21 the "family" of Jesus, who in this episode deems him insane, is pictured as being allied with the teachers of the law, who in v. 22 accuse Jesus of being "in league with Beelzebub."[31] This "family," we are later told, includes the "mother" and "brothers" of Jesus (3:31–32). The theological ramifications of this are significant for our view of Mary. Mary is portrayed as part of the family of Jesus who sets out to "take charge" of him because "he is out of his mind." This suggests assumptions on the part of Mark that are inconsistent with the view that Mary held a special status in the early church. Mark could not have subscribed to any notion of a high status for Mary and at the same time have placed her in the company of those who thought Jesus was insane.

McHugh, sensing the weight of this observation, suggests that Mary may have been an unwilling participant in this episode. He notes, "one ought to mention also that there is nothing in the text to indicate that Mary shared this belief."[32] Yet such a statement seems gratuitous. Neither is there anything in the text to indicate that the "brothers" shared this belief. One might with equal force argue that it was Mary who spearheaded this effort, and that Jesus' brothers went along only grudgingly. McKenzie argues similarly when he notes that "the presence of Mary with the brothers of Jesus in Mark 3:21 & 31–35 does not show that she shared their sentiments."[33] Yet, if not, one wonders why Mark felt a need to include Mary in this scene at all. Moreover, are we to assume that once he has identified Jesus' "family" as including his mother, Mark tacitly expected his readers to separate Mary from the sentiments of the rest of his family who deem him insane? If so, on what basis? Mark has said nothing to his readers about Mary up to this point, and it seems odd that we would be expected to make this kind of assumption about her. This view cannot be derived from the text, and McHugh and McKenzie's caveat seems to be little more than a not-so-subtle attempt to "rescue" Mary from a less than flattering picture of her.

Once Jesus' mother and brothers arrive on the scene, we are told, they are "standing outside" (ἔξω στήκοντες) of the house (v. 31), and must therefore send for Jesus by "calling him" (καλοῦντες αὐτόν) This is reiterated by those in the crowd who tell Jesus that his mother and brothers are "outside looking for him" (v. 32). The fact that Jesus' family is "seeking" him, coupled with the "outside" motif and Jesus' response to his family, is theologically loaded. R. P. Martin points out that the verb "to seek" used here always carries a negative connotation with it—

the word is always associated either with hostility or with distracting Jesus from his mission.[34] Moreover, according to Ben-Chorin, "the custom required that Jesus should get up at once and meet his mother"[35]; but Jesus does not comply. Instead, he asks the rhetorical question: "Who are my mother and brothers?"

Mark deliberately places Jesus' mother and brothers *outside* while placing his disciples *inside* "seated in a circle around him" (v. 34). Those within the circle are his "true" family, while those outside have no claim on him. "The least it seems to mean is that the physical family has no real importance in the new standard of values established by the proclamation of the kingdom."[36] The significance of the fact that Jesus seems to disown Mary cannot be missed; for "such an attitude would be considered scandalous in any society, but among Jews it would even be more strongly resented."[37] As Brown notes: "There is not only a definition [of 'true' family] but a distinction. Jesus deliberately points to those inside, not to those outside.… There is no indication in Mark that Jesus thinks of His mother and brothers in the category of family constituted by doing the will of God."[38]

Senior concurs that in this episode Jesus "emphatically distances himself" from his biological family, and then adds: "The gospel draws a sharp line between blood ties and discipleship ties and leaves no doubt that true kinship with Jesus is based on the latter."[39] Moreover, as Ruether rightly notes: "The reaction to their request showed that they were not believers and were embarrassed or opposed to his current mission and were perhaps trying to recall him to ordinary life at home."[40]

McHugh sees it possible that Mark did not view Mary and Jesus' brothers as one homogenous group based on the singularity of the verb "to come" (ἔρχεται) in v. 31 (connected with Mary, but not with "brothers")—literally, "and his mother comes, and his brothers."[41] McHugh's reason for postulated this seems to be motivated once again by a desire to "get Mary off the hook" as it were. If he can separate Mary from Jesus' brothers, then perhaps a case can be made that Mary was not complicit with them in this episode.

Yet, McHugh's observation does not help his case. First, one might argue that this observation instead provides clear evidence that the decision to "take charge" of Jesus because he was "out of his mind" was primarily Mary's idea. After all, she seems to be leading the way while his "brothers" merely follow. Second, one might argue all the more emphatically (based on McHugh's observation) that Jesus' rejection of his earthly family is directed primarily at Mary. Third, all of the more significant verbs in this passage (στήκοντες, "standing"; ἀπέστειλαν, 'they sent"; καλοῦντες, "calling"; ζητοῦσίν, "seeking") are in the plural, encompassing both his mother and his brothers. Fourth, even if McHugh's observation were taken into consideration, it does not thereby lessen the impact of Jesus' response: "Who is my mother?" Indeed, as even McKenzie notes:

> Certainly the response of Jesus to his family (Mark 3:33–35) makes no distinction between mother and brothers, nor does the anecdote express any dissociation of Mary from the brothers expressed by Mary or by any one else. If any one else were concerned, the anecdote would be read as showing *passive co-operation of Mary with the action of the brothers.*[42] *…Unbelief and hostility* would be clearly seen in Mark 3:21 & 3:31–35 if any one else but Jesus and possibly his mother were involved[43] [emphasis his].

It is not as though Jesus' mother and brothers *cannot* enter the inside circle (indeed, as we shall see, they eventually do); only that they cannot do so based on their physical relationship to him:

> Although the 'inside' vs. 'outside' staging indicates that the physical family members are not among those whom Jesus currently regards as his eschatological family, the passage in itself does not exclude the physical family members from *eventual* participation in the eschatological family. Yet they can participate only if they do the will of God.[44]

The definition of Jesus' true, *eschatological* family is to be found in Mark 10:29–30:

> "I tell you the truth," Jesus replied, "no one who has left home or brothers or sisters or mother or father or children or fields for me and the gospel will fail to receive a hundred times as much in this present age (homes, brothers, sisters, mothers,

children and fields—and with them, persecutions) and in the age to come, eternal life."

Both the statement here and the one above indicate that biological relations are inconsequential in the kingdom. This is important to note, because some Catholic exegetes who agree with the primacy of the eschatological family nevertheless argue for unique privileges for Mary since she is both disciple *and* mother of Jesus. Mary's status in Roman Catholicism as "Mother of God" gives rise to many other beliefs about her that, in light of Mark's portrayal, must be viewed with a skeptical eye. She is said to be "co-Mediatrix" because, as Jesus' mother, she is in a unique position to make requests of her son in our behalf. She is said to be "Co-Redemptress" because she gave her willing consent to bear the Son of God—without which consent, it is argued, the world could not have been redeemed.[45] Yet Tambasco is right when he notes: "What is important for Mary is not her physical relationship to Jesus, but her relationship of faith."[46] Indeed, if we were to render a decision about Mary's status in the NT based entirely on our text above, we would have to conclude not only that Mary had *no* special status, but in fact that she was not even a disciple: "One must admit that the only scene in Mark in which the mother of Jesus ever appears is not a scene that would incline one to develop a great devotion to the mother of Jesus."[47] Indeed, Mary is here portrayed not merely as someone who is not yet a disciple, but as someone who outwardly opposes Jesus' mission: "The Gospel of Mark gives us a picture of Mary that is at least verging on the negative. She is not differentiated by Mark from those members of Jesus' family who at best misunderstand and perhaps even refuse to believe in him and who oppose him."[48]

For Mark, the earthly family of Jesus—including Mary—are not counted among those who "hear the word of God and put it into practice." They are instead counted among those: "Who looked intently but did not see, listened carefully but did not understand because they had not received the mystery of the reign of God.… For Mark, they had not been given the light of faith which would have enabled them to see and understand."[49] Fortunately for Mary, we do find other texts elsewhere that lead us to believe she eventually came to faith. Yet even this does not grant her a higher status than any other "brother, sister, and mother" of Jesus. Her status as "mother" is based solely on the extent to which she "does the will of God," and not at all on her biological relationship to Jesus. "Thus Jesus turns his mother, brother and sisters away, bids them farewell. This messianic community, however, is open to all believers, including Jesus' mother and family, *not because of their blood relationship but because of their faith*"(emphasis mine).[50]

Matthew's Parallel

Many scholars, including those in the *MNT* taskforce, surmise that since Matthew's account of this episode (12:46–50) omits the charge of insanity recorded in Mark's account, that Matthew intended to "soften" the harshness of the Markan account.[51] Indeed, the taskforce goes so far as to assert not only the neutrality of Matthew in regard to Jesus' family, "but a neutrality that would probably pick up coloring from the initial positive impression given the reader at the beginning of the Gospel"[52]; namely, Mary's willing consent to her divine commission to bear the Son of God. LaVerdiere puts it this way: "Matthew has omitted everything found in Mark which presented Jesus' family in a bad light…. He avoided Mark's figurative reference to the family's being *outside* [ἔξω]. Matthew maintains the ordinary sense of being 'outside'" (italics his).[53]

One is left wondering, however, just how we can know that ἔξω is being used differently here apart from the *a priori* assumption that Matthew views the family of Jesus in a positive light. While it is true that Matthew's account is less harsh, Jesus' response in this episode is virtually identical to that found in Mark's account. In both instances Jesus asks the rhetorical questions, "Who is my mother?" and "Who are my brothers?" (Matt 12:48; Mark 3:33). The intended effect of this question is to direct his hearers away from any notion of special status with him through biological ties—indeed, to sever those biological ties, and to establish a new "family" based on obedience to the will of God. His meaning is effectively, "those who bore me and grew up with me are not my mother and brothers; rather those who are *doers of the word* are."[54] This is the point that most Catholic scholars, including Perkins, seem to miss. Perkins states that Mary's relationship to Jesus is based on faith and not "merely" her biological ties to him.[55] Yet this statement tacitly assumes something not found in the text; namely, that after Jesus spoke these words Mary's relationship to Jesus would be based on biological ties *at all*. It is not simply a matter of Mary *retaining* her status as mother on the condition that she also be a "doer of the word"; there is instead a *new* "eschatological" family order based entirely on discipleship, and Mary must enter by that gate if she is to become (not remain) a "mother" of Jesus. Yet once she enters (as we have already noted), she is afforded no higher status than any other "mother" of Jesus. Bridcut sums it up well: "That Matthew's view of the incident is similar to Mark's is seen in his placing it among illustrations of misunderstanding of and opposition to Christ's ministry.... In his reply Jesus does not separate his mother from his brothers."[56]

Luke's Parallel

What some scholars surmise about Matthew's account of this episode is often asserted even more strongly about Luke's account (8:19–21). According to Senior, Luke does not "drive a wedge" between Jesus' biological family and his family of disciples, and concludes that "a direct reading of Luke's account does not exclude the mother of Jesus from being counted among those 'who hear the word of God and do it'."[57] While this is certainly true, it must be asserted with equal force that neither do we find here special privileges for Mary. Indeed, as in the case of Matthew and Mark, Jesus is here denying that biological ties are what matters. Instead we are again told that *anyone* who does the word of God is Jesus' "mother" and "brother" (8:21). So, while Mary may very well be included among the disciples, any notion of special privileges based on her status as mother of Jesus is conspicuously absent. Wansbrough's comments are even more speculative:

> In Luke's equivalent of Mk 3:31–35 there are two significant changes: firstly, Jesus' family do not remain passively outside as though they have no place inside. Rather they remain outside only because the rest of the crowd prevents them coming to Jesus, and they join in with the crowd pressing to reach Jesus.[58]

Wansbrough misses one other difference that is proffered by Mercurio; namely, "the omission of Jesus' [rhetorical] question softened any apparent harshness suggested by His words to His Mother."[59] Brown explains:

> But when Jesus is told, "Your mother and brothers are stand-
> ing outside, desiring to see you," He does not ask, "Who are
> my mother and my brothers?"… Rather he affirms in response,
> "My mother and brothers are those who hear the word of God
> and do it."… There is no longer a contrast between a family
> of believers and a natural family—to the contrary, the natural
> family now become exemplary believers.[60]

Yet, again, Luke does in fact leave the family of Jesus "standing outside," just as do Mark and Matthew; and he never brings them inside.
On what grounds can we conclude that this is theologically significant
in the case of Mark but not in the case of Luke? Indeed, the fact that
"they were not able to get near him because of the crowd" suggests that
Luke excludes them from the inner circle of disciples in the same way
that Mark and Matthew do. In light of this, Wansbrough's conclusion
that "in Mark Jesus' mother and brothers are contrasted with true
disciples, while in Luke they are the perfect example of discipleship"[61] (along with Brown's conclusion above) seems a bit overly
optimistic.

The *MNT* taskforce sees a possible resumptive reading of Luke's
account—"My mother and my brothers—these are the ones who hear
the word of God and do it"—and adds, "Luke's notion of what constitutes discipleship…is not much different from the notion found in
Mark and Matthew…. Luke, however, is much clearer than Mark
and Matthew in insisting that Jesus' mother and brothers meet that
criterion."[62] The taskforce sees a connection with this passage to the
parable of the sower and sees Jesus' mother and brothers as the seed
that falls on "good soil." Just as the seed on good soil stands for those
with a "noble and good heart, who hear the word, retain it, and by
persevering produce a crop" (8:15), so also Jesus' mother and brothers
"are those who hear God's word and put it into practice" (8:21).

Conzelmann takes issue with those who hold that Luke softens this
passage over against Mark and Matthew, postulating instead that the
"mother and brothers" of Jesus in Luke 8:19 illustrate not 8:15, but 8:18:
"Whoever has will be given more; whoever does not have, even what
he thinks he has will be taken from him."[63] The *MNT* taskforce criticize Conzelmann's view on the basis that he misses the "exact word
parallel between 8:15 and 8:21; and he reconstructs his theology

of Luke without recourse to the picture of Mary in the infancy narratives."[64]

But the taskforce's criticism is unfounded. First, aside from the use of τὸν λόγον and ἀκούοντες there really is not an "exact word parallel" here at all; and even with the common words, the order is different (v. 15 places ἀκούοντες before τὸν λόγον; v. 21 reverses that order), and v. 21 has properly τὸν λόγον τοῦ θεοῦ, and not simply τὸν λόγον as is found in v. 15. Second, there is no necessary connection between accepting the parallel between v. 15 and v. 21, and accepting the taskforce's resumptive reading of v. 21. One can duly note the connection between these two passages without coming to the conclusion that Jesus in v. 21 must be referring to his biological family. Third, while it is true that Luke has painted a positive portrait of Mary in his infancy narrative, that does not thereby preclude Luke from using Jesus' family later as an illustrative device to reinforce the point that whereas biological ties may have been necessary in Jesus' infancy (how else would he have survived as a human baby?), they are irrelevant in the eschatological family. This point can be made even if Jesus believed his family to have met his discipleship requirements, as though Jesus is saying, "Why are you speaking about my mother and brothers as though biological ties should have any special privilege with me? Look instead to those who hear the word of and do it!" If that happens to *include* his biological family, well and good; Jesus simply does not tell us, and that is not Luke's point in any case. On the other hand, Luke (with Mark and Matthew) places Jesus' mother and brothers "outside" (ἔξω) the crowd (v. 20), and tells us that they were "unable to get near him" (v. 19). This suggests at the very least that if Jesus' mother and brothers *were* disciples at this point, they were not accorded special status or privileges based on biological ties with him.

In light of these considerations, there seems to be no good reason to assign to Luke a different meaning for this passage than we find in Mark and Matthew's account. This meaning not only makes better sense of the Lukan text, but is also more faithful to the internal unity of the Gospels. We know that at least Mark saw Jesus' mother and brothers as outside the sphere of discipleship. To assign a different meaning to Luke's account assumes an underlying, ultra-redactional method of interpretation that is unnecessary for understanding this passage. Lonsdale, after tracing Mary's developing understanding of Jesus' mission through Luke, concludes more realistically:

> Through these scenes, then, Mary grows as a believer and a disciple. At the same time, the story hints that even for Mary complete discipleship is not yet possible (Lk 2, 50–51). Her discipleship will be completed and perfected through the ministry, cross and resurrection of Jesus as she continues to search for understanding.[65]

Smith concurs: "There is strong evidence that [Mary] was not even a disciple of her enigmatic son until after the resurrection."[66] In this light, then, Mary is not portrayed in Luke as the *model* disciple (as is often assumed),[67] but rather the *epitomized* disciple. She begins in unbelief, struggles with misconceptions about Jesus—sometimes even opposing his mission!—until she receives the light of understanding and becomes a disciple. She, along with Peter and others, is sometimes on target and sometimes misses the mark. This portrait of Mary is more credible, not only because it squares more readily with the NT witnesses, but also because is makes Mary a real person by eliminating fanciful—indeed, legendary—notions about her.

Mark 6:1–6 and Parallels (Matthew 13:53–58 and Luke 4:22–24)

There is only one other episode with Marian significance that is mentioned in all three Synoptic Gospels. It is a context in which Jesus gives an assessment of his family's view of him:

> Jesus left there and went to his hometown, accompanied by his disciples. When the Sabbath came, he began to teach in the synagogue, and many who heard him were amazed. "Where did this man get these things?" they asked. "What's this wisdom that has been given him, that he even does miracles! Isn't this the carpenter? Isn't this Mary's son and the brother of James, Joseph, Judas and Simon? Aren't his sisters here with us?" And they took offense at him. Jesus said to them, "Only in his hometown, among his relatives and in his own house is

a prophet without honor." He could not do any miracles there, except lay his hands on a few sick people and heal them. And he was amazed at their lack of faith. (Mark 6:1–6)[68]

When Jesus had finished these parables, he moved on from there. Coming to his hometown, he began teaching the people in their synagogue, and they were amazed. "Where did this man get this wisdom and these miraculous powers?" they asked. "Isn't this the carpenter's son? Isn't his mother's name Mary, and aren't his brothers James, Joseph, Simon and Judas? Aren't all his sisters with us? Where then did this man get all these things?" And they took offense at him. But Jesus said to them, "Only in his hometown and in his own house is a prophet without honor." And he did not do many miracles there because of their lack of faith. (Matthew 13:53–58)

All spoke well of him and were amazed at the gracious words that came from his lips. "Isn't this Joseph's son?" they asked. Jesus said to them, "Surely you will quote this proverb to me: 'Physician, heal yourself! Do here in your hometown what we have heard that you did in Capernaum.' I tell you the truth," he continued, "no prophet is accepted in his hometown." (Luke 4:22–24)

At issue in this episode is the extent to which each gospel writer includes the mother and brothers of Jesus in the realm of those who do not honor/accept Jesus as prophet. Only Mark and Matthew actually mention the mother and brothers of Jesus—Luke's account mentions only Joseph. Based of this, we can agree in part that Luke's parallel (at least in this instance) is "kinder" to Jesus' family than both Mark and Matthew.[69] On the other hand, one can hardly conclude that Luke must have viewed Mary in a favorable light in a passage in which she is not even mentioned. The lack of any mention of Mary by Luke forces us to rely solely on Mark and Matthew for any Marian significance we might glean from this episode.

Mark's Account

Jesus has just left the house of Jarius the synagogue rule and returned to his hometown. His teaching in his hometown synagogue not only prompts his hearers to be "amazed," but also to question where he would have received such wisdom and the ability to do miracles. After all, wasn't he merely the local carpenter? Wasn't he well known as being the son of Mary, an ordinary Jewish mother; and the brother of James, Joseph, Judas and Simon, men who were of no special significance? The questions are intended rhetorically to point out Jesus' humble origins. A man with such origins could not possibly engender the honor afforded a true prophet: "and they took offence at him" (v. 3).

It is against this backdrop that Jesus gives his assessment of the situation: "Only in his hometown, among his relatives and in his own house is a prophet without honor." We stated earlier that the townspeople ask about Jesus' family to point out his humble origins. But Mark also intends it to serve as a partial connection to Jesus' response. Not only does Jesus receive no honor from those in his hometown (i.e., those who "took offence at him"), but neither does he receive it from his "relatives," nor those "in his own house" (i.e., the mother, brothers and sisters just mentioned). As Senior notes, the lesson that we are taught earlier in Mark 3:21–35 is "reinforced in the only other reference to Mary in Mark's gospel. Jesus' return to his hometown of Nazareth…is an unhappy one."[70] Jesus as prophet is not "un-honored" (ἄτιμος), except in his "hometown" (πατρίδι), and among his "relatives" (συγγενεῦσιν), and in his "own house" (τῇ οἰκίᾳ αὐτοῦ).

Matthew's Parallel

Matthew's account of this episode is nearly identical to Mark's. As with Mark's account, Matthew includes Jesus' entry into his hometown (13:54), his teaching in the local synagogue, the amazement of the people at his wisdom and ability to perform miracles, the rhetorical questions about his origin (including references to Mary, his brothers and his sisters; v. 55–56), and the offence which they take at him (v. 57). The only notable difference is that Matthew, in identifying those by whom Jesus is not "honored" (ἄτιμος), omits the reference to "his relatives" (συγγενεῦσιν), mentioning only his "hometown" (πατρίδι) and his "own house" (τῇ οἰκίᾳ αὐτοῦ). Wansbrough see this as something of a softening of Mark's harshness toward Jesus' family: "Matthew omits [Mark's reference to 'relations'], obviously deliberately and carefully, to avoid the suggestion that Jesus' relations despised him."[71]

LaVerdiere concurs: "When Jesus utters the saying in Matthew, we find no mention of his relatives. Again Matthew has edited out of the text anything which could have placed the family of Jesus, including his mother Mary, in a bad light."[72]

However, the exclusion of a reference to Jesus' family in Matthew's account is not so readily apparent. While Matthew does omit the word "relatives," he still includes the phrase "his own house" (v. 57), which, in this passage, must include at least Mary if not also his "brothers and sisters" (vv. 55–56). The differences in meaning between the two gospels are minimal, and it is doubtful that Matthew intended, by this omission, to portray Mary in a more positive light than she is portrayed by Mark.

This is precisely the point which Brown misses when, commenting on this passage, he concludes:

> Matthew phrases Jesus' words…[by] leaving out "among his own relatives." It is inconceivable to Matthew that the woman who conceived this child through the power of God would not honor her son. One begins to see how the Christian understanding of God's plan begins to color the picture of Mary.[73]

But again, it is not entirely clear how leaving out "among his own relatives" while including "in his own house" thereby exempts Mary from those who do not honor Jesus. Who else would Matthew have in mind in the phrase "in his own house"? Moreover, we must be careful to distinguish between "without honor" and "dishonor." While Matthew affirms the former about Jesus' "own house," he does not thereby suggest the latter. One can fail to honor someone worthy of that distinction (perhaps due to complacency, or the inability to recognize the greatness of someone with whom one is a bit too familiar), without suggesting in any way that one has *dis*honored that person (which implies contempt). The household of Jesus, while guilty of the former, is not necessarily guilty of the latter. Mary is thus spared from being counted among those who hold Jesus in contempt.

Concluding Thoughts on the Synoptic Portrayal of Mary

René Laurentin surveys the passages that seem to cast Mary in a negative light (viz., Mark 3:20–35; Luke 11:27–28) and concludes by labeling these passages "silent passages" since "they have no specific meaning" regarding Mary other than to "warn us against erroneous assessments of Mary from a carnal standpoint."[74] But Laurentin's assessment of these passages (as well as those typically used to support modern Roman Catholic ideas about Mary) is tendentious. He claims to be writing with an unbiased pen,[75] but then proceeds uncritically to interpret all of the pertinent Marian passages in a decidedly Roman Catholic way—all the while suggesting to us that his conclusions, contradicted though they may be by nearly all of his colleagues, are simply the natural outworking of sound exegesis.[76]

The "specific meaning" of these supposed "silent" passages lies, of course, in the fact that the modern Roman Catholic notion of honoring Mary is entirely foreign to the minds of the NT writers. Mary's status, at least so far as the Synoptic Gospels are concerned, is never elevated above the level of any other true disciple, such as we find in the dogmatic teaching of the Roman Catholic church. Indeed, in many instances in the NT Mary does not even rise to the level of disciple, at least until after the resurrection!

But what of the differences among the parallel Marian passages that we find in the Synoptic accounts? Do they really reveal differing theologies? The most we can say with certainty about the differences among Mark, Matthew and Luke's account is that Matthew and Luke seem to temper Mark's harshness towards Jesus' family.[77] That is not to suggest, however, that Matthew or Luke must necessarily see Jesus' family in a more positive light (as is often superficially concluded); only that they do not deem it necessary to make every point that Mark makes, especially redundant points. In the parallel account of Mark 3:21–35 and Matt 12:46–50, for instance, Matthew chooses to omit the fact that Jesus' family deemed him insane. But he still makes the theological point that Jesus' family "seeks" him (a word always associated either with hostility or with distraction from Jesus' mission), that they are "outside," and that Jesus (by his rhetorical question) downplays the significance of anyone's claim to him based on biological ties. In the parallel account of Mark 6:1–6 and Matt 13:53–58, Matthew omits the reference to Jesus "relatives" as those who do not honor him. But he still refers to those "in his own house," which by any objective standard must include his mother and brothers. While Matthew's omissions abbreviate Mark's account, they do not thereby diminish his theological points.

The same may be said about Luke's account vis-à-vis Mark's account. In the parallel account of Mark 3:21–35 and Luke 8:19–21, both Mark and Luke place Jesus' family "outside" the circle of disciples. Moreover, both use the physical family of Jesus to illustrate what is *not* important in the kingdom. Although Luke does not include Jesus' rhetorical question, he does include the statement by Jesus that his disciples constitute his *true* family. Again, brevity does not imply difference. The absence of the rhetorical question in Luke does not imply a different point, for Jesus' statement ("my mother and brothers are those who hear God's word and put it into practice") implies the very same point made explicit by Mark; namely, that discipleship—not biological relationship—is what counts in the kingdom.

Mark's essential theological points remain intact in both Matthew and Luke's account. Although each account may cast Mary in varying degrees of contrariety, none casts Mary in such a way as to lead us to conclude that she must enjoy a special status with Jesus. But our purpose has not been to show that Mary bears a status that is *beneath* other disciples (although one could easily conclude this based on Mark's portrayal); our purpose has simply been to show that Mary is not accorded a status *higher* than that of any other disciple. Yet without this higher status, one cannot posit special privileges for Mary such as we find in Roman Catholicism. Granted, the status afforded to Mary in Roman Catholicism is based on other passages than those currently under consideration: We shall turn to those passages momentarily. But the passages under consideration cannot simply be dismissed from an inquiry into Mary's status if we are to arrive at a balanced and biblical Mariology. These passages offer evidence that weighs against the belief that Mary's status is higher than that of any other believer. If, therefore, we are to find evidence for this Roman Catholic belief, we must look specifically at those passages used to support it. It is to these passages we will turn next.

CHAPTER V

Special Considerations About Mary in Luke–Acts

In our last chapter we examined the view of Mary's status found in the Synoptic Gospels. There are several additional passages in Luke which shed light on the status of Mary in the NT, but which have no parallels in either Mark or Matthew. These include Luke 1:26–38 (the annunciation of the angel to Mary), 1:39–56 (the visitation of Mary to Elizabeth), 2:21–35 (the presentation of the infant Jesus in the temple), 2:41–52 (the adolescent Jesus in the temple), and 11:27–28 (the woman who praises Jesus' mother). In addition, we also have one passage in Acts in which Mary is mentioned, but with little significance for our inquiry (1:14).

Luke 1:26–38

If Matthew's infancy narrative gives special prominence to Joseph, then Luke's gives prominence to Mary: She is the focal point of the narrative. Whereas in Matthew's gospel Joseph is the recipient of the angel's message, in Luke it is Mary who is the recipient. Luke's account reads as follows:

> In the sixth month, God sent the angel Gabriel to Nazareth, a town in Galilee, to a virgin pledged to be married to a man named Joseph, a descendant of David. The virgin's name was Mary. The angel went to her and said, "Greetings, you who are highly favored! The Lord is with you."[1] Mary was greatly

troubled at his words and wondered what kind of greeting this might be. But the angel said to her, "Do not be afraid, Mary, you have found favor with God. You will be with child and give birth to a son, and you are to give him the name Jesus. He will be great and will be called the Son of the Most High. The Lord God will give him the throne of his father David, and he will reign over the house of Jacob forever; his kingdom will never end." "How will this be," Mary asked the angel, "since I am a virgin?" The angel answered, "The Holy Spirit will come upon you, and the power of the Most High will over-shadow you. So the holy one to be born will be called the Son of God. Even Elizabeth your relative is going to have a child in her old age, and she who was said to be barren is in her sixth month. For nothing is impossible with God." "I am the Lord's servant," Mary answered. "May it be to me as you have said." Then the angel left her.

"Full of grace"

The angel's greeting (χαῖρε, κεχαριτωμένη) has given rise to much speculation among older Roman Catholic scholarship—as well as recent Roman Catholic apologetics—about Mary's sinlessness, and consequently her immaculate conception. Older Catholic transla-tions tend to render this greeting in a way that suggests a special status for Mary: "Hail, *full of grace*, the Lord is with thee" (*Douay Rheims Version*). Basing their argument entirely on the word χαρι-τόω, Roman Catholic apologists even today follow these translations and assert that Mary was conceived without the stain of original sin. Karl Keating, for instance, takes this word to mean "a perfection of grace," and concludes from this that Mary was "full of grace" from conception to her life's end.[2] He bases this (presumably, though he does not say explicitly) on the fact that Luke uses the perfect tense of this word: "This grace…is at once permanent and of a singular kind."[3] Laurentin is less vague when he asserts that this is a "new name" for Mary. According to Laurentin, Mary is "full of *grace* in a way that is unchanging, everlasting, definitive (shown by the word [χαριτόω] used in the perfect tense).… That is why she is 'blessed among women'."[4]

While χαριτόω is indeed used in the perfect tense here (κεχαρι-τωμένη), both Keating and Laurentin have given far too much significance to this. This word occurs in the same participial form in Sir 18:17 with no theological significance.[5] It also occurs in Eph 1:6 where it is applied to all believers. As even McHugh grants, "there is no doubt that Luke uses the word in the same sense as the author of Ephesians."[6] Are we to conclude on this basis that all believers are without original sin? Keating or Laurentin might attempt to distinguish these two occurrences on the basis that Eph 1:6 does not use the perfect tense whereas Luke 1:28 does. But this does not help their case since the perfect tense speaks only of the *current state* of the subject without reference to *how long* the subject has been in that state, or *will be* in that state.[7]

Modern scholarship has dismissed the translation "full of grace" as a nonviable rendition of χαριτόω. *BAGD*, for instance, translates the word as "one who has been favored by God." Louw and Nida has "you to whom (the Lord) has shown kindness."[8] Even a Catholic source such as Zerwick avoids the translation "full of grace," opting instead for the less theologically loaded phrases "endowed with grace; dearly loved."[9] The *MNT* taskforce translates it as "graciously favored by God,"[10] while noting that the *Douay Rheims* translation, "full of grace," "is not literal and is gradually being replaced among Roman Catholic translators."[11] The most recent standard Catholic translations, the *NAB* and the *JB*, have followed suit in their renditions (*NAB*, "O highly favored daughter"; *JB*, "So highly favored").

There is good reason for rejecting the translation "full of grace"— it makes little sense in context. This word χαριτόω is further explained in 1:30: "you have found favor with God." Contextually, the reason Mary is "highly favored" is because she "has been elected by God to conceive the Messiah"[12]; not because of some intrinsic and permanent quality of grace within Mary. Attempts by modern Catholic scholarship notwithstanding, a handful of Roman Catholic apologists and scholars still view κεχαριτωμένη as descriptive of Mary's intrinsic quality. This "grace" is seen by this group as that which Mary has to bestow as much as that which Mary has received. McHugh criticizes Protestant scholars such as Plummer for misunderstanding the Roman Catholic position on κεχαριτωμένη in relation to Mary. He insists that Catholicism teaches that Mary "owes to God every grace, every blessing, every favour she has ever received."[13] Yet, McHugh contradicts this idea in his very next statement: "Bede puts it neatly when he writes: 'Well is she called "full of grace", for she has received the grace which no *other* woman had *deserved*'."[14]

This reading, of course, is not demanded by the Vulgate's *gratia plena*, nor by the *Douay* translation's "full of grace," since both of these can be rightly interpreted as "full of grace *which you have received for the present circumstance.*" Nearly all Roman Catholic NT scholars in recent years, including Raymond Brown and Joseph Fitzmyer, agree that the older Roman Catholic interpretations of this word "clearly go beyond the meaning of Luke's text."[15]

"The Lord is with you"

Another item in this passage that has prompted some Catholic exegetes to ascribe a special status to Mary is the phrase "the Lord is with you" (ὁ κύριος μετὰ σοῦ). McHugh writes: "these words are never addressed to a person in ordinary circumstances, but always to someone for whom God has great plans."[16] He then insists that in all cases where this phrase is used, "the destiny of Israel is at stake."[17] His argument becomes even more tenuous:

> The person to whom the words are addressed is summoned by God to a high vocation, and entrusted with a momentous mission, and…the religious history of Israel (and therefore of the world) depended, at that moment, on his response to God's call. Thus if Isaac or Jacob had abandoned the faith of Abraham, the people of Israel would not have been God's instrument in redemption. If Moses had not led the people out of Egypt, there would have been no covenant at Sinai…. And if Jeremiah had not so effectively forewarned the people of impending doom, the disaster of 587 BC might well have been the final act in the drama of Israel's history.[18]

McHugh's view of this phrase and its implications is exceedingly tendentious, and it soon becomes apparent where he is headed with all this: "[Luke] must have seen that at the moment before the incarnation, Mary held in her hands the destiny of Israel, and of the world, for only when Mary utters her *Fiat* does the angel depart from her."[19] Hence, the stage is set for the Roman Catholic notion of Mary as

"Co-Redemptress," according to which Mary cooperates with God's plan of salvation, without which cooperation mankind could not have been redeemed. Since McHugh has here introduced the issue of Mary's response (or *fiat*) to the angel at the end of this pericope (v. 38), we will address that issue along with McHugh's comments on the phrase at hand.

Several criticisms may be leveled against McHugh's presentation. First, the phrase "the Lord is with you"[20] is commonly used as a salutation among Jews, and therefore says nothing special with regard to Mary. It is used, for instance, in Judg 6:12 where the angel of the Lord greets Gideon (κύριος μετὰ σοῦ); in Ruth 2:4 where Boaz greets the harvesters (κύριος μεθ' ὑμῶν); in Ex 10:10 where Pharaoh dismisses Moses and Aaron from his presence (κύριος μεθ' ὑμῶν); and in 1 Chr 22:16 where David wishes the builders of the temple success (κύριος μετὰ σοῦ).[21]

Second, McHugh's assertion that God needs the cooperation of human beings to accomplish his purpose for his people is nothing more than a gratuitous assumption on his part. He cites several examples, including those of Abraham, Isaac, Jacob, Moses, Gideon, and Jeremiah, where individuals were instrumental in the creation and/or preservation of Israel as a nation, and concludes without warrant that had any of these individuals chosen not to cooperate with God, Israel as a nation would not exist today. But McHugh's selective use of OT examples is tendentious. What are we to conclude in those examples where God's purpose is accomplished in spite of—or perhaps even *because of*—the agent's disobedience? Tamar, by posing as a prostitute, conceived an illegitimate son who was in the direct lineage to the Messiah (Genesis 38; cf. Matt 1:3). God put to death two of Judah's sons because of their disobedience, and Judah himself unwittingly became the father of Tamar's children through his own sinful relationship with her. Similarly, Pharaoh attempted to thwart God's purpose by refusing to comply with his plan to free Israel; yet Paul can cite this episode as an integral part of God's plan: "For the Scripture says to Pharaoh: 'I raised you up for this very purpose, that I might display my power in you and that my name might be proclaimed in all the earth'" (Rom 9:17).

Other examples could be multiplied without undue difficulty, including the example of Jonah, who complied with God's plan only with great reluctance—and even Judas, whose betrayal of Jesus is seen by the NT writers as entirely necessary in accomplishing salvation for the world![22] Far from endangering the preservation of the nation of Israel through their unwillingness to cooperate with God's plan, these individuals were either chastised till they did cooperate, were replaced by others who would cooperate, or became unwitting agents of the very plan they opposed!

McHugh sees in Mary's acceptance of the angel's words a *fiat* on her part (i.e., a *consent* to participate in the divine plan) rather than simply a humble submission to God's will.[23] He notes that the optative "can only be translated as an earnest wish or prayer," and that the only correct rendering of this verse is as a cry of joy: "O may it be so for me, according to thy word."[24] Other Catholic scholars concur with McHugh's reading of Mary's response. Senior argues that through Mary's consent to bear the Son of God, she "is the one who enables the life of Israel to be redeemed."[25] Beattie writes:

> There was no implicit threat in God's invitation, and no fear of punishment. If she chose the quiet life, she would be left at peace. The decision was hers and hers alone. God waited while Mary deliberated. The history of the world hung in the balance as a young girl considered the options before her."[26]

Francis J. Moloney contends that "Mary must be seen as free to respond or not to respond to this initiative of God."[27] The tacit assumption of Moloney (and the *not so tacit* assumption of others who make this same point[28]) is that the redemption of the world is contingent upon Mary's decision to accept God's course for her life. Yet, Mary's decision to accept this can be no more significant than Paul's decision to accept his commission from God to take the gospel to the Gentiles. Are we to conclude that, had Paul refused, God would have counted his losses and worked instead only with the Jews?

Bearsley argues McHugh's point from a slightly different angle:

> Her consent to God was not temporarily conditioned with an inbuilt time limit—a "yes, for now!" In accepting motherhood of the Son of the Most High, she was committing herself to something irrevocable.... Once she became mother of Christ,

he could never be other than her Son. This is the significance of Mary's perpetual virginity, her *virginitas post partum....* Henceforward she is to be hailed as the Blessed Mary Ever Virgin.[29]

Bearsley leaps from Mary's acceptance of bearing the Messiah to Mary's perpetual virginity as though the latter were somehow the natural and logical consequent of the former. But even if we were to take Mary's words "let it be to me according to your word" as a consent or *fiat*, there is still no hint that she is here agreeing to be a virgin perpetually. To consent to bear a son never implies a subsequent vow of abstinence in any other situation; why would it imply it in this case? The "yes, for now!" condition that Bearsley rejects is a red herring in that it confuses the real message of the angel—"you will bear a son"—with Bearsley's tacit (and false) assumption of the *meaning* of that message—"you will remain a virgin." The latter is nowhere to be found in the Lukan text.

There is no question that, had Mary refused the angel's directions for her, God would simply have chosen someone else for the task. To conclude otherwise seems to be a case of special pleading with regard to Mary. Earlier we mentioned that Matthew gives the same prominence to Joseph as Luke does to Mary. In Matthew's account, it is Joseph who must make the decision to take Mary as his wife. If he had refused, and had carried out his plan to divorce her, Mary (as an unwed, pregnant woman) would no doubt have been accused of adultery and ostracized from society—perhaps even stoned, killing both mother and child! Yet, oddly, none of the exegetes that see special significance in Mary's decision go so far as to speak of Joseph's *fiat*, or conclude that Joseph is somehow a "co-Redeemer" because of his decision to stay with Mary.

Sklba's comments on Mary's cooperative decision seem in comparison much more reasoned than the Roman Catholic view that Mary's free decision secured the redemption of mankind: "She took her place among the poor who had no recourse except to respond, 'be it done to me according to your word' (Lk 1:38).... She awaits the command of another. The last word on the subject is not really her own."[30] Caird concurs when he notes that Mary's response "is the only response that anyone can properly make to the free and gracious bestowal of God's favour, the response of humility, faith, and obedience."[31]

According to Børresen, the understanding of Mary's response to mean *active consent* dates only from the beginning of the eighteenth century[32]; so that when Vatican II (in its document *Lumen gentium*) deals with Mary's role as the *new Eve*: "It makes use of the patristic interpretations of Luke 1:38, but whereas for the early Fathers this text was about obedience and faith...the council document uses *consentiens* and *cooperans* (consenting and co-operating)."[33] But even for all its *fiat* language, the significance that Vatican II places on Mary's decision is mild compared to pre-Vatican II Mariology. Tambasco explains that while the older, Christotypical Mariology "from above" saw in this passage Mary's *fiat* (that is to say, Mary's *decision* to become the mother of Jesus and thereby share in the redemptive work of Christ), the post-Vatican II Mariology "from below" places a new emphasis on Mary as the "receiver of redemption."[34]

"How will this be since I do not know a man?"

The *RSV* translation of Luke 1:34, "since I have no husband," is misleading since Mary did indeed have a husband at that time.[35] Both Matthew and Luke presuppose the two-step marriage process of that day. In the first step, *'êrûsîn* (betrothal, which is a "legally ratified marriage"),[36] the couple exchanged vows before witnesses but continued to live separately for a period of about a year, although at least one conjugal visit by the husband during the interim period was not uncommon.[37] In the second step, *nîśû'în*, the husband received the woman into his home, initiated regular marital relations with her, and took financial responsibility for her.[38]

McHugh has shown from Mishnahic sources[39] that sexual relations between the betrothed were allowed in Judaism, at least after the Jewish Revolt of AD 132–135. He notes that a betrothed girl whose fiancé had died was to wait a period of three months before marrying again in order to ascertain whether or not she had conceived a child.[40] However, the apparent reason for this allowance of sexual activity prior to the second step of the marriage process was to prevent Roman soldiers in Judaea from seizing a girl on her wedding day whom they assumed to be a virgin.[41] Around AD 150 R. Judah indicates that the practice of sexual relations during betrothal had diminished except in Judaea.[42] The normal practice by and large was to abstain from normal sexual relations until *nîśû'în*. This is assumed in *Ketuboth* 1:1–5 where instructions are given for legal action to be taken by the man if after the wedding it is discovered that the girl is not truly a virgin.

Mary's words in this passage ("I do not know a man") indicate that she and Joseph abstained from sexual relations during the *'êrûsîn* ("betrothal") period of their relationship. Yet some Catholic exegetes go even farther and suggest that Mary, by these words, indicates that she had taken a prior vow of virginity. This view, first posited by fourth-century fathers such as Gregory of Nyssa, Ambrose and Augustine, argues that Mary's question makes sense only if Mary had already made up her mind to remain a virgin, "so that her objection takes on the tone of a resolve: 'How can this be since I shall not know a man?' "[43]

Keating goes so far as to suggest that any opposing view encounters "insuperable" problems.[44] According to Keating, Mary's response would make no sense if she had not taken such a vow, for why would Mary ask "how" she would be pregnant if she knew she would be having sexual relations upon marrying Joseph?[45]

> There is no reason to assume Mary was wholly ignorant of the rudiments of biology. She presumably knew the normal way in which children are conceived. If she anticipated having children and did not intend to maintain a vow of virginity, she would hardly have to ask "how" she was to have a child, since having a child the normal way would be expected by a newlywed.[46]

Keating cannot understand how Mary's response could make sense in light of the angel's announcement that she would bear a child. But Keating's objection assumes that Mary is thinking of her future relations with Joseph and does not understand the conception to be immediate. Yet we have every indication that Mary *does* understand the angel to mean that she would conceive immediately. First, Mary does not say, "How can this be, since *I will not* know a man," which is what we might expect if Mary had taken a vow of lifelong virginity. Instead, she says, "How can this be, since *I am not* knowing a man." The present tense, not the future, is used in this statement. Mary could not fathom how she was going to become pregnant *right now* since she was not currently having sexual relations with Joseph.[47] In light of our earlier observation that sexual relations were not uncommon for a betrothed

Jewish couple in the first century, it would make perfect sense (in spite of Keating's insistence to the contrary) for Mary to ask "how" this would happen since she and Joseph were not engaging in what was otherwise considered an acceptable practice: "How will this happen, since (unlike some other betrothed couples) we are not having sexual relations?"

Second, the subsequent narrative indicates that Mary *did* conceive immediately. She is already pregnant when she visits Elizabeth—who, according to v. 36, is six months pregnant at Mary's Annunciation—for Elizabeth blesses the "fruit of [Mary's] womb" (v. 42). We are further informed that Mary stayed with Elizabeth three months (v. 56), but left before Elizabeth's child was born (v. 57). If Elizabeth was six months pregnant at Mary's Annunciation, and Mary was able to be with her for three full months afterward—but before Elizabeth gave birth—then Mary's visitation to Elizabeth (as well as her pregnancy) could *only* have been immediately after her Annunciation. This is borne out by v. 39, which tells us that Mary went to Elizabeth "with haste" (μετὰ σπουδῆς). If Mary asks her question under the assumption that the angel is referring to the immediate future, then, in the words of Landry, "she turns out to be right."[48] In light of these observations, it seems tendentious to suggest that Mary may be thinking of anything other than that she will conceive immediately:

> After considering the various alternatives, it seems clear that an ancient reader would conclude that as a betrothed virgin, Mary objects because she assumes that the angel is telling her that she will become pregnant *almost immediately*, before she could possibly have sexual relations legally with her husband.[49] [emphasis in original].

Mary's question, therefore, "certainly cannot be read as a vow of virginity: There are far too many more obvious senses of the statement to make that probable."[50]

The underlying assumption that leads Keating to his conclusions is that virginity is somehow a higher calling than marital relations.[51] Senior explains: "Traditional mariology has presumed that the virginity of Mary is presented in Luke's text as a treasured virtue. But there is reason to suggest that Luke considers it an impoverishment, a promise unfulfilled and with prospect in sight."[52] Senior shows the link between Elizabeth's circumstance as a "barren woman" who is promised a son, and Mary's circumstance as a virgin with no husband who is promised a son. The angel counters Mary's protest of impossibility ("how will this be since I am not sexually active," *translation mine*) by noting Elizabeth's "impossible" conception (v. 36), and reminding Mary that nothing is impossible with God (v. 37).[53] Mary's designation of herself as "the Lord's servant" (ἰδοὺ ἡ δούλη κυρίου, v. 38) may echo the words of the mother of Samuel (1 Sam 1:18) who was also the recipient of divine intervention in regard to her pregnancy; and the angel's words, "not any word will be impossible with God" (οὐκ ἀδυνατήσει παρὰ τοῦ θεοῦ πᾶν ῥῆμα) may be an allusion to the LXX of Gen 18:14: "Is a word impossible with God?" (μὴ ἀδυνατεῖ παρὰ τῷ θεῷ ῥῆμα). Both "words" are promises of an otherwise impossible pregnancy. "The 'low estate' of Mary in Luke's narrative is her virginity. She is destined to bear the messiah but she has no husband"[54] (i.e., she was not yet married).

Keating, moreover, has introduced an historical novum; namely, that there was such a thing as a *married virgin*. Yet, such a notion cannot be supported either biblically or historically. Indeed, the very notion of a teenage girl making a vow of lifelong chastity while at the same time planning a wedding is the stuff of which myths are made: "Such an interpretation of 1:34 reads into the text later concerns; and the idea that a Galilean village girl, who had already entered into marriage, did so intending to remain a virgin and childless is out of harmony with the Jewish mentality of Jesus' time."[55]

Jewish culture looked to the bearing of children as a great blessing and considered childlessness a disgrace—hence, Elizabeth's remark that God had "taken away [her] disgrace" by giving her a son (Luke 1:25; cf. the cases of Rachel, Sarah and Hannah).[56] Moreover, though some have attempted to marshal historical evidence for this interpretation by appealing to the Qumran practice of celibacy, this offers no real support since the practice itself is uncertain and is unrelated to virginity within marriage in any case.[57]

Even more importantly, the idea of a married virgin is biblically untenable. There is never any indication from the Old or New Testaments that it is acceptable to be married and at the same time a virgin.[58] Catholic apologists often argue that Mary and Joseph planned to be married—even though Mary had taken a vow of virginity—for reasons of financial expediency, or so that Mary would have a protectorate to provide for Mary and to protect her from other suitors. Yet Paul gives just the opposite directive for virgins in 1 Corinthians 7. There he tells us that, while it is ideal to remain unmarried (ἀγάμος) so that one can better serve the Lord (vv. 32–35), this would be impractical for those not having the "gift" of celibacy (vv. 7–9). However, if one *does* marry, that person has a marital *debt* (v. 3)[59] that is owed to his or her spouse; namely, not to deprive the spouse of his or her body—which, by virtue of marriage, no longer belongs to him or her, but to the spouse (vv. 4–5). He would like unmarried widows and virgins to remain unmarried (ἀγάμος), but if their passions flare up they too should marry (vv. 8–9, 25–28).

Several points need to be made about Paul's words here. First, it is clear by these passages that Paul assumes that if one is married, he or she is also sexually active. Second, Paul maintains that if one is not sexually active within a marriage, that person is depriving his or her spouse of what is *owed* (ὀφειλὴν). Moreover, if one wants to live a life of sexual inactivity and undistracted devotion to the Lord, that person is to remain *unmarried* (ἀγάμος)—not to marry for financial expediency. Marriage between two avowed virgins violates the divinely instituted intent of marriage, which is to demonstrate the intimate relationship between Christ and his church (Eph 5:22–32). To marry for reasons of financial expediency, or the like, is to misrepresent that original intent. Unconsummated marriage, therefore, is not only unsupported biblically and historically, but also seems to be averse to biblical teaching. If this was Mary's practice, then Mary is open to these charges. In any case, as Landry notes, though the "vow of virginity" interpretation has been popular among Roman Catholics in the past, its adherents are waning: "One seldom hears this line of thought in more recent scholarship. Many scholars regard the idea of a vow of perpetual virginity in the first century as an anachronism."[60]

Luke 1:39–56

The next passage in Luke that merits consideration is Mary's visit to Elizabeth in Luke 1:39–56. The text reads as follows:

At that time Mary got ready and hurried to a town in the hill country of Judea, where she entered Zechariah's home and greeted Elizabeth. When Elizabeth heard Mary's greeting, the baby leaped in her womb, and Elizabeth was filled with the Holy Spirit. In a loud voice she exclaimed: "Blessed are you among women, and blessed is the child you will bear! But why am I so favored, that the mother of my Lord should come to me? As soon as the sound of your greeting reached my ears, the baby in my womb leaped for joy. Blessed is she who has believed that what the Lord has said to her will be accomplished!" And Mary said: "My soul glorifies the Lord and my spirit rejoices in God my Savior, for he has been mindful of the humble state of his servant. From now on all generations will call me blessed, for the Mighty One has done great things for me—holy is his name. His mercy extends to those who fear him, from generation to generation. He has performed mighty deeds with his arm; he has scattered those who are proud in their inmost thoughts. He has brought down rulers from their thrones but has lifted up the humble. He has filled the hungry with good things but has sent the rich away empty. He has helped his servant Israel, remembering to be merciful to Abraham and his descendants forever, even as he said to our fathers." Mary stayed with Elizabeth for about three months and then returned home.

Roman Catholic exegetes see significance in several phrases found in this passage. We will examine each one below.

Mary as "Blessed"

There are three phrases in this passage that may be dealt with together: They are (1) "blessed are you among women" (spoken by Elizabeth), (2) "blessed is the child you will bear" (again, spoken by Elizabeth), and (3) "from now on all generations will call me blessed" (spoken by Mary). The question for purposes of our inquiry becomes, How and to what extent is Mary "blessed"?

As we might have gathered based on his comments on the Annunciation passage, McHugh thinks Mary is blessed because she "made an outstanding contribution to the salvation of Israel," and to that extent is a "savior" of the Jewish people, much the same way that Jael, Abram, and Judith had saved the Jewish people in their day.[61] McHugh states: "That her special rank was acknowledged by the Church is implied by the text of the Magnificat, where Luke says that 'from this present time' (1:48b) all generations will call her blessed,"[62] and then asks:

> Could Luke have written that phrase if, at the time when he was writing (AD 70–80), his own generation had not begun to call her blessed? The text of Lk 1:42 would seem conclusive proof that the early Church expressed its reverence for the mother of its Lord by singing hymns in her honor.... What was more obvious or more appropriate than to place on [Elizabeth's] lips a prayer commonly used by Christians of the day to the mother of Jesus? ...In Lk 1:42 we have preserved for us the opening words of an early liturgical hymn in honour of Mary.[63]

McHugh goes on to explain that the word ἀνεφώνησεν ("said in a loud voice"; which he maintains is used in the LXX only in contexts of religious ceremonies around the Ark of the Covenant) is used here precisely because the words of Elizabeth must be seen as a liturgical formula of the early church.[64] Why else, McHugh asks, would Luke make the point that Elizabeth said this in a "loud voice"?[65]

While McHugh does make some interesting observations about this passage (the word ἀνεφώνησεν is indeed used only in the way McHugh specifies[66]), his conclusion that Mary must have enjoyed a special status in the NT church based on Elizabeth's words and reactions is a bit improvident. Regrettably, McHugh ignores the way Luke portrays Mary in the very next chapter as one who is in need of correction by the boy Jesus at the temple (2:48–49).[67] Nor does he take into account the way the other gospel writers portray Mary, and especially John who wrote his gospel at least a decade after Luke wrote his.[68] In the rest of the NT, including the Lukan writings, there is not one hint of any special status for Mary; and indeed there are many counter-examples where she has no special status at all—even as a *disciple*, much less as a *mother*.[69]

Moreover, the phrase εὐλογημένη σὺ ἐν γυναιξὶν ("blessed among women") is not exactly unique to Mary. In Judg 5:24 Deborah and

Baraka sing a song, partly in honor of Jael because she killed Sisera: "Blessed be Jael among women" (εὐλογηθείη ἐκ γυναικῶν). In Judith 13:18 (23) Uzziah addresses Judith with a similar phrase: "O daughter, you are blessed [εὐλογητὴ σύ] by the Most High God above all women on earth [παρὰ πάσας τὰς γυναῖκας τὰς ἐπὶ τῆς γῆς]."[70] Moreover, Melchizedek blesses Abram in a similar way: "Blessed be Abram by God Most High, Creator of heaven and earth. And blessed be God Most High, who delivered your enemies into your hand" (Gen 14:19–20). These examples and others have caused the *MNT* taskforce rightly to conclude: "the fact that such a blessing has been invoked upon others prevents us from taking it too absolutely, as if it meant that Mary was the most blessed woman who had ever lived."[71]

The last part of Elizabeth's blessing to Mary comes in the form of blessing to her child: "blessed is the child you will bear." The *MNT* taskforce sees this clause as an allusion to Deut 28:1–4:

> If you fully obey the LORD your God and carefully follow all his commands I give you today,… All these blessings will come upon you and accompany you if you obey the LORD your God:… The fruit of your womb will be blessed.

They conclude from this passage that the blessing of the fruit of Mary's womb is due to her show of obedience in 1:38. But this, too, seems unnecessary. The child in Mary's womb is "blessed" because of his intrinsic quality: He is called "great," the "Son of the Most High" (1:32), the "holy one," and the "Son of God" (1:35). In any case, he is not blessed because of Mary's obedience.

But what of Mary's statement about her own blessedness: "from now on all generations will call me blessed" (v. 48)? Unlike the "holy one" she would bear, there is no hint here of blessing based on Mary's intrinsic quality. Instead, she is blessed because "the Mighty One has done great things for [her]" (v. 49). "All generations" will call her blessed because of the divine favor bestowed on her in being chosen to bear the Son of God: "for he has been mindful of the humble state of his servant" (v. 48). This type of blessedness is not unique to Mary, however, but is true of anyone for whom God has assigned a unique task, including Adam and Eve (Gen 1:22), Noah and his sons (Gen 9:1), Abraham

(Gen 24:1), Isaac (Gen 25:11), Jacob (Gen 35:9), the pure in heart (Matt 5:8), those who are persecuted (Matt 5:10), etc. Indeed, this concept appears so many times in both Testaments that to single out Mary and posit that her blessing is qualitatively different from all other cases of blessedness is to engage in special pleading. Shall we conclude that when Leah states "All women will call me blessed" (Gen 30:13, a statement that is remarkably similar to Mary's statement) that she has been more highly favored by God than any other woman? Mary was indeed divinely favored; but the favor extended to her was no more conditioned on her intrinsic quality than was God's favor to King David, or any other biblical character for that matter. The difference is in the task assigned to each, not in the degree of God's favor for that task. The significance of Mary's blessing does not lie in God's choosing an extraordinary human being of superlative status to bear his son. Instead, it lies in God's choosing a "lowly," ordinary teenage girl of humble circumstances and status to accomplish his will.

"The Mother of my Lord"

This phrase in Luke 1:43 has been treated in a number of ways by various Catholic writers. Senior observes that Mary is "lauded" by Elizabeth not only for believing that God would fulfill the promise he gave her, but also for being the mother of her Lord,[72] which he labels "a powerful, royal title."[73] Some Catholic apologists go even farther and posit that the phrase "mother of my Lord" is to be equated with the later historical title "mother of God." But this is certainly not Luke's intent. We will address this issue in more detail in the appendix section.

Luke 2:21–35

In this passage, the infant Jesus is presented in the temple and receives a blessing from Simeon. The text reads as follows:

> On the eighth day, when it was time to circumcise him, he was named Jesus, the name the angel had given him before he had been conceived. When the time of their purification according to the Law of Moses had been completed, Joseph and Mary took him to Jerusalem to present him to the Lord (as it is written in the Law of the Lord, "Every firstborn male is to

be consecrated to the Lord"), and to offer a sacrifice in keeping with what is said in the Law of the Lord: "a pair of doves or two young pigeons." Now there was a man in Jerusalem called Simeon, who was righteous and devout. He was waiting for the consolation of Israel, and the Holy Spirit was upon him. It had been revealed to him by the Holy Spirit that he would not die before he had seen the Lord's Christ. Moved by the Spirit, he went into the temple courts. When the parents brought in the child Jesus to do for him what the custom of the Law required, Simeon took him in his arms and praised God, saying: "Sovereign Lord, as you have promised, you now dismiss your servant in peace. For my eyes have seen your salvation, which you have prepared in the sight of all people, a light for revelation to the Gentiles and for glory to your people Israel." The child's father and mother marveled at what was said about him. Then Simeon blessed them and said to Mary, his mother: "This child is destined to cause the falling and rising of many in Israel, and to be a sign that will be spoken against—and a sword will pierce your own soul too—so that the thoughts of many hearts will be revealed."

The Roman Catholic teaching of Mary's virginity *during* birth (*in partu*) (i.e., without rupture of the hymen) seems to be negated by Luke's phrase in v. 22 that Jesus "opened the womb" (διανοῖγον μήτραν). The sacrifice made in vv. 21–24 presupposes a normal birth process for Jesus, and many Catholic scholars note that it is unlikely that Luke would have employed this phrase if he had known of this Marian tradition.[74]

But the more significant part of this pericope is Simeon's prophecy to Mary at the end of the passage, particularly in regard to the phrase, "and a sword will pierce your own soul too." This phrase has often been taken by Roman Catholic writers to mean that Mary would experience the anguish of seeing her son suffer and die, would undergo the humiliation of being accused of the illegitimate birth of her son, and may even have died a martyr's death.[75] A connection is often made to John's gospel where we find Mary at the foot of the cross (John 19:25–27). The intent of this connection is to show Mary in tandem with Jesus in his suffering; presenting her in a positive, if not sympathetic light.

This interpretation pivots on a proposed change of thought between Simeon's statement ("and a sword will pierce your own soul too") and the rest of Simeon's words ("this child is destined to cause the falling and rising of many in Israel, and to be a sign that will be spoken against, so that the thoughts of many hearts will be revealed"); with the effect that the first statement becomes something of a parenthetical note. Yet, aside from an *a priori* connection to the scene of Mary at the cross in John's gospel, there seems to be no good reason to assume a change of thought here: "We may not safely combine the data of Luke and John to conclude that [the cross of Jesus in John] is the occasion when a sword pierces her soul."[76] The statement about Mary cannot be taken in isolation, and its meaning must flow naturally from the context in which it is found.

A correct understanding of this passage seems to be bound up with the meaning of the word "sword" (ῥομφαία). McHugh notes that this same word is used in several OT contexts as a metaphor for God's devastating anger, and in each of these cases provision is made for the salvation of the remnant (Ezek 6:2–9; 5:1–4; 12:14–16; 14:12–23; 17:21).[77] The "sword" in these passages is therefore not merely an instrument of judgment, but also an instrument by which God would separate his remnant from the rest of the people.[78]

McHugh offers a revised version of the traditional Catholic view given above. He correctly notes that the relationship between v. 35a ("and a sword will pierce your own soul too") and 35b ("so that the thoughts of many hearts will be revealed") is *prima facie* a non sequitur, and that is why many translations have placed v. 35a as a parenthetical thought (*NAB, KJV, NASB*).[79] McHugh attempts to solve the problem by introducing corporate personality into the text, according to which Mary is seen not only as representing herself, but also as the *daughter of Zion* who represents Israel.[80] Hence, there is double entendre here. Mary's personal "sword" would be the pain and sorrow she experiences in seeing the rejection, suffering and death of her son.[81] Mary's corporate-personality "sword" would be the preaching of Jesus, which in turn would become the downfall or "stumbling block" for many in Israel.[82]

McHugh makes several insightful observations that persuasively link the "sword" with Jesus' preaching. The Servant of the Lord in Isa 49:2 declares, "He made my mouth like a sharpened sword." This theme is taken up by John in the Revelation where, describing the Son of Man, John writes: "and out of his mouth came a sharp double-edged sword" (1:16). John continues this theme when he is commanded to compose a letter containing the "words of him who has the sharp, double-edged sword" (2:12). The recipients are to separate themselves from those who hold to false teachings, lest the awesome figure return and they find themselves fighting against "the sword of [his] mouth" (2:16). We find this same theme later when John describes the Rider of the white horse, whose name is "the Word of God" (19:13), and out of whose mouth "comes a sharp sword with which to strike down the nations" (19:15). John has already identified Jesus by his message in John 1:1: "In the beginning was the Word…and the Word was God." That same message, or "word of God," is elsewhere described as "the sword of the Spirit" (Eph 6:17), and "sharper than any two-edged sword" that penetrates the "soul" and "judges the thoughts and attitudes of the heart" (Heb 4:12). One cannot avoid the obvious connection between this last reference and Luke 2:35: "so that the thoughts of many hearts will be revealed. And a sword will pierce your own soul too."[83] McHugh concludes: "The meaning of Simeon's prophecy, there-fore, is that the word of revelation brought by Jesus will pass through Israel like a sword, and will compel men to reveal their secret thoughts."[84]

McHugh's thesis has much to commend it, and many of his points are no doubt valid. Still, there are several problems both with his view, and with the traditional Catholic view he has revised. First, so far as the traditional Roman Catholic view is concerned, it seems dubious that Luke would have included a statement that requires for its inter-pretation information that Luke himself does not supply.[85] Only John depicts Mary at the foot of the cross in the detailed way that this view requires (19:25–27),[86] and Luke cannot be expected to have assumed that his readers would have cross-referenced a writing that was not yet extant.

Second, McHugh's revision introduces more problems than it solves. His entire thesis turns on the acceptance of Mary as the *daughter of Zion*, which (as we shall later see) is based on scant evidence.[87] Yet, if one does not come to this text with McHugh's understanding of Mary as the *daughter of Zion* in Luke 1:28–30, one cannot possibly accept his conclusions here.[88]

Third, McHugh's presentation of Mary as the *daughter of Zion* here has fundamental differences with the *daughter of Zion* he presents to us when discussing Luke 1:28–30. There the *daughter of Zion* which Mary represents is identified as the "poor,"[89] the "destitute refugees,"[90] and the faithful "remnant" of Israel.[91] Yet here in Luke 2:34–35 we are asked to accept a *different daughter of Zion*—still represented by Mary, but one that includes both those who "rise" (i.e., the remnant) as well as those who "fall" (i.e., the rest of Israel). The latter symbol cannot simply ride on the coattails of the former, but must be firmly established on its own merit by the text itself. Unfortunately, apart from an appeal to the already precarious understanding of the *daughter of Zion* in Luke 1:28–30, there is nothing in the text of Luke 2:34–35 that can do this.

In all fairness, McHugh may simply be thinking of the remnant even here in Luke 2:34–35 (as opposed to those who "fall"). On this understanding, Mary, as the remnant *daughter of Zion*, sorrows over the rejection of the Messiah by Israel's leaders in the same way that Mary as an individual sorrows over the suffering and death of her son. In this way the identity of the *daughter of Zion* in Luke 1:28–30 is left intact in 2:34–35, and the integrity of the symbol is maintained. Indeed, McHugh subtly indicates that this may be what he in fact has in mind.[92]

Yet, this qualification has problems of its own; for in that case we are presented with three groups in Israel: those who fall in Israel, those who rise in Israel, and the remnant *daughter of Zion*. It seems *prima facie* unlikely that the phrase "a sword will *also* (καὶ) pierce *your own* soul (σοῦ [δὲ] αὐτῆς τὴν ψυχὴν) is meant to refer to one of the groups just mentioned. Yet those who "rise" in v. 34 are undoubtedly the remnant, and this precludes v. 35 from mentioning them again since Simeon presents here a distinct person.[93] McHugh's general thesis is therefore inadequate since it raises more questions than it answers.

The simplest explanation of how a sword would pierce Mary's soul is to view it in light of Simeon's words in v. 34: "This child is destined to cause the falling and rising of many in Israel, and to be a sign that will be spoken against." Jesus, Simeon declares, will be the focal point upon which some will "fall" and others will "rise." Luke is probably thinking of a "sword of division," which separates the bad (those who reject Jesus will "fall") from the good (the "hearers and doers" of the word will "rise"; Luke 8:21; 11:28). Elsewhere Luke records Jesus as saying:

> Do you think I came to bring peace on earth? No, I tell you, but division. From now on there will be five in one family divided against each other, three against two and two against three. They will be divided, father against son and son against father, mother against daughter and daughter against mother, mother-in-law against daughter-in-law and daughter-in-law against mother-in-law (Luke 12:51–53).

Matthew records the same saying this way:

> Do not suppose that I have come to bring peace to the earth. I did not come to bring peace, but a sword. For I have come to turn 'a man against his father, a daughter against her mother, a daughter-in-law against her mother-in-law—a man's enemies will be the members of his own household' (Matt 10:34–36).

Where Luke has "division" Matthew has understood "sword." The sword of division divides people into two groups. Matthew's groups are comprised of (1) those who "acknowledge" and "love" Jesus, and by taking up their cross and following him find their lives (vv. 32, 37–38); and (2) those who "disown" Jesus, love biological ties more than him, and by not taking up their cross and following him lose their lives (vv. 33, 37–38). Luke's groups are similarly composed.

Matthew (10:34) uses μάχαιραν ([short] "sword"), while Luke (2:35) uses ῥομφαία ([broad] "sword").[94] The effect nevertheless is the same. The "sword" in both cases has to do with the demands of discipleship. Everyone must be pierced by this sword, and Mary is no exception: "By directing this saying to Mary, the oracle hints that even being a member of Jesus' own family does not shield Mary from the discrimination that lies ahead."[95] As part of Israel, her "own" (αὐτῆς) soul must also be pieced "in order that it may be revealed whether her thoughts are those of a believer or the hostile thoughts (*dialogismoi*) of those who speak against the sign offered in Jesus."[96] The word "thoughts" (διαλογισμοί) is always used in the NT in a pejorative sense[97]; and Mary herself must be judged by her own response to the "child [who] is destined to cause the falling and rising of many in Israel" to see whether her "thoughts" will be revealed. Once again we see that, far from any special privileges conferred upon her as the mother of Jesus, Mary is expected to undergo the same judgments and discipleship process as everyone else: "By the imagery of the sword passing through Mary's soul, Luke describes the difficult process of learning that obedience to the word of God transcends family ties."[98]

Gaventa counters this argument by adducing evidence from Greco-Roman letters of consolation in which the grief of the mother is compared to the imagery of a sword.[99] The first two are from Seneca, and the last is from Pliny:

> Of all the wounds that have ever gone deep into your body, this latest one, I admit, is the most serious; it has not merely torn the outer skin, but pierced your very breast and vitals. But just as raw recruits cry out even when they are slightly wounded, and shudder more at the hands of the surgeons than they do at the sword, while veterans, though deeply wounded, submit patiently and without a groan to the cleansing of their festered bodies just as if these were not their own, so now you ought to offer yourself bravely to be healed. (Seneca, *To Helvia on Consolation* 3.1).
>
> That you may know that even this deep-cut wound will surely heal, I have shown you the scar of an old wound that was not less severe. (Seneca, *To Marcia on Consolation* 1:5).
>
> When she found she could no longer restrain her grief, but her tears were gushing out, she would leave the room, and having given vent to her passion, return again with dry eyes.... The action was, no doubt, truly noble, when drawing the dagger she plunged it into her breast, and then presented it to her husband with that ever-memorable,..."it does not hurt, my Paetus." ...But was it not something much greater, without the view of such powerful motives, to hide her tears, to conceal her grief, and cheerfully play the mother when she was so no more? (Pliny, *Letters* 3:16).

Yet, while in each case the imagery of "cutting," or "piercing," is clear, there are important differences with the Lukan text. In the former the "piercing" imagery is always with reference to the physical body (*To Helvia*, "body," "breast," "vitals"; *To Marcia*, "deep-cut wound," "scar of an old wound"; *Letters*, "breast"); in Luke the "piercing" imagery is with reference to the "soul" (ψυχὴν). In the former there is mention of a "sword" only in *To Helvia*—*To Marcia* makes no mention a sword, and *Letters* has "dagger." Moreover, Pliny's writing offers no parallel to Luke at all since the proposed imagery is no imagery at all. Pliny is referring to a woman's decision to die with her husband, who in turn is forced to commit suicide. The "drawing of the dagger" and "plunging it into her breast" is quite literal here, and is not to be connected to the loss of a child. The reason she is "mother no more" is because of her own impending death, not that of her child. The citation from Pliny, therefore, must be discounted from the equation entirely.

Gaventa acknowledges that her evidence does not constitute a "stock literary feature,"[100] and with that we can agree. One more dissimilarity is that in each of the remaining two writings the imagery is explicitly connected to the grief of the mother—in Luke there is no such explanation. Gaventa argues that the imagery in Luke does not have to be fulfilled in a direct way "so that the reader 'sees' the pain of Mary"[101] (e.g., through a portrayal by Luke of Mary's grief at the cross), since "the reader also does not 'see' the division of Mary's family regarding Jesus."[102] Gaventa concludes from this that the absence of Mary from the cross in Luke's gospel "is not itself particularly significant."[103]

Yet Gaventa is mistaken. As we have seen in the previous chapter, we do indeed "see" the division of Mary's family regarding Jesus: Mary is portrayed by Luke as standing "outside" the circle of true disciples, and hence divided from Jesus.[104] This theme is continued in many of the Lukan passages treated in this chapter as well.[105] The fact that the context of the passage itself suggests that "sword" means "sword of division," and that Luke nowhere else alludes to Mary's grief, makes Luke's omission of Mary at the cross (Gaventa's assertion to the contrary notwithstanding) most significant. In such a case, there is no "fulfillment" of Simeon's prophecy. After all is considered, it is best to conclude with Fitzmyer that the interpretation we have adopted:

> rules out many other attempts to explain the sword, e.g., as the sword of doubt piercing Mary during the passion of Jesus,…or as the sword of her own violent death,…or as the sword of rejection that she too experienced in the public rejection of her son; or as the sword of illegitimacy with which Jesus was

reproached because of the virginal conception; or as the sword of tragedy that she experienced at the fall of Jerusalem; or as the sword of enmity set between her seed and the seed of the serpent of Gen 3:15. All such attempts explain the sword on the basis of material extraneous to the Lucan Gospel and could scarcely have been envisaged by Luke.[106]

Our proposed understanding of this passage (which, after all, is supported by both Protestant and Catholic exegetes) is significant in still another sense. Luke has used this episode to help us anticipate—*and understand*—subsequent passages where Mary is mentioned in his gospel: "Thus, with the imagery of the sword piercing Mary, Simeon hints at the difficulty she will have in learning that obedience to the word of God will transcend even family ties. Recall how Mary will be depicted in Luke 8:21 and 11:27–28."[107] Many exegetes could aid their understanding of other Marian passages found later in Luke (including the two mentioned above by Fitzmyer) if they would simply keep the present passage in mind. It is to one such passage that we now turn.

Luke 2:41–52

In Luke 2 we find the adolescent Jesus at the temple. It is significant that this episode comes so soon on the heels of Simeon's prophecy that the *sword of division* would pass through Mary's soul. Here we have Mary's first encounter with this "sword":

> Every year his parents went to Jerusalem for the Feast of the Passover. When he was twelve years old, they went up to the Feast, according to the custom. After the Feast was over, while his parents were returning home, the boy Jesus stayed behind in Jerusalem, but they were unaware of it. Thinking he was in their company, they traveled on for a day. Then they began looking for him among their relatives and friends. When they did not find him, they went back to Jerusalem to look for him. After three days they found him in the temple courts, sitting among the teachers, listening to them and asking them questions. Everyone who heard him was amazed at his understanding and his answers. When his parents saw him, they were

astonished. His mother said to him, "Son, why have you treated us like this? Your father and I have been anxiously searching for you." "Why were you searching for me?" he asked. "Didn't you know I had to be in my Father's house?" But they did not understand what he was saying to them. Then he went down to Nazareth with them and was obedient to them. But his mother treasured all these things in her heart. And Jesus grew in wisdom and stature, and in favor with God and men.

At issue here is Mary's attempted rebuke of Jesus ("Son, why have you treated us like this? Your father and I have been anxiously searching for you") and Jesus' response to it ("Why were you searching for me? Didn't you know I had to be in my Father's house?"). The phrase ἐν τοῖς τοῦ πατρός μου has been variously rendered as "in the domain of my Father," "among the things of my Father," "among those who serve my Father," and "about my Father's business."[108] McHugh summarily rejects the rendering of v. 49 as anything other than "in my Father's house (or home)."[109] Surprisingly, though, McHugh has nothing at all to say about the tone of Jesus' reply to Mary's question in v. 48!

Reese proposes (presumably on the basis that Luke uses οὐ rather than μή) that the phrase "did you not know" (οὐκ ᾔδειτε) indicates that Mary had a "special understanding" of Jesus' role and mission: "The question in the Greek implies the answer, 'yes: I knew that you had to take this course of action.'"[110] Amazingly, Reese misunderstands both the Greek and the context of this passage. The Greek particle οὐ implies only that Mary and Joseph *should* have understood Jesus' purpose; not that they did in fact understand. Indeed, the very next verse denies Reese's thesis: "But they did not understand what he was saying to them" (v. 50).[111]

Luke paints a picture of Mary in this passage that indicates Mary did not understand—and even opposed to some degree—Jesus' mission.[112] Moreover, we have here the first hint of a future severing of biological ties between Jesus and his earthly family; Jesus responds to his mother's correction with a correction of his own.[113] Although the *MNT* taskforce generally sees Luke's treatment of Jesus' family in more benevolent terms than Mark's treatment, it is acknowledged here that "the tone of [Luke] 2:48…is somewhat closer to Mark [than to Luke's otherwise benevolent tone]."[114] What is more, Luke here portrays Jesus as *anticipating* the severing of biological ties with his mother: "Mary (and Joseph) are concerned for Jesus as the natural, blood relatives. Jesus changes the relationship by his question, 'Did you not know I must be in my Father's house?' From now on the relationship must be one of faith in Jesus as the revelation of God."[115]

Whereas Luke's first chapter portrays Mary in a somewhat positive light, Luke's second chapter turns the tide. Luke seems to be telling us that while a biological mother was essential for Jesus in his early years (in order to survive as a helpless infant), that need wanes as Jesus grows older, and Jesus indicates as much with his response to Mary:

> The question that [Jesus] asks in no way responds to Mary's concern. Indeed, it may be understood as a *rejection* of her question, perhaps even of her prerogative to ask a question. The narrator's comment that "they did not understand what he said to them" only reinforces the wedge this episode drives between Jesus and Mary (and Joseph).[116]

Yes, we are told that after this episode Jesus "went down to Nazareth with them and was obedient to them" (v. 51); but this temporary arrangement was only until "Jesus grew in wisdom and stature" (v. 52). The turning point in biological relations between Jesus and his parents occurs when he is a boy. While he continues to submit to them afterward, Jesus' response to Mary nevertheless "establishes a distance between Jesus and his earthly parents in favor of his relationship to his heavenly Father,"[117] and Luke will repeat this theme later in his gospel: "The evangelist's remark is really a commentary on the words of Simeon to Mary, about the sword of discrimination that would pierce her.… His parents did not understand because their coming to understand was a gradual process, even in the Lucan writings."[118] For Mary, then, the *sword of division* has not yet been sheathed.

Luke 11:27–28

One final passage in Luke that holds Marian significance is 11:27–28: "As Jesus was saying these things, a woman in the crowd called out, 'Blessed is the mother who gave you birth and nursed you.' He replied, 'Blessed rather are those who hear the word of God and obey it.'" In this episode a woman attempts to offer indirect praise to Jesus by praising his mother. In his response to the woman, "Jesus shunts direct praise for his mother in a different direction."[119] He points rather to the blessedness of those who are disciples. In so doing, "he firmly deflected any praise of his mother."[120] This idea seems even clearer coming on the heels of 11:23—"He who is not with me is against me, and he who does not gather with me, scatters"—and its explanation in vv. 24–26: "It provides a further commentary on the cautions he has just uttered there; but otherwise it is hard to say why Luke has put this episode here."[121] Even the *MNT* taskforce concedes that a surface reading of this text "seems to be a bit more negative toward the mother of Jesus than 8:19–21."[122]

At the end of the day, however, the taskforce arrives at a different conclusion about how Mary is viewed in this passage. The particle μενοῦν ("rather") is seen by the taskforce, not as a corrective, but as a reinforcement of the woman's statement in v. 27—"Yes, but even more"—citing Phil 3:8 as an instance where it is rendered thus.[123] "Literally, the praise is for the womb 'that bore you' and the breasts 'you sucked.'…and the beatitude of the mother may lie in the son she has produced."[124] The taskforce concludes on this basis (and on the basis of Elizabeth's praise of Mary in 1:42) that Mary herself "is truly the object of praise,"[125] and that by these words Jesus is pointing to his mother as the model disciple.

Other Catholic scholars who concur with the taskforce are not wanting. Tambasco concludes that Luke intends "to offer [Mary] as first example of the Christian who keeps God's word."[126] McHugh thinks it "regrettable that some commentators read this text as if it were pointing away from Mary as a model for all Christians."[127] Wansbrough views this "highly laudatory and positive statement on Mary's blessedness" as Luke's intentional substitute for Mark's negative portrayal of Mary: "Instead of being a prime example of failure to accept Jesus' message, she has become the prime example of its joyful acceptance."[128]

Yet perhaps the boldest assertion about Luke's portrayal of Mary comes from the pen of Mercurio: "As we hear the joyous cry of a 'certain woman,' we detect [Luke's] voice mingled with hers…. Throughout the gospel [Luke] has sung the praise of Mary."[129] Mercurio believes that in these words Jesus was "extolling" his mother[130] and raising the woman's thoughts to a "higher, loftier plane."[131] According to Mercurio, what Jesus is really saying is that his mother "should receive praise above all else for being the ideal hearer and doer of the life-giving word of God."[132]

Mercurio's rendition here is highly susceptible to misunderstanding. He does not mean by this statement that Mary should receive praise "above all others," but rather that praise for Mary should be based on, more than any other reason, her obedience to the word of God. Still, Mercurio assumes by such a statement that Luke sees Mary as the ideal disciple. Indeed, as we have already noted, this is also the assumption of Tambasco, Wansbrough, and McHugh, as well as the *MNT* taskforce.

It is just this assumption, however, that is in question. We have already noted in the previous chapter that Luke does not soften Mark's account, as this view requires. We have also seen that Jesus as a boy begins to distance himself from Mary in anticipation of severing biological ties (Luke 2:49). Hence (the *MNT* taskforce's focus on the infancy narrative notwithstanding), the last time we actually see Mary in Luke's gospel is not when Elizabeth praises her; it is instead when Luke portrays her as someone who does not understand Jesus' mission; and we have not been given any reason since then to think that she is now a disciple. The burden of proof, then, is on those who tacitly assume that Mary is portrayed both here and in Luke 8:19–21 in a positive light. For these reasons, Jesus' words here (as the *MNT* taskforce itself agrees[133]) are more naturally interpreted as deflection of praise for Mary.

Fitzmyer, relying heavily on the work of Thrall,[134] suggests that the particle μενοῦν be understood here as "yes, rather": "v. 28 admits that Jesus' mother is worthy of praise, not just because she has given birth to him, but because she too—in the Lucan story—is among those who have listened to the word of God, believed it (1:45)."[135] Fitzmyer points out three distinct usages of this particle: (1) the adversative usage ("nay, rather"), a complete rejection of what has just been said, which includes Rom 9:20 and 10:18; (2) the affirmative usage ("indeed"), an emphatic agreement of what has just been said, which includes Phil 3:8; and (3) the corrective usage ("yes, but rather"), meaning that what has just been said is true but has not gone far enough, which includes no clear NT examples (only Classical, Plato, *Rep.* 498D[136]). Fitzmyer, relying again on Thrall, further suggests that the first two usages must be eliminated from consideration, since, "when [Luke] wants to express contradiction, he uses *ouchi, legō hymin* (12:51; 13:3,5); and for the affirmative he employs *nai* (7:26; 10:21; 11:51; 12:5)."[137]

The major criticism that can be leveled against Fitzmyer's suggestion is that it relies too heavily and uncritically on Thrall, who in turn quite possibly has set up artificial categories, both in the NT usages of the particle and in the suggestion of what Luke should have used had he wanted to convey contradiction. First, it is doubtful that the usage of the particle can be subdivided into three categories, since there is no real difference between categories (2) and (3) above; both can rightly be translated "more than that." Second, while it is true that this particle can be used in contexts that emphasize ("more than that"), the only clear example of this usage is in Phil 3:8; all other NT instances are used as correctives ("on the contrary"—Rom 9:20; 10:18). When we examine Phil 3:8, we see what may account for this reversal of meaning. In Phil 3:8 the particle μενοῦν is accompanied by the construction ἀλλὰ καὶ ("but also"). When this combination occurs, the meaning is "not only this, but also"[138]; whereas in all other instances (including Luke 11:28), the particle stands alone at the beginning of a clause and, hence, takes on the adversative meaning—which is the normal meaning of the word—found in category (1) above ("nay, rather"). This unique usage in Phil 3:8 is explained by ἀλλὰ καὶ, and not by anything inherent in the particle itself.

Thrall cites only one other instance of this word (in classical Greek; Plato, *Rep.* 498D) as evidence of *meaning (3)* above; but even here the meaning is not clearly that which Thrall suggests. In this passage, Socrates is debating with a Sophist who mockingly comments on the amount of time it will take Socrates to convince Thrasymachus of his concept of how government should be structured: "A brief time, your forecast contemplates."[139] Socrates answers, "Nay [μὲν οὖν], nothing at all [εἰς οὐδὲν], as compared with eternity [ὥς γε πρὸς τὸν ἅπαντα]."[140] Though she does not explicate, Thrall apparently sees in the phrase "as compared with eternity" justification for her understanding of μὲν οὖν as "what you have said is true as far as it goes, but…" (Fitzmyer's *meaning [3]* above). However, this is to misunderstand Plato's intent. Socrates does not mean to agree that his opponent is correct in his understanding "as far as it goes"; rather he means to convey that his opponent's entire perception is faulty because it is measured by the wrong standard. Socrates' opponent measures the time it will take Socrates to persuade his friend in terms of the *usual* amount of time such an activity takes. Socrates rejects that measurement altogether and compares it instead with eternity. This is just what Jesus seems to do in Luke 11:28; he rejects the woman's praise of Mary altogether because it is based on the faulty perception that being biologically related to Jesus entails a state of blessedness. Hence, both Plato and Luke use the word μενοῦν in the same adversative sense that it is used everywhere in the NT, with the exception of Phil 3:8 whose meaning we have seen is explained on other grounds.[141] The adversative meaning in Luke 11:28 is supported by R. E. Brown ("rather"),[142] M. Zerwick ("rather"),[143] I. H. Marshall ("rather"),[144] *BDF* ("rather"),[145] *BAGD* ("rather/on the contrary"),[146] the *NASB* ("on the contrary"),[147] the *NIV* ("rather"), the *RSV* ("rather"), the *NAB* ("rather"), and the *Douay Rheims* ("rather").

Another criticism of Fitzmyer's view here is that it completely overturns his prior insistence that we should understand these Marian passages in light of the *sword of division* motif found in Simeon's prophecy (2:34–35).[148] As we have already noted, in 2:49–50 Luke leaves us with the impression that Mary is someone who does not yet understand Jesus' mission. That we should now simply assume that Mary is a model disciple (based on what evidence?) seems to us an incredible stretch. Moreover, one wonders just how Fitzmyer's suggestion for the meaning of the particle (above) explains the passage. As Fitzmyer earlier noted,[149] this episode comes on the heels of Jesus' words in v. 23: "He who is not with me is against me, and he who does not gather with me, scatters." According to this verse, one need not actively oppose Jesus to be regarded as his opposition. This "with me/against me" motif suggests that we should not expect Jesus to admit of any middle ground of "blessing." Hence, when the woman suggests that Jesus' mother must be blessed because of her biological connection to Jesus, it is not Jesus' style—anywhere else, much less here—to acquiesce to a "middle ground" and assert in essence, "well, yes, I suppose there is a blessing of sorts due to that connection—I take back what I said earlier."

Another consideration that bears on the meaning of Jesus' response is a grammatical one. In her exclamation of praise, the woman uses the singular (μακαρία ἡ κοιλία ἡ βαστάσασα; lit., "blessed is the belly that carried you"), pointing directly to the mother of Jesus and no other. If we are to understand Jesus' response as further praise of his mother (i.e., to emphasize what the woman has already said), we might have expected Jesus to use the singular as well: "she is even more blessed because she hears and does the will of God." Instead, Jesus uses the plural (μακάριοι οἱ ἀκούοντες τὸν λόγον τοῦ θεοῦ καὶ φυλάσσοντες; "blessed are *they* who hear the word of God and do it"). The change from the singular to the plural strongly suggests that Jesus cannot be thinking about his mother here, as though he were extending the degree of praise for her. Instead, he is pointing away from "the belly that carried" him to "those" who do the will of God. By so doing, Luke conveys the same severing of biological ties between Jesus and Mary that we find in the Synoptic accounts, and that Luke hints at in 2:28–52. Viewed in this light, the idea that Mary is presented in this passage as a model disciple seems contrived, if not altogether opposed to Luke's theology elsewhere.

One final statement by Mercurio deserves comment:

> We can see that in this historical setting Our Lord's words were not intended as a disparagement of Mary. He was known as 'the son of Mary.' He had lived thirty years subject to her at Nazareth. He knew very well that right-thinking men would not mistake His meaning.[150]

Mercurio has cast the matter in such a way as to place in jeopardy the right-headedness of those who wish to disagree with him here. At the risk of sounding injudicious, perhaps one ought to point out that the title "son of Mary" occurs only in Mark 6:3, and the only two references to a relational title in Luke is "Mary his mother" (Luke 2:34) and "Mary the mother of Jesus" (Acts 1:14). Moreover, whereas Jesus may well have lived with Mary all thirty years of his pre-ministerial adulthood (John 19:27), this hardly constitutes evidence that he was "subject to her" during any of his adult life. Although it is by no means clear in the Lukan passage that Jesus is *disparaging* Mary, Mercurio presents this and his view as though they were the only two options. Jesus can legitimately draw attention away from Mary in an attempt to downplay biological ties and focus attention instead on those who hear and do the word of God, without in any way disparaging Mary in the process. Mary is neither disparaged here nor is she held up as the ideal disciple. Instead, she is presented by Luke as an illustration to show that even the closest biological ties to Jesus do not grant special status with him. That status is given only to those who hear the word of God and do it. Mary eventually attained to that status, but it is not the evangelist's purpose to report it here. As Bridcut concludes:

> Through this woman Jesus says to us: 'Blessed are those who rightly hear, so concentrate on what was spoken, not on the mother of him who spoke.' In speaking like this Jesus is not rejecting his mother but showing that being mother would have been of no avail.[151]

After all options have been considered, this seems to be the most reasoned view of this passage. Mary is not rejected as a disciple; only as a biological mother. Her status as disciple is no less than any other disciple, but neither is her standing as mother any advantage.[152] Indeed, Moloney may very well have it right when he says, "in many ways this passage serves as a warning for all subsequent interpretations of the greatness of Mary."[153] If Jesus rebuffs this woman's comparatively minimalistic praise of Mary, it seems certain that he would much more forcefully rebuff the inherent praise and unique status implied in such titles as Mother of God, Queen of Heaven, Co-Redemptress, Co-Mediatrix, and the like.

Acts 1:13–14

By the time we reach Luke's sequel the resurrection has already occurred, and Jesus' mother is counted among the disciples; the *sword of division* has now been withdrawn from Mary:

> When they arrived, they went upstairs to the room where they were staying. Those present were Peter, John, James and Andrew; Philip and Thomas, Bartholomew and Matthew; James son of Alphaeus and Simon the Zealot, and Judas son of James. They all joined together constantly in prayer, along with the women and Mary the mother of Jesus, and with his brothers (Acts 1:13–14).

There is very little here that is significant for our discussion—Mary is neither rebuffed nor praised. Instead, she is portrayed merely as one of the disciples, along with Jesus' brothers and the apostles, who is awaiting the reception of the promised Holy Spirit—she is no greater and no less: "Since Mary is mentioned only once in Acts (1:14), it is clear that Luke was not concerned with exalting her role in the post-Easter community."[154] If it is argued that there is significance to the fact that there is a specific reference to her, then that same significance must also apply to Jesus' "brothers" who are also singled out in this verse.[155] What *is* significant—indeed, incredible if we are to accept the Roman Catholic view that Mary held a high status in the early church—is that Mary is never again mentioned in Luke's entire history of the early church.[156] Luke goes to great lengths to show the regard the church had for James, Peter, Paul, Barnabas, Apollos, Aquila, Priscilla, Lydia and others; but there is not one mention of the mother of Jesus—not even in retrospect[157]—so that even Laurentin (whom Brown takes to task for his tendentious approach to this issue[158]) is forced to conclude:

> Throughout all this period, the precise length of which escapes us, the mother of Jesus, having attained the light of her perfection, lived in the Church without being ever explicitly mentioned.… It was as though she herself were ignorant of the extent of her influence, and as though those about her were unaware of it. She was a living organ in the body of Christ, but not the subject of the Church's teaching.[159]

Such an admission is remarkable from a writer who goes on to assert that what was conspicuously absent from the apostolic *kerygma* legitimately found explicit expression in later centuries.[160] Yet, without disputing over whether or not such a later development was indeed legitimate, we have tacit agreement from a leading Roman Catholic polemist that the NT gives no indication of Mary's primacy in the life of the NT church.

All through Luke's narratives we find a portrait of Mary that typifies, or *epitomizes*, a disciple. In Luke's Annunciation narrative she responds in belief and humbly accepts the mission before her, but not without questioning it first. At the presentation of Jesus in the temple we are told that she herself would be "pierced" by the "sword" that separates unbelievers from the remnant. Twelve years later (when the boy Jesus teaches in the temple), we find that she misunderstands a good portion of Jesus' mission and presumes to impose her will upon his, with the effect (unwitting though it may be) of subverting that mission: She is rebuffed by Jesus for doing so. Still later we find that Mary requests special privileges of Jesus on the basis of biological ties, demonstrating once again that she misunderstands his mission: True relations in the kingdom are based on discipleship.

Finally, we find her in the company of the rest of the disciples waiting patiently for the promise, neither claiming special privileges to Jesus nor opposing his mission: "Neither the 'sword' that threatened her nor her own inability to understand Jesus prevented her from becoming one of those gathered in the upper room."[161] She has, through her sometimes-on/sometimes-off process of following Jesus, typified discipleship. This same process may be found in Matthew's Peter, who sometimes hits the mark (Matt 16:16), and sometimes misses it very badly (Matt 16:22–23). Mary is therefore to be seen, not as having a special status, but as being in league with every other true disciple of Jesus.[162]

CHAPTER VI

Marian Symbolism in Luke

Before we go on to the other literature of the NT, we need to examine one final aspect of Luke's gospel that may hold Marian significance. Many scholars, particularly those on the Roman Catholic side, see in Luke's gospel an attempt by Luke to portray Mary as a symbol. This symbol, which varies from scholar to scholar, includes Mary as *Model Disciple*, Mary as *daughter of Zion*, Mary as *Ark of the Covenant*, and Mary as *Anawim* (the poor).[1] All but the first are found by these scholars in Luke's birth narrative (Luke's *model disciple* symbolism is based on his overall portrait of Mary). We will examine the arguments for these symbols below, and then propose what we believe is Luke's true intent.

Mary as Model Disciple

Throughout discussions about the way in which Mary is presented in Luke, one theme more than any other emerges by those who see a special status for Mary; namely, that Mary is deliberately portrayed by Luke as *model disciple, symbol of discipleship, perfect disciple*, or the like. Mary, it is argued, was the first to "hear the word of God and do it" when she accepted her divine mission.[2] Lonsdale writes: "Her response [in Luke 1:38]…shows that she is already prepared to be a member of Jesus' eschatological family; she is already a believer for whom God's word is enough."[3] Senior concurs: "[Mary's] response is clear and exemplary from Luke's point of view: …Mary's credentials as hearer and doer of the word are impeccable."[4]

Bearsley, who seems intent on defending the title of Mary as mother of God, is willing to admit that Luke sees Mary's discipleship of much more value than Mary's motherhood of Jesus, and proposes to use the former as a paradigm for understanding the latter: "Her motherhood should be understood in light of her discipleship, and not vice versa."[5] Yet the conclusions he later draws from such a paradigm contradict his initial premise: "That she is the mother of God is the most glorious thing about her; it is her greatest privilege. Nothing, not even her perfect discipleship, may be permitted to detract from her sublime dignity as mother of the God-made-man, Jesus Christ."[6]

In Senior's opinion, Mary shows herself to be the model disciple, one who "hears the word and does it," by the intense pondering in which Mary engages about her son (Luke 2:19, 51).[7] Brown believes this theme emerges in the book of Acts as well:

> After the death, Resurrection and Ascension of Jesus [Mary] is shown as having remained faithful, waiting for the Spirit. Thus she serves as the most consistent disciple in the whole Gospel narrative. This is a tremendous development in the line of the New Testament reflection on Mary. The development comes after Mark was written and begins to move us toward what will happen in the subsequent church.[8]

It is little wonder, then, that those who see the inception of this theme in Luke 1, and the culmination of it in Acts 1, would find it in the rest of Luke's Gospel as well. Hence, the underlying assumption of these exegetes becomes clear when we come to passages such as Luke 8:19–21 ("my mother and my brothers are those who hear the word of God and do it") and 11:27–28 ("blessed rather are those who hear the word of God and do it")—and even 2:48–52 ("did you not know I had to be in my father's house?"). In short, it seems to be the desire on the part of these writers to see continuity in the way Mary is presented by Luke that results in the otherwise seemingly contrived interpretations of these texts. But if Luke presents Mary as the model disciple, why does she so suddenly disappear into obscurity after the Resurrection? The *MNT* taskforce explains:

> The relative Lucan silence [of Mary in Acts] is startling, granted the great interest Luke has shown in Mary in the

infancy narrative. However, once we realize that such an interest was not primarily in Mary as a person but in Mary as a symbol of discipleship, Luke's shift of attention becomes more intelligible. When Jesus was an infant, the mother was really the only appropriate figure to illustrate discipleship.... But in the narrative of Jesus' ministry, there is a wider range of figures who can illustrate discipleship, especially the twelve.[9]

Yet, as we have already noted, the other gospel writers do not present Mary as the first disciple—indeed, Mark does not present her as a disciple at all! Matthew presents Joseph as the first disciple (1:24–25); and Mark presents John the Baptist as the first "doer of the word," as does John's gospel (1:6; cf. 1:15–35). Yet no scholar seems to be looking for symbolism in either Joseph or the Baptist. One wonders, then, why we should just assume that Mary is the object of special attention in Luke. The answer seems to lie in other Marian symbolism that many Catholic exegetes see in Luke's gospel. We shall now examine this symbolism in depth below.

The "Daughter of Zion" Symbolism

One popular symbol for Mary is that of the *daughter of Zion*. On this view, Mary corporately represents Israel. This symbolism is based primarily on the word χαῖρε in Luke 1:28 ("*Greetings*, you who are highly favored!"). Proponents of this view argue that χαῖρε should here be translated as "Rejoice!,"[10] connecting it to such passages as the following:

Rejoice [χαῖρε] greatly, O Daughter of Zion! Shout, Daughter of Jerusalem! See, your king comes to you, righteous and having salvation, gentle and riding on a donkey, on a colt, the foal of a donkey (Zech 9:9).

Sing, O Daughter of Zion; shout aloud, O Israel! Be glad and rejoice with all your heart, O Daughter of Jerusalem! The LORD has taken away your punishment, he has turned back your enemy. The LORD, the King of Israel, is with you; never again will you fear any harm (Zeph 3:14–17).

It is further argued that Luke typically uses εἰρήνη, not χαῖρε, in Semitic contexts (cf. Luke 10:5; 24:36). Moreover, in the LXX translation of the books originally written in Hebrew (i.e., the OT books of the Protestant canon) the imperative χαῖρε is never once found as the equivalent of the ordinary greeting שלום (which is invariably translated as εἰρήνη).[11] Further support is adduced from the fact that παρθένος ("virgin") is used in both Luke and many of the LXX passages that speak of the *daughter of Zion* (cf. 2 Kings 19:21; Isa 37:22; Lam 2:13—"Virgin Daughter of Zion").

McHugh sees significance in the fact that the only three OT passages that use the present imperative χαῖρε (with the exception of Lam 4:21, Prov 24:19 and Hos 9:1, the first of which uses it as irony, and the latter two of which use it with the negative) use it in connection with the *daughter of Zion* (Zeph 3:14; Joel 2:21; Zech 9:9)—although he acknowledges that the Joel passage gives no direct reference to the *daughter* of Zion, but rather the *children* of Zion. This evidence, coupled with the fact that Luke uses the form χαῖρε only here,[12] causes the proponents of this view to conclude that Luke intends to portray Mary as the new *daughter of Zion*.

Difficulties with the Daughter of Zion View

The image of the *daughter of Zion*, often attributed to Mary by conservative Catholic scholars, is doubted by most moderates.[13] The phrase is used frequently in the OT to denote a sinful and shameful Israel—not exactly the kind of imagery Catholics would like to apply to Mary.[14] The *MNT* taskforce does not mince words in assessing the tenability of this symbolism: "Drawing heavily on a concordance to the LXX, the proponents of this symbolism often contend that since a term used by Luke is found in a certain Old Testament passage, Luke intended to invoke that passage, its context, and other related passages."[15]

The taskforce notes several difficulties with this view.[16] First, χαῖρε is further clarified in 1:29: "Mary was greatly troubled at his words and wondered what kind of *greeting* (ἀσπασμός) this might be," indicating that the proper translation is "greeting," not "rejoice." Second, χαῖρε is a term that normally denotes a simple greeting (Matt 26:49; 28:9), or is used at the beginning or ending of a letter (Jas 1:1; Phil 3:1; 4:4), and was as common then as "hello" and "goodbye" are today. The notion that Luke would have used εἰρήνη and not χαῖρε had he intended a normal greeting is pure speculation. Third, the connection between Mary and the *daughter of Zion* via the use of παρθένος does not help the case of the proponents of this view "since almost all the Old Testament references to the virgin Zion or virgin Israel are uncomplimentary, portraying her in a state of oppression, waywardness, and lust."[17] Fourth, χαῖρε is also found in the LXX addressed to the Daughter of Edom:

> Rejoice and be glad, O Daughter of Edom, you who live in the land of Uz. But to you also the cup will be passed; you will be drunk and stripped naked. O Daughter of Zion, your punishment will end; he will not prolong your exile. But, O Daughter of Edom, he will punish your sin and expose your wickedness (Lam 4:21–22).

On what basis do we assign to Mary the symbolism of the *daughter of Zion* and not the Daughter of Edom since χαῖρε is used for both? Moreover, as McHugh himself has already conceded (above), only two of the six OT passages that use the present imperative form of χαῖρε are used with the phrase *daughter of Zion*—hardly enough of a pattern to justify our finding the technical meaning for this word that McHugh implies in his thesis!

In answer to the first two objections above, McHugh grants that this is a greeting, but asks what *kind* of greeting it is: "Does it have Old Testament overtones or not?"[18] In answer to this, we must ask the further question, Can the OT passages to which McHugh appeals be considered true greetings? In fact, neither the Zephaniah passage nor the Zechariah passage uses χαῖρε as a greeting. But if neither one of the two OT passages that can be adduced in support of McHugh's view is a true greeting, then the connection between those passages and the Lukan passage breaks down even further. Moreover, as even McHugh concedes,[19] Luke may have chosen χαῖρε instead of εἰρήνη simply because he intended a wordplay with κεχαριτωμένη which immediately follows.

Against the fourth objection above, McHugh, while conceding that a phrase such as "Rejoice and be glad, O Daughter of Zion" would certainly have made Luke's purpose clearer, nevertheless maintains that this would be out of step with Luke's style.[20] He cites other instances where Luke alludes to OT passages without providing direct quotations, such as 1:31 which alludes to Isa 7:14,[21] and 1:32–33 which alludes to Isa 9:7 and 2 Sam 7:12–16. Yet in each of the cases McHugh cites, the OT allusions are Christological, not Mariological. Moreover, even McHugh grants that his view of χαῖρε as an allusion to the *daughter of Zion* is historically innovative, and that "before 1939, nearly all writers took the word χαῖρε to be simply an everyday greeting, devoid of doctrinal significance, the Greek equivalent of the Hebrew *shalôm* or the Aramaic *shelam* ('Peace!')."[22]

On the other hand, McHugh has argued persuasively for a connection between the *daughter of Zion* passages and the Annunciation via the use of the present imperative χαῖρε. If there is no intended connection, it is indeed odd (the attendant difficulties set aside for the moment) that Luke never again uses this form of the word for a greeting, and that all the instances of it in the LXX where a positive command is given also refer to Zion. Still, all this *must* mean is that Luke intends an allusion of *some* kind. It would not be at all surprising that Luke might allude to these passages given their salvation-historical theme. For Luke, the Messiah has come, and with him the ultimate cause for Israel's rejoicing. If Luke portrays Mary as the recipient of the greeting "Rejoice!," it is not so much that Mary is being portrayed as the *daughter of Zion* as that Mary, as a member of the class of Israel, is also a member of the *daughter of Zion*. At the end of the day, if McHugh has sought to equate the person of Mary with the eschatological *daughter of Zion*,[23] he has not established his case. For there is clearly a difference between connecting the *daughter of Zion* passages in the OT to the Lukan passage by means of the common theme of the final redemption of Israel, and the further, unmerited step of equating the *daughter of Zion* with the person of Mary. While the evidence McHugh adduces (though scant in light of the objections above) might support the former contention, it certainly cannot bear the weight of the latter.

The Ark of the Covenant Symbolism

Some Roman Catholic scholars see in Luke's portrayal of Mary the symbolism of the Ark of the Covenant, or the Tabernacle.[24] The word ἐπισκιάσειν ("overshadow") in Luke 1:35 ("The Holy Spirit will come upon you, and the power of the Most High will *overshadow* you") is also used in reference to the cloud overshadowing the Tabernacle in the desert (Exod 40:35; cf. Num 9:18, 22 where σκιάζειν is used), and in reference to cherubim "overshadowing" (συσκιάζοντες) the Ark of the Covenant (Exod 25:20; cf. 1 Chr 28:18, σκιαζόντων).[25] No Jewish reader of Luke, McHugh insists, could fail to see in this word an allusion to the *Shekinah*.[26]

McHugh examines further evidence for this theme, adduced by some Catholic scholars (though apparently he is not convinced by it[27]), from Elizabeth's greeting to Mary in Luke 1:43: "But why am I so favored, that the mother of my Lord should come to me?" This is taken as a "Christian midrash" to David's words in 2 Sam 6:9: "How can the ark of the LORD ever come to me?"[28] Just as the Ark of the Lord stayed in the house of Obed-Edom the Gittite for three months (2 Sam 6:11), so also Mary (the Ark of the Lord) stayed with Elizabeth for three months (Luke 1:56).[29] A cross-reference over to John 1:14 shows that Jesus "tabernacled among us" (ἐσκήνωσεν ἐν ἡμῖν), and by logical extension in the womb of Mary.[30]

McHugh notes further parallels between the "journey" Mary takes and the one the Ark (via David) takes: both Mary and David "arise" (ἀναστᾶσα, Luke 1:39; ἀνέστη, 2 Sam 6:2) and "set out" (ἐπορεύθη in both).[31] Both the Ark and Mary are greeted with "shouts of joy" (2 Sam 6:12, 15; Luke 1:42, 44).[32] Elizabeth's greeting to Mary upon her arrival is described by the verb ἀνεφώνησεν ("exclaimed"). According to McHugh, this word is used in the LXX only in contexts of liturgical ceremonies centered around the Ark.[33]

Objections to Mary as Ark/Tabernacle

Many of McHugh's points made in support of viewing Mary as Ark/ Tabernacle are badly in need of nuance. The word ἐπισκιάσειν (along with its variants σκιάζειν and συσκιάζειν, "overshadow") is used in many other OT contexts beside the one McHugh selectively cites. It is used, for instance, of Mount Zion (Isa 4:50; cf. Wis 19:7), of the Israelites (Num 10:34[36]), of God's chosen ones (Deut 33:12; Ps 91[90]:4; 140[139]:7), and even of the plant that grew over Jonah's head (Jonah 4:6). Moreover, the parallelism demanded by this view is inconsistent. We are told sometimes that Mary is paralleled with David (both "arise" and "set out"), while other times that Mary is paralleled with the Ark. Moreover, the statement of David in 2 Sam 6:9, "How can the ark of the LORD ever come to me?," changes the parallelism from Mary/David to David/Elizabeth.

Yet even if we were to allow for this inconsistency, there are still other incongruities. First, the Ark *did not* immediately come to David (as Mary does to Elizabeth) but was taken to the house of Obed-Edom for three months. Second, David's words are said in frustration, whereas in the case of Elizabeth, the words are stated in humility. Third, Mary *did* stay with Elizabeth for three months, as opposed to David who complains that the Ark can never come to him—again changing the parallelism, this time from Elizabeth/David to Elizabeth/Obed-Edom. There is a difference not only in the intent of the saying, but also in just where the "Ark" stayed in relation to the speaker. The fluctuation of the parallelism from Mary/Ark to Mary/David to David/Elizabeth to Elizabeth/Obed-Edom seems too capricious to be valid, and is for that reason alone rightly rejected by most scholars.[34] Mary's three-month stay with Elizabeth is more naturally explained on the basis that Elizabeth is six months pregnant when Mary arrives. After the baby is born (three months later), Mary would naturally return home to take care of her own advancing pregnancy.

At the end of the day, if McHugh's parallel between Mary and the Ark is to be maintained ("like the Ark of the Covenant, [Mary] became the Dwelling-place of the Most High"[35]), then it must be nuanced—the value of the Ark lay in its Dweller and not in the Ark itself which, apart from the Dweller, has no intrinsic value of its own. If Mary is to be seen as the Ark, it must have been a temporary status lasting only the duration of her pregnancy. Once the Dweller leaves, so also the value of the Ark diminishes.[36]

Mary as the Anawim

Still another Marian symbolism that some have seen in the Lukan Annunciation passages is Mary as *anawim*. This symbolism is not taken from any one passage in the OT, but rather the common theme inherent in the Hebrew word *'ânâw* ("poor, humbled, afflicted"). Mary is seen on this view to represent the lowly. The members of the *MNT* taskforce, who are usually hesitant to accept other proposed symbolism for this passage, make an exception in this case—they see an *anawim* theme in Mary's canticle: "From now on all generations will call me blessed" (Luke 1:48). If we may compare this to Leah's words in Gen 30:13, "All women will call me blessed," we see how an *anawim* theme might emerge. In both passages the subject discovers she is pregnant. The context of each passage assumes a prior state of humility for the subject (though for different reasons[37]).

There may also be an allusion to the "low estate" and exultation of Hannah in 1 Samuel 1–2.[38] In this narrative, Hannah is childless and, as a result, is taunted by her rival Peninnah (1:6). She prays to the Lord to relieve her of her misery by giving her a son, and vows to devote her son to the Lord (1:11). After she conceives a child, she sings a canticle in honor of God. It is here—and even beyond— that there are similarities to Mary's canticle and Jesus' subsequent childhood. (See table on page 170.)

McHugh sees Mal 3:12 as the appropriate parallel: "All the nations will call you blessed" (a reference to Israel) on the basis that it is "closer in thought" to the Magnificat than is Gen 30:13.[39] The "thought" McHugh has in mind is the eschatological overtone in each.

Tambasco sees in the Lukan passage a possible allusion to the lives of Abraham and Sarah:

> One of the midrashes [*sic*] shows Mary as reliving in an eminent way the roles of Abraham and Sarah.... Mary proclaims that God has remembered his mercy to Abraham.... Mary's faith leads to the one who will be the final blessing for all nations. There needs to be God's intervention. Abraham and Sarah both ask, "Shall Sarah who is ninety bear a child?" ...Mary asks, "How shall this be done?"[40]

To this we might add the response given to each woman's objection, both Sarah and Mary are told that "nothing is impossible with God" (Luke 1:37; cf., "Is anything too hard for the Lord?" Gen 18:14).

With the exception of McHugh's suggestion that the Lukan text refers to Mal 3:12, each of the views above has much to commend it.[41] However, there does not seem to be any sense in which a direct reference to a specific OT passage is intended. It is perhaps better to avoid

I Sam 2:1–11, 26	Luke 1:45–55; 2:22–52
(1) My heart rejoices in the LORD; in the LORD my horn is lifted high.	(46–47) My soul glorifies the Lord and my spirit rejoices in God my Savior,
(1–2) My mouth boasts over my enemies, for I delight in your deliverance. There is no one holy like the LORD; there is no one besides you; there is no Rock like our God.	(48–50) for he has been mindful of the humble state of his servant. From now on all generations will call me blessed, for the Mighty One has done great things for me—holy is his name. His mercy extends to those who fear him, from generation to generation.
(3–4) Do not keep talking so proudly or let your mouth speak such arrogance, for the LORD is a God who knows, and by him deeds are weighed. The bows of the warriors are broken, but those who stumbled are armed with strength. [(6–8) The LORD brings death and makes alive; he brings down to the grave and raises up. The LORD sends poverty and wealth; he humbles and he exalts. He raises the poor from the dust and lifts the needy from the ash heap; he seats them with princes and has them inherit a throne of honor.] [(9–10) It is not by strength that one prevails; those who oppose the LORD will be shattered. He will thunder against them from heaven; the LORD will judge the ends of the earth. He will give strength to his king and exalt the horn of his anointed.]	(51–52) He has performed mighty deeds with his arm; he has scattered those who are proud in their inmost thoughts. He has brought down rulers from their thrones but has lifted up the humble.
(5) Those who were full hire themselves out for food, but those who were hungry hunger no more.	(53) He has filled the hungry with good things but has sent the rich away empty.
(9) He will guard the feet of his saints, but the wicked will be silenced in darkness.	(54–55) He has helped his servant Israel, remembering to be merciful to Abraham and his descendants forever, even as he said to our fathers.
(11) Then Elkanah went home to Ramah, but the boy ministered before the LORD under Eli the priest.	(2:22–25) When the time of their purification according to the Law of Moses had been completed, Joseph and Mary took him to Jerusalem to present him to the Lord.... Now there was a man in Jerusalem called Simeon.
(26) And the boy Samuel continued to grow in stature and in favor with the LORD and with men.	(2:52) And Jesus grew in wisdom and stature, and in favor with God and men.

the temptation to adopt one passage over the other. Instead, a general allusion to all those who have been raised up from a humble, childless circumstance may be intended.

It must be noted, however, that this does not imply the use of *symbolism* by Luke. Luke can allude to similarities between Mary's circumstances and those of her predecessors without intending to portray Mary as some sort of *symbol* of those circumstances; or of anything else for that matter. We will close this chapter by asking whether Luke intends any Marian symbolism at all in his gospel.

Is Marian Symbolism Intended by Luke?

We may now return to our original question regarding the validity of the *model disciple* symbolism for Mary. None of the other symbols for Mary have held up under close scrutiny except perhaps for the *anawim* motif. Any evidence for Mary as model disciple must therefore stand on its own without the support of the other symbols. Flanagan asks what he sees as "persisting questions" in regard to the way in which the NT writers see Mary as a symbol:

> Why was it precisely Mary who was chosen as the symbol of discipleship, of attentive hearer, as doer of the word, as the blessed among women? Why not someone else? Why is it Mary who appears at the foot of the cross as representative of Christ's spiritual family? Why not someone else? Why not the Beloved Disciple by himself? …Is it even possible to imagine that Luke paints his annunciation scene, as John his Calvary scene, without knowing through historical information that Mary was a worthy, if not superworthy, model?[42]

Yet, as we have already seen, every uniquely Marian passage that is cited by Roman Catholic scholars as evidence of this symbolism is more naturally taken in the opposite sense. One wonders, therefore, whether looking for Marian symbolism in these passages is legitimate in the first place; or, indeed, if the character were someone other than Mary, whether *anyone* would see symbolism in Luke at all.

If we are to see Marian symbolism in Luke based on allusion to the OT, why do we not see Josephine symbolism in Matthew based on similar OT allusion? After all, "it is true that Mary is mentioned in the infancy narrative of Matthew, but the account centers on Joseph."[43] In Matthew's infancy narrative we find in at least four instances that Joseph is connected with "dreams" (1:20; 2:13, 19, 22); not unlike the Joseph of Genesis who is also connected with "dreams" (Gen 37:5–11, 19; 40:8–18; 41:16–32).[44] Both Matthew's Joseph and the Joseph of Genesis are called sons of "Jacob" (Gen 35:22–24; Matt 1:16). Both are objects of special attention for the biblical writers (the OT Joseph is "loved," Gen 37:3; the NT Joseph is "righteous," Matt 1:19). Both go down to Egypt under duress (Gen 37: 28; Matt 2:13–15). In Matt 2:18 we read a quotation from Jer 31:15 which pictures "Rachel weeping for her children and refusing to be comforted." This is directly connected to the "slaughter of the innocents" that prompts the NT Joseph to go down to Egypt. We know from texts such as Gen 35:24 that Rachel is the OT Joseph's mother, who, when told of the supposed death of her son (Gen 37:31–33), no doubt "mourned" (37:34) and "refused to be comforted" (37:35) along with her husband Jacob—how could anyone fail to see here an intended connection between the Rachel of Genesis and the Rachel of Matthew? Finally, we read in Genesis 41–47 that the OT Joseph, by his trip to Egypt, saved the world from certain destruction and was highly exalted by Pharaoh (placed second in command over all Egypt). The NT Joseph, too, saved the world from certain destruction by taking the child Jesus to Egypt thus preserving his life and paving the way for his death on the cross, which would secure eternal redemption for the world. One can safely assume, therefore, that just as the OT Joseph was highly exalted and placed second in command, so also the NT Joseph must be highly exalted by God and his church, and (perhaps) placed second in command in the Kingdom of God.

The foregoing "symbolism" is of course to be completely rejected. But the exegesis that leads to it is little different than that which we find in the supposed Marian symbolism claimed for Luke's gospel by countless Roman Catholic scholars. Lonsdale's caveat against McHugh's exegetical practice in this regard may serve as a warning to all of us: "John McHugh's general tendency is to try to combine theological and historical interpretations of incidents in the infancy narratives, a combination which is often uneasy and unsatisfying."[45] McHugh, of course, is not the only exegete who falls prey to this—

unfortunately the majority of modern Roman Catholic interpreters, with few exceptions,[46] have fallen prey to it as well. This is not to say that there is no symbolism in the gospels. Far from it; but the symbolism in the gospels is decidedly Christocentric rather than Mariocentric. Yet it is precisely this Mariocentric exegesis—which is in reality a special pleading with regard to Mary in the NT—that continues to stifle constructive dialogue, and continues to prevent Protestant scholars from seeing much value in Roman Catholic contributions on these issues. Until all sides cease to look for Marian significance in passages that if any other character were involved would hold absolutely no significance, it is doubtful that we can arrive at a common New Testament Mariology.

CHAPTER VII

Mary in the Gospel of John (Part One)

There are only two scenes in John's gospel where an encounter between Jesus and his mother evidence possible Marian significance.[1] The first of these, John 2, is set at the wedding feast in Cana; the second, John 19, is set at the cross. In each scene speculation abounds as to how Mary is to be viewed. At one end of the spectrum Mary is seen in the most mundane terms, or even in opposition to his mission; while at the other end Mary is seen as our heavenly intercessor, mother of the church, and a crucial player in God's plan of salvation. We suspect that the true picture of Mary in John lies somewhere in between. A detailed look at these two passages will be necessary to complete the overall portrait of Mary among the evangelists.

Jesus and Mary at Cana—John 2:1–5

The first scene in which Mary appears is that of a wedding celebration. The backdrop of this scene as a wedding banquet plays a crucial part in the meaning of this passage, as we shall later see. Here John recounts the events at this wedding:

> On the third day a wedding took place at Cana in Galilee. Jesus' mother was there, and Jesus and his disciples had also been invited to the wedding. When the wine was gone, Jesus' mother said to him, "They have no more wine." "Dear woman, why do you involve me?" Jesus replied. "My time has not yet come." His mother said to the servants, "Do whatever he tells you."

The events at this scene actually extend to v. 11 of this passage; but since Mary's significance stops at v. 5, so shall our inquiry. The tension in this scene begins with John's narration that "the wine was gone," followed by Mary's echo of this crisis to Jesus: "They have no more wine." Stephen Hartdegen surveys the various views on the significance of Mary's words.[2] Some exegetes take this to imply nothing more than anxiety on Mary's part over the obviously embarrassing situation for the bridal couple.[3] Others see in Mary's words a request by Mary for Jesus to relieve the potentially embarrassing situation, though not necessarily by means of a miracle.[4] Still others see this as an observation by Mary that Jesus interprets as a command.[5] Finally, some see this as an express request from Mary for Jesus to perform a miracle.[6] Hartdegen himself falls into this last category, although in a nuanced way.[7]

Eamon Carroll depicts Mary's words this way: "Mary, inspired by the Spirit, was requesting the messianic fulfillment."[8] Other depictions are equally unsatisfying because of their at-all-cost tendency to cast Mary artificially in symbolic terms:

> At Cana, she could represent the church as a concerned mother asking for the new wine of the spirit and presenting obedience to Jesus' word understood in light of his death as a means to obtain it. A second possible way is that of Mary as a heavenly intercessor. This is not found in the Fourth Gospel by any kind of direct evidence. However, it would fit in with the Gospel and be in no way contradictory to it; it would also be supported by acceptable biblical models.[9]

Similarly, the suggestion of Hartdegen and others who see in Mary's words a request for a miracle is to be rejected on the basis that, for John, this is "the *first* of his miraculous signs" (2:11). To portray Mary as expecting Jesus to perform a miracle—something that until now he had never done—seems anachronistic. How could she have tacitly expected something for which there was no historical precedent? Moreover, Hartdegen's additional point that Mary's words are to be seen as a "delicate request" that are said "without any restriction of [Jesus'] complete freedom of action,"[10] is likewise contradicted by the passage. If Mary's words are to be viewed as a request at all, then Jesus' response—"what to me and to you"—implies at the very least that she was overstepping her bounds (see discussion below). Before turning our attention to this phrase, we must conclude that the simplest explanation of Mary's words here is that they are to be understood in the sense of a simple expression of anxious concern on her part, laced with an appeal to help her come up with a solution ("They have run out of wine. What do you suggest?"). This makes sense of what we are told before Mary utters these words, as well as of how Jesus responds in turn. Carson notes that the fact that Mary, Jesus and his disciples were all invited to this event (2:1–2) suggests the wedding was for a close friend or relative.[11] According to Carson, it is not at all unlikely that Mary may have had some responsibility for coordinating the event, "hence her attempt to deal with the shortage of wine."[12] This seems also to be supported by her seemingly covert knowledge of that wine shortage, as well as her tacit assumption in v. 5 that the banquet servants would be willing to comply with her command to "do whatever he tells you." If she did have such a role, this would certainly explain Mary's anxiety about the situation. But Mary had, no doubt, also learned to count on her son's "resourcefulness"[13]; hence, she brings the matter to Jesus. In any case, if we accept Hartdegen's additional point—namely, that Mary's words are a request for a miracle and imply no restriction on Jesus to do as he pleases—then we must conclude by his response that Jesus misunderstood her; for his response suggests that she has indeed overstepped her bounds.

"What to me and to you?"—v. 4

There has been much speculation about the precise intent of Jesus' response to his mother. Reese characterizes it as a "loving appeal."[14] McHugh thinks it should be taken as a suggestion of common disinterest ("why should *we* be concerned about that?")[15] Yet, as even McHugh admits, both Augustine[16] and Chrysostom[17] believed that Jesus was reprimanding his mother in this passage.[18] This understanding of Jesus' words as a reprimand is not uncommon in the patristic writings; it shows up as well in Irenaeus, who understands Jesus' tone toward Mary to be harsh in this passage: "When Mary pressed on toward the admirable sign of the wine and wanted prematurely to participate in the anticipated cup, the Lord said, repelling her untimely haste: 'Woman, what have I to do with you.'"[19] It may also be found in Theodoret, who, commenting on our passage, writes: "At one time

[Jesus] gives honor to his mother as to her that gave him birth; at another time he rebukes her as her Lord."[20] Our passage is also commented on by Gregory the Great, who, in a treatise on the distinction between Christ's deity and humanity, paraphrases Jesus' words in John 2:4: "In the miracle, which ability comes not from your nature, I do not acknowledge you."[21]

In order to decide on a meaning for this phrase we must look at how it is used elsewhere. The *MNT* taskforce sees two meanings of this phrase in the OT: (1) an injured party may say to his perpetrator, "What have I done that you should do this to me" (citing Judg 11:12; 2 Chr 35:21; 1 Kgs 17:18); and (2) a person uninterested in involving himself in affairs not his business may say, "That is your business; how am I involved?" (citing 2 Kgs 3:13; Hos 14:8).[22] We agree with this general assessment of the meaning of the phrase. However, as we shall see, there are some who hold out Jesus' words to Mary as an exception to these meanings. Only by examining the full weight of the evidence for the meaning of this phrase will we be able to put to rest the notion that Jesus' words to Mary do not constitute a distancing reproof.

The Greek text of Jesus' response to his mother's words reads τί ἐμοὶ καὶ σοί, γύναι—literally, "what to me and to you, woman," a phrase that implies some degree of reproach. Some Catholic scholars are uncomfortable with the notion that the Son of God is here rebuffing his mother. As a result, many Catholic scholars have attempted to soften the meaning by interpreting Jesus' words as something such as "What has changed between us?,"[23] or "What would you have me do?"[24] Yet, the philological evidence is squarely against such an interpretation. Hartdegen provides a useful survey of the occurrences of this phrase elsewhere in Scripture and in secular Greek literature.[25] The identical construction occurs in Judg 11:12, where Jephthah inquires of the Ammonite king who is attacking his countrymen: "*What do you have to do with me* that you have attacked our country?" In 2 Sam 16:10, King David responds to Abishai's offer to decapitate Shimei who is cursing David, "*What do you and I have in common*, you sons of Zeruiah? If he is cursing because the LORD said to him, 'Curse David,' who can ask, 'Why do you do this?'" In 1 King 17:18, the widow of Zarephath whose son has just died cries out in despair to Elijah, "*What do you have against me*, man of God? Did you come to remind me of my sin and kill my son?" In 2 King 3:13, the prophet Elisha says to Joram, the wicked king of Israel, "*What do we have to do with each other?* Go to the prophets of your father and the prophets of your mother." And in 2 Chron 35:21, Neco the king of Egypt asks Josiah the king of Judah why he is coming against him in battle: "*What do you have to do with me*, O king of Judah? It is not you I am attacking at this time, but the house with which I am at war. God has told me to hurry; so stop opposing God, who is with me, or he will destroy you." On this basis, Wansbrough is able to say: "However Jesus' reply to [Mary] is construed, whenever [this] phrase…occurs in the Old Testament it always in some way distances the speaker from the interlocutor."[26]

This same negative connotation is carried over to the NT writings as well. There are several NT passages where the identical Greek construction appears, and in *every one* of them the idea of distancing and/or reproach is involved. It is used in Matt 8:29 of the demon-possessed men who shout to Jesus, "*What do you want with us*, Son of God? …Have you come here to torture us before the appointed time?" It is similarly used in Mark 1:24 of the demon-possessed man who calls out to Jesus, "What *do you want with us*, Jesus of Nazareth? Have you come to destroy us? I know who you are—the Holy One of God!" It is used again of still another demon-possessed man in Mark 5:7 who, we are told, shouts at the top of his voice, "*What do you want with me*, Jesus, Son of the Most High God? Swear to God that you won't torture me!" It is used in Luke 4:34, the parallel to Mark 1:24, again of a demon-possessed man, "Ha! *What do you want with us*, Jesus of Nazareth? Have you come to destroy us? I know who you are—the Holy One of God!" Finally, it is used in Luke 8:28, Luke's parallel to Mark 5:7, "*What do you want with me*, Jesus, Son of the Most High God? I beg you, don't torture me!"

As Hartdegen notes, in each case "a negative, never a positive, answer is expected to the rhetorical question."[27] The meaning of the phrase is roughly "why are you bothering me" (or better) "leave me alone!" and carries the intent of distancing the two parties in question, with an overtone of reproach.[28] Hartdegen further notes that this very same connotation is found in all its occurrences in the literature of classical Greek, koine and later hellenistic Greek, and in classical and later Latin.[29]

After surveying the evidence, Hartdegen summarizes that the preponderance of evidence "clearly indicates a lack of common bond between persons relative to the particular situation found in the context. Though the question is formulated positively, a negative reply is expected."[30] Incredibly, Hartdegen concludes, in spite of all the evidence he has adduced, that in John 2:4 the phrase is "uttered in a tone of friendliness in this context, not of reproof."[31] McHugh follows suit when he says: "In the Old Testament texts cited, and in the mouth of the possesses, a harsh protest is demanded by the context. But downright rudeness by Jesus to his mother would be unthinkable."[32] McHugh suggests that we should ignore the way this phrase is used everywhere else and interpret it as "Why should I, why should you, be concerned with such a trivial mishap?"[33]

It should now be clear why we had to trouble ourselves with examining the meaning of this phrase. To conclude with Hartdegen and McHugh that John 2:4 is to be seen as the only exception to the clear meaning of this phrase everywhere it is found is to abandon all exegetical objectivity. If anyone but Mary were the recipient of Jesus' words here, it is doubtful that we would have so many attempting to posit an exception (in the case of John 2:4) to the consistent meaning of this phrase everywhere else it is found. Our understanding of this passage must be guided by the language used, and not vice versa. If in every place it occurs—whether in the LXX, the NT, classical Greek literature, hellenistic Greek literature, or classical and later Latin literature—this phrase always and without exception carries a negative connotation of reproach, it is precarious in the extreme to suggest we should render it differently in our present passage just because Mary happens to be the recipient. Such exegesis should be avoided not merely because it is tendentious, but because it is a case of special pleading with regard to Mary.

We must therefore be suspicious of Reese's assessment of this phrase: "[it] retains all the openness of a loving appeal."[34] Certainly we do not want to conclude that Jesus' words to Mary are in any way *un*loving; but Reese's spin on this episode flattens the intended rebuff that John wants us to see. Indeed, rather than seeing a rebuff in this passage, Reese concludes just the opposite: "[Jesus] is painting the transition from one bond to a deeper one."[35] Similarly, McHugh's objection that to adopt the normal meaning of this phrase would be "unthinkable" because it would have Jesus engaging in "downright rudeness" toward his mother does not seem to be sufficient reason for rejecting this meaning for the phrase. Jesus does not shy away from this kind of "rudeness" (in reality, reproof) in other contexts toward his own disciples who presume to suggest a course of action for him (John 13:8; cf. Matt 16:22–23), not to mention his adversaries (John 7:3–7), and McHugh gives us no good reason to decide contrary to the syntactical evidence of this construction found everywhere else.[36]

Bearsley suggests that Josh 22:24–25 provides an instance in which this phrase implies "a question of whether there is something which unites the two parties."[37] He concludes on this basis that in the Cana story "Jesus is not refusing his mother's request nor is he reproving her."[38] Yet, aside from the fact that the phrase used here is not the identical phrase as is found in John 2:4—nor, for that matter, in any of the passages cited above (Josh 22:24 has τί ὑμῖν κυρίῳ τῷ θεῷ Ισραηλ)— Bearsley's understanding of the Joshua passage is incorrect. In context, the tribes of Reuben and Gad and the half tribe of Manasseh are explaining to the angry heads of the other tribes why they have erected an altar on the border of Canaan. Their rationale for building it is as follows:

> We did it for fear that some day your descendants might say to ours, "*What do you have to do with the* LORD, *the God of Israel?* The LORD has made the Jordan a boundary between us and you—you Reubenites and Gadites! You have no share in the LORD." So your descendants might cause ours to stop fearing the LORD.

The phrase "What do you have to do with the LORD, the God of Israel?" does not suggest that something might *unite* them; rather it suggests that they have *nothing in common* with the God of Israel, and is used therefore as a distancing reproach (as are all occurrences of the phrase proper). At the end of the day, this phrase is, at the very least, "a measured rebuke,"[39] if not a "Hebrew expression of either hostility… or denial of common interest."[40] In light of the fact that it can properly be translated in all other instances as "why are you bothering me?" we would not be too far wrong translating it this way in John 2:4 as well.[41]

"Woman"—v. 4

Just as significant for the meaning of this passage in John is Jesus' address to Mary as "woman." Once again, speculation abounds as to Jesus' intent by this term. Wansbrough argues that:

> Jesus' form of address to his mother, 'Woman'…may well be an allusion to Eve…. Eve invites Adam to disobey, just as Mary seems to invite Jesus to depart from his 'hour'…. As Christ is in Paul so prominently the Second Adam, so in John there is at least the suggestion that Mary is the new Eve.[42]

Others have attempted to interpret Jesus' address of Mary as "woman" in more endearing terms than the Greek allows, including "dear woman," or "mother."[43] But this is without justification. Even Catholic scholars acknowledge that the title "woman" (γύναι) is "unattested in reference to one's mother."[44] As Hartdegen observes:

> Neither in antiquity nor today does the usage prevail of a son addressing his mother as 'woman.' …This change from the name 'mother' to woman at this time would seem to indicate that Jesus did not wish the relationship of natural motherhood and authority to be the basis of Mary's dealings with him in His public life and ministry of salvation.[45]

Unfortunately, Hartdegen takes the further, unwarranted step of seeing in the word "woman" a singling out of Mary for a special role in the divine plan:

> Both 'Son of Man' and 'woman' would indicate in the first place that both belonged to the ordinary race of human beings, but also that both enjoyed an altogether and singular position, Christ, that of Son of God and Messias besides mere man, and Mary that of 'the woman' in God's plan of salvation, i.e. the Mother of messianic people.[46]

It is discouraging to see Hartdegen make so many salient exegetical points about the text, and then consistently draw all the wrong conclusions.[47] As Hartdegen has noted above, so also other scholars have noted, "there is no precedent in Hebrew or, to the best of our knowledge, in Greek, for a son to address his mother [as 'woman']."[48] The use of the word "woman" certainly does not suggest that Mary is somehow singled out for a special task, for Jesus uses the same address for other women as well. It is used to address the Samaritan woman at the well (4:21). It is used to address the woman caught in adultery (8:10). It is used to address the mother of Jesus, not only in the present passage but also in 19:26 where Mary appears at the foot of the cross. It is also used to address Mary Magdalene after the resurrection (20:15).[49] The *MNT* taskforce notes that "for Jesus to address his mother in the same way he addresses the Samaritan woman (4:21) and Mary Magdalene (21:13) may mean that he places no special emphasis on her physical motherhood."[50] Perhaps the more significant point theologically is that Jesus *never* refers to Mary as "mother." It is simply remarkable, then, that Hartdegen can compare the title "Son of Man"—which is uniquely applied to Jesus in the gospels, and is used no fewer than eighty-three times, twelve of which occur in John—to the supposed title "Woman"—which is applied to at least three other women in John's gospel besides the mother of Jesus (to whom it refers only twice out of its nine occurrences in all the gospels)—in order to come to the conclusion that John wants us to see in all this the spiritual motherhood of Mary![51]

Other Catholic exegetes exhibit this same tendency. Reese, for instance, connects this pericope to John's prologue, and in particular to the opening phrase "In the beginning" (John 1:1; which he connects to Gen 1:1), but then takes the unwarranted step in concluding that "Jesus assumes the role of the new Adam, and Mary is Eve, His helpmate.... He is calling her to enter a new relationship with Him in the work of redemptive Incarnation."[52] While Reese's connection between John 1:1 and Gen 1:1 is certainly a sound one,[53] the *conclusion* he reaches based on his connection between John 1:1 and 2:4 cannot be sustained, for it cannot be reconciled with the phrase that accompanies the word "Woman"; namely, "what do we have in common?"[54]

However much Wansbrough has tempered his assertion (see above) by seeing a negative as well as a positive aspect of the symbolism ("Eve invites Adam to disobey, just as Mary seems to invite Jesus to depart from his 'hour'"[55]), such an assertion seems contrived rather than derived from the text. If the word "woman" is the key to seeing an allusion to Eve, then, as we have noted above, the connection is tenuous.

There needs to be much more of a parallel than that which may be derived from a single word, which after all is used commonly in other contexts without thought of any OT allusion. Moreover, in Paul (to whom Wansbrough compares his symbolism) the connection between Adam and Christ is explicit, and we are not left wondering about his intent.

On the whole, it seems much more reasonable to conclude with the *MNT* taskforce that the word woman "is not an impolite address, and the various Gospels attest that it is Jesus' normal way of speaking to women."[56] And so, while we must not conclude that Jesus is being *rude* by using this title, neither can we conclude that he is thereby singling out Mary for a special role. Yet we must add a caveat to the taskforce's conclusion above: "Though thoroughly courteous, [this word] is not normally an endearing term, nor the form of address preferred by a son addressing a much-loved mother."[57] It is certainly true that Jesus commonly addresses women this way in the NT (as we have already shown above). However, this is not to say that this is the *only* way Jesus addresses women. In the case of women with whom he is particularly close, he sometimes uses the woman's proper name. In Luke 10:41 he refers to "Martha" (cf. John 11:5 which tells us that "Jesus loved Martha and her sister and Lazarus"). In John 20:16 he refers to Mary Magdalene by name. In other words, when there is a special relationship between Jesus and a woman who is a known disciple, he often uses more personal addresses. The title "woman," by contrast, seems to be used to establish *distance* between Jesus and the other party.[58] One might expect, then, that had Jesus intended to convey an intimate relationship with his mother—one that was unencumbered by distance—he would have chosen "mother" or "Mary" or the like. Instead, he uses an address that is polite but distancing. Indeed, the fact that Jesus never once in all the gospels calls Mary by the title "mother" indicates not only that there is no special emphasis on Mary's physical motherhood, but may also indicate something much more significant; namely, that Mary's physical motherhood is quite intentionally downplayed. That seems to be the case in the present passage.[59] Even an exegete such as Bearsley, who must be placed in the category of those who do not see a reproach in this passage, nevertheless agrees that the title "woman" in place of "mother" "shows that Jesus no longer sees himself vis-à-vis his mother on the level of a natural family."[60]

"My hour has not yet come"—v. 4

There are two main issues bound up in this short phrase. The first one is the mood of the statement οὔπω ἥκει ἡ ὥρα μου. Is this an indicative statement ("My hour has not yet come") or an interrogative ("Has not my hour come?")? The answer depends on the second main issue in this phrase; namely, To what does "hour" (ὥρα) refer? Those who take this phrase as an interrogative also take "hour" as a reference to Jesus' public ministry.[61] Those who take the phrase as an indicative statement usually (though not always) see "hour" as a reference to the events surrounding his death (passion, death, ascension, glorification).[62]

Bearsley takes the view that this phrase should be interpreted as an interrogative: "Has not my hour come?"[63] He argues that the "hour" of Jesus "is not limited to his moment on Calvary. The 'hour' begins at Cana…and reaches its climax at Calvary."[64] Bearsley also concludes from this that the former biological relationship between Jesus and Mary is, at these words of Jesus, "transformed into a new relationship because his hour is now beginning with the sign which he will work in response to her intervention."[65]

But this view encounters insuperable difficulties. First, it requires that the word οὔπω ("not yet") be left untranslated.[66] This word occurs twenty-six times in the NT, and in each case the word is translated either "not yet" (when the statement is indicative) or "still not" (when the statement is interrogative). The word οὔπω used with the interrogative is extremely rare, occurring only four times in the NT. Yet even here the word must be translated in order for the passage to make sense. The first instance, Matt 16:9, has οὔπω νοεῖτε ("Do you still not understand?"); the second, Mark 4:40, has οὔπω ἔχετε πίστιν ("Do you still have no faith?"); the third and fourth instances are both found in Mark 8:17–21 which is the Markan parallel of Matt 16:9 (οὔπω νοεῖτε οὐδὲ συνίετε, "Do you still not see or understand?"; and καὶ ἔλεγεν αὐτοῖς· οὔπω συνίετε, "Do you still not understand?"). In each case it is found with the interrogative, οὔπω must be translated to complete the sense of the passage. Yet in order to sustain the view that John 2:4 is interrogative we must leave οὔπω untranslated—"Has not my hour come?"; for to translate it would make no sense of the text—"Has my hour not yet/still not come?" The latter would be a question of true inquiry instead of the rhetorical question that this view requires.

Moreover, the view that Jesus is here saying that his hour "has come" conflicts with other statements later in John. Carson notes that the "hour" of Jesus "constantly refers to his death on the cross and the exultation bound up with it (7:30; 8:20; 12:23, 27; 13:1; 17:1), or the consequences deriving from it (5:28–29), so it would be unnatural to take it in any other way here."[67] In John 7:30 we read; "At this they tried to seize him, but no one laid a hand on him, because his hour had not yet come" (οὔπω ἐληλύθει ἡ ὥρα αὐτοῦ). A similar statement is found in 8:20; "Yet no one seized him, because his hour had not yet come" (οὔπω ἐληλύθει ἡ ὥρα αὐτοῦ). Clearly both of these passages refer to an "hour" when Jesus *would* be seized (i.e., arrested and put to death).[68] In John 12:23 Jesus says; "The hour has come for the Son of Man to be glorified." That this refers to his death is clear from v. 27; "Now my heart is troubled, and what shall I say? 'Father, save me from this hour'? No, it was for this very reason I came to this hour"; as well as from vv. 32–33; "'But I, when I am lifted up from the earth, will draw all men to myself.' He said this to show the kind of death he was going to die." Another indication that "hour" refers to the events surrounding his death is found in 13:1; "It was just before the Passover Feast. Jesus knew that the hour had come for him to leave this world and go to the Father." Finally, Jesus indicates in his prayer to the Father (17:1) that his "hour" refers to his death; "Father, the hour has come. Glorify your Son, that your Son may glorify you." The "glorification" of Jesus occurs at his death as is evidenced in 7:32: "By this he meant the Spirit, whom those who believed in him were later to receive. Up to that time the Spirit had not been given, since Jesus had not yet been glorified." We can safely take "glorified" here as a reference to Jesus' death since we are told elsewhere that the Spirit cannot be given until Jesus leaves the earth and sends him to us; "But I tell you the truth: It is for your good that I am going away. Unless I go away, the Counselor will not come to you; but if I go, I will send him to you" (16:7). It is best then to reject the interrogative view and take Jesus' words in John 2:4 as "my hour has not yet come."

Moreover, Jesus' response as an indicative statement makes perfect sense of the present context. Mary has just mentioned a need for "wine" in mundane terms; and she has done this in the context of a wedding banquet. In typical fashion Jesus is quick to establish a connection between the mundane and his mission. He engages in this same activity with the Samaritan woman who asks about something as mundane as "water" (4:7–15; "whoever drinks the water I give him will never thirst," v. 14), as well as with the crowd who asks about "bread" (6:31; "I am the bread of life. He who comes to me will never go hungry," v. 35). In our present passage he establishes that same kind of connection by indicating that *his* time to provide an abundance of wine has not yet arrived. Jesus is here referring eschatologically to the messianic banquet (alternatively called "the wedding supper of the Lamb," Rev 19:7–9) that will take place in the kingdom at the end of the age (Luke 13:28–29; Matt 22:1–14; cf. Isa 25:6: "On this mountain the LORD Almighty will prepare a feast of rich food for all peoples, a banquet of aged wine—the best of meats and the finest of wines").[69] That John is familiar with this concept is evident just one chapter later when he records the words of John the Baptist who refers to Jesus as "the bridegroom" (3:27–30).[70]

The *MNT* taskforce notes that some, taking the "hour" as a reference to Jesus' glorification, see in this phrase an implicit promise to Mary that she would have a role after Jesus' glorification. They connect this to Mary's presence at the foot of the cross during which Jesus supposedly gives his mother to the church.[71] This theme will be dealt with in more detail later when we address John's scene at the cross in chapter 19.

"Do whatever he tells you"—v. 5

All of the other phrases we have examined in this passage have generated some degree of Marian significance, and the present phrase is no exception. Not surprisingly, this phrase has become a major proof-text in Roman Catholicism for seeing Mary as Intercessor. Bearsley's comments are comparatively mild to those of some of his colleagues: "As a mother, she brought others to follow him as his disciples."[72] Hartdegen is much more open about seeing Mary as Intercessor in this passage:

> Mary's part in obtaining this miracle applies also the effects of the miracle. She is therefore the *instrumental cause* of [the disciples'] faith in the messiaship of Christ, and of the beginning of their faith in His divinity. And since even the beginning of faith in Christ's divinity is also the commencement of the new life of grace, we see here the beginning or sign of

Mary's spiritual motherhood.… This role of Mary of dispos-
ing people to obey, and through obedience to come to believe
in Christ, is another phase of collaboration in the messianic
activity of her Son.[73]

Grassi concurs, though with a bit more restraint:

> A second possible way is that of Mary as a heavenly interces-
> sor. This is not found in the Fourth Gospel by any kind of
> direct evidence. However, it would fit in with the Gospel and
> be in no way contradictory to it; it would also be supported by
> acceptable biblical models.[74]

Grassi goes on to adduce even more possible support for Mary's role
as Intercessor from examples in 2 Maccabees and the Revelation in
which characters are shown to have "interceded" for Israel or the
church.[75] He concludes: "In line with these models, perhaps the Johannine community considered Mary as continuing her function as a loving mother by offering their petitions to her son."[76]

But Grassi's conclusions (not to mention those of Hartdegen and
others) seem gratuitous. He himself grants that they are based on no
explicit biblical support. The examples he adduces from 2 Maccabees
and the Revelation could just as readily be held out to support Paul as
a heavenly intercessor. After all, did not Paul "intercede" in prayer for
the church on more than one occasion? What prevents us then from
establishing Paul as a "co-Mediator" to whom we should pray in our
time of need? In the words of Carson: "On this reasoning, one wonders why everyone who ever asked Jesus for help and found in him the
solution to some pressing need, should not be elevated to the status of
mediator or mediatrix."[77] Framed in this way, it becomes impossible to
accept either Grassi's or Hartdegen's thesis without an *a priori* appeal
to Roman Catholic theology.

Moreover, Grassi has confused categories. The burden of his thesis
is to demonstrate to us that John 2 offers indirect evidence of Mary's
role as Intercessor. By "Intercessor" Grassi does not mean merely that
Mary makes intercession through prayer to her son on our behalf. If
that were the case then no one could disagree, and there would be no
need to write an article convincing us of such. For members of Christ's

body to pray for one another has explicit biblical support, and there is no need to assume that the ability to pray for Christ's body ceases once a Christian dies. Rather, by "Intercessor" Grassi wants us to accept the notion that we can pray *to* Mary to ask her for her intercession (hence, her role in Roman Catholicism as Mediatrix)—not simply that she might pray for us. But this goes well beyond not only the text of John, but also both 2 Macc 15:11–16 and Rev 5:8. In John, Mary asks Jesus for a favor (more wine). In both 2 Maccabees and the Revelation, biblical characters are in some sense offering prayers to God in behalf of other members of God's people. But in no case do we find an example of someone praying *to* a heavenly being (other than to God himself) to ask for intercession. We must therefore conclude with Perkins that "Mary's role in the wedding at Cana is not direct evidence for Marian intercessory power as older [Catholic] exegetes held."[78] Indeed, Lonsdale calls this interpretation "old fashioned," and adds: "It makes better sense to see [Mary] as one of the people who, despite their good intentions, misunderstand Jesus."[79]

A more novel view comes from Reese, who compares Mary's words here to those of Pharaoh in regard to Joseph when the starving Egyptians were crying out for food: "This is not some trivial sentence but a quote from an important scene in the Book of Genesis."[80] However, the parallels are not as close as Reese would have us believe; it is in any case certainly not a "quote." The Greek of each passage reads thus:

John 2:5:　　ὅ τι ἂν λέγῃ ὑμῖν ποιήσατε

Gen 41:55:　　ὃ ἐὰν εἴπῃ ὑμῖν, ποιήσατε.

Only the first word and the final two words are identical, and the dissimilarities of both the language and the setting cause us to think that any "parallel" here cannot bear the weight of Reese's conclusion: "Mary accepted the invitation to play a role in the unfolding of Jesus' messianic mission."[81]

Returning to the flow of the passage itself, Bearsley offers one final defense of his thesis that Jesus' words do not constitute a distancing from Mary. He speculates that since Mary speaks again she must not feel rebuffed and she must not feel as though the relationship has been strained[82]: "It is too strong to maintain that the relationship of mother and son is broken or even replaced; it is transcended."[83] Similarly,

McHugh contends that interpreting this passage as a rebuff of Mary would result in a *non sequitur*, for Mary's instructions to the servants ("Do whatever he tells you") combined with Jesus' subsequent miracle cannot follow from a statement of refusal.[84] What McHugh does not appear to understand is that his own proposed solution does not clear up the *non sequitur* that he contends is there. As we have noted, McHugh argues that Jesus' words τί ἐμοὶ καὶ σοί ("what to me and to you") should be understood as an assumed common disinterest of the current crisis ("Why should I, why should you, be concerned with such a trivial mishap?"). But if Jesus is asserting that neither he nor Mary should be concerned with such trivial matters as a shortage of wine, and then rectifies the problem anyway, McHugh's *non sequitur* remains.

Other Catholic exegetes agree with Bearsley and McHugh that Mary must have understood Jesus' prior response as an affirmative answer to her initial "request" to provide wine.[85] But given the reasons (above) for rejecting Mary's words in v. 3 as a direct "request" *per se*, it seems more natural to see the present phrase as an indication that Mary now understands her diminished role in Jesus' life and ministry. Although her words in v. 3 were borne out of anxiety over the situation with only minimal thought of a request to Jesus to help solve it, the seemingly disjointed response Jesus gives her is intended to *shock* her (as he often does to his audience)[86] into wondering whether something more will happen: "if Jesus acts, it will be in accord with *his* own conscious purpose and design, not that of others."[87] In this case, it works. Hence, whereas before Jesus uttered his response Mary was anxiously concerned about the situation, afterwards she seems hopeful and content, even if a bit cautious: "She still does not know what he would do; but she has committed the matter to him, and trusts him."[88]

Moreover, the view that Jesus' words must have been an affirmative response to Mary's request does not take into account the pattern of *request-rebuff-compliance* found throughout the gospels. This same pattern occurs in John 4:46–54 (the "second miraculous sign" at Cana, v. 54). There Jesus is asked by a man to heal his son (v. 46–47). Jesus initially rebuffs the request in v. 48: "Unless you people see miraculous signs and wonders you will never believe." The man persists in his request (v. 49); and Jesus finally complies (v. 50). John 7:1–10 gives us another example of the pattern. There Jesus' brothers make a request that he "go to Judea" (vv.3–4). Jesus initially rebuffs the request

(vv. 6–9), and then complies (v. 10). A Synoptic example of this pattern may be found in Matt 15:21–28. There a Canaanite woman requests of Jesus that her daughter be healed of demon possession. Jesus rebuffs this request twice: once in v. 24 ("I was sent only to the lost sheep of Israel") and the second time in v. 26 ("It is not right to take the children's bread and toss it to their dogs"). After much persistence Jesus finally complies (v. 28).[89]

This same pattern is evident in our present passage as well. Mary has, by her anxious words, tacitly requested Jesus' help in solving a crisis (v. 3). Jesus in turn initially rebuffs the request, placing distance between him and Mary (v. 4), but then complies (v. 6–7). This renders Bearsley's statement—namely, "Mary is obviously an important figure in the story. She cannot be put there merely to have her request rejected and to be told that her maternal status has no claims on Jesus in his public life"[90]— completely without warrant. Nor can we conclude that the reason Jesus complies is because Mary, as his mother, is uniquely related to Jesus and the object of his special affection. In that case, what would explain the fact that Jesus complies in all the *other* instances where we find this pattern? All agree that John's gospel presents a high Christology. It would not be at all inconsonant for John to show right from the beginning that biological ties had no claim on Jesus. The fact that John refers to Mary as "the mother of Jesus" in this episode, whereas Jesus refers to her as "woman," speaks more of the necessity for John to identify just what relationship is being severed than it does of an ontological status for Mary.

Theological Implications

One final question about this text is two-fold: Why does Jesus feel a need to rebuff Mary in this episode, and what implications are there for our overall view of Mary? The *MNT* taskforce warns us against an over-exaggeration of the negative side of the picture of Mary in John 4: "the very fact that Jesus finally *does* supply the wine requested makes it virtually impossible to maintain that the scene contains a polemic against his mother."[91] While it is certainly true that John did not intend a polemic against Mary, the fact that Jesus complies with the request does not offer support for the taskforce's assertion. After all, as we have already seen, Jesus also complies with the request of his unbelieving brothers (7:3–5, 10), and it is certain that John there intended us to view his brothers in a negative light. In any case, it is clear that Jesus does not alleviate Mary's concern over the shortage of wine because of any special relationship to her; he seems instead to grant the request *in spite of* the requester, as an illustrative tool, both to show his own glory and to teach others not to assume they have a right to request anything from him based on biological ties. As Tambasco notes: "His relation to Mary and to all his family is no longer the blood relationship."[92] Hartdegen echoes this sentiment when he states: "In commencing His public life attention must be drawn to his divinity veiled by His humanity, and to a new relationship of Mary to Christ since she in not the mother of His divinity."[93]

Also interesting to note is that John chooses to record this episode in the first place. One must ask why he felt this was important for his readers to know. Prescinding from the Catholic proposal that Mary is to be seen as an Intercessor of sorts (which we have already investigated and rejected), the only reasonable explanation is that John wanted to show clearly that Jesus was indebted to no one—not even to his own mother. This is significant since John is the apostle who took Mary in to live with him after Jesus' death (John 19:26–27). If anyone knew Mary on an intimate basis, John did. Yet, far from exalting Mary as the spiritual mother of the church, or the heavenly intercessor, or the like, John portrays her in a decidedly unflattering way! Cast in this light, Mary must be seen as epitomizing discipleship: "Mary represents the disciple on the painful and puzzling road to acceptance and belief."[94] This "road" entails not only blessings, but often times rebuke from Jesus due to presumptuousness on the part of the disciple. In the case of Mary, that presumptuousness is due to special privileges she assumed she had as Jesus' mother. Carson puts it succinctly: "In short, in 2:3 Mary approaches Jesus as his mother, and is reproached; in 2:5, she responds as a believer, and her faith is honoured."[95]

Hence we have some evidence for concluding that this episode signals the beginning of Mary's faith, as Brown notes: "Already at Cana the portrait begins to shade over into the more positive picture of Matthew and Luke. Even though Jesus has rebuffed her family claim, she says to the waiters, 'Do whatever he tells you.' "[96] Brown cautions against both an *in*flated view and a *de*flated view of Mary's import in this passage:

Perhaps nowhere in John is the difference of theological predisposition between Catholic and Protestant more painfully evident that [*sic*] in the exegesis of ii 4. There is an enormous amount of Catholic literature on this verse, much of it not rising above the level of pious eisegesis; yet most Protestant commentators pass over the verse as if it were unthinkable that Mary played a role in Johannine theology.[97]

While Brown's caution is duly noted and the tendency Brown criticizes is studiously avoided in this work (which, see below), Brown himself directly ignores his own advice by proposing that we "draw on" Revelation 12 (the "woman clothed with the sun")—which in turn Brown gratuitously links to Genesis 3:15[98]—in order to understand John's intended theological points about Mary at Cana.[99] But Brown's suggested points are based on so many tendentious and speculative connections from John 2:4 to Rev 12:1–6, from Rev 12:1–6 to Gen 3:15, and from Gen 3:15 back to John 19:25–27, that it is difficult to see how he thinks it would convince someone who is not looking for Marian significance in this passage—not to mention the fact that such a connection is anachronistic, and could not have been understood this way by John's first readers (and therefore could not have been intended by John) since the Revelation had not yet been composed.[100] It is a tenuous suggestion indeed to hold that John would have attached significance to a term that requires for its interpretation information that did not yet exist. In any case, this issue is more appropriately taken up in our discussion of Revelation 12.

Bearsley takes Brown to task on another point he makes regarding 2:4:

> Brown's interpretation casts Mary in a role that is limited to her natural motherhood. It is not until Jesus' 'hour' on Calvary that she is seen as also a disciple. But this ignores the context in which the Cana story is set. John recounts the episode immediately after his account of the calling of the first disciples, and he links Mary with these disciples in the opening verse of the Cana episode.[101]

But Bearsley ignores two facts relevant to this scene. First, we cannot conclude that Mary is portrayed here as a disciple merely because she is linked with his disciples in the opening verse, for then we would have to conclude that Jesus' brothers are disciples based on their link to the disciples in 2:12. Yet we are explicitly told several chapters later that these brothers are still unbelievers (7:1–8). Second, Brown has not stated that Mary's role is limited to her physical motherhood; rather he concludes that Mary, at least at the end of this episode, is portrayed in a more positive light than at first, and that her faith comes to fruition at the foot of the cross. This is the view of most scholars: "Mary's request for a sign, demonstrating perhaps a certain naïve confidence and imperfect understanding, leads ultimately to solid faith.... It is only on Calvary that she finally becomes a model for believers."[102]

This should not be misconstrued to mean that Mary is portrayed here by John as having a special status. Indeed, what Mary experiences here is not unlike what the typical disciple experiences. Lonsdale cites other similar instances of this kind of misunderstanding, including the woman at the well and Nicodemus (both of whom later became disciples) and concludes that this may be a Johannine literary device.[103] Hence, rather than conclude that Mary is portrayed as the *model* disciple—as is so often simply assumed in the literature without much evidence of serious reflection about just what that title implies; namely, a standard toward which we should ever strive—it is more in keeping with John's intent to conclude that Mary is portrayed as the *epitomized* disciple; that is, a true picture of the typical believer, blemishes and all, who struggles in her understanding not only as she comes to faith, but afterward as well. John seems to portray Mary as an *incipient* disciple, if only at the end of this episode.[104] What she becomes later at the foot of the cross is yet to be seen. It is to that scene that we may now turn.

CHAPTER VIII

Mary in the Gospel of John (Part Two)

We must examine one final passage in John's gospel before turning our attention elsewhere. No passage in the NT has engendered more support for the spiritual maternity of Mary than has John 19:25–27:

> Near the cross of Jesus stood his mother, his mother's sister, Mary the wife of Clopas, and Mary Magdalene. When Jesus saw his mother there, and the disciple whom he loved standing nearby, he said to his mother, "Dear woman, here is your son," and to the disciple, "Here is your mother." From that time on, this disciple took her into his home.

The current state of conservative Roman Catholic understanding of this passage is well represented by the comments of Bearsley: "Mary's virginal consent at the Annunciation enabled her to be the mother of [Jesus], and her consent was sustained right through to Calvary, where she was declared mother of the disciples. Truly she is the Virgin Mother of the Church."[1] Bearsley merely states this without attempting to support exegetically his notion that in this passage Mary becomes the mother of "disciples" (plural) rather than the mother of John the disciple (singular). Hartdegen follows suit: "Just as her intercession obtained the miracle of the wine at Cana, her presence at the foot of the cross, and her share in Christ's passion, helped to obtain for all Christ's followers the saving gift of His life-giving Blood."[2] Again, no attempt to support this assertion exegetically; just an affirmation that this is what the passage means. The same view is found in Flanagan: "She becomes the new woman who shares in the victory of her son, as the OT woman shared the defeat of her husband, Adam…. Woman of the victory, she also becomes mother to the Beloved Disciple, she becomes symbol of Mother Church."[3] Not all attempts on the Roman Catholic side to deal with this passage are as blatantly absent exegetical considerations. But it is just this widely held assumption that we should see Marian significance in this passage in the first place that prompts our inquiry.

Support for the Spiritual Maternity of Mary

Tambasco explains the thought process that leads to the traditional Catholic view: "Put in its most general way, the argument is: Mary brings forth the source of spiritual life for all Christians; the one who brings life is a mother; therefore, Mary is in some way our spiritual mother."[4] The argument actually begins with Jesus' words to the beloved disciple: "behold, your mother"; these words, it is argued, are intended to introduce Mary into a new role.[5] Similarly, Jesus' words to his mother, "behold, your son," are seen to cast John symbolically as representing all disciples. Mary is thereby given status as "mother of all disciples," hence, "mother of the church"[6]:

> The use again of "woman" to address Mary, plus the fact that actual names are not used for the mother or the beloved disciple, indicates that John is concerned primarily with expressing new ties between Jesus and Mary and symbolic roles for both Mary and the disciple…. Mary is given as mother to the community symbolized by the beloved disciple.[7]

Ceroke proposes that the key to seeing Mary as the mother of the church in this passage lies in the OT allusion invoked by the word γυνή. He expands on Gächter's thesis[8] that there are five distinct episodes in John's scene at the cross, three of which are bounded by *inclusio*.[9] Ceroke sees importance in this literary structure because in his opinion all episodes except the present one (Jesus' words to Mary and John) contain "either express citation of the OT or a clear allusion to OT texts."[10] The only one unaccounted for is the present episode. Since the OT citations/allusions in the surrounding episodes suggests that we should find something similar in the present episode as well, and since only the word γυνή could invoke an OT allusion in this episode, we must search for possible allusions based on this word. Ceroke admits to the fact that why John has not been more explicit with an OT allusion in this episode is a "puzzle," and that the tendency among Roman Catholic scholars automatically to assume a reference to Genesis 3 in light of other equally good options (Jer 13:21; Isa 26:17–18; 37:3; 66:7–8) is to be avoided.[11] Ceroke concludes that we are to view the word γυνή in light of Jesus' redemptive mission to defeat Satan (John 12:31; 13:2, 27; 14:30; 16:11). The culmination of this conflict occurs at the foot of the cross: "In the theological thought of the gospel, the consolation offered to Mary by Jesus revolves about his conflict with Satan.… The words to Mary from the cross, 'Woman, behold thy son,' can only mean for the evangelist an announcement that concerns the fulfillment of Jesus' universal mission."[12] It is here that the allusion to Gen 3:15 becomes clear for Ceroke. The offspring of the woman would "crush the head" of the serpent; Jesus is that offspring and the "woman" is Mary.[13] All of this, in Ceroke's mind, "necessarily suggests a maternity over the beloved disciple that is religious in nature"[14]; and, "since Jesus' mission is universal, the maternity that rests on His announcement of its fulfillment must be universal."[15] Not surprisingly, Flanagan concurs with this: "The evidence points strongly to a symbolic birthing of the Church. The two unnamed individuals beneath the cross represent all beloved disciples and mother Church."[16]

Ceroke's thesis is not without difficulties, however. At its very foundation, the exact import of noting *inclusio* in John's scene at the cross is not entirely clear. As Ceroke himself notes, two of the episodes in this scene do not have *inclusio*; and even those that are purported to be bound by *inclusio* are suspect.[17] This calls into question any pattern one wishes to establish in the literary structure of the five episodes that Ceroke sees in this scene. Moreover, Ceroke has asserted that each of the episodes in this scene—with the exception of the third (Jesus' words to Mary and John)—contains a clear OT citation or allusion. But this is simply not the case. Neither does the first episode (the title on the cross) contain an OT citation or allusion. Again, assuming the correctness of the five-episode model, there is inconsistency in the pattern. In fairness, Ceroke may be referring to the general OT theme that the Messiah would be "king" (hence, the title on the cross "King of the

Jews"); yet this alleged allusion—indeed, the very idea that OT *allusion* (not to say *citation*) is intended in this passage at all—seems out of step with John's overall approach to this pericope. When he wants us to see reference to the OT, he doesn't *allude* to Scripture; rather he cites it directly and accompanies it in each case with the phrase "so that the Scripture might be fulfilled" (vv. 24, 28, 36). Significantly, he does not do this with the reference to γυνή ("woman") in the episode of Jesus' words to Mary and John. This is especially odd if Ceroke's thesis is correct; for Ceroke has argued that this episode is the very climax of Jesus' entire mission to defeat Satan! Wouldn't John have wanted to make it clear to his readers that this was said "so that the Scripture might be fulfilled: 'I will put enmity between you and the woman, and between your offspring and hers,' and 'he will crush your head'"?

But the five-episode model on which Ceroke bases his conclusions is itself suspect. Why does the model begin in vv. 19–22 rather than in vv. 16–18, which also includes an "episode" at the scene of the cross? Is it because there is no clear instance of *inclusio* or OT allusion? Excluding this episode seems completely arbitrary if we are to establish sound literary patterns from this scene, especially since some of the other episodes at this scene likewise lack *inclusio* or OT allusion. As it stands, the pattern proposed by Ceroke seems too artificial to use as a basis for concluding something as weighty as that Mary is to be regarded as the mother of the church.

Another way this has been taken is to see a revelation pattern. On this view, when a prophet points specifically to a person with the word ἴδε ("behold"), what follows is a statement about that person's mission. Examples cited include John 1:29 ("Behold, the Lamb of God, who takes away the sin of the world!"). According to this argument, John points to the "mission" of Mary in 19:26—she is the mother of the church.

But this suggestion, too, seems exegetically dissatisfying. In response to the last suggestion (that the word ἴδε signals a statement of mission), John 1:47 seems to be an exception ("Behold, a true Israelite, in whom there is nothing false"). Are we to conclude that Jesus is here telling us that Nathanael's *mission* is that he would uniquely become the quintessential Israelite? This also doesn't seem to work in the case of Jesus' words to Mary regarding John, "Behold, your son" (19:26). If we are to see Mary's "mission" in 19:27 as that of "mother of the church," what then is John's mission? To be the symbolic son of Mary? Even if we agree that John represents the church, does anyone really want to argue that the church's "mission" is to be the "son" of Mary? In any case, 1:47 seems sufficient to discount the pattern.

Laurentin is another who sees Mary's universal maternity at the cross. He argues his case on the basis of the use of the article in this passage:

> In the gospel (Jn 19:25–27) Jesus makes Mary aware that her motherhood is being transferred—from him to the disciple, type of every disciple.… The possessive "*his* mother," in reference to Christ, is dropped from the sentence where John merely says "*the* mother" (twice), in reference to nobody, as if this motherhood were unoccupied, vacant. Then the possessive re-appears, this time in reference to the disciple: "*your* mother."[18]

Two observations may be raised against Laurentin's view. First, the article in the second clause is properly anaphoric ("the previously mentioned mother"). One wonders if we should treat every anaphoric article as though it refers to some "unoccupied" position. Second, in his eagerness to make Mary the mother of all disciples, Laurentin has unwittingly removed Mary's motherhood from Jesus, so that she can no longer be called "mother of God." The first observation renders Laurentin's suggestion exegetically untenable; the second renders it theologically untenable from a Roman Catholic perspective.

Mary's Significance at the Foot of the Cross in John

How then should we view Mary in John's scene at the cross? At the most fundamental exegetical level it must be acknowledged that, whatever view one finally adopts for the meaning of this passage, John takes Mary to his home *based on* Jesus' words: "From that hour, this disciple took her into his home." At the very least, this statement indicates that John understood Jesus to mean "take care of her," rather than that Mary now had a maternal role over him.[19] This is a point that is often missed in Roman Catholic exegesis of this passage: "It is sometimes said that Jesus by his words made Mary mother of the church (represented by

John). But Jesus wasn't asking Mary to look after John; he was asking John to take care of her."[20]

This is not to criticize all Roman Catholic exegetes; for some, such as McKenzie and Ceroke, have reached this same conclusion with regard to the present passage. McKenzie states: "She is expressly committed to the care of the disciples."[21] Ceroke raises pointed questions against the spiritual maternity view of Mary—a view that he nevertheless eventually adopts: "If Jesus did intend to proclaim from the cross the spiritual maternity of Mary over mankind, it is strange that the text of John would not provide clear and simple evidence of this meaning."[22] Ceroke notes further not only that "there was no exegetical tradition among [the fathers] that advanced the spiritual maternity of Mary" based on Jesus' words in this passage, but also that "the three great Fathers, St. John Chrysostom, St. Cyril of Alexandria, and St. Augustine propounded only the filial piety of Christ toward Mary in connection with our text"[23]; Brown mentions three more—Athanasius, Epiphanius, and Hilary.[24] Perkins agrees that at this time in the history of the church, "this passage [had] not yet developed the symbolism of Mary as mother of the church that would emerge from twelfth century Marian piety."[25]

The *MNT* taskforce admits that "a reading of these verses on their own merits would incline us to judge that neither figure is clearly more important than the other"; but then adds: "However, this should not lead us to conclude that the evangelist's *primary* interest is biographical, i.e., to report simply that after Jesus died his mother went to live in the home of a favorite disciple."[26] While we do not want to downplay the possible symbolism in this passage (most scholars agree that John seems to use symbolism elsewhere in his gospel), the symbolism cannot be used to overturn the plain meaning of the passage. The taskforce has already put forward that a plain reading of the passage disallows us to view Mary in any superior way; and it is clear in the passage that the "giving" here is completely reciprocal—Mary is given to John, but John is also given to Mary. If one wants to argue that Mary is here given to the church as its mother, then one could just as readily argue that John is here given to the church as a son. The tendency among Catholic exegetes to view Mary as a singular and literal person while viewing John as a corporate personality representing the church seems completely arbitrary and tendentious. If Jesus were interested in establishing Mary as "mother of the church," his intent would have been clearer if he had simply told John, "here is your mother," and left it at that.

Moreover, Jesus' words suggest an emphasis on the sheltering care of his mother by John. To extrapolate from this a symbolism that suggests the opposite—namely, Mary's sheltering care for the church as its mother—is to oppose the plain reading of the text. This view in turn is usually based on the notion that there is a future promise implicitly bound up in Jesus' words to Mary at Cana in John 2. Now that Jesus is glorified and his "hour" has come, Mary is able to make requests of Jesus that would benefit her "son," the church.[27] But again, perhaps the biggest difficulty with this view is that it inconsistently treats Mary as a literal individual but John as a symbol who represents the church: "an ordinary symbolic pattern would treat both as individuals or both as general [symbols]."[28]

Commenting on the oft-raised objection that Jesus should have left his mother in the care of his brothers since they had primary responsibility for her in Jewish culture,[29] Ben-Chorin writes:

> The present scene simply shows that Jesus had given up *all contact with his brothers and sisters*. However far apart he and his mother might be, he did not want to leave her in the company and care of these brothers and sisters, especially as she had not left him in the hour of his martyrdom. So he asked the disciple to look after her and in this way tried to inaugurate a new mother-and-son relationship.[30]

Moreover, the objection itself assumes that material welfare is all that is at stake in the care of Jesus' mother. Certainly that is included—within the Christian community believers are to view each other as family members who take care of one another.[31] But also included are emotional consolation and spiritual oversight. John has already portrayed Jesus' brothers as unbelievers (7:5), and he gives us no indication that that situation has changed.[32] Jesus would have been remiss to have left his mother, now a disciple, in the care of those who had a history of hostility to Jesus and his mission. On the other hand, John is portrayed in this passage (and elsewhere in this gospel) as "the disciple whom Jesus loved." He had walked with Jesus and had become an intimate friend. The solace that John could provide to Mary far outweighed the obligation to hand Mary over to unbelieving relatives. Hence, spiritual, emotional and physical concern for his mother are bound together in Jesus' words to John.

Ceroke does not seem fully to understand this when he states that Jesus' request to John on the cross:

> does not explain why John is anxious to inform us that his care of Mary was a controlling interest of his life. His original concern for Mary lay in the circumstances of her bereavement. This motive would endure throughout the period of bereavement. But with the resurrection of Jesus the original motive for John's care of Mary would have ceased altogether.[33]

Such a statement assumes that Mary continued to live with John in the post-resurrection era. However, this is not necessary. The Greek phrase, ἀπ' ἐκείνης, used in this passage tells us when an event begins without necessarily implying that the event continues without ceasing. The phrase is used only three times in the NT; once in Matthew (22:46), and the other two in John (11:53 and the present passage). In the Matthean passage we are told, "*from that* day on no one dared to ask him any more questions." This does not mean that absolutely *no* questions were entertained, for the disciples themselves ask Jesus about the end of the age just two chapters later (24:3). What is meant in 22:46 is that no one *beginning on that day* asked him questions in a confrontational way with the intent of leading him to his demise. Yet even with this qualification the time frame is not absolute; "so Jesus' enemies went underground *for a short time* before the crucifixion,"[34] but then resurfaced later and did indeed reengage him in confrontational questions designed to implicate him (26:62–63).

The same may be said about the other instances of ἀπ' ἐκείνης as well. In John 11:53 we read: "So *from that* day they plotted to take his life." We must not envision this "plotting" as something that the Jews did for the rest of their natural lives. Rather, the plotting occurred for a short time, until the purpose of that plotting was satisfied. In the same way we must not assume that when John takes Mary to his home "from that hour," that this necessarily implies a permanent arrangement. Mary is bereaved. Jesus' brothers are currently unbelievers and hostile to the faith. The current situation dictates to Jesus that he must provide his earthly mother with a source of emotional and spiritual comfort from an intimate associate, at least until the resurrection.[35] After the resurrection, when Mary discovers that her son has conquered death, when her other sons become convinced of the true identity of Jesus and themselves become disciples, we then find Mary reunited with Jesus' brothers (Acts 1:14).[36]

Ceroke also objects to the view that Jesus, by these words, is giving Mary to John as his new "mother," on the basis that "such an action…appears implausible" since John already had a mother (Salome) who would, by this action, be replaced.[37] But such an objection ignores the fact that in Christ's body all older women in the faith are to be treated as "mother" (1 Tim 5:1–2). Jesus could not have left his own mother (whom John here portrays as a disciple) with his as yet unbelieving siblings (7:5); such an act would be the essence of Christian infidelity (1 Tim 5:8). Ceroke himself seems to recognize this later when he writes: "Jesus, solicitous of the suffering of His Mother, requested the beloved disciple to undertake the responsibility for the care that she would require upon His death and burial."[38]

The Theological Meaning of John 19:25–27

If we must discount the view that by his words in this passage Jesus is conferring on Mary a spiritual maternity over the disciple, the church, or mankind, then it remains to be seen what John's intent is for including this episode in his gospel in the first place. Grassi objects that "the words cannot be simply a last command on Jesus' part that a favorite disciple took care of his mother upon his death."[39] Similarly, Flanagan: "The least that should be deduced from this is the presentation of mother (of Christ) Mary as symbol of mother (of Christians) Church. This same interpenetration…is evident in Revelations [sic] 12."[40]

But neither Grassi nor Flanagan seems to have considered that there is another theological point John is making here; namely, the theologically poignant point that, at the hour of his departure from this life, Jesus is signifying final severance of any and all biological ties to him. Lindars holds that if we are to see significance in this passage, far from indicating Mary's spiritual motherhood over all believers, it is used to signify the end of special earthly relationships.[41] Lonsdale thinks that

Mary's spiritual motherhood can and should be retained, but only with reference to John:

> As she stands at the foot of the cross, Jesus gives his physical mother a 'spiritual' role as mother of the disciple. In this way Jesus' physical family is replaced by the beloved disciple who is not a natural relative but someone particularly loved. Jesus' physical mother, however, does become part of this 'eschatological' family, since the beloved disciple is given to her as a her son. An interpretation along this line seems the most fruitful and plausible of those recently offered.[42]

On this view, Mary's relationship to Jesus and the church is predicated upon and viewed in light of the relationship between the beloved disciple and Jesus, and not vice versa. She becomes part of the eschatological family by virtue of her new relationship to the beloved disciple. There is much to be commended in Lonsdale's position. It at once satisfies the tendency to see the spiritual significance of an otherwise mundane passage in a book that is replete with symbolism, and offers restraint against seeing far too much significance in a character who up to this point has given us little reason to think she is the object of some divine mission.

The *MNT* taskforce reaches essentially the same view when it points out that there may be significance in the fact that John "brings together two figures for whom John never gives us personal names."[43] This may mean that it is the role of each figure, rather than the person that is important here. This new mother/son relationship is based entirely on a common belief in Christ and parallels the eschatological family based on discipleship found in the Synoptic Gospels. While Mary may have "lost" her other sons because of her commitment to Jesus, she has here gained another (Luke 18:28–30); and John has gained a mother.[44]

Along this same theme of severing biological ties, Bridcut makes an interesting observation regarding Matthew 22 and the issue of familial bonds in heaven. There Jesus makes it clear that no one will be married (i.e., retain marital status) in eternity, but will be like the angels "with no partners, parents, or children."[45] He notes that the first and closest human relationship in the Scriptures is that of husband and wife, from which all other relationships arise: "If, as Jesus makes clear, there is no husband and wife in heaven, there is, as regards continuing relationship, no mother and son either."[46] He further notes that Augustine subscribed to a similar view when he speaks of the heavenly realms "where no one says, my father; but all say to God, our Father, and no one says, my mother, but all say to that other Jerusalem, our mother."[47]

Implications for Mary's Role in the Church

Raymond Brown ends his discussion of this passage with these words:

> John thus moves in the same direction as Luke. These two Evangelists know of Jesus' 'de-emphasis' of the natural family that is so strong in the tradition. Yet, as they face the reality of Mary, they recognize that, while she was natural family, she was part of the family of believers and even had a *preeminent* place in it.[48]

It is discouraging to see so fine a scholar as Brown reach such tendentious conclusions after engaging in such clear exegesis of the text. Nothing in the text, nor in Brown's observations about the text, would lead us to conclude that John "faces a reality of Mary" that, at the end of the day, is at odds with what he has plainly written about her. If, as Brown notes, John portrays Jesus as "de-emphasizing" Mary, how do we conclude on that basis that, in reality, John intends to give her a place of preeminence? Are we likewise to conclude that John, who is singled out in the same gospel as "the disciple that Jesus loved," held a preeminent place over the other apostles? If not, why not? After all, what we are presented with in the case of John's preeminence are clear and direct statements, while what we are left with in the case of Mary is pure speculation. To suggest that the latter has preeminence based on such tenuous evidence seems to be a clear case of special pleading. No other biblical character, it seems, is given the kind of spiritual advances that are gratuitously assigned to Mary by many Catholic exegetes. Bridcut's words are relevant here:

> There is no evidence that Mary had any influence in the early Church which could have given rise to belief in a spiritual

motherhood in relation to the Church.... If Mary had been given such a position it would be hard to explain how Luke doesn't even mention her presence at the Cross if he knew she were there.... [Moreover] there is nothing in his words about the relationship between mother and son being continued or reknit in the heavenly realms.[49]

Ceroke, like Brown, reads far too much into John's text when he concludes from Jesus' words that just as John was to provide for the immediate material welfare of Mary, so it is "clear" that Mary was to "uphold the faith of John in the messianic mission of Jesus."[50] But why this should be "clear" is not readily apparent. The much simpler explanation—and the one that we have seen makes more sense of the text—is that Mary's role as "mother" to John is one of *recipient*, not one of *giver*. Jesus is not envisioning that Mary can actually *do* anything for John; rather the reverse is intended—John does something for Mary; namely, he becomes a source of comfort and strength in her bereavement. That this was John's understanding of Jesus' words is evident from John's diligence to obey: "From that hour, this disciple took her into his home."

This, on the whole, seems to be the most reasoned view of Mary in John's gospel. We find Mary at the beginning of John misunderstanding both Jesus' mission and her proper role in relation to him. She learns quickly in this episode that she can no longer curry favor as Jesus' biological mother; for Jesus, in anticipation of "his hour" is severing biological ties. We leave this episode with the impression that she is now an *incipient* disciple (i.e., one in whom are the beginnings of faith, but who is yet confused and cautious). She then disappears from John's mind altogether only to reappear again at the foot of the cross, this time as a disciple. Yet discipleship implies a recognition of changed relationships. Mary is no longer Jesus' biological mother. She is now to be seen in relation to all other disciples in the eschatological family. Just as Paul would later extrapolate from Jesus' teaching that new relationships in the eschatological family entail that Jesus' disciples view each other as "brother," "sister," "father," and "mother" (1 Tim 5:1–2), so also Mary becomes John's mother and John becomes her son. "It is her faith, a faith shared by other figures like the beloved disciple, and not her biological relationship to Jesus which secures her special place in the gospel."[51] It is true, as Perkins notes, that when the incarnation in John's prologue is combined with the infancy narratives of the Synoptics, "Mary's biological relationship to Jesus comes to the fore. She is the source of Jesus' 'humanity.'"[52] It is equally true, however, that this relationship is downplayed and shown not only to be temporary but also insufficient for admission into the eschatological family.

It is at this point that we may see a connection with the only other episode in which the mother of Jesus is presented in John's gospel. Returning to the scene at Cana, we noted that Jesus rebuffs Mary by asking her why she is bothering him since his hour had not yet come. The scene itself, with its wedding banquet backdrop and its shortage of wine, prompted us to see Jesus' "hour" as the events surrounding his death; and more specifically to that time in his kingdom when he would provide an abundance of wine at the wedding supper of the Lamb. However, once we read about the events at the foot of the cross—the only other place that Jesus' mother appears—it becomes exceedingly difficult not to see a backward reference to Jesus' words to Mary at Cana—"my hour has not yet come."

This is not unlike the relationship between John 6:22–58 and the Lord's Supper. In what is known as the "bread of life" discourse, Jesus tells us in v. 51–53: "I am the living bread that came down from heaven. If anyone eats of this bread, he will live forever…unless you eat the flesh of the Son of Man and drink his blood, you have no life in you." Although it is anachronistic to see in these words a *direct* reference to the Lord's Supper, it is, nevertheless,

> hard to imagine that the Evangelist, writing several decades after the institution of the Lord's supper, could produce these words without noticing that many readers, even if they understood the passage aright, would in all likelihood detect some parallels with the eucharist…[yet] "John 6 is not about the Lord's Supper; rather, the Lord's Supper is about what is described in John 6."[53]

Put another way, while the first hearers of Jesus' words in John 6 could never have come to the conclusion that Jesus is referring to the institution of the Lord's Supper (which chronologically happened later in his life, even if John doesn't include it in his account), once we know about the institution itself, it is difficult *not* to see a backward reference to Jesus' teaching in John 6. Hence, while we cannot see the Lord's Supper in John 6, we cannot *but* see John 6 in the Lord's Supper.

The same may be said of our present passage. At the cross, Jesus' hour has come, and Mary is there. The astute reader is at once reminded that in the only other place Jesus addresses his mother he referred to his "hour." Looking back on the Cana episode from this vantage point, the two statements of Jesus at Cana take on another nuance (not to say new meaning). At Cana, his hour had not yet come; at the cross, it has come. At Cana, his desire for his mother was that she not bother him with her mundane concerns; at the cross, he is now ready to make final arrangements for her welfare. It is as though at Cana his words take on a cryptic subplot: "Why are you bothering me now, woman? My hour (during which time I will address concerns of yours that are more important than your current concern) has not yet come." This does not make Jesus' "hour" *equivalent to* his words to Mary and John in John 19 (as some mistakenly assert[54]). Rather, his hour (as we have seen in the previous chapter) must be taken as the timeframe for the events surrounding his death.[55] His addressing of Mary's "concern" at the cross falls within that "hour," and consists of leaving her in John's care to console her and look after her. Hence, while John does not intend for us to see in Jesus' "hour" (in John 2) a reference to how he will address Mary at the foot of the cross in John 19—that is to say, it cannot be anticipated there since it is not what is primarily involved in Jesus' "hour"—he does in fact intend for us to see a reference to Mary's request in John 2 when he finally addresses Mary in John 19.

Concluding Thoughts

Ceroke's stated purpose of writing his monograph has been that:

> Catholic exegetical opinion has not been swayed decisively to the acceptance of Mary's spiritual maternity as the clear teaching of the evangelist in his record of Jesus' words from the cross…[and that this doctrine] has as yet been placed on an acceptable foundation by the science of biblical exegesis.[56]

Yet Ceroke and his colleagues have demonstrated neither that the universal maternity of Mary is John's "clear" meaning—nor that it is even a convincing secondary meaning—nor that this doctrine has now safely been placed on a sound exegetical foundation. He himself concedes as much in his final summary:

> At this point the exegesis of the text, grammatical and philological analysis of the verbal content and literary structure break down. The evangelist has not intended to supply any direct data that bear upon the nature of this religious maternity of Mary. In lieu of direct data, he supplies us with a religious mystery in the term gynê.[57]

If Ceroke's goal has been to convince the skeptic that the Roman Catholic understanding of this passage is the right one, then he has not attained that goal. In the final analysis, Ceroke has given us little more reason than we already had for adopting the Roman Catholic reading of this passage, and that reading must be rejected on both exegetical and theological grounds. John's Revelation offers one final place of inquiry that may hold Marian significance. It is to there we now turn.

CHAPTER IX

Mary in Revelation 12

Revelation 12 serves as our final passage of inquiry into Mary's status and role in the NT. The relevant points of the passage read as follows:

> A great and wondrous sign appeared in heaven: a woman clothed with the sun, with the moon under her feet and a crown of twelve stars on her head. She was pregnant and cried out in pain as she was about to give birth. Then another sign appeared in heaven: an enormous red dragon with seven heads and ten horns and seven crowns on his heads. His tail swept a third of the stars out of the sky and flung them to the earth. The dragon stood in front of the woman who was about to give birth, so that he might devour her child the moment it was born. She gave birth to a son, a male child, who will rule all the nations with an iron scepter. And her child was snatched up to God and to his throne. The woman fled into the desert to a place prepared for her by God, where she might be taken care of for 1,260 days.… When the dragon saw that he had been hurled to the earth, he pursued the woman who had given birth to the male child. The woman was given the two wings of a great eagle, so that she might fly to the place prepared for her in the desert, where she would be taken care of for a time, times and half a time, out of the serpent's reach. Then from his mouth the serpent spewed water like a river, to overtake the woman and sweep her away with the torrent. But the earth helped the woman by opening its mouth and

swallowing the river that the dragon had spewed out of his mouth. Then the dragon was enraged at the woman and went off to make war against the rest of her offspring—those who obey God's commandments and hold to the testimony of Jesus (Rev 12:1–17).

Before embarking on our discussion of the *meaning* of this text, and whether or not Mary is to be seen as a referent of the "woman clothed with the sun," a few preliminary comments are in order. First, it is acknowledged up front that the dubious nature of the Revelation itself, including whether the events it records should be interpreted as sequential or as recapitulation, should caution us against argumentation that relies too heavily on the context of the passage itself.[1] Moreover, as McHugh notes, the current diversity of opinion on this passage mirrors that of the early church.[2] Almost entirely without exception, the fathers saw the "woman" in this passage as representing the "church"—interpreted variously as the church of the new covenant or the church as the people of God under both covenants—or simply as Israel.[3] Indeed, "it is fair to say that in the first eight centuries no one identified the woman in the Apocalypse as Mary to the positive exclusion of the Church"[4]; by which is meant that even if a few writers during this time saw Mary as the exemplar of the church, it was in this way—and only in this way—that they connected Mary with the woman of Rev 12, which they saw primarily as a reference to the church.[5]

The Setting of Revelation 12

Chapter 12 seems to have three sections or "scenes," which may be divided as follows:[6]

Vv. 1–6: the scene in heaven (the woman, the child, and the dragon)
Vv. 7–12: another scene in heaven (Michael and the dragon)
Vv. 13–17: the scene on earth (the dragon, the woman, and the woman's offspring)

Most of what concerns us is included in the first and last sections, the second section acting as an aside. John tells us that there are two *signs* in this passage; a woman with child, and a dragon. Both signs are said to have "appeared in heaven," though just which "heaven" is in mind is uncertain.[7] Is it the abode of God (as in 4:2; 11:19)? The sky (6:14; 11:6)? Or outer space (12:4)? The context suggests the last option. The woman is "clothed with the sun," the moon is under her feet, and twelve stars make up her crown.[8] Moreover, the dragon has swept "a third of the stars" with his tail. All of this suggests that the scene takes place in the constellations; although the conflict itself seems to take place on the earth, since the woman flees "into the desert" (v. 6) and the child is "snatched up" to heaven (v. 5).[9] Some, such as Caird, see in the scene an allusion to the zodiac.[10] Both the woman (v. 1) and the dragon (v. 3), we are told, represent constellations of stars, though not *actual* constellations (i.e., there is no "woman" constellation). The dragon, which physically symbolizes a government power (cf. 13:1) and spiritually symbolizes Satan (12:9), casts "a third of the stars" down to earth (v. 4),[11] and stands prepared to devour the child once it is born.[12] The similarities between this symbolism and that of the ancient pagan world forces Beasley-Murray to conclude that these events represent a "Jewish–Christian adaptation of what can only be described as an international myth, current throughout the world of John's day."[13] Johnson explains:

> The basic plot of the story was familiar in the ancient world. A usurper doomed to be killed by a yet unborn prince plots to succeed to the throne by killing the royal seed at birth. The prince is miraculously snatched from his clutches and hidden away, until he is old enough to kill the usurper and claim his kingdom.[14]

Johnson goes on to tell us that in the Greek myth the woman was Leto, the male child she was about to bear was Apollo, and the usurper was Python. In the Egyptian myth the woman was Isis, her male child she was about to bear was Horus, and the usurper was Set the red dragon.[15] Other suggested sources for John's vision include Qumran,[16] the Testament of Naphtali (5:1–8),[17] the story surrounding the death of Emperor Domitian's son,[18] and, of course, the OT, particularly Gen 37:9: "Then [Joseph] had another dream, and he told it to his brothers. 'Listen,' he said, 'I had another dream, and this time the sun and moon and eleven stars were bowing down to me.'"[19] This final source has the advantage of explaining the "crown of twelve stars" as representing the twelve tribes of Israel[20] (also mentioned elsewhere, cf. Rev 7:4–8; 21:12); and, in keeping with the imagery representing the people of God both before and after the coming of Christ, also the twelve apostles (Rev 21:14—see below). Although we cannot say with certainty, it seems possible that John may have blended elements from several of these sources when writing this section.[21] Even if this is the case, Johnson cautions us against relying too heavily upon this blending: "Regardless of the sources or allusions, John reinterprets the older stories and presents a distinctively Christian view of history in the imagery of the woman and her child."[22] Moreover, Thomas shows that it is entirely possible to reject allusion to pagan or Qumran sources altogether since the differences are greater than the similarities.[23]

On the other hand, the imagery of a woman travailing in birth and a male child who is to become the deliverer is not entirely foreign to Scripture. For one thing, "the story told in this chapter and the next reads like an interpretation of God's curse on the serpent in Genesis 3:15."[24] Indeed, this "interpretation" becomes pivotal for the Roman Catholic view that identifies the *woman* as Mary; which view we shall address momentarily. The imagery is also found with reference to the sufferings of Israel. In Isa 26:16–18 we read:

> LORD, they came to you in their distress; when you disciplined them, they could barely whisper a prayer. As a woman with child and about to give birth writhes and cries out in her pain, so were we in your presence, O LORD. We were with child, we writhed in pain, but we gave birth to wind. We have not brought salvation to the earth; we have not given birth to people of the world.

The passage goes on to speak of deliverance for Israel (Isa 27:1–12). This idea is found elsewhere in the OT as well, mostly in the Prophets: "Terror will seize them, pain and anguish will grip them; they will writhe like a woman in labor.... See, the day of the LORD is coming— a cruel day, with wrath and fierce anger—to make the land desolate and destroy the sinners within it" (Isa 13:8–9).[25] The parallels found here are sufficient to show that the "birth pangs" in our present passage are undoubtedly the afflictions of the people of God that culminate in the coming of the Messiah,[26] so that no appeal to outside literature, such as Qumran—much less pagan mythology—is necessary.

The identification of the "woman" (γυνή) in v. 1 turns in part on the meaning of "to have birth pangs" (ὠδίνω) in v. 2, and in part on the meaning of "male son" (υἱὸν ἄρσεν) in v. 5. Beale, along with most scholars, sees the birth pangs as "a picture of…the suffering of the ideal city of God resulting from oppression (Jer 4:31)."[27] These "sufferings" act as a prelude to the coming of the Messiah,[28] who, on this view, is the "male son." The *woman*, therefore, is "a picture of the faithful community, which existed both before and after the coming of Christ."[29] This "faithful community"[30] is alternatively titled the "people of God,"[31] the "Israel of God,"[32] or the "Messianic community,"[33] all of which may be taken as virtual synonyms. This view of the *woman* is that which has been adopted by the vast majority of scholars who write on this passage, though perhaps nuanced in various ways.[34]

Few today follow Thomas' view that the "woman" is "national Israel" (i.e., Israel consisting of both believers and unbelievers).[35] Thomas objects to the view that these are the "people of God" on the basis of the distinction in v. 17 between the woman and "the rest of her offspring," as well as the fact that the OT people of God and the NT church have already been distinguished in 7:1–8.[36] However, prescinding from Thomas' point regarding 7:1–8,[37] there can be no real objection to viewing the "woman" as the *collective* people of God throughout history, distinguishing her from manifestations of those same people of God in any given era; in this case, the "rest of her offspring" are the "people of God" after the coming of Messiah (i.e., the church).[38] This distinction is found outside of the OT and NT as well.[39]

Another novel view comes from Michaels, who identifies the *woman* as the *earth* or *mother earth*: "The earth is personified over against the dragon."[40] But this is unsatisfying because it ignores the allusion to the faithful remnant as the woman's "offspring." Surely John is not saying that the dragon pursues *all* people as the "offspring" of the earth, regardless of whether or not they are part of the faithful community! Michaels himself is inconsistent with this imagery because he later identifies the "rest of her offspring" as the Christian community.[41]

The "male son" is most likely the Messiah at his first coming, for "he will rule all the nations with an iron scepter" (v. 5; cf. 2:26–27; Ps 2:6–9). This, again, is the view of the majority of scholars. Against this view, Ford has advanced the idea that "the Messiah is not mentioned in this part of our text," and that "in our present text there seems to be no Christological reference."[42] Ford concludes instead that the "male son" is to be identified as some governmental figure, perhaps a Roman emperor. Such an interpretation is especially interesting because Ford is a Roman Catholic, who would have everything to gain by first seeing a messianic reference here in order to take the further step of identifying Mary as the *woman* who gives birth to the Messiah.

Most scholars believe that v. 5 represents a "telescoping" of Christ's life: "She gave birth to a son, a male child, who will rule all the nations with an iron scepter. And her child was snatched up to God and to his throne."[43] The exact elements of Jesus' life that are included in this "telescoping" are debated. Some, such as Beale, think it includes Jesus' birth, destiny of kingship, and ascension (with no mention of his ministry or death).[44] Most agree that the purpose of the telescoping is to place emphasis on the victory of Christ's resurrection and ascension: "The essential truths of the vision could be best served by brevity."[45] The imagery of the dragon (who is later identified as Satan, v. 9) who is standing in front of the woman "so that he might devour her child" (v. 4) may be an allusion to the suffering and death that Satan inflicted upon Jesus during his earthly life. The child is "caught up" (ἁρπάζω) to God and to his throne—likely a reference to the ascension of Jesus[46] (Acts 1:9); or, less likely, to his resurrection.[47]

Responding to the claim by some modern critics that John's "telescoping" in this passage represents a "curious and lamentable anomaly" since it jumps from the nativity to the ascension without once mentioning the life of Jesus, Caird suggests that the "birth" in this passage represents not the nativity but the cross.[48] Feuillet has taken up this cause as well.[49] He surveys the usage of the verb βασανίζειν, and notes that it refers primarily to "the extraordinary pains or torments which God inflicts upon the evil, the demons or the damned," and that there is not a single instance of the word in the LXX, NT, Apocrypha, papyri, or patristic literature where it refers to the pain of childbirth.[50]

He concludes from this that what is depicted in Rev 12:2 is not the pains of childbirth, but rather the pains of the suffering, death and resurrection of Christ.[51] He adduces support for this from Ps 2:7 ("You are my Son; today I have begotten you"), which in turn is quoted in Acts 13:33 as Scripture fulfilled in the resurrection of Jesus (cf. Acts 13:30, 34–37).[52] Caird points out that Paul affirms this understanding when he writes that Jesus Christ was "declared with power to be the Son of God *by his resurrection from the dead*" (Rom 1:4).

Both Beasley-Murray and Mounce see this view as attractive, but doubtful.[53] But even if we do not accept all of Caird and Feuillet's conclusions, Feuillet's observation regarding the word βασανίζειν is revealing in that it renders unlikely any interpretation of this passage that finds a reference to a literal woman giving birth—most notably, the Marian interpretation. The "birth" of the male child likely cannot denote the actual incarnation of the Messiah *per se*,[54] "much less…a description of the Virgin Mother giving birth to Jesus."[55] Rather, it denotes the *Christ event* in general, with no thought of the details of that coming.[56] There is therefore no allusion to a literal woman giving birth in this passage. There is much more to be said regarding the Marian interpretation, and it is to there we now turn.

The Marian Interpretation

As we have shown above, the vast majority of exegetes see in the woman a symbol of the people of God. There are still those today, however—particularly among Roman Catholic exegetes—who see in our passage an allusion to Mary, either as the primary referent or as secondary. Laurentin simply assumes it when he says that the spiritual motherhood of Mary "does seem to find confirmation in Revelations [*sic*]."[57] Bearsley concedes that "the woman in Revelation is a symbol of the people of God,"[58] but then adds:

> Although the primary symbolism to this mysterious figure undoubtedly points to the chosen people of God of both the old and new dispensations, all reference to Mary is not thereby excluded…. Since the woman is presented as the mother of the Messiah, it is not unreasonable to see Mary in the symbol too.[59]

Tambasco is much more cautious: "To make any application at all of Revelation 12 to Mary is problematic, because she is not mentioned by name. The 'woman' seems certainly the church with the *possibility* that the image of Mary is superimposed as a second image."[60] Raymond Brown gives perhaps the best defense of the Catholic perspective.[61] He begins by pointing out the allusion to Genesis 3 in this passage:

> There can be no doubt that Revelation is giving the Christian enactment of the drama foreshadowed in Gen iii 15 where enmity is placed between the serpent and *the woman*, between the serpent's seed and her seed, and the seed of the woman enters into conflict with the serpent.[62]

Brown continues that the "dragon" is expressly connected to the "ancient serpent" and identified as "Satan" (12:9), making the allusion to Gen 3:15 indisputable.[63] Brown admits that that there is general agreement that the "woman" is a symbol for the "people of God." He himself notes that elsewhere in the Revelation, the church is portrayed as a "bride" (19: 7), and hence, a *woman*.[64] This agreement notwithstanding, Brown argues that collective figures are often based on historical figures in the Bible: "The figure of Eve in Gen iii 15 is the background for the description of the woman in Rev xxii; and it is important that from the earliest days of Christianity Mary was seen as both a symbol of the Church and the New Eve."[65] Brown cites Justin, *Trypho* 100.5; and Irenaeus, *Against Heresies* 3,22.4 for support of this.[66]

Brown further notes several parallels with the woman in Rev 12:1–6 and the "woman" (i.e., Mary) at the foot of the cross in John 19:25–27: (1) both are called by the title "woman," which title "needs an explanation"; (2) there is an unmistakable connection between Rev 12:1–6 and Gen 3:15, based (presumably) on the reference to the "ancient serpent" (Rev 12:9; cf. Gen 3:1–5, 13–15) and the "birth pangs" of the "woman" (Rev 12:1–2; cf. Gen 3:16), which may be associated with the death of Christ in John 19; (3) the "woman" of Revelation 12 has other "offspring (v. 17), and Mary is made the "mother" of other "offspring" in that she is made the mother of the "Beloved Disciple" who represents the church.[67]

While we can agree that there is indeed a probable allusion to Gen 3:15 in our passage (though it is not as certain as Brown thinks), Brown's thesis turns on a great number of exegetical leaps based on some rather questionable inferences. Against his first point, we have already seen that the title *woman* does indeed have an "explanation," both in our present passage and in John 19[68]—but in each case, that explanation is far removed from any connection between Mary and Gen 3:15, or between Revelation 12 and John 19. Against his second point above, Brown himself admits that while a connection between Rev 12:1–6 and Gen 3:15 is "unquestionable," the connection between Gen 3:15 and John 19 "is more difficult to discern."[69] He attempts to connect the two passages based on the conflict between Jesus and Satan evident in our present passage and that found in the whole of John's gospel. But even if we allow that John intends for us to see this "conflict" motif in his gospel, that motif does not finally make its way to John 19. In all of the OT citations John provides us in John 19 to show that the Scripture is being fulfilled in the suffering of Christ, there is not one citation, not one allusion to Gen 3:15. If John has intended for us to see at the cross of Jesus the culmination of the conflict of the two "seeds" (Gen 3:15)—the point in time at which the salvation of all mankind is at stake, the very apex of salvation history, no less the very focal point of "all the law and the prophets" fulfilled in this one dramatic event; namely, Jesus' final conflict with Satan in which he crushes the serpent's head—then we have to conclude that he has done a poor job of it.

After all, John takes pains to ensure that we would not fail to see the fulfillment of Scripture in the comparatively insignificant detail of the soldiers casting lots over Jesus' garment: "This happened that the Scripture might be fulfilled" (19:24). He is also careful not to omit the fact that Jesus' thirsting was itself "so that the Scripture would be fulfilled" (v. 28), and that the soldiers' decision both to pierce Jesus' side and refrain from breaking his legs were in fulfillment of Scripture as well (vv. 36–37). It seems odd, given John's attention to how the Scripture is fulfilled in all these minute details, that he would then fail to make the same connection between Jesus' calling his mother "woman" and the seed of the woman in Gen 3:15 based on Jesus' conflict with Satan. Feuillet sums it up this way:

The relationship of these two passages to each other would be much more in evidence if we could be certain that the fourth Gospel places Christ's Passion in relation to the Protoevangelium, as does the Apocalypse. But it is more difficult to establish this than we might wish to think.... And it would certainly be a vicious circle to invoke the Apocalypse in order to place this element in John XIX:25–27, if we are to make use of this fourth Gospel text in order to give a marian interpretation of Apocalypse XII. Given the unresolved state of this entire question, we consider it more prudent to refrain from invoking an unproven similarity between the fourth Gospel and the Apocalypse.[70]

These sound words of advice notwithstanding, Feuillet proceeds to make the very connection he insists we should avoid. He maintains that since the Revelation and the fourth gospel originate from "the same school" (if not from the same author), it would not be incorrect to explain one by the other.[71] Feuillet then advances the same arguments for seeing Mary in the Revelation based on the same relationship between the Revelation and John's gospel that Brown has made above.[72] In addition to all that we have already said in response to this, one wonders just how Feuillet thinks he has escaped his own prior criticism of others who make that connection.

McHugh defends the Marian interpretation on other grounds. He asserts that:

To identify the woman with the Christian church, while excluding both Mary and the people of Israel before the birth of the Messiah, is to do violence to the plain meaning of the text.... In the Old Testament, the community gives birth to the community, but only an individual woman gives birth to the person of the Messiah.[73]

While we can agree with McHugh's first statement that this text cannot be a reference to the church of the new covenant only (without reference also to Israel), his second statement is fallacious because it is designed to leave a reference to Mary as the only option. As we have already shown above, the symbolism of a woman bearing a male son, though it certainly refers to the Messiah, does not refer to the incarnation *per se* (as McHugh's statement assumes), but rather to the Christ event; hence McHugh's argument falls to the ground. Moreover, in spite of McHugh's insistence to the contrary, there are indeed many statements in the OT that speak of the Messiah coming "out of" (hence, being born from) a community. Micah 5:2 is one example of this: "But you, Bethlehem Ephrathah, though you are small among the clans of Judah, *out of you* will come for me one who will be ruler over Israel, whose origins are from of old, from ancient times."

Feuillet takes to task those who see in Revelation 12 proof for the Roman Catholic teaching of the *assumption* of Mary.[74] This "proof" is adduced not only from the image of a glorified woman, but also from vv. 6 and 14 which tells us that the woman "fled into the desert to a place prepared for her by God." The phrase "prepared by God" (and phrases like it) often carries with it eschatological connotations (Matt 24:44; 25:10; Luke 12:40; John 14:2; Rev 21:2).[75] However, the place where the woman goes is not "my Father's house" (John 14:2), but the "desert."[76] And the duration of her stay there is the same as the length of time in which the Gentiles will trample on the "holy city" (Rev 11:2) and that God's two witnesses will prophesy before they are put to death (Rev 11: 3), and is remarkably similar to the length of time found in Daniel's prophecy to indicate how long the "boastful" ruler (Dan 7:11, 20; Rev 13:5–6) of the "beast with ten horns" (Dan 7:7, 24; Rev 13:1) will "wage war against the saints" (Dan 7:21, 25; Rev 13:7) just before the "son of man" sets up his kingdom (Dan 7:26–27; cf. Rev 19–21)— namely, "a time, times, and half a time" (Rev 12:14; cf. Dan 7:25), 1,260/1,290 days (Rev 11:3; 12:6; Dan 12:11), "42 months" (Rev 11:2; 13:5).

Beasley-Murray is right when he notes that the tendency among Catholic exegetes to see in the symbol *woman* a double referent to the people of God and to Mary is "difficult to sustain…in view of the lack of support for such an estimate of Mary in the rest of the New Testament," and also because v. 17 portrays the church as the children of the woman.[77] Moreover, it is significant that the 144,000 Jews chosen from the twelve tribes of Israel (7:3–8) are "sealed" so that no harm comes to them (v. 3), and that we find them peacefully resting on Mount Zion in the presence of the Lamb while the "beast" reigns upon the earth (14:1–5; cf. 13:11–18; 14:6ff). Yet we are also told that the beast is "given power to make war against the saints and to conquer them" (13:7), and that some will "die in the Lord" for refusing to receive his mark (14:13; cf. vv. 9–12); hence, there is a distinction to be made between the 144,000 "sealed" from the twelve tribes of Israel (to which no harm comes), and the "saints" who may "die" during the reign of the beast.

All of this suggests that the *woman* in Revelation 12 is to be identified with the 144,000 chosen "people of God." The "place God has prepared for her" in the desert is "Mount Zion," where she is kept from any harm by the dragon/beast (12:17; 13:7), who now turns to pursue her "offspring" (12:17). Her offspring are identified as "those who obey God's commandments and hold to the testimony of Jesus," both in 12:7 and in 14:12. McHugh sees the *woman* as the church and "the rest of her offspring" as individual members of the church.[78] If by "church" McHugh means the remnant of Israel, then we can accept his interpretation. Although we concluded earlier that the literature sometimes portrays the people of God *collectively* with one figure and those same people of God *individually* with another, it is unlikely that John would make a distinction between the "church" and its collective members in this passage. It is the "offspring" (i.e., the church)[79] that is persecuted and put to death and *not* the *woman* (i.e., the 144,000 chosen out of the twelve tribes of Israel); the latter instead is given "two wings of a great eagle" so that she may flee to "the desert"[80]—a fairly obvious allusion to Exod 19:4 in which God reminds Israel of His great deliverance: "You yourselves have seen what I did to Egypt, and how I carried you on eagles' wings and brought you to myself."[81] There are two opposite destinies in mind for the woman and her offspring, making it impossible for them to be one and the same. And, of course, it hardly needs to be said that all of this "goes beyond anything that could have been said about Mary and her children."[82]

With this in mind, the allusion to Genesis 37 evoked by the mention of the woman "clothed with the sun," with the "moon under her feet," and wearing a "crown of twelve stars," is significantly strengthened because it embodies all who are included in the family of Israel (=Jacob).[83] In Joseph's dream, the sun is Jacob/Israel, the moon is Rachel, and the stars are the sons of Jacob who are patriarchs of the twelve tribes.[84] This, as the simplest solution (because it is the one that best explains the passage in both its immediate context, and its apocalyptic context vis-à-vis Daniel), renders any allusion to Mary here as little more than a foreign contrivance.

Further evidence against seeing Mary in our passage is the fact that the dragon is explicitly identified as an individual (viz., Satan), whereas no such identification is given to the woman as an individual. Indeed, she is rather to be seen in juxtaposition to the *woman on the beast* in chapter 17:1–18[85]—who, incidentally, is likewise not identified as an individual, but rather as a city (v. 18). This strongly suggests to us that the woman in chapter 12 cannot symbolize *any* literal individual, let alone Mary. If we allow the antithetical parallelism in these two chapters to rule the day, then we must conclude that just as the unrighteous woman of chapter 17 symbolizes the evil city of the antichrist, so also the righteous woman of chapter 12 symbolizes the "city of God."

At the end of the day, we can do no better than to conclude with Wansbrough:

> [In] the Book of Revelation, the figure of the Woman Robed with the Sun (Rv 12) is so ambivalent that no teaching about Mary may safely be derived from it; it seems much more likely that the woman represents the holy people of God who give birth to the Messiah.[86]

The Patristic Writings

One final consideration that bears on the interpretation of our text is the view of the fathers. The number of patristics writings that even address this issue is scarce, much less those that view the *woman* in this passage as Mary: "Almost all of the Church Fathers in the East and the West, as well as the Reformers and modern exegetes who interpreted this text, have seen in this image the Church."[87] Even Laurentin grants the "rarity of texts" among the Greek patristic writings through the fifteenth century that speak of Mary's spiritual motherhood.[88] It was not, in any case, a prevailing concept; nor is it today, in spite of the contradictory and confusing assertion of Feuillet to the contrary.[89]

Le Frois has written perhaps the most exhaustive treatment of the patristic views on this passage.[90] He surveys the works of all the church authors who write on this passage in the first eight centuries of church history, and finds four distinct views of the identity of the *woman* in our text: (1) the people of God in the New Covenant (i.e., the church); (2) the people of God in both the Old Covenant and the New; (3) Mary; and (4) a combination of (1) and (3) above. Le Frois' survey is extremely helpful and he is to be commended for the hard work he has done. However, while the categories he outlines above are accurate and may be useful for investigating the various nuances of beliefs among the fathers, they are at the same time misleading since they suggest an artificial distinction between categories (1) and (2). The purpose of Le Frois' inquiry—as well as that of our own—is not to breakdown every conceivable nuance of the identity of the *woman*, but rather to disclose whether and to what extent the fathers adopted the *Marian* interpretation. Similarly, Le Frois' category (4) above is not a *distinct* view (excluding all other views) but rather a *combined* view, a combination of Le Frois' categories (1) and (3) above. For the purpose of our inquiry, therefore, we may safely combine Le Frois' categories (1), (2) and (4) together as representing the *people of God* interpretation, and place that over against the combination of Le Frois' categories (3) and (4) as representing the *Marian* interpretation. To the extent that a writer sees in the woman a symbol of the people of God, he will be included in the *people of God* category. To the extent that same writer sees in the woman a symbol of Mary, he will be included in the *Marian* category as well.

The *Woman* as the People of God

Le Frois cites Hippolytus as representing the *people of God* view: "By the 'woman then clothed with the sun,' he meant most manifestly the Church, endued with the Father's word, whose brightness is above the sun."[91] Not only does Hippolytus represent the view that the *woman* is the church, but (writing in the 2nd—3rd cent.) he is also the first patristic writer who addresses the issue. Writing toward the end of the third century, Victorin(us) writes: "The woman clothed with the sun, and having the moon under her feet, and wearing a crown of twelve stars upon her head, and travailing in her pains, is the ancient Church of fathers, and prophets, and saints, and apostles."[92] Writing about the same time, Methodius (3rd—early 4th cent.) confirms this view:

> The woman who appeared in heaven clothed with the sun…is
> certainly, according to the accurate interpretation, our
> mother…whom the prophets…have called sometimes Jerus-
> alem, sometimes a bride, sometimes Mount Zion, and some-
> times the Temple and Tabernacle of God.… It is the Church
> whose children shall come to her with all speed after the res-
> urrection, running to her from all quarters. She rejoices receiv-
> ing the light which never goes down, and clothed with the
> brightness of the Word as with a robe.[93]

Methodius goes on to identify the "male child" that is borne by the
woman, not as Christ, but as representative of all those who are baptized.[94] Moreover, Methodius notes that this is the "accurate interpretation," strongly implying that his was a widely held view. Other
patristic writers who hold this view include Pseudo-Cyprian (4th
century), Tyconius (4th century), Jerome (4th–5th centuries), Augustine (4th–5th centuries), Pseudo-Augustine[95] (5th–6th centuries),
Primasius (6th century), Gregory the Great (6th century), Paterius
(6th century) Alulfus (6th century), Andrew of Caesarea (6th–7th
centuries), Bede (7th–8th centuries), and Beatus de Liébana (8th
century).[96]

The details of the views of each of these patristic writers need not
detain us here since their adherence to the *people of God* interpretation
of this passage is not in dispute. The *people of God* view is well established, both in its distribution of fathers and in its early date. What is
in question is at what point in history and to what extent the early
church adopted the Marian interpretation of our text. That this view
was accepted by the sixth century is beyond dispute. Oecumenius clearly held that Mary was the primary referent of Revelation 12: "But what
does he really say? A great sign…a woman clothed etc.… As was said
before, it is the mother of our Savior that he speaks to us."[97] What is
at issue is whether or not there is sufficient evidence that would lead
us to conclude that others held this view before Oecumenius. Le Frois
suggests that such evidence does exist, and he places six writings that
predate Oecumenius in the category of Marian interpretation. It will
be helpful to examine these writings in depth to see whether what Le
Frois has posited holds up under close scrutiny.

The *Woman* as Mary

It needs to be noted at the outset that there are three writings that predate Oecumenius historically that are thought by some to contain an allusion to Mary in the Revelation; namely, a passage in the apocryphal *Gospel According to the Hebrews*, a passage in Clement of Alexandria (*Paed.* 1, 6, 41–42), as well as a passage in Ignatius (*Epist. to the Ephesians* 19:1). However, adopting this view of these passages in turn requires adopting so many prerequisite and questionable interpretations of the details of Revelation 12 that no clear allusion can possibly be adduced from them. To his credit, Le Frois examines and rightly dismisses these as providing no evidence for the Marian interpretation. Consequently, these passages need not detain us.

Hippolytus

Although Le Frois has placed Hippolytus among those who hold that the *woman* of Revelation 12 is the church, he nevertheless contends that Hippolytus may also have seen a double referent to Mary as the *woman*.[98] This is not based on some explicit statement by Hippolytus, but rather on the theory that since Hippolytus sees the woman as the church, and the son who is born as Christ, then he must also have seen "Mary as the church" for "the mission of Mary and the Church is identical."[99] Such reasoning is clearly tendentious; one must first accept the dubious assertion that "the mission of Mary and the Church is identical," and then accept the dubious inference that where we see the church we should also see Mary, before he can accept Le Frois' rationale here. Indeed, why not simply postulate this for *everyone* who identifies the woman as the church in Revelation 12? Le Frois' suggestion here seems driven more by the desire to see a Marian interpretation of Revelation 12 that is at least as early as the *people of God* interpretation, than by an objective evaluation of Hippolytus' view of this issue.

Andrew of Caesarea—"Some before Methodius"

The attentive reader will recall that we included Andrew of Caesarea as a sixth-/seventh-century proponent of the *people of God* interpretation of our text—as well he is. Although not disputing this fact, Le Frois is of the opinion that Andrew alludes to a Marian interpretation that predates Methodius, one which both Methodius and Andrew reject. Le Frois' thesis is based on the following passage from Andrew:

Some have interpreted the woman clothed with the sun to be the all-holy Mother of God; they held that she underwent all the things that follow in order here.… But that was before that divine birth was properly understood. But the great Methodius referred them to the Church, deeming that the things mentioned in this passage little befitted the mystery of the Lord's birth.[100]

Le Frois concludes from this that "the length and trouble that St. Methodius went to, to convince his hearers of his point…only shows that the opposite opinion had a solid hold on them, and that it was the opinion of some men of authority."[101] This thesis, if true, would supply hard evidence for the existence of adherents of the Marian interpretation sometime in the late third century.

But both Andrew and Le Frois certainly misunderstand Methodius on this point. While it is doubtless true that Methodius seems to be writing a polemic against a view that he himself rejects, both Andrew and Le Frois simply assume that view must be the Marian interpretation. This assumption is adduced from Methodius' statement to wit: "The woman who appeared in heaven clothed with the sun…is certainly, according to the accurate interpretation,…the Church"[102]; a statement that could support the existence of almost any rival interpretation of the identity of the woman. If Methodius had left it at that, then we might have put more stock in Andrew's assessment of the historical situation surrounding Methodius' polemic. However, Methodius proceeds in the very next chapter to tell us just what view it is he rejects:

If anyone…should be vexed and reply to what we have said: 'But how, O virgins, can this explanation seem to you to be according to the mind of Scripture, when the Apocalypse plainly defines that the church brings forth a male, while you teach that her labor pains have their fulfillment in those who are washed in the laver [of regeneration]?' We will answer; but, O faultfinder, not even you will be able to show that Christ himself is the one who is born [in this passage]. For long before the Apocalypse [was written], the mystery of the Incarnation of the Word was fulfilled.… [But here] the Church labors and gives birth to those who are baptized.[103]

Methodius quite clearly believes that the *woman* is the church (the New Covenant people of God), and the "male son" is the baptized believer. The view he is opposing is not that the *woman* is Mary, but rather that the *woman* is Israel (the Old Covenant people of God) and that the "male son" is Christ. In other words, Methodius is defending his view from the charge that the woman could not be the New Covenant church since the church does not give birth to the Messiah, Israel does. As we have already seen, Victorin held to the very view that Methodius rejects; namely, that the woman represents the "ancient church" (combining all believers in the New Covenant and the Old). We also know that Victorin writes just before (if not contemporaneously to) Methodius. In light of all this, it is exceedingly precarious to suggest that Methodius is not writing against Victorin's view (a view we know existed in his day), but rather the Marian interpretation (a view whose existence cannot be verified at such an early date). Commenting on this, Schaff notes the following:

> Wordsworth, and many others of the learned, sustain [Methodius'] comment on this passage. So Aquinas, ad loc., Bede, and many others. Methodius is incorrectly represented as rejecting the idea that "the woman" is the Blessed Virgin Mary, for no such idea existed for him to reject. He rejects the idea that the man-child is Christ; but that idea was connected with the supposition that the woman was the Church of the Hebrews bringing forth the Messiah.[104]

All the evidence suggests, therefore, that both Andrew and Le Frois have misread Methodius. If we are to adduce evidence for the Marian interpretation of Revelation 12 before the time of Oecumenius, we must look elsewhere for it.

Epiphanius

The evidence for the Marian interpretation from the fourth-century father Epiphanius is considerably stronger than what we found in Methodius. Discussing the question as to whether or not Mary died, Epiphanius writes:

Scripture does not tell us whether Mary died or whether she did not die. Scripture is silent about this because of the surpassing miracle of her departure, lest minds of men be overcome by the marvel.... Some indeed, understand the prophecy of Simeon (Lk. 2, 35) as meaning that she was to be slain with the sword. On the other hand, she may have been exempt from death, for that which John tells us in the Apocalypse may have been fulfilled in her: 'The dragon hastened to the woman who had brought forth the man-child, and there were given to her the wings of an eagle, and she was born into the desert lest the dragon seize her' (Ap. 12, 14). For my part I will not say whether she remained immortal or whether she died. I refrain because Scripture which transcends the grasp of the human mind, has left the matter in the dark for the honor of her body.[105]

Le Frois argues from this passage that even if Epiphanius did not himself hold to the Marian interpretation of Revelation 12 he must have "taken for granted" its existence in his day.[106] Honesty compels us to admit that Epiphanius must have known of a Marian interpretation in his day; but the details are still unclear. First, Epiphanius distinguishes the Lukan passage from the Johannine passage by saying of the former, "some understand" the passage as meaning *x*, whereas no such confirmation is given about the latter. In the latter Epiphanius simply says, "On the other hand, she *may* have been exempt from death," and that Revelation 12 "*may* have been fulfilled in her." This may be understood to indicate either that Epiphanius personally considered (and subsequently rejected) seeing Mary in Revelation 12, or that he knew of someone who held this view, but did not see it as adhered to widely enough to suggest that "some understand" it this way. In any case, if this is a case of seeing Mary in the Revelation, it is clear that Epiphanius did not see much merit in this view; for he concludes nevertheless that "Scripture does not tell us" about Mary's *assumption*, that "Scripture is silent about this," and that Scripture has "left the matter in the dark." If the vision of Mary in the Revelation forces us also to see her *assumption* in the words "the woman fled into the desert to a place prepared for her by God," then Epiphanius rejects this view.[107]

Ephraem

Le Frois suggests that another fourth-century writer, Ephraem, may have seen Mary in the Revelation. He cites two passages that may allude to Revelation 12. The first says this: "Said Mary: The Child whom I bore, took me up and placed me between his mighty wings, and carried me away high in the air, and said: The heavens and the deep belong to thy Son."[108] The second says this:

> The Son of the Most High came and took up within me His dwelling, and I became his Mother. He who was born of me granted me a rebirth[109] likewise; and whereas His body clothed itself in the flesh of His Mother I have clothed myself in His glory.[110]

In the first of these, Le Frois suggests that there are three similarities to Revelation 12: (1) the divine child; (2) who is Lord of the world; and (3) the mother is carried off by "the wings of a great eagle."[111] In response, the first two can hardly be seen as allusions to Revelation 12, for these are Christian staples found in so many other places (in Scripture as well as in popular belief by Ephraem's day) that no allusion to Revelation 12 is necessary. Le Frois has embellished the third similarity by adding the words "wings of a great eagle," found in the Revelation, but not found in the citation by Ephraem. This could just as easily be an allusion to one of any number of other passages in Scripture.[112]

Moreover, the dissimilarities are greater than the similarities. If this is an allusion to Revelation 12, one might expect some reference to a "desert," or to a "place prepared by God"—or, indeed, to the child "ruling with an iron scepter." In Revelation 12, the son is "snatched up" whereas the woman "flees." In Ephraem, the son carries the mother. In Revelation 12, the woman herself is the one with wings. In Ephraem, the mother is carried by the wings of another. Le Frois concludes that if there is an allusion to Revelation 12 here, "the probability is slight."[113] The second passage from Ephraem (above) is even less convincing as an allusion to Revelation12, as even Le Frois admits.[114] We must conclude, therefore, that Ephraem does not provide evidence for the Marian interpretation of Revelation 12.

Augustine

Augustine represents a fifth-century writer who unequivocally holds to the *people of God* view of Revelation 12, but whom Le Frois nevertheless sees as possibly holding to the Marian interpretation as well.[115] The evidence that Le Frois offers us is that since Augustine interprets the "wilderness" or "solitary place" in Revelation 12 as a symbol of Christ's virgin birth, and the *woman* as the "ancient city of God," we should therefore take this "as an indication of the transition in the mind of Augustine from Mary to the Church."[116] But this is completely unnecessary. The "ancient church" for Augustine is the collection of the people of God regardless of Old or New Covenant. Mary is seen to be part of this "ancient church" (in this case the Old Covenant) which gives birth to the Messiah. That does not imply that Augustine saw a double referent to Mary *and* the church; rather he saw Mary as *part of* the church. There is no more an indication in Augustine of the Marian interpretation than there is among exegetes today who hold that the woman is the *people of God* of both Covenants, and that the "birth" of the male child refers to the birth of Christ, without seeing a double referent to Mary as the *woman*.

Quodvultdeus

Quodvultdeus, a fifth-century writer who is thought to have been a friend and disciple of Augustine, is the first known writer historically to associate the *woman* of Revelation 12 with Mary:

> In the apocalypse of John the Apostle it is written that "the dragon stood before the woman who was about to bring forth, that when she had delivered her child, he might devour it.... No one of you is ignorant of this: that the dragon is the devil; nor of this: that the woman signifies the Virgin Mary, who being inviolate, brought forth our Head inviolate; at the same time she represented in her person Holy Church in figure, that as she remained a virgin in bringing forth her Son, so also the Church brings forth His members at all times, without any loss to her virginity.[117]

While Quodvultdeus clearly says that the woman signifies Mary, Le Frois' further, unwarranted assertion that "we can take for granted that

St. Augustine's own doctrine is reflected in his disciple's teaching"—
by which he means that this must also have been the view of Augustine—begs the question. Le Frois would no doubt reject this same rationale in other situations.[118] Moreover, Quodvultdeus' words must be
kept in context. These words are taken from a work that attempts to
show that types and figures permeate the biblical text. If one is *looking*
for a "type" in the symbolism of the *woman* who gives birth to the
Messiah in Revelation 12, one cannot help but see Mary. Yet even here
Quodvultdeus is careful to distinguish the symbolism of the "dragon,"
which he says *is* the devil (i.e., John specifically identifies him as such),
and the "woman," which he says "signifies" Mary who represents the
church, which Quodvultdeus sees as John's *true* symbolism in this passage. In other words, Quodvultdeus sees Mary not as the primary
referent, but as a derived referent only. This is far removed from the
popular belief among conservative Catholic scholars and apologists
today that Marian symbolism is John's intent in this passage.

With Quodvultdeus we exhaust the writers thought to hold the
Marian interpretation of Revelation 12 before the time of Oecumenius.
The evidence Le Frois has submitted in support of the Marian interpretation for most of these writers falls to the ground. The only exceptions may be Epiphanius and Quodvultdeus. In the case of Epiphanius,
we do not know whether he himself held Mary to be the woman while
rejecting the notion that Revelation 12 supports her *assumption* into
heaven; or that he himself, while having considered them, rejected both
ideas. In any case, he provides no statement that would serve as evidence of a widely held Marian interpretation during his day—nor,
indeed, that anyone of repute was a proponent of it. He seems instead
to suggest just the opposite since he connects the phrase "some understand" with a possible interpretation of Luke 2, but provides no such
statement in regard to the Marian interpretation of Revelation 12. The
most we can say with certainty is that the Marian interpretation (so far
as the known evidence is concerned) finds its genesis in Epiphanius,
who considered and then rejected it.

In the case of Quodvultdeus we find the first instance of the woman as double referent to the church and Mary. Yet, even here there is
no thought that Quodvultdeus thinks John envisions Mary as the *woman*—only that Mary may be seen as a *type* or *figure* that represents the
church, the true woman in Revelation 12. It is not until we arrive at the

sixth century that we find (in Oecumenius) the view that Mary is the primary referent of Revelation 12, to the exclusion of the people of God.

Interestingly, Quodvultdeus (5th cent.) is the first saint canonized by Rome to suggest that the Marian referent is a valid one (though only in a secondary way). Even Oecumenius, the first true proponent of the full-orbed Marian interpretation, is not considered a canonized father of the church. Indeed, even in the list Le Frois provides, the only canonized father in the first eight centuries to make mention of the Marian view (in which Mary is the primary referent) is Epiphanius who may have actually *rejected* the view. The number of patristic writers in the first six centuries who subscribe to the *people of God* view of Revelation 12 (at least sixteen known to us, counting Quodvultdeus, nine of whom are canonized saints) far exceeds the number of those who see Mary as the primary or secondary referent (only two, none of whom are canonized fathers of the Roman church). The implications of these statistics are telling against the Roman Catholic view of this passage:

> The fact that the mariological emphasis on Revelation 12 is relatively recent raises the question of whether it represents an exegesis of the text itself or simply an imaginative theological application as part of a search for biblical support for Marian doctrine.[119]

Concluding Thoughts

Many Roman Catholic interpreters who see the *woman* in Revelation 12 as a reference to Mary (if only in a secondary sense) do so on the basis of the implausibility of an early Christian reader seeing no reference to Mary in a passage that speaks of the birth of the Messiah. Feuillet writes: "It is inconceivable that a Christian writer, much less the Apostle John,…could have spoken of the Mother of the Messiah, without having a thought of Mary, the Mother of Jesus."[120] Yet, as we have seen, such a view assumes what it seeks to prove; namely, a status for Mary that was nonexistent in the NT church. Moreover, if (as we have seen) the *woman* in Revelation 12 is to be understood as the *people of God* embodied in Israel rather than Mary, and the "birth" of the male child symbolizes the *Christ event* rather than the Incarnation, it would not be implausible at all that the first Christians could read this passage without seeing any reference to Mary. Indeed, what Feuillet has called "inconceivable" is precisely what we find in the ancient church.

There are other factors that lead us in this direction as well. First, from a purely literary standpoint, it is significant that although the dragon in Revelation 12 is identified by John as Satan, the woman remains unidentified. Moreover, when we compare this woman to the antithetical woman of Revelation 17, we find that both represent collective entities—the former consists of the "city of God," whereas the latter consists of the "city of the beast." Second, the description in Revelation 12 does not fit the Gospel portrayal of the events surrounding the birth of Jesus. The birth, the snatching up, and the woman fleeing are all situated in heaven. Third, if one holds to the virginity of Mary *in partu*, which implies a painless delivery and which is "looked upon as a dogma of the faith by many Roman Catholics,"[121] then one has a problem explaining the "birth pains" in this passage.

Fourth, no church writer for the first several centuries saw any reference to Mary in this passage at all. It is not until the fifth century (in Quodvultdeus) and the sixth century (in Oecumenius) that we find positive evidence for seeing, respectively, Mary as a secondary referent unintended by the author of the Revelation and Mary as the primary referent in the interpretation of this text.[122] In any case, the Marian interpretation was never the majority opinion in the early church. The majority viewed the "woman" as the *people of God*, both the ancient church and the New Covenant church.[123] Lonsdale's statement that "ancient christian liturgical and exegetical traditions have seen in the figure of the woman in Revelation 12 an image of Mary"[124] is therefore misleading. He later nuances this statement when he writes: "Early christian writers did not interpret Revelation 12 mariologically."[125]

Fifth, as McHugh allows, "it is possible to give a wholly satisfactory explanation of Apoc 12 without postulating any allusion to Mary the mother of Jesus."[126] McHugh goes on to insist, however, that if this is read in conjunction with the fourth Gospel, it is difficult to escape the allusion to Mary as "mother of all whom Jesus loves."[127] Yet, this reading depends on McHugh's prior understanding of Mary's role at the foot of the cross in the fourth Gospel—a view we have examined and

rejected as untenable. If one rejects that understanding, he is not altogether likely to accept an allusion to Mary in Revelation 12. In the
words of Lonsdale:

> Most contemporary scholars agree that this [Marian] in-
> terpretation has real difficulties…[and] the safe conclusion is
> that an intended reference to Mary in Revelation 12 is very
> unlikely…. The woman appears [instead] to be primarily
> intended as an image of the people of God, the messianic
> community.[128]

At the end of the day, then, we must satisfy ourselves with the fact that
Revelation 12 provides us with no significance for our inquiry into the
New Testament's view of Mary.

Toward a New Testament Mariology

We have examined all the major NT passages that bear on our understanding of Mary's status and role in the early church. Though the passages are few when compared to other NT characters (such as Paul or Peter), they are significant nevertheless. Taken together they portray Mary as someone who initially receives the word of God with great enthusiasm; who then struggles to understand her true role vis-à-vis the conflict between her old role as *mother* of Jesus (in which she exercises her will over him) and her new role as *servant* of Jesus (in which she humbly submits to his will); who at times gets it right, while other times not; who at times even opposes Jesus' mission and sides with those who deem Jesus "insane"; who then finally becomes a full-fledged disciple.

The desire on the part of Catholic exegetes to downplay the negative side of Mary while focusing on her positive contributions has led some to see Mary as a *model* disciple or *symbol* of discipleship. The NT evidence warrants neither of these conclusions. Mary is instead portrayed as an *epitomized* disciple; that is to say, a disciple who experiences the same normal successes and failures that characterize all disciples to varying degrees. She receives the word with gladness, experiences setbacks, opposes Jesus' mission to some extent, is the object of Jesus' reproof and rebuff, submits to Jesus as she comes to terms with her new relationship with him, and is at last found in the company of the disciples she once opposed.

What this means for our view of Mary is that she is a normal human being who has been redeemed in the very same way that all disciples are. What this means for the Roman Catholic view of Mary is that there is great disparity between the biblical data and Roman Catholic dogma. Raymond Brown opines that while distinctive Catholic beliefs about Mary cannot be found in the NT itself, those beliefs are not at variance with the NT witness:

> The wrong question (the one unfortunately almost unfailingly posed by the very literal minded and conservative) is: Are the Marian doctrines found in the New Testament? …The correct question to pose is: Are such Marian doctrines along lines of development that proceed from the New Testament? Part of the genius of Catholicism is that it does not confine itself to the limited insight of the first century…but sees that tradition has continued to grow in a believing community of other centuries.[1]

While the doctrinal development principle Brown mentions is indeed a valid consideration when formulating a full-orbed Christian theology, it does not help his case for a Roman Catholic Mary. It is one thing to postulate, for instance, the Christian doctrine of the Trinity, which is little more than the full composite of the theological "pieces" provided to us by the biblical writers.[2] The Marian doctrines are a different case entirely. Whereas in the former we are simply putting together the pieces that we find in the NT, in the latter we are asked to believe in something diametrically opposed to the teaching of the NT.

In the NT, Mary weds as a virgin who, after the birth of Jesus, engages in normal marital relations with her husband resulting in biological brothers and sisters of Jesus; in Roman Catholicism, Mary is a perpetual virgin, unblemished by "the stain of carnal commerce." In the NT, Mary is "blessed" by virtue of her privilege to carry and bear the one who would redeem the world; in Roman Catholicism, Mary is "blessed" because she is inherently "full of grace," and is singularly privileged to have been born without the stain of original sin. In the NT, Mary humbly accepts her fate as directed by God to become the mother of Messiah; in Roman Catholicism the fate of all mankind hangs in the balance and rests in the hands of Mary who is free to choose one way or the other whether she wants to bear the Messiah—without this *fiat* on Mary's part, God counts his losses and man is eternally lost; hence, this *fiat* results in Mary's exalted role as

Co-Redemptress. In the NT, Mary fails to understand Jesus' mission and at times actively opposes it; in Roman Catholicism, Mary is always in complete harmony with Jesus and his mission. In the NT, Mary attempts to exercise her privilege as mother, and is rebuffed by Jesus on several occasions; in Roman Catholicism, Jesus never rebuffs his mother, but always honors her by submitting to her, and grants her every request; hence, her exalted role as Co-Mediatrix. In the NT, just as there is only one God, so also there is only one mediator between man and God—the man Jesus Christ; in Roman Catholicism Mary is co-Mediatrix, one who intercedes on our behalf to Christ. In the NT, Mary struggles with the conflict of her changed relationship to Jesus as he severs biological ties with his earthly family in favor of his new eschatological family, which is based solely on discipleship; in Roman Catholicism, the biological ties between Mary and Jesus are never severed, and in fact become the basis for exalting Mary as "Mother of God." In the NT, Mary is given to John for her ongoing physical care and spiritual comfort after the death of her son; in Roman Catholicism, Mary takes care of John, who is a symbol of all disciples, by protecting him and nurturing him; hence, Mary's exalted role as "Mother of the Church."[3]

We are not, at the end of the day, being asked by Roman Catholicism to believe a *development* of NT Marian doctrine; rather, we are being asked to believe something that lies in direct contradiction to the New Testament's witness about Mary. Far from seeing such beliefs as a legitimate *development* of Mariology, there is not even a hint in the NT "of such doctrines as the Immaculate Conception or the Assumption, let alone Mediatrix of Graces"[4]; and indeed these beliefs run contrary to the evidence we find in the NT. If it is argued that these beliefs developed from Mary's role as Mother of Jesus, then it must also be insisted that "the obvious teaching of the Bible is that the office of mother to the Lord carried with it no permanent prerogatives."[5]

This final point is evidenced not only by the witness of the evangelists in which Jesus severs biological ties with his mother, but also by the ongoing life of the church in which Mary plays no part. She does show up one time at the beginning of Acts; but we are told simply that she was there with the rest of the disciples, and there is no hint that she holds any special status among them. Similarly, although in the Roman Catholic view Mary plays a central role in God's plan of salvation (she is both the instrument of salvation and our ongoing mediatrix), she is never once mentioned in the *kerygma* of the NT church, although the contrary has sometimes been advanced: "In presenting Jesus as one 'born according to the flesh of the offspring of David' (*Rom.* 1, 3), the first preachers must necessarily have spoken of Mary His Mother."[6] But Mercurio's thesis seems forced, and it is summarily dismissed by Wansbrough: "In assessing the Pauline evidence the task is brief: merely to point out that passages which have sometimes been considered by an over-inventive piety to refer to Mary have in fact no such import."[7] Indeed, one wonders just why mention of Mary would be *necessary* to convey the fact that Jesus was born the offspring of David. The very fact that Paul can communicate the true humanity and kingly line of Jesus by phrases such as "born of a woman" (Gal 4:4), "made in the likeness of man" (Phil 2:7), and "born according to the flesh of the offspring of David"—and yet not once mention Mary—makes it all but certain that the early *kerygma* did not "necessarily" include reference to Mary as Mercurio contends. Lonsdale sums it up this way:

> Commentators have tried to quarry insights about Mary from the letters of Paul, but without much positive yield.… These passages [Gal 1:19; 4:4–5, 28–29; Rom 1:3–4; Phil 2:6–7], taken singly and together, throw very little light…on the mother of Jesus.… We are led, therefore, to the conclusion that just as Paul was not particularly interested in the earthly life of Jesus, so he does not pay attention, in any significant way, to the conception, birth or mother of Jesus.[8]

Yet, Lonsdale's words are a bit misleading in that they compare the silence of any mention of Mary to the relative "silence" of Jesus' earthly ministry in Paul's writings. In fact, Paul does speak of the suffering, death and resurrection of Christ—all of which are part of Jesus' earthly ministry, and all of which are absolutely central to Paul's gospel (1 Cor 15:1–4; Rom 4:25; Phil 2:6–8; 3:10–11; etc.). For Paul, this *is* the gospel. Moreover, as Lonsdale hints at above, the greatness of the heavenly status of the risen Christ is a recurring theme in Paul, and presented as central to the Christian life (Phil 1:20–21; 2:9–11; 3:10–11; etc.). Yet, where in the ongoing life of the church do we find any similar mention of Mary's *fiat* in her earthly ministry; or any ongoing mediation in her supposed heavenly ministry—both of which are absolutely central to the Roman Catholic gospel? The question is not difficult to answer: "Mary plays no part in the earliest layers of kerygmatic formulation, except as she is very obliquely referred to in Galatians 4:4."[9]

It is in this light that we should assess Bearsley's lamentation that, in current discussions about Mary, there is too much insistence on viewing Mary in negative terms and that she is of interest only in relation to Christ. This Bearsley sees as a "deficiency."[10] Such an assertion is astounding in light of our inquiry here. One might rather legitimately ask why we should view Mary any differently than the picture given to us by the NT writers. Given that there are so few references to Mary in the NT to begin with, that most of these portray Mary in a negative light,[11] and that arguably all of these portray Mary in relation to Jesus (Mary is never spoken of independently of Christ or the Christ event, except for perhaps Acts 1), it seems odd that Bearsley should lament the fact that our view of Mary is in line with what we are actually told about her.

Bearsley's further clarification is telling: "Mariology does not develop in a logical fashion from a bedrock of principles; it does not unfold from a germ idea. Rather, Mariology grows through reflection on the data of revelation."[12] But this is precisely where the problem of Bearsley's position arises. If we are not constrained by "bedrock principles" of exegesis and instead allow ourselves to by guided only by an unbridled prior devotion to Mary, we will no doubt see all sorts of fanciful musings about the mother of Jesus. Such an approach could be used to justify any and every aberrant belief imaginable.[13] A biblical Mariology can grow only from sound exegesis of the biblical text.

Perhaps even less subtle are the comments of Kugelman cited earlier in this work:

> In his endeavor to plumb the profound meaning of Sacred Scripture, the Catholic exegete enjoys a unique privilege. He is not left solely to the resources of patient scholarship. He is directed in his study and guided by the divinely appointed custodian and the authentic interpreter of the inspired word, the Magisterium. The Holy Spirit, whom the glorified Jesus sent upon his Church, teaches her all things.[14]

Kugelman's words are revealing. According to Kugelman, NT exegesis for the Roman Catholic interpreter is not an exercise in ascertaining the meaning of the biblical text through examination of the Greek words, the literary context, and the original intent of the writer. Far from it; it consists rather in listening to what the Roman Catholic Magisterium has already said the meaning is, and then looking for ways that that meaning can be defended from Scripture.[15] The fact that such strained exegesis must be applied to the Marian texts in order to arrive at the conclusion at which Roman Catholic interpreters would like us to arrive suggests to us that the Roman Catholic interpretation of these texts is tendentious at best.

Yet even some who do attempt exegesis of the text seem to do so almost out of a sense of obligation, as though this exercise is solely for the benefit of those who are reluctant to accept an untenable view—all the while seeming to be completely unaware that it is painfully obvious to those of us who do not hold prior loyalties to Rome that such "exegesis" comes not from the text itself but from an a *priori* belief in Mary's spiritual maternity. The text is simply made to "fit" the foregone conclusion. It is not as though *no* progress has been made toward a common understanding of Mary among Protestants and Roman Catholics. On the whole, Roman Catholic scholarship on this issue has begun to lean toward the Protestant view, though there are still those who hold to a pre-Vatican II understanding of this issue. And, Protestants seem much more willing to embrace the notion that there are some positive things to say about Mary, particularly in the fact that she is among the "blessed," that she is counted among the disciples, and that she epitomizes, through her successes as well as her failures of faith, true discipleship—such a notion is entirely biblical (as we have seen), and we should not hesitate to embrace it. But until the Roman Catholic side can evaluate Mary's status and role more openly and honestly, being guided solely by the NT witness instead of by a desire to salvage outdated elements of Mariology that have been shown to be unbiblical, we cannot hope to reach a common understanding on this issue.

A Breakdown of the Various Usages of ἕως in the New Testament

The breakdown of the various usages of ἕως when used by itself and with ἄν, οὗ, or ὅτου is illustrated in the tables below. Each table has five headings: *Verse, Text, Meaning, Cat.* (category), and *Or.* (order). The letters *S, E,* and *T* in the Category column stand for *Spatial, Extent,* and *Temporal* respectively. Where there are two letters (e.g., S/E), the first signifies the primary meaning of ἕως in the present passage, while the second letter signifies a lesser, secondary connotation. The Order (Or.) column is of no significance to the reader as it acts only as a sorting field to place the verses back in their original order.

1. Ἕως Alone (104 Occurrences)
1a. Spatial

Verse	Text	Meaning	Cat.	Or.
Mt 2:9	[The star] went ahead of them until it stopped over the place where the child was	to a spatial point, but no further	S	4
Mt 20:8	beginning with the last ones hired and going on to the first	to a certain point, but no further	S	17
Mt 26:58	But Peter followed him at a distance, right up to the courtyard	to a spatial point	S	26
Mk 14:54	Peter followed him at a distance, right into the courtyard of the high priest	to a spatial point	S	41
Lk 2:15	Let's go to Bethlehem and see this thing that has happened	to a spatial point	S	45
Lk 4:29	and took him to the brow of the hill on which the town was built	to a spatial point	S	47
Lk 4:42	The people were looking for him and when they came to where he was	to a spatial point	S	48
Lk 23:5	He started in Galilee and has come all the way here	to a spatial point	S	59
Lk 24:50	When he had led them out to the vicinity of Bethany	to a spatial point	S	61
Jn 2:7	so they filled them to the brim	to a spatial point	S	62
Ac 8:40	preaching the gospel in all the towns until he reached Caesarea	to a spatial point	S	74
Ac 9:38	desiring that he would not delay to come to them.	to a spatial point	S	75
Ac 11:19	traveled as far as Phenice	to a spatial point	S	76
Ac 11:22	that he should go as far as Antioch	to a spatial point	S	77
Ac 13:47	that you may bring salvation to the ends of the earth	to a spatial point	S	79
Ac 17:14	the brethren sent away Paul to go as it were to the sea	to a spatial point	S	80
Ac 17:15	The men who escorted Paul brought him to Athens	to a spatial point	S	81
Ac 21:5	All the disciples and their wives and children accompanied us out of the city accompanied us out of the city	to a spatial point	S	82
Ac 23:23	seventy horsemen and two hundred spearmen to go to Caesarea	to a spatial point	S	83
Ac 26:11	I even went to foreign cities to persecute them	to a spatial point	S	84
2 Co 12:2	such an one caught up to the third heaven	to a spatial point	S	95
Mt 11:23	will you be lifted up to the skies	to a spatial point/extent	S	8

continued

Mt 11:23	No, you will go down to the depths	to a spatial point/extent	S	9
Mt 24:31	from one end of the heavens to the other	to a spatial point	S	22
Mt 27:51	the curtain of the temple was torn in two from top to bottom	From one spatial point to another	S	29
Mk 15:38	The curtain of the temple was torn in two from top to bottom.	From one spatial point to another	S	43
Lk 10:15	will you be lifted up to the skies?	to a spatial point	S	50
Lk 10:15	No, you will go down to the depths	to a spatial point	S	51
Ac 1:8	and to the ends of the earth	to a spatial point	S	70
Mt 1:17	fourteen generations in all from Abraham to David	to a spatial point, but no further	S	1
Mt 1:17	fourteen from David to the exile to Babylon	to a spatial point, but no further	S	2
Mt 1:17	fourteen from the exile to the Christ	to a spatial point, but no further	S	3
Mt 22:26	The same thing happened to the second and third brother, right on down to the seventh	to a spatial point, but no further	S	18

33 instances where the *spatial* idea is primary: 21 S; 8 S/E; 4 S/T

1b. Extent

Verse	Text	Meaning	Cat.	Or.
Mt 18:21	Up to seven times?	to a certain point, but no further	E	13
Mt 18:22	not up to seven times	to a certain point, but no further	E	14
Mt 18:22	but up to seventy-seven times	to a great extent	E	15
Mt 26:38	My soul is overwhelmed with sorrow to the point of death	to a great extent	E	25
Mk 6:23	I will give you, up to half my kingdom	extent	E	32
Mk 14:34	My soul is overwhelmed with sorrow to the point of death	to a great extent	E	40
Lk 22:51	But Jesus answered, "No more of this!"	extent	E	58
Ac 8:10	all the people from the greatest to the least	extent	E	73
Ro 3:12	there is no one who does good, not even one. [OT]	extent	E	86
2 Co 1:13	And I hope that, as you have understood us in part, you will come to understand fully	extent	E	93
Heb 8:11	from the least of them to the greatest	extent	E	98
Mt 24:27	lightning that comes from the east is visible even in the west	to a great spatial (unlimited or all-encompassing) extent	E/S	21
Mk 13:27	from the ends of the earth to the ends of the heavens	to a great spatial (unlimited or all-encompassing) extent	E/S	37

13 instances where *extent* is primary; 11 E; 2 E/S

1c. Temporal

Verse	Text	Meaning	Cat.	Or
Mt 2:15	where he stayed until the death of Herod	until a specified time (but not after)	T	5
Mt 11:12	from the days of John the Baptist until now	up to a specified time, with no reference to cessation or continuance	T	6
Mt 11:13	all the Prophets and the Law prophesied until John	until a specified time (but not after?)	T	7
Mt 13:30	let both grow together until the harvest	until a specified time (but not after)	T	10
Mt 18:30	into prison until he could pay the debt	until a specified time (but not after)	T	16
Mt 24:21	unequaled from the beginning of the world until now	until a specified time (and continuing)	T	20
Mt 24:39	nothing about what would happen until the flood came	until a specified time (but not after)	T	23
Mt 26:29	I will not drink of this fruit of the vine from now on until that day	until a specified time (but not after)	T	24
Mt 27:8	that is why it has been called the Field of Blood to this day	up to a specified time, with no reference to cessation or continuance	T	27
Mt 27:45	from the sixth hour until the ninth hour darkness came over all the land	until a specified time (but not after)	T	28
Mt 27:64	so give the order for the tomb to be made secure until the third day	until a specified time (but not after)	T	30
Mt 28:20	I am with you always, to the very end of the age	until a specified time (and continuing)	T	31
Mk 13:19	unequaled from the beginning, when God created the world, until now—and never to be equaled again	until a specified time (and continuing)	T	36
Mk 14:25	I will not drink again of the fruit of the vine until that day when I drink it anew in the kingdom of God.	until a specified time (but not after)	T	38
Mk 15:33	at the sixth hour darkness came over the whole land until the ninth hour	until a specified time (but not after)	T	42
Lk 1:80	and he lived in the desert until he appeared publicly to Israel.	up to a specified time, with no reference to cessation or continuance	T	44
Lk 2:37	and then was a widow until she was eighty-four.	up to a specified time, with no reference to cessation or continuance	T	46

continued

[1c cont.]

Lk 12:59	you will not get out until you have paid the last penny.	until a specified time (but not after)	T	53
Lk 13:35	you will not see me again until you say, Blessed is he	until a specified time (but not after)	T	54
Lk 15:4	and go after the lost sheep until he finds it?	until a specified time (but not after)	T	55
Lk 22:34	before the rooster crows today, you will deny three times that you know me.	until a specified time (but not after)	T	57
Lk 23:44	darkness came over the whole land until the ninth hour	until a specified time (but not after)	T	60
Jn 2:10	but you have saved the best till now.	until a specified time (but not after)	T	63
Jn 5:17	my Father is always at his work to this very day	until a specified time (and continuing)	T	64
Jn 10:24	how long will you keep us in suspense?	until a specified time (but not after)	T	66
Jn 16:24	until now you have not asked for anything in my name	until a specified time (but not after)	T	67
Jn 21:22	if I want him to remain alive until I return	up to a specified time, with no reference to cessation or continuance	T	68
Jn 21:23	if I want him to remain alive until I return	up to a specified time, with no reference to cessation or continuance	T	69
Ac 1:22	beginning from John's baptism to the time when Jesus was taken up	until a specified time (and continuing)	T	71
Ac 7:45	it remained in the land until the time of David	until a specified time (and continuing)	T	72
Ac 13:20	God gave them judges until the time of Samuel the prophet	until a specified time (but not after)	T	78
Ac 28:23	from morning till evening he explained and declared to them the kingdom of God	up to a specified time, with no reference to cessation or continuance	T	85
Ro 11:8	and ears so that they could not hear, to this very day [OT]	until a specified time (and continuing)	T	87
1 Co 1:8	he will keep you strong to the end	until a specified time (and continuing)	T	88
1 Co 4:13	up to this moment we have become the scum of the earth	until a specified time (and continuing)	T	89
1 Co 8:7	some people are still so accustomed to idols	until a specified time (and continuing)	T	90

continued

[1c cont.]

1 Co 15:6	most of whom are still living	until a specified time (and continuing)	T	91
1 Co 16:8	but I will stay on at Ephesus until Pentecost	until a specified time (but not after)	T	92
2 Co 3:15	even to this day when Moses is read, a veil covers their hearts	until a specified time (and continuing)	T	94
2 Th 2:7	will continue to do so till he is taken out of the way	until a specified time (but not after)	T	96
1 Ti 4:13	until I come, devote yourself to the public reading	up to a specified time, with no reference to cessation or continuance	T	97
Heb 10:13	since that time he waits until his enemies are made his footstool	until a specified time (but not after)	T	99
Jas 5:7	be patient, then, brothers, until the Lord's coming.	up to a specified time, with no reference to cessation or continuance	T	100
Jas 5:7	until he receive the early and latter rain	up to a specified time, with no reference to cessation or continuance	T	101
1 Jn 2:9	anyone who claims to be in the light but hates his brother is still in the darkness	until a specified time (and continuing)	T	102
Re 6:10	how long, Sovereign Lord, holy and true, until you judge	until a specified time (but not after)	T	103
Re 6:11	they were told to wait a little longer, until the number of their fellow servants	until a specified time (but not after)	T	104
Lk 17:8	wait on me while I eat and drink; after that you may eat	until a specified time (but not after)	T	56
Mk 6:45	go on ahead of him to Bethsaida, while he dismissed the crowd	While (during the period in which)	T	33
Jn 9:4	while it is day, we must do the work of him who sent me	While (during the period in which)	T	65
Mk 14:32	sit here while I pray.	While (during the period in which)	T	39
Mt 17:17	how long shall I stay with you?	until a specified time (but not after)	T/E	11
Mt 17:17	how long shall I put up with you?	until a specified time (but not after)	T/E	12
Mk 9:19	how long shall I stay with you?	until a specified time (but not after)	T/E	34
Mk 9:19	how long shall I put up with you?	until a specified time (but not after)	T/E	35

continued

[1c cont.]

Mk 9:19	how long shall I put up with you?	until a specified time (but not after)	T/E	35
Lk 9:41	how long shall I stay with you and put up with you?	until a specified time (but not after)	T/E	49
Lk 11:51	from the blood of Abel to the blood of Zechariah	up to a specified time, with no reference to cessation or continuance	T/S	52
Mt 23:35	from the blood of righteous Abel to the blood of Zechariah son of Berekiah	up to a specified time, with no reference to cessation or continuance	T/S	19
58 instances where the *temporal* meaning is primary: 51 T; 5 T/E; 2 T/S				

2. Ἕως ἂν (20 Occurrences)

Verse	Text	Meaning	Cat.	Or.
Mt 2:13	take the child and his mother and escape to Egypt. Stay there *until* I tell you	until a specified time (but not after)	T	1
Mt 5:18	*until* heaven and earth disappear, not the smallest letter, not the least stroke of a pen, will by any means disappear	up to a specified time, with no reference to cessation or continuance	T	2
Mt 5:18	will by any means disappear from the Law *until* everything is accomplished	up to a specified time, with no reference to cessation or continuance	T	3
Mt 5:26	you will not get out *until* you have paid the last penny	until a specified time (but not after)	T	4
Mt 10:11	stay at his house *until* you leave	until a specified time (but not after)	T	5
Mt 10:23	you will not finish going through the cities of Israel *until* the Son of Man comes	up to a specified time, with no reference to cessation or continuance	T	6
Mt 12:20	a smoldering wick he will not snuff out, un *til* he leads justice to victory	up to a specified time, with no reference to cessation or continuance	T	7
Mt 16:28	some who are standing here will not taste death *until* they see the Son of Man coming in his kingdom	up to a specified time, with no reference to cessation or continuance	T	8
Mt 22:44	sit at my right hand *until* I put your enemies under your feet	up to a specified time, with no reference to cessation or continuance	T	9
Mt 23:39	you will not see me again *until* you say, 'Blessed is he	until a specified time (but not after)	T	10
Mt 24:34	this generation will certainly not pass away *until* all these things have happened	up to a specified time, with no reference to cessation or continuance	T	11
Mk 6:10	whenever you enter a house, stay there *until* you leave that town	until a specified time (but not after)	T	12
Mk 9:1	some who are standing here will not taste death *until* they see the kingdom of God come with power	up to a specified time, with no reference to cessation or continuance	T	13
Mk 12:36	Sit at my right hand *until* I put your enemies under your feet	up to a specified time, with no reference to cessation or continuance	T	14
Lk 9:27	some who are standing here will not taste death *until* they see the kingdom of God	up to a specified time, with no reference to cessation or continuance	T	15

continued

[2 cont.]

Lk 20:43	[sit at my right hand] *until* I make your enemies a footstool for your feet	up to a specified time, with no reference to cessation or continuance	T	16
Lk 21:32	this generation will certainly not pass away *until* all these things have happened	up to a specified time, with no reference to cessation or continuance	T	17
Ac 2:35	[sit at my right hand] *until* I make your enemies a footstool for your feet	up to a specified time, with no reference to cessation or continuance	T	18
1 Co 4:5	therefore judge nothing before the appointed time; wait *till* the Lord comes	until a specified time (but not after)	T	19
Heb 1:13	sit at my right hand *until* I make your enemies a footstool for your feet	up to a specified time, with no reference to cessation or continuance	T	20
20 instances where the *temporal* meaning is primary				

3. Ἕως ὅτου (5 Occurrences)

Verse	Text	Meaning	Cat.	Or.
Mt 5:25	Settle matters quickly with your adversary who is taking you to court. Do it *while* you are still with him on the way	while (the duration of which)	T	1
Lk 12:50	But I have a baptism to undergo, and how distressed I am *until* it is completed!	until a specified time (but not after)	T	2
Lk 13:8	leave it alone for one more year, while I dig around it and fertilize it	while (the duration of which)	T	3
Lk 22:16	I will not eat it again *until* it finds fulfillment in the kingdom of God	until a specified time (but not after)	T	4
Jn 9:18	The Jews still did not believe that he had been blind and had received his sight *until* they sent for the man's parents	until a specified time (but not after)	T	5
5 instances where the *temporal* meaning is primary				

4. Ἕως οὖ (17 Occurrences)

Verse	Text	Meaning	Cat.	Or.
Mt 1:25	But he had no union with her *until* she gave birth to a son	until a specified time (but not after)	T	1
Mt 13:33	The kingdom of heaven is like yeast that a woman took and mixed into a large amount of flour *until* it worked all through the dough	until a specified time (but not after)	T	2
Mt 14:22	Jesus made the disciples get into the boat and go on ahead of him to the other side, *while* he dismissed the crowd	while (the duration of which)	T	3
Mt 17:9	Don't tell anyone what you have seen, *until* the Son of Man has been raised from the dead	until a specified time (but not after)	T	4
Mt 18:34	his master turned him over to the jailers to be tortured, *until* he should pay back all he owed	until a specified time (but not after)	T	5
Mt 26:36	Sit here *while* I go over there and pray	while (the duration of which)	T	6
Lk 13:21	It is like yeast that a woman took and mixed into a large amount of flour *until* it worked all through the dough	until a specified time (but not after)	T	7
Lk 15:8	Does she not light a lamp, sweep the house and search carefully *until* she finds it?	until a specified time (but not after)	T	8
Lk 22:18	For I tell you I will not drink again of the fruit of the vine *until* the kingdom of God comes	until a specified time (but not after)	T	9
Lk 24:49	but stay in the city *until* you have been clothed with power from on high	until a specified time (but not after)	T	10
Jn 13:38	the rooster will by no means crow *until* you have disowned me three times	until a specified time (but not after)	T	11
Ac 21:26	[Paul] entered into the temple to signify the accomplishment of the days of purification, *until* an offering might be offered for every one of them	until a specified time (but not after)	T	12
Ac 23:12	and bound themselves with an oath not to eat or drink *until* they had killed Paul	until a specified time (but not after)	T	13
Ac 23:14	We have taken a solemn oath not to eat anything *until* we have killed Paul	until a specified time (but not after)	T	14
Ac 23:21	They have taken an oath not to eat or drink *until* they have killed him	until a specified time (but not after)	T	15
Ac 25:21	I ordered him held *until* I could send him to Caesar	until a specified time (but not after)	T	16
2 Pe 1:19	you will do well to pay attention to it, as to a light shining in a dark place, *until* the day dawns and the morning star rises in your hearts	until a specified time (but not after)	T	17

17 instances where the *temporal* meaning is primary

Table of Usages for the Phrases ἕως οὗ and ἕως ὅτου in the LXX

The following tables contain all instances of ἕως οὗ and ἕως ὅτου in the LXX. Each table has five headings: *Verse*, *Text*, *Meaning*, *Cat.* (category), and *Or.* (order). The Category (*Cat.*) column contains an abbreviation of that meaning (E=extent; T=temporal; B=before; R=result; S=spatial; una=until, not after; unr=until, no reference; and w=while). The Order (*Or.*) column is of no significance to the reader as it acts only as a sorting field to place the verses back in their original order.

1. Ἕως οὗ in the LXX

Verse	Text	Meaning	Cat.	Or.
Ge 26:13	The man became rich, and his wealth continued to grow until he became very wealthy	to the extent that	E	1
Dt 9:21	And I took your sin, the calf which you had made, and burnt it with fire, and stamped it, and ground it very small, until it was as small as dust: and I cast the dust thereof into the brook that descended out of the mount	to the extent that	E	4
2 Sa 23:10	but he stood his ground and struck down the Philistines until his hand grew tired and froze to the sword.	to the extent that	E	13
2 Ki 6:25	And there was a great famine in Samaria: and, behold, they besieged it, until a donkey's head was sold for eighty pieces of silver	to the extent that	E	17
2 Ki 17:20	Therefore the LORD rejected all the people of Israel; he afflicted them and gave them into the hands of plunderers, until he thrust them from his presence	to the extent that	E	18
2 Ki 21:16	Moreover Manasseh shed innocent blood very much, until he had filled Jerusalem from one end to another	to the extent that	E	20
2 Ch 26:15	His fame spread far and wide, for he was greatly helped until he became powerful	to the extent that	E	26
Da 3:19	He ordered the furnace heated seven-fold, until it was completely burning up. [Theodotion]	to the extent that	E	53
Da 4:33	His body was drenched with the dew of heaven until his hair grew like the feathers of an eagle [Theodotion]	to the extent that	E	58
Da 8:11	he magnified himself even to the prince of the host [Theodotion]	to the extent that	E	63
Jdg 4:24	And the hand of the Israelites grew stronger and stronger against Jabin, the Canaanite king, until they destroyed him [ms Fam. B; ms Fam. A omits οὗ]	to the extent that/ with the result that	E/R	7
Ps 57:8	[58:7] They will amount to nothing as water that flows away. He will stretch his bow until they will be weak.	to the extent that/ with the result that	E/R	30
Ec 2:3	I sought in my heart to give myself to wine—all the while leading my heart with wisdom—and to lay hold of folly, until I might see what was good for the sons of men to do under the heaven all the days of their life.	with the result that	R	39

continued

[1 cont.]

Is 33:23	Your rigging hangs loose: The mast is not held secure, the sail is not spread. Until an abundance of spoils will be divided and even the lame will carry off plunder	with the result that	R	46
Dt 2:15	The LORD's hand was against them until he had completely eliminated them from the camp	with the result that/ to the extent that	R/E	3
1 Ki 17:17	Some time later the son of the woman who owned the house became ill. He grew worse and worse, until he finally stopped breathing	with the result that/ to the extent that	R/E	15
2 Ki 17:23	[The Israelites persisted in all the sins of Jeroboam and did not turn away from them] until the LORD removed them from his presence	with the result that/ to the extent that	R/E	19
2 Ch 21:15	You yourself will be very ill with a lingering disease of the bowels, until the disease causes your bowels to come out	with the result that/ to the extent that	R/E	24
2 Ch 24:10	All the officials and all the people brought their contributions gladly, dropping them into the chest until it was full	with the result that/ to the extent that	R/E	25
Jdt 15:5	And those in Galaad and in those in Galilee chased them in a great slaughter until they had passed Damascus and her borders.	until a spatial point is reached (prepositional)	S	74
Ps 131:5	132:5] [I will allow no sleep to my eyes, no slumber to my eyelids] until I find a place for the LORD, a dwelling for the Mighty One of Jacob	temporal/before/ until a specified time (but not after)	T/B/ una	36
Ec 12:2	[Remember your Creator in the days of your youth...] until the sun and the light and the moon and the stars grow dark, and the clouds return after the rain	temporal/before/ until a specified time (but not after)	T/B/ una	40
So 2:7	Do not arouse or awaken love until it so desires	temporal/before/ until a specified time (but not after)	T/B/ una	42
So 3:4	Scarcely had I passed them when I found the one my heart loves. I held him and would not let him go until I had brought him to my mother's house, to the room of the one who conceived me.	temporal/before/ until a specified time (but not after)	T/B/ una	44
Eze 24:13	Because I tried to cleanse you but you would not be cleansed from your impurity, you will not be clean again until my wrath against you has subsided	temporal/before/ until a specified time (but not after)	T/B/ una	50
Da 6:25	[6:24] And they did not reach the floor until the lions had overpowered them	temporal/before/ until a specified time (but not after)	T/B/ una	60

continued

[1 cont.]

Tob 1:21	And not fifty days passed before two of his sons killed him	temporal/before/ until a specified time (but not after)	T/B/una	66
Dt 2:15	The LORD's hand was against them until he had completely eliminated them from the camp	temporal/until a specified time (but not after)/ (to the extent that?)	T/una/E	3
Dt 2:14	And the space in which we came from Kadeshbarnea, until we were come over the brook Zered, was thirty and eight years; until all the generation of the men of war were wasted out from among the host, as the LORD swore unto them	temporal/until a specified time (but not after)	T/una	2
Jdg 3:30	So Moab was subdued that day under the hand of Israel. And the land had rest eighty years. *[And Ehud judged them until he died] [*in LXX, not Hebrew]	temporal/until a specified time (but not after)	T/una	6
Jdg 5:7	Village life in Israel ceased, ceased until I, Deborah, arose, [until I] arose a mother in Israel [ms Fam. B has the second occurrence of ἕως οὗ]	temporal/until a specified time (but not after)	T/una	8
Jdg 19:26	At daybreak the woman went back to the house where her master was staying, fell down at the door and lay there until daylight [B omits οὗ]	temporal/until a specified time (but not after)	T/una	9
Ru 2:23	So Ruth stayed close to the servant girls of Boaz to glean until the barley and wheat harvests were finished. And she lived with her mother-in-law	temporal/until a specified time (but not after)	T/una	11
Ru 3:3	Wash and perfume yourself, and put on your best clothes. Then go down to the threshing floor, but don't let him know you are there until he has finished eating and drinking	temporal/until a specified time (but not after)	T/una	12
1 Ki 11:40	Solomon tried to kill Jeroboam, but Jeroboam fled to Egypt, to Shishak the king, and stayed there until Solomon's death	temporal/until a specified time (but not after)	T/una	14
1 Ki 18:29	Midday passed, and they continued their frantic prophesying until the time for the evening sacrifice. But there was no response, no one answered, no one paid attention	temporal/until a specified time (but not after)	T/una	16
1 Ch 6:17	[6:32] They ministered with music before the tabernacle, the Tent of Meeting, until Solomon built the temple of the LORD in Jerusalem	temporal/until a specified time (but not after)	T/una	21

continued

[1 cont.]

2 Ch 8:16	All Solomon's work was carried out, from the day the foundation of the temple of the LORD was laid until its completion. So the temple of the LORD was finished	temporal/until a specified time (but not after)	T/una	22
2 Ch 9:6	But I did not believe what they said until I came and saw with my own eyes	temporal/until a specified time (but not after)	T/una	23
2 Ch 29:34	The priests, however, were too few to skin all the burnt offerings; so their kinsmen the Levites helped them until the task was finished and until other priests had been consecrated, for the Levites had been more conscientious in consecrating themselves than the priests had been.	temporal/until a specified time (but not after)	T/una	28
La 3:50	[My eyes will flow unceasingly, without relief,] until the LORD looks down from heaven and sees	temporal/until a specified time (but not after)	T/una	47
Eze 4:8	I will tie you up with ropes so that you cannot turn from one side to the other until you have finished the days of your siege.	temporal/until a specified time (but not after)	T/una	48
Eze 21:32	[21:27] A ruin! A ruin! I will make it a ruin! It will not be restored until he comes to whom it rightfully belongs; to him I will give it.	temporal/until a specified time (but not after)	T/una	49
Da 4:8	[but they could not interpret the dream for me] until Daniel came into my presence and I told him the dream. [Theodotion]	temporal/until a specified time (but not after)	T/una	54
Da 4:23	Let him be drenched with the dew of heaven; let him live like the wild animals, until seven times pass by for him. [Theodotion]	temporal/until a specified time (but not after)	T/una	55
Da 4:25	Seven times will pass by for you until you acknowledge that the Most High is sovereign over the kingdoms of men [Theodotion]	temporal/until a specified time (but not after)	T/una	56
Da 4:32	Seven times will pass by for you until you acknowledge that the Most High is sovereign over the kingdoms of men [Theodotion]	temporal/until a specified time (but not after)	T/una	57
Da 5:21	and his body was drenched with the dew of heaven, until he acknowledged that the Most High God is sovereign over the kingdoms of men [Theodotion]	temporal/until a specified time (but not after)	T/una	59
Da 7:22	[As I watched, this horn was waging war against the saints and defeating them,] until the Ancient of Days came and pronounced judgment in favor of the saints of the Most High, and the time came when they possessed the kingdom [Theodotion]	temporal/until a specified time (but not after)	T/una	62

continued

[1 cont.]

Ho 5:15	Then I will go back to my place until they admit their guilt	temporal/until a specified time (but not after)	T/una	64
Jon 4:5	Jonah went out of the city, and sat on the east side of the city, and there made him a booth, and sat under it in the shadow, until he might see what would become of the city	temporal/until a specified time (but not after)	T/una	65
Tob 2:4	And before I had tasted anything, I got up and took him up into a room until the sun went down [ms fam. BA]	temporal/until a specified time (but not after)	T/una	67
Tob 2:10	moreover, Achiacharus took care of me until he left for Elymais. [ms fam. BA]	temporal/until a specified time (but not after)	T/una	68
Jdt 6:5	you will see my face no more from this day until I take vengeance on this nation that came out of Egypt.	temporal/until a specified time (but not after)	T/una	70
Jdt 6:8	And you will not perish until you are destroyed with them.	temporal/until a specified time (but not after)	T/una	71
Jdt 10:10	and the men of the city looked after her until she had gone down the mountain and until she had passed the valley and could see her no more.	temporal/until a specified time (but not after)	T/una	72
Jdt 14:8	Then Judith declared to him in the midst of the people all that she had done, from the day that she left until she spoke to them.	temporal/until a specified time (but not after)	T/una	73
Sir 4:17	For at first she will walk with him by crooked ways, and bring fear and dread upon him, and torment him with her discipline until she may trust his soul and try him by her laws.	temporal/until a specified time (but not after)	T/una	75
Sir 13:7	[the rich man] will disgrace you with his food, until he has drained you two or three times, and at the end he will scorn you.	temporal/until a specified time (but not after)	T/una	76
Sir 29:5	Until he has received, he will kiss a man's hand, and for his neighbor's money he will speak submissively; but when payment is due, he disappoints him.	temporal/until a specified time (but not after)	T/una	77
Jos 4:10	Now the priests who carried the ark remained standing in the middle of the Jordan until everything the LORD had commanded Joshua was done by the people, just as Moses had directed Joshua	temporal/until a specified time (but not after)/ while (during the period in which)	T/una /W	5
Ru 1:13	would you wait until they grew up? Would you remain unmarried for them?	temporal/until a specified time (but not after)/ while (during the period in which)	T/una /W	10

continued

[1 cont.]

So 2:17	Until the day breaks and the shadows flee, turn, my lover, and be like a gazelle or like a young stag on the rugged hills.	Temporal/until a specified time, with no reference to cessation or continuance	T/unr ?	43
So 4:6	Until the day breaks and the shadows flee, I will go to the mountain of myrrh and to the hill of incense.	Temporal/until a specified time, with no reference to cessation or continuance	T/unr ?	45
2 Ch 29:28	The whole assembly bowed in worship, and the singers sang and the trumpeters played. All this continued until the sacrifice of the burnt offering was completed	Temporal/until a specified time, with no reference to cessation or continuance	T/unr	27
Ps 71:7	[72:7] In his days the righteous will flourish; prosperity will abound until the moon is no more	Temporal/until a specified time, with no reference to cessation or continuance	T/unr	31
Ps 93:15	[94:15] [For the LORD will not reject his people; he will never forsake his inheritance] until judgment returns to righteousness: and all the upright in heart will follow it	Temporal/until a specified time, with no reference to cessation or continuance	T/unr	33
Ps 111:8	[112:8] His heart is established, he will by no means be afraid, until he binds his enemies	Temporal/until a specified time, with no reference to cessation or continuance	T/unr	34
Ps 141:8	[142:7] Set me free from my prison, that I may praise your name. The righteous will await on me until you return to me.	Temporal/until a specified time, with no reference to cessation or continuance	T/unr ?	38
4 Mac 7:3	[The reasoning of Eleazar] in no way turned the rudder of godliness until it sailed into the harbor of victory over death.	Temporal/until a specified time, with no reference to cessation or continuance	T/unr ?	78
Ps 56:2	[57:1] I will take refuge in the shadow of your wings until the disaster has passed.	Temporal/until a specified time, with no reference to cessation or continuance/ until a specified time (but not after)	T/unr /una	29

continued

[1 cont.]

Ps 56:2	[57:1] I will take refuge in the shadow of your wings until the disaster has passed.	Temporal/until a specified time, with no reference to cessation or continuance/ until a specified time (but not after)	T/unr /una	29
Ps 122:2	[123:2] as the eyes of a maid look to the hand of her mistress, so our eyes look to the LORD our God, until he shows us his mercy	Temporal/until a specified time, with no reference to cessation or continuance/ until a specified time (but not after)	T/unr /una	35
Da 2:9	You have conspired to tell me misleading and wicked things, until [hopefully] the situation changes [Theodotion; Old Greek has ἕως ἄν]	Temporal/until a specified time, with no reference to cessation or continuance/ until a specified time (but not after)	T/unr /una	51
Ps 93:13	[94:13] you grant him relief from days of trouble, until a pit is dug for the wicked	temporal/while (during the period in which)	T/w	32
Ps 140:10	[141:10] Let the wicked fall into their own nets, while I pass by in safety	temporal/while (during the period in which)	T/w	37
So 1:12	While the king was at his table, my perfume spread its fragrance	temporal/while (during the period in which)	T/w	41
Da 2:34	You were watching until a rock was cut out, but not by human hands [Theodotion; Old Greek has ἕως ὅτου]	temporal/while (during the period in which)	T/w	52
Da 7:4	The first was like a lion, and it had the wings of an eagle. I watched until its wings were torn off and it was lifted from the ground [Theodotion; Old Greek has ἕως ὅτου]	temporal/while (during the period in which)	T/w	61
Tob 10:7	and she did not cease during the nights to bewail her son Tobias until the fourteen days of the wedding were accomplished. [ms fam. BA]	temporal/while (during the period in which)	T/w	69

2. Ἕως ὅτου in the LXX

Verse	Text	Meaning	Cat.	Or.
1 Mac 14:10	He provided food for the cities and set up arms in them *until* his glorious name was renowned to the ends of the earth	extent/until a specified time (but not after)	E/T/una	8
Ec 12:6	[Remember your creator in the days of your youth] *until* [before] the silver cord be loosed, or the golden bowl be broken	temporal/before/ until a specified time (but not after)	T/B/una	10
1 Sa 30:4	So David and his men wept aloud *until* they had no strength left to weep	temporal/until a specified time (but not after)/extent	T/una/E	2
1 Ki 10:7	But I did not believe these things *until* I came and saw with my own eyes	temporal/until a specified time (but not after)	T/una	3
1 Ki 11:16	Joab and all the Israelites stayed there for six months, *until* they had destroyed all the men in Edom	temporal/until a specified time (but not after)	T/una	4
Ne 4:5	[4:11] And our adversaries said, "They will not know, neither see, *until* we come in the midst among them, and slay them, and cause the work to cease"	temporal/until a specified time (but not after)	T/una	6
Tob 5:3	And we will pay him *until* you come; and you take from him this silver [based on the inferior Sinaiticus reading]	temporal/until a specified time (but not after)	T/una	7
Eze 39:15	As they go through the land and one of them sees a human bone, he will set up a marker beside it *until* the gravediggers have buried it in the Valley of Hamon Gog	temporal/until a specified time (but not after)	T/una	11
2 Ki 2:17	But they persisted *until* he was too ashamed to refuse. So he said, "Send them."	temporal/until a specified time (but not after)/extent	T/una / E	5
1 Sa 22:3	Would you let my father and mother come and stay with you *until* I learn what God will do for me?	temporal/while (the duration of which)	T/w	1
Ec 12:1	Remember now your Creator in the days of your youth, *while* the evil days are still not here	temporal/while (the duration of which)	T/w	9
Da 2:34	You were watching *until* [while] a rock was cut out, but not by human hands [Old Greek; see Θ citation]	temporal/while (the duration of which)	T/w	12
Da 7:4	The first was like a lion, and it had the wings of an eagle. I watched *until* [while] its wings were torn off and it was lifted from the ground [Old Greek; see Θ citation]	temporal/while (the duration of which)	T/w	13
Da 7:9	I watched *until* [while] the thrones were cast down, and the Ancient of days sat	temporal/while (the duration of which)	T/w	14

A Theological Inquiry into Selected Marian Titles

While we have been able to address most of the Marian issues in the main text of this work, there remain two beliefs about Mary that we have not addressed fully because (1) there is no NT text that addresses the Marian beliefs in question, (2) the beliefs in question are more theological than exegetical in nature, and/or (3) in at least one case, the NT texts that do have something to say regarding the belief have absolutely nothing to say about Mary. These two beliefs include Mary as Mediatrix and Mary as Mother of God.

Mary as Mediatrix

We have dealt somewhat with this issue in our discussion of John 2. There we saw that in spite of the insistence of many Roman Catholic interpreters to the contrary, Mary's mediation cannot be found in the words "do whatever he tells you." There is a NT passage, however, that though it says nothing specifically in regard to Mary, may be adduced as evidence that the NT writers did *not* see Mary as Mediatrix. That passage is 1 Tim 2:5: "For there is one God and one mediator between God and men, the man Christ Jesus." Here we are told in no uncertain terms that there is only *one* mediator, and that mediator is Christ. Roman Catholic interpreters often counter that Mary's mediation is not to be seen on a level with Christ's mediation.[1] We all mediate for each other in prayer, we are told, and that fact does not seem to militate against Christ's unique mediation.[2] There is indeed only one mediator at Christ's level, it is argued, but that does not prevent us from seeing in Mary a mediator who is at once at a lower level than Christ *and* who shares in a unique way in his mediation.

In response to this, two things may be said. First, it is not the case that we are being asked to believe in a Marian mediation on par with every other believer who prays for the church. If that were the case, then there would be no cause for concern. On the contrary, Marian mediation is said to be of a singular kind. She alone is Co-Redemptress with Christ.[3] Second, the parallel that Paul gives us, and with which we are to view the oneness of Christ's mediation, is the oneness of God himself. Just as there is "*one* [εἶς] God," Paul says, so also there is "*one* [εἶς] mediator" between God and man. There is no hint here of seeing the possibility of a *demigod*, who is halfway between the one God and all the rest of us—the oneness of God excludes that notion. So also, to preserve the parallel that Paul gives us, we must conclude that there is no hint here of seeing the possibility of a *demi-mediator* (as it were)— a sort of mediator between the one mediator and the rest of us. As far as the text is concerned, the only mediator that exists—or is even needed—between God and man is Christ.

Mother of God

In our discussion of Luke 1:43 we saw that some Roman Catholic interpreters see in Elizabeth's words, "why am I so favored, that the mother of my Lord should come to me?," evidence for the title Mother of God. Senior observes that Mary is "lauded" by Elizabeth not only for believing that God would fulfill the promise he gave her, but also for being the mother of her Lord,[4] which he labels "a powerful, royal title."[5] Some Catholic apologists go even farther and posit that the phrase "mother of my Lord" is to be equated with the later historical title "mother of God." But this is certainly not Luke's intent. The word "Lord" (κύριος) used here refers, as Senior has noted above, to a position of majesty, and not to a divine nature.

As we have already seen, the origins of the nomenclature "Mother of God" finds its basis in the term *theotokos*, which was used by the framers of the councils of Ephesus (430) and Chalcedon (451). Yet, as we have also seen, neither the title "Mother of God," nor any of its implied privileges, is consonant with the original intent of the term *theotokos*:

The title *Theotokos*, is used not so much to say something about Mary as to say something about Jesus.... Recent Christology, emphasizing an approach 'from below,' finds the formula of Chalcedon in need of reformulation. The language has little meaning for contemporary society, and the formulation does not seem to allow enough room for a full treatment of the humanity of Jesus.[6]

Tambasco points out that the title Mother of God came about through a logical syllogism: "the Bible says Mary is the mother of Jesus; it also says Jesus is God; therefore, it says equivalently that Mary is mother of God."[7] We have dealt with the logical fallacy of this argument elsewhere and the reader is referred there for the full discussion.[8] In short, the syllogism suffers from the fallacy of the undistributed middle term due to the mistaken notion that each of the premises is a categorical statement. The same fallacy exists in the syllogism "Mary is the mother of God, God is a Trinity, therefore Mary is the mother of the Trinity"! Returning to the former syllogism, the first premise, "Mary is the mother of Jesus," is indeed a categorical statement (i.e., "*all* of Mary is the mother of Jesus"). However, the second premise, "Jesus is God," is not; for it is not the case that "*all* of Jesus is God." *Some* of Jesus (viz., his humanity) is not God, and the premise is better stated as a particular statement ("*some* of Jesus is God"). With this in mind, the syllogism to which Tambasco refers can no longer be thought to support the conclusion it is made to support; for the conclusion, "Mary is the mother of God," does not necessarily follow the premises, "Mary is the mother of Jesus," and "some of Jesus is God"; for it very well could be (and indeed is the case) that Mary is mother of only the *non*-God part of Jesus.[9]

Some Catholic writers take issue with this, insisting that Mary is not the mother of a *nature*, but of a person. Yet that argument, too, falls to the ground. Properly speaking, God is not a person, but a *being* that subsists in three persons. God is a Trinity; yet it cannot be said that since Jesus is God then Jesus must be a Trinity! Catholic apologists have not made the necessary theological distinction between person, nature, and being. Some Catholic apologists have argued for an exception in the case of Jesus, asserting that Jesus is a "divine person" who took on a human nature. Such an argument, however, encounters innumerable difficulties. First, the instant one uses the phrase "divine person," one has already violated the distinction above. "Divine person" is just another way of saying "person with a divine nature." Yet, the instant the incarnation occurred, the "person" in question was something more—namely, he was a "person with a divine nature and a human nature"; and it was to *this* person that Mary gave birth. Moreover, if one insists that we must regard Mary as the mother of God on the basis that Mary gave birth to a "divine person," we must then ask some probing questions. Luke tells us that "Jesus grew in wisdom" (Luke 2:52); since Jesus is God are we then to conclude that God grew in wisdom? Jesus did not know the precise day and hour of his return (Matt 24:36); since Jesus is God, are we to conclude that God did not know this information? Jesus was "tempted in every way just as we are" (Heb 4:15); since Jesus is God, do we conclude that God was tempted? Jesus died on the cross; since Jesus is God, are we to conclude that God died?

The biblical view, of course, is that God has always possessed all wisdom; that God knows all things, including the time-frame for Christ's return (Matt 24:36); that God cannot be tempted with evil (Jas 1:13); and that God cannot die since death is a corporeal condition, affecting humans (1 Cor 15:22; "in Adam, all die"), but not God (Ps 82:6–7; "I said, 'you are gods.'…but you will die like mere men"), nor even angels (Luke 20:36; "they can no longer die, for they are like the angels"). How is it then that Jesus grew in wisdom, was limited in knowledge, was tempted, died—and yes, was born? Quite simply, only by virtue of his humanity, and not by virtue of his divinity. God, in his divinity, cannot be conceived and born any more than he can die. It cannot therefore be said of Mary that she bore God (and hence, bears the designation "mother of God"), any more than it can be said of the Jews that they killed God. Jesus in his humanity had a mother; Jesus in his divinity was "without father or mother, without genealogy, without beginning of days or end of life" (Heb 7:3).

This was also the view of the earliest thinkers of this relationship between Jesus and his mother. Augustine, commenting on John 2, writes: "At that time, therefore, when about to engage in divine acts, He repelled, as one unknown, her who was the mother, not of His divinity, but of His [human] infirmity."[10] He shares the same sentiment elsewhere as well: "It was as if [Jesus] said [in John 2], 'You did not give birth to my power of working miracles, it was not you who gave birth to my divinity. But you are the mother of all that is weak in me."[11] Clearly, Augustine made a distinction between the relation Mary enjoyed with Jesus' humanity, and that which she enjoyed with Jesus' divinity. Augustine goes on to explain what he means in the very next chapter of his work:

> Why, then, said the Son to the mother, "Woman, what have I to do with thee? mine hour is not yet come?" Our Lord Jesus Christ was both God and man. According as He was God, He had not a mother; according as He was man, He had. She was the mother, then, of His flesh, of His humanity, of the weakness which for our sakes He took upon Him. But the miracle which He was about to do, He was about to do according to His divine nature, not according to His weakness; according to that wherein He was God not according to that wherein He was born weak. But the weakness of God is stronger than men. His mother then demanded a miracle of Him; but He, about to perform divine works, so far did not recognize a human womb; saying in effect, "That in me which works a miracle was not born of thee, thou gavest not birth to my divine nature; but because my weakness was born of thee, I will recognize thee at the time when that same weakness shall hang upon the cross." This, indeed, is the meaning of "Mine hour is not yet come." …How then was He both David's son and David's Lord? David's son according to the flesh, David's Lord according to His divinity; so also Mary's son after the flesh, and Mary's Lord after His majesty. Now as she was not the mother of His divine nature, whilst it was by His divinity the miracle she asked for would be wrought, therefore He answered her, "Woman, what have I to do with thee?"[12]

Gregory the Great, commenting on John 2 and 19 states: "As if to say plainly, That I can do a miracle comes to me from my Father, not from my mother. For he who from the nature of his Father did miracles, had it from his mother that he could die."[13] Both Gregory and Augustine share the view we have posited above for the distinction between Mary's relationship to Jesus in his humanity and the same to Jesus in his divinity. There can be no objection, then, from the Roman Catholic who dismisses this view as ahistorical. It is based not only on better logic than the "mother of God" formula, but also has support from some of the early church's best minds.

BIBLIOGRAPHY

Aland, Kurt et al, eds. *The Greek New Testament*, ed. K. Aland, M. Black, C.M. Martini, B.M. Metzger, and A. Wikgren. New York: United Bible Societies, 19753.

__________ et al. *Novum Testamentum Graece*, 26th ed. Stuttgart: Deutsche Bibelgesellschaft, 1988 (=1979).

Abbot, Walter M., ed. *The Documents of Vatican II*. New York: Guild Press, 1966.

Barrett, C. K. *The Gospel According to St. John*, 2nd ed. Philadelphia: Westminster, 1978.

Bauckham, Richard. *Jude and the Relatives of Jesus in the Early Church*. Edinburgh: T. & T. Clark, 1990.

__________. "The Brothers and Sisters of Jesus: An Epiphanian Response to John P. Meier," *CBQ* 56/4 (1994): 686–700.

Bauer, Walter et al, ed. *A Greek-English Lexicon of the New Testament and Other Early Christian Literature*, 2d ed. Rev. and augmented by F. W. Gingrich and F. W. Danker; Chicago: University of Chicago, 1979.

Beale, G. K. *The Book of Revelation: A Commentary of the Greek Text*. NIGTC. Ed. I. Howard Marshall & D. A. Hagner. Grand Rapids: Eerdmans, 1999.

Bearsley, Patrick J. "Mary the Perfect Disciple: A Paradigm for Mariology," *Theological Studies* 41/3 (1980): 461–504.

Beasley-Murray, G. R. *The Book of Revelation*. NCB. London: Oliphants, 1974.

Beattie, Tina. *Rediscovering Mary: Insights From the Gospels*. Liguori, MO: Triumph Books, 1995.

Ben-Chorin, Schalom, "A Jewish View of the Mother of Jesus," in *Mary in the Churches*. Ed. Hans Küng and Jürgen Moltmann. ETr. Marcus Lefébure. New York: T. & T. Clark, 1983.

Benko, Steven. *Protestants, Catholics and Mary*. Valley Forge: Judson, 1968.

Best, E. "Mark iii.20,21,31–35," *NTS* 22 (1975–76): 309–19.

Blass, F. and A. Debrunner, eds. *A Greek Grammar of the New Testament and Other Early Christian Literature*. ETr. and ed. R. W. Funk. Chicago: University of Chicago, 1961.

Blomberg, Craig. *Matthew*. The New American Commentary, vol. 22. Ed. David S. Dockery. Nashville: Broadman Press, 1992)

Børresen, Kari, "Mary in Catholic Theology," in *Mary in the Churches*. Ed. Hans Küng and Jürgen Moltmann. ETr. Marcus Lefébure. New York: T. & T. Clark, 1983.

Brenton, L. C. L. *The Septuagint with Apocrypha*. Peabody, MA: Hendrickson, 1986.

Bridcut, William. "Our Lord's Relationship with His Mother," *One in Christ* 22/2 (1986): 364–70.

Brown, Raymond. *Biblical Exegesis and Church Doctrine*. Mahwah: Paulist, 1985.

__________. *The Birth of the Messiah*. Garden City: Doubleday, 1977.

__________. *The Gospel According to John*, 2 vols. Garden City: Doubleday, 1966–70.

__________ et al, eds. *Mary in the New Testament*. Philadelphia: Fortress Press, 1978.

__________. "Mary in the New Testament and in Catholic Life," *America* (May 15, 1982): 375–79.

__________. "More Polemic than Instructive: R. Laurentin on the Infancy Narratives," *Marianum* 47 (1985): 188–207.

__________. "The Annunciation to Mary, the Visitation, and the Magnificat (Luke 1:26–56)," *Worship* 62/3 (May 1988): 249–259.

__________. "The Meaning of Modern New Testament Studies for an Ecumenical Understanding of Mary," in *Biblical Reflections on Crises Facing the Church*. London, 1975.

Brunner, F. D. *The Christbook: A Historical/Theological Commentary*. Waco: Word Books, 1987.

Caird, G. B. *Luke*. The Pelican Gospel Commentaries. New York: Penguin Books, 1963.

__________. *A Commentary on the Revelation of St. John the Divine*. Ed. H. Chadwick. London: Adam and Charles Black, 1966.

Carroll, Eamon. "Mariology," in *An American Catechism*, an issue of *Chicago Studies* (Fall 1973): 295–303.

__________. "Theology on the Virgin Mary," *Theological Studies* 37 (1976): 253–289.

__________. "The New Testament Charisms of the Blessed Virgin Mary," *One in Christ* 22/2 (1986): 356–364.

Carson, D. A. *The Gospel According to John*. Grand Rapids: Eerdmans, 1991.

__________. "Matthew," *Expositor's Bible Commentary*. 12 vols. Frank E. Gaebelein, ed. Grand Rapids: Zondervan, 1976.

Ceroke, Christian. "Jesus and Mary at Cana: Separation or Association?" *Theological Studies* 17 (1956): 1–38.

__________. "Mary's Maternal Role in John 19, 25–27," *Marian Studies* 11 (1960): 123–51.

Charlesworth, J. H., ed. *The Old Testament Pseudepigrapha*, vol. 2. Garden City: Doubleday, 1985.

Cole, W. J. "Scripture and the Current Understanding of Mary Among American Protestants," *Maria in Sacra Scriptura* (Acta congressus mariologici-mariana internationalis) 6 (1967): 95–161.

Collins, R. *The Combat Myth in the Book of Revelation*. HDR 9; Missoula: Scholars, 1976.

__________. "Mary in the Fourth Gospel: A Decade of Johannine Studies," *Louvain Studies* 3 (1970): 99–142.

Conzelmann, H. *The Theology of St. Luke.* New York: Harper & Row, 1960.

Craghan, John. F. *Mary: The Virginal Wife and the Married Virgin: The Problematic of Mary's Vow of Virginity.* Rome: Gregorian University Press, 1967.

__________. "Mary's 'Ante Partum' Virginity: The Biblical View," *AER* 162 (1970): 361–72.

Crossan, J. D. "Mark and the Relatives of Jesus," *NovT* 15 (1973): 81–113.

Currie, David. *Born Fundamentalist: Born Again Catholic.* San Francisco: Ignatius Press, 1996.

Deiss, Lucien. *Mary, Daughter of Sion.* Collegeville, MN: Liturgical Press, 1972.

Donnelly, Doris, ed. *Mary Woman of Nazareth: Biblical and Theological Perspectives.* New York: Paulist, 1989.

Elliott, J. K. *The Apocryphal New Testament.* Oxford: Clarendon Press, 1993.

Erasmus, *The Handbook of the Militant Christian.* ETr. John P. Dolan. New York, 1965.

Feuillet, A. "The Messiah and His Mother According to Apocalypse XII," in *Johannine Studies.* Staten Island, NY: Alba House, 1965.

Fitzmyer, Joseph. *The Gospel According to Luke*, 2 vols. Ed. W. F. Albright and D. N. Freedman. Garden City, NY: Doubleday, 1981–85.

Flanagan, Donal. *The Theology of Mary*, no. 30, Theology Today Series. Hales Corner, WI: Clergy Book service, 1978.

__________. "Eschatology and the Assumption," *Concilium* 41 (1969): 135–46.

Flanagan, Neal M. "Mary of Nazareth: Woman for all Seasons," *Marianum* 48 (1986): 154–69.

__________. "The Mother of the Lord: An Ecumenical Presentation," *Marianum* 37 (1975): 253–61.

Ford, J. Massyngberde. *Revelation.* The Anchor Bible. Ed. W. F. Albright and D. W. Freedman. Garden City, NY: Doubleday, 1975.

France, R. T. *Matthew.* Tyndale New Testament Commentaries. Leicester: InterVarsity Press, 1985.

Fuller, Reginald H. "New Testament Roots to the Theotokos," *Marian Studies* 29 (1978): 46–64.

Gardner, Richard B. *Matthew.* Believers Church Bible Commentary. Scottsdale, P.A.: Herald Press, 1991.

Gaventa, Beverly R. *Mary: Glimpses of the Mother of Jesus.* Columbia: University of South Carolina, 1995.

Gibson, Elsie. "Mary and the Protestant Mind," *Review for Religious* 24 (1965) 397.

Gottfried, Maron, "Mary in Protestant Theology," in *Mary in the Churches.* Ed. Hans Küng and Jürgen Moltmann. ETr. Marcus Lefébure. New York: T. & T. Clark, 1983.

Graef, Hilda. Mary: *A History of Doctrine and Devotion*, 2 vols. New York: Sheed and Ward, 1964–65.

Grassi, Joseph A. "The Role of Jesus' Mother in John's Gospel: A Reappraisal," *CBQ* 48/1 (1986): 67–80.

Graystone, G. *Virgin of all Virgins: The Interpretation of Luke 1:34*. Rome: Pio X, 1968.

Gregg, J. A. F. *The Primitive Faith and Roman Catholic Developments*. Dublin, 1928.

Gundry, Robert. *Matthew: A Commentary for His Handbook on a Mixed Church Under Persecution*, 2d ed. Grand Rapids: Eerdmans, 1994.

Hartdegen, Stephen. "The Marian Significance of Cana," *Marian Studies* 11 (1960): 85–103.

Hartmann, G. "Mark 3,20f.," *BZ* 11 (1913): 249–79.

Hughes, P. E. *The Book of Revelation: A Commentary*. Leicester, ENG: IVP, 1990.

Humenay, Robert L. "The Place of Mary in Luke: A Look at Modern Biblical Criticism," *American Ecclesiastical Review* 168/5 (May 1974): 291–303.

Isaacs, M. E. "Mary in the Lucan Infancy Narrative," *The Way Supplement* 25 (1975): 80–95.

Jelly, Frederick. "Mary's Intercession: A Contemporary Reappraisal," *Marian Studies* 32 (1981):76–95.

Johnson, Alan. "Revelation," *Expositor's Bible Commentary*, vol. 12. Ed. F. Gaebelein; Grand Rapids: Zondervan, 1981.

Johnson, Elizabeth. "Mary and the Image of God," in *Mary Woman of Nazareth: Biblical and Theological Perspectives*. Ed. Doris Donnelly. New York: Paulist, 1989.

Kalogirou, John. *Maria, the Ever-Virgin Theotókos according to the Orthodox Faith*. Salonica, 1957.

Keating Karl, *Catholicism and Fundamentalism : The Attack on "Romanism" by "Bible Christians."* San Francisco: Ignatius Press, 1988.

Kress, R. "Immaculate Conception—God's Gift to the World," *Emmanuel* 85 (1979): 636–41.

Kugelman, Richard. "The Object of Mary's Consent in the Annunciation," *Marian Studies* 11 (1960): 60–84.

Küng, Hans and Jürgen Moltmann, eds. *Mary in the Churches*. ETr. Marcus Lefébure. New York: T. & T. Clark, 1983.

Lambrecht, J. "The Relatives of Jesus in Mark," *NovT* 16 (1974): 241–58.

Landry, David T. "Narrative Logic in the Annunciation to Mary (Luke 1:26–38)," *JBL* 114/1 (1995): 65–79.

Laurentin, René. *Queen of Heaven*. London: Burns, Oates and Washbourne, 1956.

__________. *The Question of Mary*. ETr. I. G. Pidoux. New York: Holt, Rinehart and Winston, 1965.

__________. *The Truth of Christmas Beyond the Myths*. Petersham, MA: St. Bede's Publications, 1986.

__________. "Pluralism about Mary: Biblical and Contemporary," *The Way suppl.* 45 (1982): 78–91.

LaVerdiere, Eugene. "His Mother Mary," *Emmanuel* 93 (1987): 191–97.

__________. "The Virgin's Name Was Mary," *Emmanuel* 92 (1986): 185–89.

Le Frois, B. *The Woman Clothed with the Sun (Ap. 12): Individual or Collective?* Rome: Orbis catholicus, 1954.

Lightfoot, J. B. *The Epistle of St. Paul to the Galatians*. Second reprint ed. Grand Rapids: Zondervan, 1957.

Lindars, Barnabas. *The Gospel of John*. London: Oliphants, 1972.

Lonsdale, David, S.J. "Mary and the New Testament," *The Way* 24 (1984): 133–45.

Louw, Johannes P. and Eugene A. Nida, eds. *Greek-English Lexicon of the New Testament Based on Semantic Domains*. Second edition. New York: United Bible Society, 1989.

Luz, Ulrich. *Matthew 1–7: A Commentary*. ETr. W. C. Linss. Minneapolis, 1989.

Madrid, Patrick. *Any Friend of God's is a Friend of Mine*. San Diego: Basilica Press, 1996.

Maloney, George. Mary: *The Womb of God*. Denville, NJ: Dimension Books, 1976.

Marshall, I. Howard. *The Gospel of Luke: A Commentary on the Greek Text*. NIGTC. Grand Rapids: Eerdmans, 1978.

Martin, Ralph P. *Mark: Evangelist and Theologian*. Grand Rapids: Zondervan, 1973.

May, Eric E. "The Problems of a Biblical Mariology," *Marian Studies* 11 (1960): 21–59.

McHugh, John. *The Mother of Jesus in the New Testament*. Garden City: Doubleday, 1975.

McKenzie, John. "The Mother of Jesus in the New Testament," in *Mary in the Churches*. Ed. Hans Küng and Jürgen Moltmann. ETr. Marcus Lefébure. New York: T. & T. Clark, 1983.

Meier, John P. *A Marginal Jew: Rethinking the Historical Jesus*, vol. 1. New York: Doubleday, 1991.

__________. "The Brothers and Sisters of Jesus in Ecumenical Perspective," *CBQ* 54/1 (1992): 1–28.

__________. "Jesus in Josephus: A Modest Proposal," *CBQ* (1990): 76–103.

Mercurio, Roger. "Some Difficult Marian Passages in the Gospels," *Marian Studies* 11 (1960): 104–122.

Metzger, B. M. *A Textual Commentary on the Greek New Testament*. Stuttgart: Biblia-Druck, 1975 (=1971).

Michaels, J. Ramsey. *Revelation*. IVP New Testament Commentary Series. Ed. Grant Osborne. Downers Grove, IL: IVP, 1997.

M'Neile, A. H. *The Gospel According to St. Matthew*. New York: St. Martin's Press, 1961.

Moloney, Francis J. *Mary: Woman and Mother*. Collegeville: Liturgical Press, 1988.

Moltmann, Jürgen. "Editorial: Can there be an Ecumenical Mary?," in *Mary in the Churches*. Ed. Hans Küng and Jürgen Moltmann. ETr. Marcus Lefébure. New York: T. & T. Clark, 1983.

Morris, Leon. *The Gospel According to Matthew*. Grand Rapids: Eerdmans, 1992.

__________. *The Gospel According to John*. NICNT; Grand Rapids: Eerdmans, 1971.

Most, William G. "The Nature of Marian Mediation," *Ephemerides Mariologicae* 26 (1976): 177–94.

————. "Unscriptural Marian Doctrine?" *HomPasRev* 94 (1994): 60–63.

Mounce, Robert H. *The Book of Revelation*. NICNT. Ed. F. F. Bruce. Grand Rapids: Eerdmans, 1977.

Nelson, Richard D. "David: A Model for Mary in Luke?," *Biblical Theological Bulletin* 18/4 (Oct. 1998): 138–142.

Nissiotis, Nikos, "Mary in Orthodox Theology," in *Mary in the Churches*. Ed. Hans Küng and Jürgen Moltmann. ETr. Marcus Lefébure. New York: T. & T. Clark, 1983.

Oberman, Heiko. *The Harvest of Medieval Theology*. Cambridge, MA: Harvard University Press, 1963. (see esp. "Mariological Rules," 304–308.

————. *The Virgin Mary in Evangelical Perspective*. Philadelphia: Fortress, 1971.

O'Carroll, Michael. *Theotokos: A Theological Encyclopedia of the Blessed Virgin Mary*. Willmington, DE: Michael Glazier, Inc., 1982

O'Connor, J. T. "Mary, Mother of God and Contemporary Challenges," *Marian Studies* 29 (1978): 26–45.

————. "Modern Christologies and Mary's Place Therein: Dogmatic Aspects," *Marian Studies* 32 (1981): 51–75.

O'Connor, William R. "The Spiritual Maternity of Our Lady in Tradition," *Marian Studies* 3 (1952): 142–173.

Papadopoulos, S. "The ever Virgin Mary," *Religious and Ethics Encyclopedia*, vol. 1. Athens, 1962.

Pelikan, Jaroslav. *Reformation of Church and Dogma (1300–1700)*. Chicago: University of Chicago Press, 1984.

————. *The Growth of Medieval Theology*. Chicago: University of Chicago, 1978.

Perkins, Pheme. "Mary in the Johannine Traditions," in *Mary Woman of Nazareth: Biblical and Theological Perspectives*. Ed. Doris Donnelly. New York: Paulist, 1989.

Piepkorn, Arthur. "Mary's Place Within the People of God According to Non-Roman Catholics," *Marian Studies* 18 (1967): 46–83.

Plummer, A. *An Exegetical Commentary on the Gospel According to S. Matthew*. London: Paternoster, 1909.

Rahner, Karl. *Mary, Mother of the Lord*. ETr. W. J. O'Hare. New York: Herder and Herder, 1963=1956.

Reese, James M. "The Historical Image of Mary in the New Testament," *Marian Studies* 28 (1977): 27–44.

Reuther, Rosemary R. *Mary—The Feminine Face of the Church*. London, 1979.

————. "The Collision of History and Doctrine: The Brothers of Jesus and the Virginity of Mary," *Continuum* 7/1 (1969–70): 93–105.

Ridderbos, H. *The Gospel of John*. ETr. John Vriend. Grand Rapids: Eerdmans, 1991.

Rohr, Richard. "The Church Without Mary," in *Mary, The Spirit, and the Church*. Ed. Vincent Branick. New York: Paulist, 1980.

Schepers, B. "The Holy Remnant and the Immaculate Virgin," *The Bible Today* (1965): 1376–82.

Schillebeeckx, Edward. *Mary, Mother of the Redemption*. ETr. N. D. Smith. New York: Sheed and Ward, 1964=1954.

Schnackenburg, R. *The Gospel According to St. John*, 3 vols. New York: Seabury Press, 1980.

Schreck, Alan. *Catholic and Christian: An Explanation of Commonly Misunderstood Catholic Beliefs*. Ann Arbor: Servant Books, 1984.

Senior, Donald. "Gospel Portrait of Mary: Images and Symbols from the Synoptic Tradition," in *Mary Woman of Nazareth: Biblical and Theological Perspectives*. Ed. Doris Donnelly. New York: Paulist, 1989.

Sherwood, P. "Byzantine Mariology," *Eastern Churches Quarterly* 14 (8, 1962): 384–410.

Shinners, John, Jr. "The Cult of Mary and Popular Belief," in *Mary Woman of Nazareth: Biblical and Theological Perspectives*. Ed. Doris Donnelly. New York: Paulist, 1989.

Sklba, Richard J. "Mary and the 'Anawim," in *Mary Woman of Nazareth: Biblical and Theological Perspectives*. Ed. Doris Donnelly. New York: Paulist, 1989.

Smith, Patricia. "Will the Mary of History Please Stand Up? *Emmanuel* 93 (1987): 187–213.

Svendsen, Eric. *Evangelical Answers: A Critique of Current Roman Catholic Apologists*. Lindenhurst, NY: Reformation Press, 1999.

__________. *The Table of the Lord: An Examination of the Setting of the Lord's Supper in the New Testament and its Significance as an Expression of Community*. Atlanta: New Testament Restoration Foundation, 1996.

Tambasco, Anthony J. *What are They Saying About Mary?* New York: Paulist, 1984.

Thomas, Robert L. *Revelation 8–22: An Exegetical Commentary*. Chicago: Moody Press, 1995.

Thrall, M. E. *Greek Particles in the New Testament: Linguistic and Exegetical Studies*. Grand Rapids: Eerdmans, 1962.

Turner, Nigel. *Syntax: A Grammar of New Testament Greek*, vol. III. Ed. J. H. Moulton. Edinburgh: T. & T. Clark, 1963.

Unger, Dominic. "Does the New Testament Give Much Historical Information about the Blessed Virgin or Mostly Symbolic Meanings?" *Marianum* 39 (1977): 323–47. [conservative]

Wall, Robert W. *Revelation*. NIBC. Ed. W. W. Gasque. Peabody, MA: Hendrickson, 1991.

Wansbrough, H. "Mark iii.21—Was Jesus Out of His Mind?" *NTS* 18 (1971–72): 233–35.

__________. "Mother and Disciple," *Priests & People* 2 (1988): 125–29.

Wenham, D. "The Meaning of Mark III.21," *NTS* 21 (1974–75): 295–300.

Westcott, B. F. *The Gospel According to St. John*. Grand Rapids: Eerdmans, 1958.

White, James R. *Mary—Another Redeemer?* Minneapolis: Bethany House, 1998.

Willoughby, A. *St. Matthew*. ICC. New York: Charles Scribner's Sons, 1913.

Zerwick, Max. "The Hour of the Mother—John 19:25–27," in *The Bible Today Reader*. Collegeville: Liturgical Press, 1973.

__________. *A Grammatical Analysis of the Greek New Testament*, 3d rev. ed. Rome: Pontifical Biblical Institute, 1988.

Eric Svendsen holds a Master of Arts in New Testament studies from Trinity Evangelical Divinity School, a Doctorate in Theological Studies from Columbia Evangelical Seminary, and has recently completed his dissertation for a Ph.D. in New Testament from Greenwich School of Theology, U.K. He is the founder and director of New Testament Research Ministries, an apologetics ministry specializing in Roman Catholic/Evangelical dialogue. He has authored several books, including *Evangelical Answers: A Critique of Current Roman Catholic Apologists* (Lindenhurst, N.Y.: Reformation Press, 1999), *The Table of the Lord: An Examination of the Setting of the Lord's Supper in the New Testament and Its Significance as an Expression of Community* (New Testament Restoration Foundation, 1996), *Getting To Know Your Bible: A Two-Year Plan for Becoming a Bible Expert in Just 30 Minutes a Day!* (Denver: New Testament Research Ministries, 2001), and *Learning to Master Your Bible: A Guide to Plumbing the Depths of God's Word* (Denver: New Testament Research Ministries, 2001). Dr. Svendsen is active in engaging anti-Christians in public debate, and has appeared as a guest on numerous Christian radio talk shows. You may contact Eric Svendsen through his ministry's web site at www.ntrmin.org.

NOTES

Prolegomena—An Overview of Mariology

1. The authors of *Mary in the New Testament* (Raymond Brown et al, eds., Philadelphia: Fortress Press, 1978) devote an entire chapter to cryptic Marian references in Romans, Galatians and Philippians with no substantial findings (33-49). (The aforementioned work is commonly known as *MNT*, and its authors as the *MNT* taskforce. This nomenclature will be used throughout this work). See also Raymond Brown ("Mary in the New Testament and in Catholic Life," *America* [May 15, 1982]), who points out that "the great Apostle of the Gentiles could preach the gospel and yet not mention Mary," and that "we know not a single New Testament detail about Mary in history after Pentecost" (374-75). There are indeed a few Pauline passages that have indirect Marian significance—those that mention the "brothers" of Jesus—but none of these is favorable to the Roman Catholic view of Mary. These passages will be dealt with in a subsequent chapter that specifically examines Jesus' biological relations, so that no special examination of Paul's writings is necessary.
2. Maron Gottfried, "Mary in Protestant Theology," in *Mary in the Churches* (ed. Hans Küng and Jürgen Moltmann; Etr. Marcus Lefébure; New York: T. & T. Clark, 1983), 45-46.
3. *MNT*, 8 n. 15.
4. Küng, "Editorial," in *Mary in the Churches* (ed. Hans Küng and Jürgen Moltmann; Etr. Marcus Lefébure; New York: T. & T. Clark, 1983), vii.
5. John McKenzie, "The Mother of Jesus in the New Testament," in ibid., 4.
6. Jürgen Moltmann, "Editorial: Can there be an Ecumenical Mary?" in ibid., xii.
7. Anthony J. Tambasco, *What Are They Saying About Mary?* (New York: Paulist, 1984), 3.
8. Ibid., 8.
9. Ibid., 10.
10. Ibid., 5.
11. Ibid., 10.

12. Ibid., 9-11 passim.

13. Ibid., 11.

14. Ibid., 16. Tambasco goes on to ask whether confessional formulas, such as "born of the Virgin Mary," are simply symbolic (as opposed to historical) statements intended to convey truths about the divinity of Jesus (ibid., 19), and concludes that it is legitimate to view this as a mere theological symbol "which has simply been presumed to be historical" (ibid., 23).

15. Walter M. Abbot, ed., *The Documents of Vatican II*, 730-731.

16. McKenzie, 9. McKenzie's words are stated in relation to the teaching of the NT, not to the teaching of the Roman Catholic church.

17. Elizabeth Johnson, "Mary and the Image of God," in *Mary Woman of Nazareth: Biblical and Theological Perspectives* (ed. Doris Donnelly; New York: Paulist, 1989), 38-39.

18. Tambasco, 74.

19. Ibid.

20. Nikos Nissiotis, "Mary in Orthodox Theology," in *Mary in the Churches* (ed. Hans Küng and Jürgen Moltmann; Etr. Marcus Lefébure; New York: T. & T. Clark, 1983), 36.

21. Kari Børresen, "Mary in Catholic Theology," in ibid., 55.

22. Richard Kugelman, "The Object of Mary's Consent in the Annunciation," *Marian Studies* 11 (1960): 75.

23. Børresen, 51.

24. Ibid.

25. Nissiotis, 31.

26. See Pope Pius XII's *Bull Munificentissimus Deus* (1950).

27. Some who affirm that Mary died point to Pius XII's *Munificentissimus Deus*, in which he mentions Mary's "death" several times. There are theological ramifications, however, if Mary, who was supposedly sinless, died. According to John Damascene (from whence this tradition originates):

> St. Juvenal, Bishop of Jerusalem, at the Council of Chalcedon (451), made known to the Emperor Marcian and Pulcheria, who wished to possess the body of the Mother of God, that Mary died in the presence of all the Apostles, but that her tomb, when opened, upon the request of St. Thomas, was found empty; wherefrom the Apostles concluded that the body was taken up to heaven.

According to this tradition Mary was not put to death, but rather died of natural causes. But since death is the consequence of sin (Rom 6:23), that naturally raises the question as to how someone who is sinless can die in this way.

28. Nissiotis, 33.

29. See chapter 9 of this work. Even as late as the 13th century, Aquinas rejects this interpretation in favor of identifying the "woman" as the church.

30. *MNT*, 266.

31. Ibid.

32. Ibid.

33. Donald Senior, "Gospel Portrait of Mary: Images and Symbols from the Synoptic Tradition," in *Mary Woman of Nazareth: Biblical and Theological Perspectives* (ed. Doris Donnelly; New York: Paulist, 1989), 92.

34. Tambasco, 39.

35. Ibid., 40.

36. Ibid., 46-48 passim.

37. Pheme Perkins, "Mary in the Johannine Traditions," in *Mary Woman of Nazareth: Biblical and Theological Perspectives* (ed. Doris Donnelly; New York: Paulist, 1989), 110.

38. McKenzie, 4 (emphasis in original).

39. This survey makes no pretence of being a complete history of Mariology. Such an endeavor would require an entire work be devoted to it. For such a treatment, see the two volume set by Hilda Graef, *Mary: A History of Doctrine and Devotion* (New York: Sheed and Ward, 1964-65). Indeed, there are many historical considerations not addressed in this survey that will be taken up when examining the specific passages related to Mariology in the NT.

40. Perkins, 116; cf. also Børresen, 50.

41. Perkins, 116.

42. Ibid.

43. Ibid.

44. One exception to this is the second-century apocryphal work, the *Protoevangelium of James*. This writing will be examined in depth in chapter 3 of this work.

45. *MNT*, 65, n. 116.

46. Tambasco, 24.

47. McKenzie, 7.

48. The first instance is found in Caelius Sedulius, *Salve sancta parens*.

49. Moltmann, vii-viii.

50. Johnson, "Mary and the Image of God," 31.

51. Ibid., 32.

52. John Shinners, Jr., "The Cult of Mary and Popular Belief," in *Mary Woman of Nazareth: Biblical and Theological Perspectives* (ed. Doris Donnelly; New York: Paulist, 1989), 164.

53. Børresen, 48-49.

54. Ibid., 49.

55. Johnson, "Mary and the Image of God," 36.

56. Shinners, 164-65.

57. McKenzie, 4 (emphasis in original).

58. Shinners, 170.

59. Cited in Shinners, 170.

60. Cited in ibid. (italics mine).

61. Johnson, "Mary and the Image of God," 34.

62. Shinners, 172.

63. Erasmus, *The Handbook of the Militant Christian*. Etr. John P. Dolan. New York, 1965, p. 66.
64. Shinners, 172.
65. McKenzie, 7. This "fittingness" argument is usually traced to Duns Scotus.
66. Johnson, "Mary and the Image of God," 35.
67. Ibid., 35.
68. Ibid., 36.
69. Patricia Smith, "Will the Mary of History Please Stand Up? *Emmanuel* 93 (1987): 188.

I. Marian Issues in Matthew 1:18–25

1. For a detailed summary of this discussion see D. A. Carson, "Matthew," *The Expositor's Bible Commentary*, vol. 8 (ed. Frank E. Gaebelein; Grand Rapids: Zondervan, 1976), 71-81; and John McHugh, *The Mother of Jesus in the New Testament* (Garden City: Doubleday, 1975), 278-342.
2. There are two instances of variant readings in the phrase "the birth of Jesus Christ" (Ἰησοῦ Χριστοῦ ἡ γένεσις). The reading adopted by NA26 for the first variant, Ἰησοῦ Χριστοῦ, is supported by 𝔓¹ ℵ C L Z Δ Θ *f*1 28 33 565 579 700 892 and a good number of minuscules, enjoying wide geographic distribution. Aside from the aid of B in the reading Χριστοῦ Ἰησοῦ, the other two variants have only scant support (the other variant is Χριστοῦ). The second part of the phrase adopted by NA26 is γένεσις, which gains support from many of the aforementioned mss. (𝔓¹ ℵ C Θ *f*¹ 579), but this time also from B. The variant γέννησις is supported primarily (though not insignificantly) by L *f*¹³ 28 33 565 700 892, and has much additional minuscule and patristic support as well.
3. Several witnesses, including D 267 954 1582*vid and it^{a?b,c,d}, have Ἡσαΐου before τοῦ προφήτου. However, its absence from the majority of mss., as well as its limited distribution, point here to a scribal gloss; see B. M. Metzger, *A Textual Commentary on the Greek New Testament* (Stuttgart: Biblia-Druck, 1975), 8.
4. NA26 has adopted the reading υἱόν, supported by ℵ B Z *f*¹ *f*¹³ and 33. The variant τὸν υἱὸν αὐτῆς τὸν πρωτότοκον, almost certainly a harmonization of Luke 2:7, is supported less significantly by C D^C (D* and L omit αὐτῆς) W Δ 28 565 579 892 and a handful of minuscules.
5. All quotations of Scripture in this work are taken from the *NIV* unless otherwise noted.
6. Both Chrysostom (*Homily on the Gospel of St. Matthew* 4:5) and Jerome (*Against Helvidius* 1:4) subscribed to the former.
7. Cf. the lexicons of Liddell & Scott and *BAGD*. Wis 7:2 seems to be the only other occurrence with this meaning in the literature of the OT, NT and Apocrypha. W. Mundle, "Come," *The New International Dictionary of New Testament Theology*, vol. 3 (ed. Colin Brown; Grand Rapids: Zondervan/Exeter: Paternoster, 1975–78), 322, cites 1 Cor 7:5 ("Then

come together again so that Satan will not tempt you") as an instance of συνέρχομαι. Unfortunately, the Greek has πάλιν ἐπὶ τὸ αὐτὸ ἦτε, not συνέρχομαι.

8. McHugh, 158.

9. The evidence for this is more appropriately addressed in a discussion of Luke's birth narrative, and so will be taken up in that chapter of this work. This and other first-century Jewish marriage practices are detailed in *MNT*, 83-84.

10. McHugh, 163.

11. Matthew alludes here to the two-step marriage process of that time. In the first step, *'êrûsin* (betrothal, which is a "legally ratified marriage" [*MNT*, 114 n. 241]), the couple exchanged vows before witnesses but continued to live separately for a period of about a year. In the second step, *nîśû'in*, the husband received the woman into his home, initiated regular marital relations with her, and took financial responsibility for her (ibid., 84).

12. Our understanding of the phrase "before they came together" is undoubtedly the earliest one. Irenaeus writes: "To this effect [the prophets, elders, apostles] were [saying,] that before Joseph had come together with Mary, *while she therefore remained in virginity*, she was found with child of the Holy Ghost'," *Against Heresies* 3.21. Such a statement clearly shows that Irenaeus understood the phrase to be speaking of a time before normal marital relations ensued.

13. Senior, 98.

14. *MNT*, 84-85 n. 174.

15. Ibid.

16. McHugh, 165.

17. Ibid., 166.

18. Ibid.

19. Ibid.

20. Ibid.

21. Ibid., 166-67.

22. Ibid., 167-68.

23. Ibid., 168. This word is translated variously as "publicly expose" (Douay-Rheims), "expose to public disgrace" (*NIV*), "disgrace" (*NASB*), "make a public example" (*KJV*), "expose to shame" (*NAB*), and "put to shame" (*RSV*).

24. Ibid.

25. Ibid., 169.

26. McHugh is no doubt correct when he notes that the angel's title for Joseph as "son of David" is Matthew's way of showing the necessity of Joseph's role in ensuring that the Messiah would be born in the line of David: "Matthew assumes [the virginal conception], and seeks to resolve the consequent problem: if Jesus was virginally conceived, how could he be of the line of David," 172.

27. McHugh, 171.

28. Ibid.

29. John 19:7: "The Jews insisted, 'We have a law, and according to that law he must die, because he claimed to be the Son of God.'" Cf. John 18:31, "But we have no right to execute anyone."

30. The rest of the passage reads: "and if after she leaves his house she becomes the wife of another man, and her second husband dislikes her and writes her a certificate of divorce, gives it to her and sends her from his house, or if he dies, then her first husband, who divorced her, is not allowed to marry her again after she has been defiled. That would be detestable in the eyes of the LORD" (Deut 24:2-4).

31. Carson, "Matthew," suggests that Joseph may have viewed Num 5:11-31 (as interpreted by the Mishnah *Sotah* 1:1-5) as his guide in this situation (75). But the differences in the respective actions of Joseph and the husband of Numbers 5 seem too great for a parallel to be sustained.

32. McHugh, 169.

33. See also Max Zerwick, *A Grammatical Analysis of the Greek New Testament* (3d rev. ed.; Rome: Pontifical Biblical Institute, 1988), 1, who has "make an example of."

34. "Secretly," Zerwick, *Grammatical Analysis*, 1.

35. McHugh admits that this was the view of Augustine, Jerome and Chrysostom, 170. He also cites some less significant patristic witnesses to his own view; Eusebius of Caesarea, Pseudo-Basil, and Pseudo-Origen.

36. Beverly Gaventa, *Mary: Glimpses of the Mother of Jesus* (Studies on Personalities in the New Testament; ed. D. Moody Smith; University of South Carolina Press, 1995), 41.

37. Φοβέω has the same connotation here as it does in 2 Cor 11:3, 12:20 and Gal 4:11, and simply means "concern."

39. Carson, "Matthew," 75.

39. Ibid., "It would leave his righteousness…and his compassion intact." Although Carson insists that "righteousness" be viewed here as "conformity to the law," he nevertheless sees the element of compassion as bound up in this definition.

40. As it does in the case of Mary's statement in Luke 1:34. See also Gen 4:1 and 1 Sam 1:19.

41. F. D. Brunner, *The Christbook: A Historical/Theological Commentary* (Waco: Word Books, 1987), 37; R. T. France, *Matthew* (Tyndale New Testament Commentaries; Leicester: InterVarsity Press, 1985), 80; and to some extent, Craig Blomberg, *Matthew* (The New American Commentary, vol. 22; ed. David S. Dockery; Nashville: Broadman Press, 1992), 61.

42. Karl Keating, *Catholicism and Fundamentalism: The Attack on "Romanism" by "Bible Christians"* (San Francisco: Ignatius Press, 1988), 285. So also D. J. Harrington, *The Gospel of Matthew* (Collegeville: Liturgical Press, 1991), 36.

43. Keating, 285. He also cites the apocryphal passage 1 Macc 5:54.

44. Ibid. Roman Catholic apologists often cite Calvin's comments on this

passage as though he were in support of Mary's perpetual virginity. However, in so doing they misrepresent Calvin who says simply:

> Let us rest satisfied with this, that no just and well-grounded inference can be drawn from these words of the Evangelist, as to what took place after the birth of Christ…. It is said that Joseph knew her not till she had brought forth her first-born son: but this is limited to that very time. What took place afterwards, the historian (Matthew) does not inform us. Such is well known to have been the practice of the inspired writers. Certainly, no man will obstinately keep up the argument, except from an extreme fondness for disputation (*Harmony of the Gospels*, vol. 1).

All Calvin intends to relay to us is that we do not know *from this passage* whether or not Mary remained a virgin (although, even here it must be noted that Calvin shows no knowledge of the usage of the Greek phrase used in this passage, for which see below). Yet, when this is compared to Calvin's comments elsewhere, his belief that Mary in fact did not remain a virgin clearly emerges (see the note on Luke 1:34 later in this work).

45. Keating's use of Gen 8:7 is unfortunately based on a bad translation of the Hebrew and does not make the point Keating thinks it does. Keating cites the Douay-Rheims version of the passage ("went forth and did not return, till the waters were dried up") and then states: "In fact, we know the raven never returned at all," ibid. The Hebrew וַיֵּצֵא יָצוֹא וָשׁוֹב עַד־יְבֹשֶׁת הַמָּיִם, however, is better reflected in the newer Catholic translation the *NAB*: "It flew back and forth until the waters dried," which is essentially the same rendition given by the *NIV* ("it kept flying back and forth until the water had dried up") and the *NASB* ("which went forth to and fro, until the waters were dried up"). Obviously, the flying back and forth could have lasted only until the water dried up and need not have continued after that point, making Keating's use of this passage precarious.

46. The argument of Ulrich Luz, *Matthew 1–7: A Commentary* (Etr. W. C. Linss; Minneapolis, 1989), 124, and Alan Schreck, *Catholic and Christian: An Explanation of Commonly Misunderstood Catholic Beliefs* (Ann Arbor: Servant Books, 1984), 175, are similarly flawed; as is that of David Currie, *Born Fundamentalist: Born Again Catholic* (San Francisco: Ignatius Press, 1996), 158, who cites Ps 110:1 ("Sit at my right hand until I make your enemies a footstool for your feet") in support of the Catholic interpretation of Matt 1:25. Unfortunately for Currie, the writer there uses ἕως ἄν, not ἕως οὗ.

47. There are 1,564 occurrences in the OT and Apocrypha.

48. F. Blass and A. Debrunner, eds. (*A Greek Grammar of the New Testament and Other Early Christian Literature* [ETr. and ed. R. W. Funk; Chicago: University of Chicago, 1961], §216 [3]), cite other constructions as well, including ἕως πότε, ἕως κάτω, ἕως ἄρτι, ἕως σήμερον. But these types of

constructions are outside of our scope since each of the accompanying words are stand-alone words and not mere particles.

49. 1,454 times in the OT and Apocrypha.

50. Leon Morris, *The Gospel According to Matthew* (Grand Rapids: Eerdmans, 1992), 32, has rightly noted that, because of the number of occurrences, "until" is primarily a Matthean word.

51. It is not likely that this should be seen primarily as a reference to time (i.e., "from *the time of* Abraham to *the time of* David") since the author intends to count generations here, not to show spans of time.

52. According to *BDF*, ἕως was "originally entirely a conjunction and became a preposition only in the Hellenistic period," §216. See also N. Turner, *Syntax: A Grammar of New Testament Greek*, vol. III (ed. J. H. Moulton; Edinburgh: T. & T. Clark, 1963), 276.

53. The only instance where it has the conjunctive meaning "until" is found in Matt 2:9, "[The star] went ahead of them *until* it stopped over the place where the child was."

54. *BDF*, §216 (3).

55. But perhaps only twenty-eight if we exclude from this subset Matt 11:13 and Luke 17:8.

56. Perhaps thirteen if we include Matt 11:13 in this subset.

57. Though Luke 17:8 may be included in this category as well, putting the total at four.

58. There are 105 occurrences in the OT and Apocrypha.

59. The four exceptions are Matt 2:13, 5:26, 10:11, and Mark 6:10. The latter two are parallel passages.

60. There are six altogether. In addition to Matt 10:11 we may also mention Matt 2:13; 5:26; 23:39; Mark 6:10; and 1 Cor 4:5.

61. There are fourteen occurrences of this construction in the OT and Apocrypha.

62. See, e.g., *BDF*, §383.

63. There are eighty-five occurrences in the OT and Apocrypha.

64. Contra the puzzling statement by *BDF* that ἕως οὗ "only means 'until' as in classical," §455. But see *BAGD*.

65. See Eric Svendsen, *The Table of the Lord: An Examination of the Setting of the Lord's Supper in the New Testament and its Significance as an Expression of Community* (Atlanta: New Testament Restoration Foundation, 1996), 111-145 passim.

66. Luke 15:8 is not included in this category since the negative there is used to introduce a question, not to negate the action of the main clause.

67. *MNT*, 86.

68. Ibid., 86-87, n. 177. So also Harrington, 36: "The text neither confirms nor denies the perpetual virginity of Mary." Protestant scholars who take this view include Robert Gundry, *Matthew: A Commentary for His Handbook on a Mixed Church Under Persecution*, 2d ed. (Grand Rapids: Eerdmans, 1994), 25, who says, "By itself ἕως οὗ, which belongs to Matthew's preferred

diction (4,2), does not necessarily imply that Joseph and Mary entered into normal sexual relations after Jesus' birth"; Richard B. Gardner, *Matthew* (Believers Church Bible Commentary; Scottsdale, P.A.: Herald Press, 1991), 41, who states that "the language of the text leaves open the question of how Joseph and Mary related to each other *after* Jesus' birth"; and to some degree Blomberg who states, "The grammatical construction translated 'until' strongly suggests (but does not prove) that Mary and Joseph proceeded to have normal sexual relations after Jesus' birth" (61). Protestant scholars who see significance in this phrase include Brunner, who notes that "the burden of proof rests on those who would contest the simple meaning of the word *until*" (37); and France who states that "the Greek expression for *not until* would normally suggest that intercourse did take place after the end of this period.... There is no biblical warrant for the tradition of the 'perpetual virginity' of Mary" (80).

69. The meaning of ἕως οὗ in the LXX (and the other literature related to the NT) will be the subject of another study in this work.

70. Nor does ἕως ὅτου have this meaning.

71. Contra Keating's unfortunate statement that "until" in the Bible "means only that some action did not happen up to a certain point; it does not imply that the action did happen later," 285. A. H. M'Neile, *The Gospel According to St. Matthew* (New York: St. Martin's Press, 1961), 10, swings too far in the opposite direction when he applies this rule to ἕως categorically (but he does not consider Matt 24:21, although this rule certainly seems to apply to ἕως ὅτου with the negative).

72. This point is strengthened by the observation of A. Plummer, *An Exegetical Commentary on the Gospel According to S. Matthew* (London: Paternoster, 1909), that the imperfect ἐγίνωσκεν is more forceful than even the aorist would have been: "it hardly needs argument that, in such a context, 'he used not to' or 'he was not in the habit of' means more than 'he did not.' It is quite true that the aorist, 'he knew her not until,' would have implied that she subsequently had children by him. But the imperfect implies this still more strongly," 9. See also A. Willoughby, *St. Matthew* (ICC; New York: Charles Scribner's Sons, 1913), 10. Contra McHugh (204) who argues just the opposite.

73. Cf. also Matt 10:23; 12:20; 16:28; 22:44.

74. Contra Currie, who thinks, "there is simply no Bible passage that refutes Mary's perpetual virginity.... There [is] no proof either way in Scripture," 158-59. In support of his view of Matthew 1:25, Currie appeals to Ps 110:1 and 2 Sam 6:23 where the English word "until" implies no continuation of the action of the main clause after the action of the subordinate clause. Unfortunately, neither passage has the construction found in Matthew 1:25. Currie betrays his loyalties early on in his discussion of Mary: "On reflection, Mary's perpetual virginity makes the most sense. Even without a vow of celibacy, can anyone doubt that Joseph would have refrained from marital relations with the woman who bore the very Son of God?," 159.

Currie's reasoning is clouded by his *a priori* devotion to Mary. It is only the mindset that views marital relations as somehow "impure" (as Currie, citing Rev 14:4, later implies, 160), or views Mary as a supernatural being—or both—that could then conclude that Joseph, as her husband, must refrain from sexual relations with her. In any case, such a conclusion is certainly not based on exegesis of the passage.

75. Compare this to the ratio of thirty to twenty-five for the entire NT. Matthew reverses the normal NT usage.

76. Just over the six to fourteen ratio for the entire NT.

77. The ratio for these two constructions combined is seven to zero (Matthew) and twenty-two to zero (the NT).

II. The Phrases ἕως οὗ and ἕως ὅτου Outside of NT

1. All translations of the LXX and the non-biblical literature that follows are the author's own unless otherwise noted.

2. There is still an intervening verb (παρῆλθον) which technically prevents ἕως οὗ from being a true preposition. Nevertheless, if we were to remove the verb and take ἕως οὗ as a prepositional phrase ("chased them to Damascus"), little would be changed as far as the meaning is concerned.

3. Based on B; A omits οὗ.

4. This usage occurs thirty-three times in the LXX.

5. Both families of the LXX text have the verb in the third person (the indicative ἀνέστη in A, and the subjunctive ἀναστῇ in B), while most translations (following the Hebrew שַׁקַּמְתִּי) render the verb in the first person.

6. Here *goal* is in mind as well, suggesting a possible telic connotation.

7. Old Greek = LXX.

8. Based on MS family BA. ℵ has μέχρι.

9. MS family BA. ℵ has πρὸ.

10. Alternatively, the first instance of ἕως οὗ may be rendered *while*: "kept her in view *while* she descended the mountain."

11. Since both 4:17 and 29:5 have *goal* in mind a secondary telic connotation may be intended.

12. This phrase also expresses a goal, and so a telic connotation cannot be ruled out.

13. Both of the Daniel texts are based on θ'; in each case the Old Greek has ἕως ὅτου.

14. E.g., 1 Enoch 89:44, 47.

15. The translation of L. C. L. Brenton, *The Septuagint with Apocrypha* (Peabody, MA: Hendrickson, 1986), 31, takes the phrase with what comes before, while the *NAB* takes it with what follows.

16. A true instance of the temporal meaning *while* usually (though not always) renders the meaning *until* senseless in the passage (cf. Cant 1:12 and John 9:4).

17. If indeed the psalmist is even thinking of such a distinction.

18. Based on θ'; the Old Greek has ἕως ἄν.

19. Based on the inferior ℵ text. BA has ἕως alone.

20. There are four other passages that may fall into this category as well; but their meanings, as we have seen, are too vague to qualify as evidence of this usage.

21. Dionysius of Halicarnassus, *Roman Antiquities* (the Loeb Classical Library; Cambridge: Harvard University Press, 1962), 4.68.2.

22. Ibid., 7.1.1.

23. Ibid., 7.59.7.

24. Alternatively known as *The Life of Adam and Eve*.

25. *The Apocalypse of Moses* 31.4, *The Old Testament Pseudepigrapha*, vol. 2 (ed. J. H. Charlesworth; Garden City: Doubleday, 1985).

26. Ibid., 40.4-6.

27. 1 Clement 50:4, *The Apostolic Fathers* (ed. Lightfoot and Harmer; Grand Rapids: Baker Books, 1984).

28. Flavius Josephus, *Jewish Antiquities* 5.19, Loeb.

29. Ibid., 6.248. Loeb actually has ἕως ἄν here; it is the Thesaurus Linguae Graecae that has ἕως οὗ.

30. Ibid., 6.272; cf. 6.273, "But David…withdrew from the city."

31. Ibid., 8.62.

32. Ibid., 8.103.

33. Ibid., 10.80.

34. Ibid., 10.134.

35. Ibid., 13.11. Loeb has ἕως ἄν here, while the Thesaurus Linguae Graecae has ἕως οὗ.

36. Ibid., 7.12.8.

37. Ibid., 13.398.

38. Ibid., 13.411–13.418. Loeb has ἕως alone; the Thesaurus Linguae Graecae has ἕως οὗ.

39. Flavius Josephus, *The Life of Josephus* 63.3–64.1, Loeb.

40. Josephus, *Jewish Antiquities*, 3.155.

41. Ibid., 3.279.

42. Heron of Alexandria, *Pneumatica* 1.2.21. The task of dealing with many of the first-century BC/AD authors is a complex one. Neither Heron's works nor (later in this work) those of Dioscorides, Archigenes, or Vitae Aesopi are readily available in English translation, if such translations exist at all. To complicate matters further, many of the passages that contain the constructions under consideration are highly fragmented, and the context is quite often missing. Consequently, all translations of these works presented in this work are the author's own. I have used dynamic equivalence where there is little question as to the meaning of the passage. In those cases where the meaning is vague or ambiguous, however, I have provided a woodenly literal translation to allow the reader to make personal exegetical judgments as to the meaning. In a few instances a Greek word used in a given passage has such a vast semantic range—or the known options make

so little sense in the context—that a firm decision in translation was impossible. In such cases I have supplied the Greek word as well as the semantic options found in the major lexicons.

43. Heron of Alexandria, *Pneumatica*, 1.2.45.

44. Ibid., 2.30.26.

45. Ibid., 2.31.14.

46. Represents an omission due to fragmentation.

47. Heron of Alexandria, *Metrica* 1.32.14.

48. Heron of Alexandria, *Dioptra* 7.19.

49. Ibid., 14.10.

50. Ibid., 16.21.

51. Ibid., 17.14.

52. Ibid., 34.71.

53. Heron of Alexandria, *Geometrica* 20.1.4.

54. Heron of Alexandria, *De automatis* 24.3.2.

55. Discorides, *de materia medica* 1.30.2.

56. Ibid., 1.68.4.

57. Ibid., 5.74.6.

58. Ibid., 5.79.6.

59. Archigenes, *Fragmenta* 11.13.

60. Represents an omission due to fragmentation.

61. Ibid., 11.15.

62. A firm decision is impossible to reach since we do not have the entire sentence to examine. However, in light of the nuance given to this phrase by Archigenes just two verses earlier, we may safely conclude that this instance follows suit.

63. *Vita W* 29.2.

64. *Vita G* 140.4.

65. 1 Enoch 89:44.

66. Ibid., 89.47.

67. Josephus, *Jewish Antiquities*, 13.343.

68. Ibid., 14.295–14.296.

69. Appian, *Roman History: Prooemium* 12, Loeb.

70. Plutarch's *Moralia: Ancient Customs of the Spartans* 240.B.3, Loeb.

71. Diodorus of Sicily, *Bibliotheca Historica* 19.108 Loeb.

72. Ibid., 19.107.

73. Ibid., 17.92 (vol. 8, 1970).

74. The time period referenced in the letter of Aristeas for the commission of the LXX is during the reign of Ptolemy II Philadelphus (283-264 BC). Although many of the claims made in the letter of Aristeas are embellished, historians generally accept as reliable the time period given for the genesis of the LXX. As for the latest date for completion of the LXX, the prologue to Sirach specifically tells us that the author found a "reproduction of our valuable teaching" (which he defines as "the law, the prophets, and the other books") while in Egypt the thirty-eighth year of the reign of Euergetes (132

BC), and therefore felt "duty bound" to likewise translate his grandfather's writings into Greek (viz., the Book of Sirach). Most scholars take the phrase "reproduction of our valuable teaching" as a reference to the LXX in its completed form. See John L. McKenzie, *Dictionary of the Bible* (New York: MacMillan Publishing, 1965), 786-87; also Sidney Jellico, *The Septuagint and Modern Study* (Winona Lake, IN: Eisenbrauns, 1989), 29-58; and the Editor's Preface of the Septuaginta (ed. A. Rahlfs; Deutsche Bibelgesellschaft Stuttgart, 1979), LVI: "As the Prologue to the Book of Ecclesiasticus [Sirach] shows, there was in existence towards the end of the 2nd century BC a Greek translation of the whole, or at least of the essential parts, of the O.T."

75. This assumes a dating of Matthew sometime after Mark's gospel (AD 50-65) and before the destruction of the temple (AD 70).

76. Nearly half of the NT occurrences of ἕως without a particle have this connotation, as do 75% of the occurrences of ἕως ἄν.

III. The Brothers of Jesus

1. All biblical references are taken from the *NIV* unless otherwise noted.

2. McHugh, 200.

3. We know of Helvidius' work only through Jerome's response to it in his *Adversus Helvidium de Virginitate beatae Mariae*.

4. A view defended by J. B. Lightfoot in his excursus "The Brethren of the Lord" included in his commentary, *The Epistle of St. Paul to the Galatians* (second reprint ed.; Grand Rapids: Zondervan, 1957), 252-91. This view has been advanced more recently by Richard Bauckham in his work, *Jude and the Relatives of Jesus in the Early Church* (Edinburgh: T. & T. Clark, 1990), 19-36. See also his defense of this view in "The Brothers and Sisters of Jesus: An Epiphanian Response to John P. Meier," *CBQ* 56/4 (1994): 686-700.

5. John P. Meier has defended this view in a number of places, including his *A Marginal Jew: Rethinking the Historical Jesus. Volume One: The Root of the Problem and the Person* (New York: Doubleday, 1991), 316-32; and in his article, "The Brothers and Sisters of Jesus in Ecumenical Perspective," *CBQ* 54/1 (1992): 1-28. Meier also points to other Catholic exegetes, such as Rudolph Pesch and the Catholic committee on the *MNT* taskforce, who likewise subscribe to the "true sibling" view, if only on a redactional level. On Pesch, Wansbrough, "Mother and Disciple" (*Priests & People* 2 [1988]: 128), notes: "Catholic scholar Rudolf Pesch published his view in 1976 that the brothers of Jesus were full brothers (*Das Markusevangelium*, p.322-325) without incurring any anathemas." Other Catholic scholars who subscribe to this view include R. Brown, J. A. Fitzmyer, J. McKenzie, and E. LaVerdiere, among others.

LaVerdiere, "His Mother Mary" (*Emmanuel* 93 [1987]: 194), explains that a Roman Catholic can at once believe that the gospels present Jesus' brothers as true siblings and that Mary remained a virgin: "We are able to accept the normal meaning of "brothers" as blood brothers. We also respect the teaching of the Church that Jesus was Mary's only child.... The reason [this] has been so problematic for many is our proneness to jump too quickly from our philological analysis of the text to historical consider-ations." In other words, in order to maintain the perpetual virginity of Mary one may accept the NT witness about her but must view these witnesses as ahistorical. The gospel writers present to us biological siblings of Jesus only so that they can in turn present Jesus rejecting these siblings in favor of "true" siblings (i.e., those who do the will of the Father), and then in turn (according to LaVerdiere) to present Mary as the model disciple who is a "figure for the life of the Church" (ibid.). A detailed analysis of LaVerdiere's "figure for the church" thesis cannot be dealt with here, but is more appro-priately developed later in this work. Suffice it here to say that, prescinding from historical considerations (which is not within the scope of this study), the scholarly consensus on both the Roman Catholic and Protestant sides is that the gospel witnesses present to us true biological siblings of Jesus.

6. McHugh, 202.

7. Lightfoot, *Galatians*, 258-59. R. Ruether, "The Collision of History and Doctrine: The Brothers of Jesus and the Virginity of Mary" (*Continuum* 7 [1969-70]), observes the historical climate of Jerome's treatise: "Jerome was in Rome at this time where he aroused no little controversy with his avid preaching of the ascetic monastic life and his corresponding denigration of marriage, child-bearing, and everything connected with the 'body.' ...The most important [opposing voice] was a monk named Jovinian.... Jerome responded to [his] criticisms with such vitriolic excesses that even his sup-porters were somewhat embarrassed.... [Jerome argued] that Joseph was not Mary's real husband, but only her putative husband,...[and concluded] by praise of the superiority of virginity over marriage and a morbid descrip-tion of marriage that removed it barely one step from the brothel" (93-94).

8. McHugh, 203-207.

9. This issue will be dealt with in detail later in this work.

10. Meier, "Brothers," 7.

11. McHugh, 224. McHugh gives no support for the fourth meaning, and doesn't include the fifth meaning in his discussion although it has strong support in the NT.

12. Ibid., 246.

13. Ibid., 244-47.

14. Both Matthew and Mark essentially name the same brothers (Mark has "Joses," the diminutive form of Matthew's "Joseph"), but Matthew reverses the order of the second pair ("Simon and Judas" rather than Mark's "Judas and Simon"). McHugh explains this reversal as evidence of his thesis that the second pair of brothers are not full blood-brothers of the first pair; and since both pairs are equally called "brothers" (ἀδελφός) of the Lord, this may set a precedent for taking ἀδελφός as something other than full broth-ers (McHugh, 242).

15. Several observations support this thesis, including (1) Joseph is never mentioned by the NT writers as a living person during this period; (2) Joseph is never mentioned in those texts that include the household of Jesus (namely, Mary and Jesus' brothers) during Jesus' ministry (Mark 3:31-32); (3) Mary is portrayed as an independent, "unmarried" woman in that she is able to follow Jesus wherever he goes (John 2:12); (4) Mary is portrayed in the upper room with the disciples and with Jesus' brothers, but without Joseph (Acts 1:14). See also Smith, 213.

16. So that Anthony Tambasco, who writes nine years after McHugh, can say: "The arguments [explaining the "brothers" of Jesus] are still that the word "brothers" means either blood-brothers, or step-brothers (children of Joseph by a previous marriage), or cousins" (23).

17. Meier ("Brothers") comments that McHugh has "tried to defend something similar to Jerome's position," but in doing so has been forced to adopt "convoluted theories of relationships within families of Joseph and Mary that simply cannot be verified"; and then concludes: "What is gratuitously asserted may be gratuitously denied" (22).

18. Ibid., n.38.

19. LaVerdiere, "His Mother Mary," 193.

20. Meier, "Brothers," 14.

21. Ibid., 14 n. 23. McHugh, following Lagrange, sees no ill intent on the part of Jesus' brothers in John 7, and explains the episode in terms of their over-eagerness for Jesus to display his power and to attract proper attention (250). But this does injustice to John's own commentary on the episode: "For even his own brothers did not believe in him."

22. Keating objects to the notion that these "brothers" of Jesus could have been real brothers since John portrays them as giving advice to Jesus. Since, Keating argues, a younger sibling in Jewish culture could not have given advice to an older sibling without seeming disrespectful, these must instead be older cousins (283). Incredibly Keating misses the point of the biting sarcasm (not advice) issued by his "brothers" in this passage. Older sibling or not, if one believes his sibling is deluded (Mark 3:21, 31) he is not going to offer the normal respect he might otherwise give. Contra Keating, McHugh (251) sees in this very passage evidence that Jesus' brothers must have been younger than Jesus since they still lived at home (cf., Matt 13:55-56; Mark 6:3).

23. So Keating, 282-84.

24. Tob 5:14, 17 is ambiguous and could mean either "friend" or "relative."

25. Meier suggest that 1 Chron 23:22 is the only clear example where the meaning "cousin" can be found in the LXX, and concludes that "it is simply not true that *adelphos* is regularly used in the Greek OT to mean cousin, and the equivalence cannot be taken for granted" ("Brothers," 17).

26. Cf. "close sister" (ἀδελφῇ...τῇ ἐγγιζούσῃ αὐτῷ) in Lev 21:3.

27. In ℵ only. BA does not have συγγενὴς.

28. Included here are the disputed passages that mention the brothers of Jesus.

29. "With 'full brother' and 'half-brother' we exhaust the literal meaning of *adelphos* found in the NT. ...it never means stepbrother (the solution of Epiphanius), [or] cousin (the solution of Jerome)" (Meier, "Brothers," 20-21).

30. With the exception of "rich neighbors," each of the groups mentioned above has its own article: μὴ φώνει τοὺς φίλους σου μηδὲ τοὺς ἀδελφούς σου μηδὲ τοὺς συγγενεῖς σου μηδὲ γείτονας πλουσίους.

31. Meier, "Brothers," 17. Some who hold to the Hieronymian view argue that the phrase "brothers of the Lord" has its roots in the earliest Aramaic-speaking Christian community, and that the woodenly literal phrase in Aramaic (which had no precise word for "cousin," and so used the Hebraism) was handed down to the subsequent Greek-speaking community in the form of *hoi adelphoi tou kyriou*, which then made its way into the NT. However, Meier has shown that Josephus, when referring to James, designates him *ho adelphos tou kyriou* (*The Jewish Antiquities* [20.9.1 §200], cited in John P. Meier, "Jesus in Josephus: A Modest Proposal," *CBQ* [1990]: 76-103). This is significant, for not only did Josephus write independently of the NT writers or other Christian influences, but it is clear that Josephus knew of the distinction between ἀδελφὸς and ἀνεψιὸς (he uses the latter for "cousin" twelve times in his works; see Meier, "Brothers," 19 n. 33), even clarifying the Hebrew of Gen 29:12 (where the Hebrew has אָח and the LXX has ἀδελφὸς) with a more precise paraphrase: "For Rebekah my mother is the sister of Laban your father. They had the same father and mother, and so we, you and I, are cousins [ἀνεψιοὶ]" (cited in Meier, "Brothers," 19). Hence, "when Josephus calls James 'the brother of Jesus,' there is no reason to think he means anything but brother," ibid.

32. Meier, "Brothers," 20.

33. Joseph Fitzmyer, *The Gospel According to Luke, Luke, I-IX* (New York: Paulist, 1989), 724.

34. John McKenzie, "The Mother of Jesus in the New Testament," 6.

35. McKenzie, "The Mother of Jesus in the New Testament," 6. Contra Francis J. Moloney (*Mary: Woman and Mother* [Collegeville: Liturgical Press, 1988]), who, when commenting on whether the meaning of ἀδελφὸς in the texts under consideration is "brother" or "cousin," writes "The New Testament text itself is open to *either* interpretation. The Church's traditional teaching on the perpetual virginity of Mary must guide both the faithful and the exegete in their interpretation of these passages" (7 n. 10). Moloney bases his conclusion solely on LXX usage, and gives us no indication that he is aware that the NT usage weighs against his view.

36. McHugh notes that the common assertion by Roman Catholics that in the Hebrew and Aramaic there is no special word for "first cousin" falls flat because both languages have a special word for "uncle" (*dodh*, Lev 10:4; Num 34:11) and "aunt" (*dodhah*, Exod 6:20; Lev 20:20): "the word for 'cousin' is not needed, for it is always possible to talk about 'my uncle's son' or 'the daughter of my aunt'" (253-54). In any case, not even this is needed since, as we have already shown, the Greek has words readily available for both

"cousin" and "relative": "it was not for a lack of a wider vocabulary that the evangelists wrote about the 'brothers' of Jesus" (ibid., 254). In the end, the view that "brother" in the NT means "cousin" is to be rejected (ibid., 253).
37. McHugh, 209.
38. Bauckham, "The Brothers and Sisters of Jesus," 689.
39. Ibid., n. 9.
40. Ibid., 690.
41. Ibid.
42. Ibid., 692.
43. Ibid.
44. Ibid., 693-94.
45. His citation of Lev 18:11 as a possible reference to a stepsister is contradicted (as even Bauckham himself admits) by all major translations and the LXX itself.
46. Meier, "Brothers," 22.
47. Ibid., 15-16.
48. It is odd then that Bauckham (who is *not* a supporter of Mary's perpetual virginity) opts for this view. His rationale for adopting the Epiphanian view over the Helvidian view seems to be based almost entirely on his assessment of the historical evidence for the identity of Jesus' brothers that we find in the post-apostolic church (see Bauckham, *Jude and the Relatives of Jesus*, 15-26). Lightfoot, *Galatians*, adopts the Epiphanian view on similar grounds (273-288). We will examine this evidence later in this chapter.
49. Meier, "Brothers," 16.
50. "The author who tells us in 1:25a that Joseph did not have relations with Mary until she bore a son is the same author who tells us in 13:55 that Jesus' mother is called Mary and his brothers James, Joseph, Simon, and Jude.... The combination of the 'until' statement in Matt 1:25a with the naming of Jesus' mother and brothers all in the same verse (13:55) creates the natural impression that Matthew understood 1:25a to mean that Joseph and Mary did have children after the birth of Jesus," Meier, "Brothers," 10-11.
51. Plummer: "it hardly needs argument that, in such a context, 'he used not to' or 'he was not in the habit of' means more than 'he did not.' It is quite true that the aorist, 'he knew her not until,' would have implied that she subsequently had children by him. But the imperfect implies this still more strongly" (9).
52. See the previous two chapters of this work in which we show that the phrase ἕως οὗ ("until") in Matt 1:25—a construction that McHugh does not deal with—implies just the opposite of what McHugh concludes for the imperfect.
53. *MNT*, 153.
54. "Her Firstborn Son," *AER* 108 [1943]: 1-13.
55. Meier, "Brothers," 14 n. 24.
56. McHugh, 345.

57. *MNT*, 72.

58. Meier, "Brothers," 11.

59. Carson, "Matthew," 583.

60. D. A. Carson, *The Gospel According to John* (Grand Rapids: Eerdmans, 1991), 615.

61. McHugh, 232.

62. This is the majority view of scholars today. So Ceroke, "Mary's Maternal Role in John 19, 25-27" (*Marian Studies* 11 [1960]: 129), and C. K. Barrett (*The Gospel According to St. John*, 2nd ed. [Philadelphia: Westminster, 1978], 551).

63. Carson, "Matthew," 583.

64. Ibid.; cf. 430.

65. See Meier ("Brothers"), who concludes that the James and Joses whose mother is at the cross is not the same James and Joses earlier listed as Jesus' brothers. He also concludes that Jesus' mother does not appear at the cross in Matthew and Mark, but only in John (11-12 n. 21). If this is the case, then perhaps it is John's "Mary the wife of Clopas" who is to be equated with Matthew and Mark's "Mary mother of James and Joses."

66. This is almost certainly the case in earlier episodes of all four gospels. See the treatment of this motif later in this work.

67. Eusebius (*Ecclesiastical History* 3.11) notes that Hegesippus records this in his *Memoirs*. Cf. 32.2.

68. Ibid. 3.11.

69. Ibid. 2.1.

70. In Papias, *From the Exposition of the Oracles of the Lord*, 10, we read the following identification of the Marys at the foot of the cross in John's gospel:

> Mary the mother of the Lord; Mary the wife of Cleophas or Alphaeus, who was the mother of James the bishop and apostle, and of Simon and Thaddeus, and of one Joseph; Mary Salome, wife of Zebedee, mother of John the evangelist and James; Mary Magdalene. These four are found in the Gospel. James and Judas and Joseph were sons of an aunt of the Lord. James also and John were sons of another aunt of the Lord. Mary, mother of James the Less and Joseph, wife of Alphaeus was the sister of Mary the mother of the Lord, whom John names of Cleophas, either from her father or from the family of the clan, or for some other reason. Mary Salome is called Salome either from her husband or her village. Some affirm that she is the same as Mary of Cleophas, because she had two husbands.

But Papias is almost certainly wrong in his assessment of the relationship between "Mary, the mother of James the Less and Joseph" and Mary the mother of Jesus, for he calls the two "sisters." It is extremely unlikely that two sisters in the same household would bear the same name. The suggestion that "sister" here is intended to denote a "cousin" or other close relative is to be rejected on the basis that this "sister" of Mary the mother of Jesus is also identified as "wife of Alphaeus," who in turn was previously identified as the mother of "James and Joseph," who later are identified as "sons of an aunt of the Lord" (Papias first identifies the four Marys, then offers more details on each in the same order that he first mentions them); hence, "sister" must mean biological sibling. Papias likewise has it wrong on the identification of "James the bishop and apostle." James the bishop (also the brother of the Lord) is distinct from James the apostle (the son of Zebedee), yet Papias treats them as the same person. Papias himself indicates that he has no first-hand knowledge of the identification of these women when he concludes, "some affirm that [Mary Salome] is the same as Mary of Cleophas." A statement such as this, combined with the other discrepancies mentioned above, suggests to us that Papias may not be an altogether reliable witness for determining the identification of the women at the cross. In any case, reliance on Papias' testimony should be tempered by the utmost caution.

71. Ignatius, *Letter to the Ephesians* 19.1.

72. *MNT*, 271. We mention this only because Catholic apologists sometimes use this phrase in support of Mary's perpetual virginity.

73. Eusibius, *Ecclesiastical History*, 2.23.

74. Ibid., 3.22.

75. Ibid., 4.22. This last reference may also support McHugh's revised view that Joseph adopted his brother's children. However, Hegesippus never makes that connection, and the other objections cited against McHugh's view would still render it unlikely. Hegesippus is both inconsistent and farfetched in his treatment of history, at one point portraying James was an ascetic Nazarite who had access to the holy place of the temple (ibid., 2.23), which most scholars reject as pure legend. Those who hold to the Hieronymian view often appeal to this passage in Hegesippus to support the "cousin" argument; but, as Ruether points out, it proves just the opposite: "There is no need to imagine that this Simeon is the same as the Simon who is listed among the Lord's brothers. It is quite usual for cousins to have the same name" ("The Collision of History and Doctrine," 100). In any case, our use of Hegesippus is merely to show that he knew of the difference between "brother" and "cousin": "His phrase, 'his brother after the flesh,' decisively points to the Jerusalem tradition that these brothers were known as siblings of Jesus" (ibid.).

76. McHugh denies the evidence that suggests Tertullian believed that Jesus had biological brothers, citing that these "brothers" are never called "sons of Mary" (448-50). But Meier takes McHugh to task for glossing over the strongest evidence, and for simply assuming that Tertullian's point of view would be mariological rather than christological: "Hence all the relationships are defined from the vantage point of Jesus, not Mary" (Meier, "Brothers," 25, n. 44). The *MNT* taskforce (271) likewise concludes that Tertullian explicitly denied Mary's virginity during birth (*in partu*).

77. *Against Marcion* 4.19.

78. *On the Flesh of Christ* 7.

79. Ruether, "The Collision of History and Doctrine," 99.

80. *On Monogamy* 8.

81. Cf. Meier, "Brothers," 25 n. 44.

82. Ibid.

83. *Against Heresies* 3.21.10.

84. Ibid., 3.22.4. Cf. Meier, "Brothers," 25 n. 44.

85. *Against Heresies*, 3.21

86. As a third-century witness, Origen writes: "that these disasters happened to the Jews as a punishment for the death of James the Just, who was a brother of Jesus (called Christ)—the Jews having put him to death, although he was a man most distinguished for his justice. Paul, a genuine disciple of Jesus, says that he regarded this James as a brother of the Lord, not so much on account of their relationship by blood, or of their being brought up together, as because of his virtue and doctrine," *Against Celsus* 1.47 (cf. 2.13). Origen is not denying that James was the biological brother of Jesus, only that this relationship was not the most important compared to James' spiritual relationship to Jesus.

87. *Protevangelium of James* 9:2. Cf. 17:1; 18:1.

88. Ibid., 11:4.

89. Ibid., 19:3–20:1. Another apocryphal work, the *Ascension of Isaiah*, affirms this about Mary's virginity *in partu*:

> And after two months of days while Joseph was in his house, and Mary his wife, but both alone. It came to pass that when they were alone that Mary straight-way looked with her eyes and saw a small babe, and she was astonied. And after she had been astonied, her womb was found as formerly before she had conceived.

This late first-/early-second century work is the product of Jewish Christians who were steeped in Gnosticism (see Graef, vol. 1, 34-35). A passage in the second-century *Odes of Solomon* (19) hints at virginity *in partu*, but does not explicate. Instead, it states merely that Mary "labored" but without pain.

90. Bauckham, "The Brothers and Sisters of Jesus," 696-97.

91. Ibid., 696.

92. So Meier, "Brothers," 6 n. 11. Meier characterizes the *Protevangelium of James* as "a wildly imaginative folk-narrative that is outrageously inaccurate about NT events as well as things Jewish," Ibid., 16. Similarly, J. K. Elliott, *The Apocryphal New Testament* (Oxford: Clarendon Press, 1993), tells us in his preface to the *Protevangelium of James* that its historical value is "insignificant" (51), citing numerous inaccuracies and inconsistencies. Graef, who is sympathetic with the Roman Catholic view of Mary, notes that it betrays "great ignorance of Jewish conditions" and is therefore of "little theological significance" (36).

93. *Infancy Gospel of Thomas* 16.1-2.

94. This episode comes between two other episodes where we are told his age. In the previous episode he is eight (12.2), and in the next episode he is twelve (19:1).

95. Origen, *Commentary on Matthew* 10.17.

96. Meier, "Brothers," 6 n. 11.

97. Even Bauckham concedes this point, "The Brothers and Sisters of Jesus," 696 n. 22.

98. Meier, "Brothers," 26.

99. Both Meier ("Brothers," 16) and Bauckham ("The Brothers and Sisters of Jesus," 698) agree on this point.

100. Meier, "Brothers," 16.

101. Ruether, "The Collision of History and Doctrine," 101.

IV. The Status of Mary in the Synoptics

1. We have dealt with Matthew's infancy narrative in a previous chapter of this work, and we will deal with Luke's in a later chapter.

2. Senior, 93.

3. Some manuscripts, including A, D, and 700 (representing wide geographic distribution from significant Byzantine, Western, and Caesarean witnesses respectively) have καὶ αἱ ἀδελφαί σου after ἡ μήτηρ σου καὶ οἱ ἀδελφοί σου in v. 32 of Mark's account. The omission of this phrase, on the other hand, gains strong Alexandrian support from ℵ, B, 33 and 892, and Caesarean support from f^1 and f^{13}, Θ, 28 and 565. However, the lack of significant support for the omission from both Western and Byzantine witnesses has earned it a C rating from UBS⁴. While the majority of the committee thought the longer reading was to be preferred, Metzger prefers the shorter reading and explains the longer reading as a "mechanical expansion" originating from the Western text (B. M. Metzger, *A Textual Commentary on the Greek New Testament* [Stuttgart: Biblia-Druck, 1975 (=1971)], 82).

4. The bracketed text in Matthew's account, which includes all of v. 47, is in question textually; and its inclusion has merited a C rating from UBS⁴. The most significant Alexandrian support in its favor includes the first corrector of ℵ and the minuscules 33 and 892. But it gains strong support from its wide geographic distribution, including the Western witness D, the Caesarean witnesses of f^1 and f^{13}, Θ, 28, 565, 700, arm and geo, and the Byzantine witnesses of E, F and G. In contrast the omission of the verse enjoys strong Alexandrian support from the first hand of ℵ, as well as B and L, but little by way of geographic distribution. The text is probably original, and most likely was accidentally omitted due to homoeoteleuton caused by the word λαλῆσαι which occurs at both the end of v. 46 and the end of v. 47 (Metzger, 32). Roger Mercurio ("Some Difficult Marian Passages in the Gospels," *Marian Studies* 11 [1960]: 108) cites Lagrange, Allen and Bénoit as representative of scholars who see the omission as genuine.

5. J. Lambrecht, "The Relatives of Jesus in Mark," *NovT* 16 (1974): 250.

6. R. P. Martin, *Mark: Evangelist and Theologian* (Grand Rapids: Zondervan, 1973), 116.

7. Though E. Best ("Mark iii.20,21,31-35," *NTS* 22 [1975-76]) holds to the traditional view, he concedes: "οἱ παρ' αὐτοῦ is certainly more easily understood to refer to the 'adherents' of Jesus than to his 'kinsmen'; evidence for the latter meaning exists but is scanty" (311).

8. *MNT*, 55.

9. See also Raymond Brown, "Mary in the New Testament and in Catholic Life," 375.

10. *MNT*, 55.

11. Best, 311.

12. See the *RSV*.

13. See Best who does not hold this view but cites it as a mediating position (313). See also the *NEB* which renders it this way.

14. H. Wansbrough, "Mark iii.21—Was Jesus Out of His Mind?" *NTS* 18 (1971-72): 233-35.

15. Ibid., 235.

16. Best, 313.

17. Cf. Mark 14:1-2 where the subject of ἔλεγον ("they were saying") is the very group who wanted to seize Jesus to kill him. Cf. also Mark 12:12 where a similar construction is used.

18. See 2:13, 3:9, 3:32, 4:1-2, 6:34, 6:45-46, 7:14, 8:2, 8:34, 9:14, 9:15-16, 10:1, 15:8, 15:11, and 15:15.

19. "According to Markan usage we should therefore have αὐτοῦς if he intended us to understand the crowd," Best, 311.

20. Ibid.

21. See 2:12, 5:42, and 6:51.

22. Best, 312.

23. See G. Hartmann, "Mark 3,20f.," *BZ* 11 (1913): 249-79; and H. Wansbrough, "Mark iii.21," 233-35. But cf. the revision by D. Wenham, "The Meaning of Mark III.21," *NTS* 21 (1974-75): 295-300.

24. Best, 312.

25. Ibid., 311.

26. Ibid., 313.

27. See Ibid.

28. Ibid., 313.

29. "Since 'sandwiching' (ABA´) is a favourite Markan literary technique used also elsewhere in his gospel, one can hold without much risk of illusion that the tendency to structurize…is not accidental," Lambrecht, 252.

30. Wansbrough, "Mother and Disciple," 125.

31. Senior, 93.

32. McHugh, 247.

33. McKenzie, 6.

34. Martin, 168.

35. Schalom Ben-Chorin, "A Jewish View of the Mother of Jesus," in *Mary in the Churches* (ed. Hans Küng and Jürgen Moltmann; Etr. Marcus Lefébure; New York: T. & T. Clark, 1983), 14.

36. *MNT*, 53.

37. Ben-Chorin, 15.

38. Raymond Brown, "Mary in the New Testament," 375.

39. Senior, 93.

40. R. R. Ruether, "The Collision of History and Doctrine," 95.

41. McHugh, 239, n 11.

42. McKenzie, 8.

43. Ibid., 6.

44. *MNT*, 53-54, emphasis in original.

45. These two beliefs will be dealt with more fully when we examine the selected texts in Luke, John and the Revelation, which are used as a basis for these beliefs.

46. Tambasco, 27.

47. Brown, "Mary in the New Testament," 375. Based on this passage, Tertullian stresses the exclusion of Jesus' mother from the community of disciples:

> He was justly indignant that persons so very near to him [biologically] *stood without*, while strangers were *within* hanging on his words, especially as they wanted to call him away from the solemn work he had in hand. He did not so much deny [their existence] as disavow them.... He transferred the names of blood relationships to others whom he judged to be more closely related to him by reason of their faith...teaching them by his own actual example that whosoever preferred father or mother or brethren to the Word of God was not a disciple worthy of him (*Against Marcion*, 19).

Tertullian goes on to speak of Jesus' "unwillingness to acknowledge" his mother and brothers "because of their offense," and that his disciples constituted "worthier" relatives than did his mother and brothers (ibid.). When commenting on this same passage in another writing, he pictures Jesus as "denying" his mother and brothers "in indignation"; yet not denying their existence, but rather "censuring their faults" (*On the Flesh of Christ*, 7). He also pictures Mary in this episode as the "separated mother" who represents the Jewish Synagogue (ibid.).

48. Lonsdale, "Mary and the New Testament," *The Way* 24 (1984): 138. So also R. Reuther, *Mary—The Feminine Face of the Church* (London, 1979), 31. See also Martin who says: "Ties of family life are severed as his kinsfolk prove hostile (3:21, 31-35).... As [Jesus] met with opposition from his kinsfolk,...so [his disciples] must anticipate a forsaking of all earthly ties (10:28-30)," (208).

49. Eugene LaVerdiere, "His Mother Mary," 196.

50. Moltmann, "Editorial," xiii.

51. *MNT*, 99. See also Senior, 96; and Wansbrough, "Mother and Disciple,"
126, who says: "By omitting Mark's v. 32 and substituting 'his disciples' for
'those sitting in a circle around him' Matthew somewhat softens the contrast."
52. *MNT*, 103.
53. LaVerdiere, "His Mother Mary," 195-96.
54. That Chrysostom understands it this way as well is evident in at least two
of his writings:

> And therefore He answered thus in this place, and again else-
> where, "Who is My mother, and who are My brethren?" (Matt.
> xii. 48), because they did not yet think rightly of Him; and
> [Mary], because she had borne Him, claimed, according to the
> custom of other mothers, to direct Him in all things, when she
> ought to have reverenced and worshiped Him. This then was the
> reason why He answered as He did on that occasion. For con-
> sider what a thing it was, that when all the people high and low
> were standing round Him, when the multitude was intent on
> hearing Him, and His doctrine had begun to be set forth, she
> should come into the midst and take Him away from the work
> of exhortation, and converse with Him apart, and not even en-
> dure to come within, but draw Him outside merely to herself.
> This is why He said, "Who is My mother and My brethren?"
> (*Homily on John* 21, 2).... But today we learn in addition another
> thing, that even to have borne Christ in the womb, and to have
> brought forth that marvelous birth, has no profit, if there be not
> virtue.... But He said, 'who is my mother, and who are my
> brethren?' And this He said, not as being ashamed of His
> mother, nor denying her that bare Him, ...but as declaring that
> she has no advantage from this, unless she do all that is required
> to be done. For in fact that which she had attempted to do was
> of superfluous vanity; in that she wanted to show the people that
> she has power and authority over her Son, imagining not as yet
> anything great concerning Him; whence also her unseasonable
> approach (*Homily on Matthew*, 44).

55. Perkins, 113.
56. William Bridcut, "Our Lord's Relationship with His Mother," *One in
Christ* 22/2 (1986): 366-67.
57. Senior, 95.
58. Wansbrough, "Mother and Disciple," 126.
59. Mercurio, 118.
60. Brown, "Mary in the New Testament," 376-77.
61. Wansbrough, "Mother and Disciple," 127.
62. *MNT*, 168.
63. H. Conzelmann, *The Theology of St. Luke* (New York: Harper & Row,
1960), 35, 47-48.

64. *MNT*, 170 n. 382.

65. Lonsdale, 141.

66. Smith, 189.

67. Cf., LaVerdiere, "His Mother Mary," who says: "By presenting his disciples as his mother and brothers, Jesus has prepared the way for Matthew to reverse the image and to introduce Mary as a figure for the life of the Church" (94).

68. There are three textual variants in this passage; but only one is as low as a C rating (the other two are A and B respectively), and none affects the interpretation of the passage.

69. *MNT*, 166-67.

70. Senior, 93.

71. Wansbrough, "Mother and Disciple," 126. See also Senior, 96; as well as the *MNT* taskforce, who thinks that Jesus' family is excluded from Matthew's account of this passage (*MNT*, 100).

72. LaVerdiere, "His Mother Mary," 197.

73. Brown, "Mary in the New Testament," 376.

74. René Laurentin, "Pluralism about Mary: Biblical and Contemporary," *The Way* suppl. 45 (1982): 81.

75. Ibid., 80.

76. Perhaps nothing in Laurentin's treatment of Mary in the NT is more telling of his allegiances than the fact that while he finds theological "silence" with regard to the negative synoptic passages given above, he is nevertheless somehow able to find Marian significance in the writings of Paul (ibid., 81-83), as well as a reference to Mary's virginity in the prologue of John's Gospel (ibid., 86)—both of which are dismissed by Laurentin's colleagues as having no Marian significance at all.

77. Lonsdale, 139.

V. Special Considerations about Mary in Luke–Acts

1. The *RSV* and the *NAB* also include the textually dubious "Blessed are you among women," which is a reading based primarily on the Vulgate, and which has limited manuscript support (A, C, D, Θ). It is almost certainly a later addition by a scribe who confused this with Elizabeth's greeting to Mary in Luke 1:42.

2. Keating, 269.

3. Ibid.

4. Laurentin, "Pluralism," 84.

5. Sir 18:17: οὐκ ἰδοὺ λόγος ὑπὲρ δόμα ἀγαθόν καὶ ἀμφότερα παρὰ ἀνδρὶ κεχαριτωμένῳ ("Behold, is not a word better than a good gift? But both accompany a favored man"). The same form of the word shows up in Sym. Ps 17 [18]:26, also with no theological significance: "to the pure [κεχαριτωμένῳ; "favored"] you show yourself pure, but to the crooked you show yourself shrewd."

6. McHugh, 47.

7. Cf., e.g., John 14:29: "I have told you now before it happens, so that when it does happen you will believe." The word "told" here is in the perfect tense, but certainly does not mean that Jesus has told them from the beginning of their lives, but rather that he just now told them. Cf. also Acts 7:56, 10:45, and Matt 13:46, all of which use the perfect tense, but none of which implies a *permanent* state or condition.

8. *Greek-English Lexicon of the New Testament Based on Semantic Domains*, 2nd ed. (New York: United Bible Society, 1989).

9. Zerwick, *Grammatical Analysis*, 171.

10. *MNT*, 127.

11. Ibid., 127-28.

12. Ibid., 127.

13. McHugh, 48.

14. Ibid., emphasis mine.

15. *MNT*, 128.

16. McHugh, 48.

17. Ibid.

18. Ibid., 49.

19. Ibid., 52.

20. There is no verb here, and the phrase may be taken either as an optative ("may the Lord be with you"), or as an indicative ("the Lord is with you").

21. In the latter two passages the phrase is used at the *end* of an encounter rather than at the beginning.

22. "The Son of Man will go as it has been decreed, but woe to that man who betrays him" (Luke 22:22). Cf. Matt 26:23 and Mark 14:20.

23. McHugh, 65. Cf., William G. Most, "Unscriptural Marian Doctrine?" (*HomPasRev* 94 [1994]): 61.

24. McHugh, 65. In spite of McHugh's insistence to the contrary, the optative does not have to be taken as an earnest wish or desire. It is often used without any expression of emotion at all (e.g., Luke 1:62), and is here more naturally read as humble submission to the angel's prophecy.

25. Senior, 107.

26. Tina Beattie, *Rediscovering Mary: Insights From the Gospels* (Liguori, MO: Triumph Books, 1995), 23.

27. Moloney, 19. Irenaeus also sees Mary's choice as instrumental in the salvation of mankind when he states: "[Just as Eve], having become disobedient, was made the cause of death, both to herself and to the entire human race; so also did Mary, having a man betrothed [to her], and being nevertheless a virgin, by yielding obedience, become the cause of salvation, both to herself and the whole human race," *Against Heresies* 3.22. Irenaeus' interpretation is based on a general tendency among the early fathers to see in Mary an antitype of Eve (cf. the Prolegomena of this work).

28. See, e.g., Neal M. Flanagan, "Mary of Nazareth: Woman for all Seasons" (*Marianum* 48 [1986]): 167, who, in his Marian Creed, writes: "I believe

that Mary's Fiat initiated the Christian era.… I believe that Mary's Fiat inserted her intimately into Christ's salvific work."

29. Patrick J. Bearsley, "Mary the Perfect Disciple: A Paradigm for Mariology," *Theological Studies* 41/3 (1980): 500.

30. Richard J. Sklba, "Mary and the 'Anawim," in *Mary Woman of Nazareth: Biblical and Theological Perspectives* (ed. Doris Donnelly; New York: Paulist, 1989), 124-26. Contra Kugelman, whose statement that "God asks and receives Mary's free consent" is listed as one of four "facts" that Luke's annunciation narrative "expresses very clearly" (65). It simply doesn't occur to Kugelman that someone might question that premise, for he offers no defense for just why we should view it as a "fact."

31. G. B. Caird, *Luke* (the Pelican Gospel Commentaries; New York: Penguin Books, 1963), 53.

32. Børresen, 56 n.16.

33. Ibid., 35.

34. Tambasco, 41.

35. So Fitzmyer, *Luke, I-IX,* 348. Cf. "betrothed" in Luke 1:27. In Matthew Joseph is called "her [Mary's] husband" (ὁ ἀνὴρ αὐτῆς) while still in this betrothed state (Matt 1:19).

36. *MNT,* 114 n. 241.

37. Ibid., 83 n. 173.

38. Ibid., 84.

39. *Kiddushin* "Betrothals," and *Ketuboth* "Marriage Deeds."

40. McHugh, 161 n. 20.

41. See the Babylonian Talmud, *Ketuboth* 3b; and the Jerusalem Talmud, *Ketuboth* 1:25c.

42. *Yebamoth* 4:10.

43. *MNT,* 114-115.

44. Keating, 283.

45. Ibid.

46. Ibid.

47. Many current-day Catholic apologists argue that the present tense here is to be taken as a futuristic present. Yet they do so without warrant. A present tense verb can be labeled a futuristic present only when it is obvious from the context that the verb is future referring. For instance, in John 14:2-3 Jesus tells his disciples: "I am going [πορεύομαι] to prepare a place for you. And if I go and prepare a place for you, I will come back [ἔρχομαι] and take you to be with." Both πορεύομαι ("I am going") and ἔρχομαι ("I am coming") are present-tense verbs, but both are unambiguously future referring and are therefore futuristic presents. Such is not the case with γινώσκω in Luke 1:34. The present tense makes good sense in its context as a present-referring verb, and so is not a legitimate example of a futuristic present.

48. David T. Landry, "Narrative Logic in the Annunciation to Mary (Luke 1:26-38)" (*JBL* 114/1 [1995]): 74. Both Fitzmyer (*Luke I-IX,* 348-350) and

Brown (*The Birth of the Messiah* [Garden City: Doubleday, 1977], 303-308) reject the historical reading of Mary's question, seeing it instead as a literary device intended to introduce *to the reader* how the birth would take place. However, both agree that of all the "psychological" explanations, the immediate-conception view is the strongest, and their only objection to this interpretation seems to be that the angel's words are in the future tense ("you *will* conceive"): "But Luke's Greek is clearly future.... The conception is yet to happen" (Brown, ibid., 306); "[The immediate-conception view] tends to obscure the future tense that the angel used in v. 32 and will use in v. 35" (Fitzmyer, Ibid., 350). Yet, curiously enough, both of these scholars seem to miss the point of the immediate-conception view. Landry takes Fitzmyer to task for this objection by noting the (seemingly) obvious. Quoting J. Schaberg's work, Landry notes that Fitzmyer's objection is valid only if "the conception is thought of as 'then and now' but not if [it is thought of] in the future before the still distant home-taking," Landry, 75 n. 36.

49. Landry, 73.

50. H. Wansbrough, "Mother and Disciple," 128. Calvin's comments on this phrase of Mary are lucid:

> The conjecture which some have drawn from these words, that she had formed a vow of perpetual virginity, is unfounded and altogether absurd. She would, in that case, have committed treachery by allowing herself to be united to a husband, and would have poured contempt on the holy covenant of marriage; which could not have been done without mockery of God. Although the Papists have exercised barbarous tyranny on this subject, yet they have never proceeded so far as to allow the wife to form a vow of continence at her own pleasure. Besides, it is an idle and unfounded supposition that a monastic life existed among the Jews (*Harmony of the Gospels*, vol. 1).

51. No appeal can legitimately be made to 1 Corinthians 7 in support of Keating's position. There Paul tells his readers that it is better to remain single so that one can serve the Lord in an undistracted way. The text is referring to singleness, not virginity *per se*. Even if we grant that Mary took a vow of virginity, she was nevertheless still a married woman with a son, and so was obligated to devote herself to the mundane distractions of life to which Paul refers in this text. It is singleness, not married virginity that is the higher calling.

52. Senior, 104.

53. Ibid., 104-105.

54. Ibid., 106.

55. *MNT,* 114-115.

56. McHugh, 179-180.

57. *MNT,* 115 n. 245. So also Brown, *The Birth of the Messiah* (Garden City: Doubleday, 1977), who notes that the "vow of virginity" view is "totally

implausible" because: "In our knowledge of Palestinian Judaism, there is nothing that would explain why a twelve-year-old girl would have entered marriage with the intention to preserve virginity and thus not to have children" (304). Moreover, the celibacy practiced at Qumran "throws no light whatsoever on the supposed resolve of virginity made by a young village girl *who had entered matrimony*," ibid., 305 (emphasis in original).

58. So Fitzmyer, *Luke I-IX*, who says, "the words in themselves merely express a simple denial of sexual intercourse and have nothing to do with an antecedent vow or resolve of perpetual virginity; the context in which they occur scarcely implies anything of the sort…. A vow of virginity is unknown in the OT," 349.

59. The Greek word used here, ὀφειλὴν, means "that which is owed."

60. Landry, 66 n. 2.

61. McHugh, 71.

62. Ibid.

63. Ibid., 71-72.

64. Ibid., 72.

65. Ibid.

66. It occurs five times in the OT—all of them in 1& 2 Chronicles (1 Chron 15:28; 16:4; 16:5; 16:42; and 2 Chron 5:13)—and only once in the NT (the passage under consideration).

67. See below for a full discussion.

68. See the discussion on John's portrayal of Mary later in this work.

69. Cf. discussions on Luke 8:19-21 in the previous chapter, and Luke 11:27-28 below.

70. It is interesting to note that Judith cites a canticle in 16:1-17 similar to Mary's canticle in Luke 1:46-56. McHugh, however, sees any allusion to Judith in the Lukan text as "highly improbable" and one that may be "confidently rejected" since there is no evidence that Luke knew the book of Judith (McHugh, 71).

71. *MNT*, 136. Calvin is right when he writes: "The word *Blessed* does not, in my opinion, mean, Worthy of praise; but rather means, Happy" (*Harmomy of the Gospels*, vol. 1).

72. Senior, 95.

73. Ibid., 107.

74. See *MNT*, 153 n. 344.

75. Ibid., 156.

76. Wansbrough, "Mother and Disciple," 128.

77. McHugh, 106; so also Moloney, 26; and Gaventa, 64.

78. McHugh, 106. Wis 5:20 also identifies God's wrath as a sword: "He will sharpen stern wrath into a sword."

79. The *NIV* has avoided the parentheses by rearranging the order of v. 35a and b. The Greek reads, καὶ σοῦ [δὲ] αὐτῆς τὴν ψυχὴν διελεύσεται ῥομφαία —ὅπως ἂν ἀποκαλυφθῶσιν ἐκ πολλῶν καρδιῶν διαλογισμοί, and the NIV has translated it: "so that the thoughts of many hearts will be revealed.

And a sword will pierce your own soul too." Even UBS[4] and NA[26] have placed v. 35a as a parenthetical thought.

80. See the discussion of the *Daughter of Zion* motif in the next chapter.

81. McHugh, 111.

82. Ibid., 112.

83. Ibid., 108.

84. Ibid., 109.

85. *MNT,* 156.

86. Luke's account mentions the women who followed Jesus (23:49), and even names them (24:10; cf. 23:55), but does not mention Mary.

87. See discussion in the following chapter.

88. Unfortunately, this problem looms large over a good portion of McHugh's work; and it serves only to undermine his arguments for additional, otherwise sound points he wishes to make about Mary.

89. McHugh, 33.

90. Ibid., 32.

91. Ibid., 33: "The expression 'Daughter of Zion' is closely (and perhaps intrinsically) linked with the notion of the remnant and of the poor."

92. Ibid., 112.

93. In addition to the abrupt change from the implied third person plural in v. 34 to the second person singular in v. 35a, we might also mention that καὶ in v. 35a is likely to be taken as "also" in the sense of "in addition to the other two groups mentioned," rather than as a simple conjunction or connective. Support for this understanding of καὶ comes from (though is by no means dependent on) the disputed inclusion of δὲ which is omitted by B but gains support from ℵ, A, D, Θ, f^1, and f^{13}. The quality of the manuscripts that include this word, coupled with their wide geographic distribution (all textual traditions are represented), causes the external evidence to lean decisively toward its inclusion. Its omission by B can be explained by its seeming redundancy with the presence of καὶ. But if we view δὲ as the connective (which, if it is to be included, would have to be its function here), then καὶ cannot have this function and, in that case, must have the meaning given above.

94. Fitzmyer, *Luke I-IX*, also sees allusion to the LXX of Ezek 14:17, "Let a sword go through the land that I may cut off from it man and beast"; as well as the *Sibylline Oracle* 3.316, "A sword shall go through the midst of you" (see also Ezek 5:1-2 and 6:8-9), 430. Implicit in these passages is the idea that a "sword singles out some for destruction and others for mercy," ibid.

95. Gaventa, 64.

96. *MNT,* 156.

97. So Fitzmyer, *Luke I-IX*, 430. There are fourteen instances of this word in the NT, six of which are found in Luke (2:35; 5:22; 6:8; 9:46,47; 24:38).

98. *MNT,* 157. The notable church father, Basil, takes a similar view:

> About the words of Simeon to Mary, there is no obscurity or variety of interpretation.... Here I am astonished that, after passing

by the previous words as requiring no explanation, you should en-
quire about the expression, "Yea, a sword shall pierce through thy
own soul also." To me the question, how the same child can be for
the fall and rising again, and what is the sign that shall be spoken
against, does not seem less perplexing than the question how a
sword shall pierce through Mary's heart. My view is,…by a sword
is meant the word which tries and judges our thoughts, which
pierces even to the dividing asunder of soul and spirit and of the
joints and marrow, and is a discerner of our thoughts.… Simeon
therefore prophesies about Mary herself, that when standing by
the cross, and beholding what is being done, and hearing the
voices, after the witness of Gabriel, after her secret knowledge of
the divine conception, after the great exhibition of miracles, she
shall feel about her soul a mighty tempest.… This is the sword.
"That the thoughts of many hearts may be revealed." He indicates that after the offence at the Cross of Christ a certain swift
healing shall come from the Lord to the disciples and to Mary
herself, confirming their heart in faith in Him (*Letter* 260.6-9).

Basil interprets the sword as "the word which tries and judges our
thoughts," applies it to Mary's doubting at the cross (thereby indicting her
with sin), and characterizes this interpretation as universally accepted ("no
obscurity or variety of interpretation"). This, of course, presents an internal
contradiction for Roman Catholic exegetes who rely on the authority of
patristic tradition for their understanding of the interpretation of Scripture
and who hold to the Roman Catholic teaching that Mary's sinlessness was
part and parcel of that same tradition.

99. Gaventa, 65-66.
100. Ibid., 66.
101. Ibid.
102. Ibid.
103. Ibid.
104. See the discussion of Luke 8:19-21 in the previous chapter.
105. Oddly enough, even Gaventa recognizes this fact only two pages later in
   her discussion of Luke 2:41-52 (68).
106. Fitzmyer, *Luke I-IX*, 430.
107. Ibid.
108. McHugh, 118-119.
109. Fitzmyer, *Luke I-IX*, is less certain of the meaning, but concludes that "in
   my Father's house" is probably the best option (443).
110. James M. Reese, "The Historical Image of Mary in the New Testament,"
   Marian Studies 28 (1977): 32-33.
111. Cf. Fitzmyer, *Luke I-IX*: "Attempts to tone down the evangelist's statement
   about the misunderstanding of these words must be resisted," 444. Some
   Catholic exegetes (such as J. Cortés and F. M. Gatti, *Marianum* 32 [1970]:
   404-418) have translated Luke's comment as "But they had not understood

what he had previously told them [regarding where he was going to be that day]." But, as Fitzmyer notes, this interpretation relies on a fairly significant detail that Luke never mentions (viz., that Jesus had told his parent that he would be going somewhere): "One has the suspicion that Luke's Greek text is being manipulated in the interest of preventing Luke from admitting that Mary…did not understand Jesus' fundamental relation to his heavenly Father. It smacks of eisegesis; and I prefer to avoid it," *Luke I-IX*, 445.

112. "Despite all that Mary has been told about her child in the earlier episodes of the infancy narrative, she is here portrayed as uncomprehending and gently rebuking," Fitzmyer, *Luke I-IX*, 443.

113. "Jesus' own question has something of a reproach in it too," Ibid.

114. *MNT*, 161.

115. Tambasco, 29.

116. Gaventa, 68; italics in original.

117. *MNT*, 161.

118. Fitzmyer, *Luke I-IX*, 445.

119. Senior, 94.

120. Ben-Chorin, 15.

121. Fitzmyer, *Luke X-XXIV*, 926.

122. *MNT*, 171. This was certainly Tertullian's view of the passage: "Now he had in precisely similar terms rejected his mother and his brothers [Luke 8:21], while preferring those who heard and obeyed God" (*Against Marcion*, 26).

123. *MNT*, 171.

124. Ibid., 171-72.

125. Ibid., 172.

126. Tambasco, 28.

127. McHugh, 347.

128. Wansbrough, "Mother and Disciple," 127.

129. Mercurio, 120.

130. Ibid.

131. Ibid., 121.

132. Ibid.

133. *MNT*, 171.

134. M. E. Thrall, *Greek Particles in the New Testament: Linguistic and Exegetical Studies* (Grand Rapids: Eerdmans, 1962), 34-36.

135. Fitzmyer, *Luke X-XXIV*, 927.

136. Fitzmyer has Plato, *Rep. 489D*, but his reference is incorrect (928).

137. Ibid., 928.

138. *BDF*, §448(6).

139. Cf. Loeb. The meaning is, "no doubt only a brief time according to you."

140. Ibid.

141. Thrall, 35.

142. Thrall's observation that when Luke wants to express contradiction he uses οὐχί, λέγω ὑμῖν, ἀλλ' (as in 12:51; 13:2-5) does not account for every instance. In Luke 7:24-25, Jesus asks his hearers about John the Baptist: "what

did you go out to see?" To the first suggestion ("A reed swayed by the wind?") he answers ἀλλά. To the second suggestion ("A man dressed in fine clothes?") he answers ἰδού (lit., "behold"). Both answers are intended to convey contradiction: "On the contrary, those who wear expensive clothes and indulge in luxury are in palaces." Luke's use of μενοῦν in 11:28, therefore, is best accounted for by stylistic variation rather than a difference in meaning.

143. Raymond Brown, "The Annunciation to Mary, the Visitation, and the Magnificat (Luke 1:26-56)" (*Worship* 62/3 [May 1988]), "He corrected the woman in the crowd," 255.

144. Zerwick, *Grammatical Analysis*, 225.

145. I. Howard Marshall, *The Gospel of Luke: A Commentary on the Greek Text* (NIGTC; Grand Rapids: Eerdmans, 1978), 482.

146. *BDF*, §450(4).

147. Walter Bauer, *A Greek-English Lexicon of the New Testament and Other Early Christian Literature* (ed. W. Bauer; ETr. and adapted by W. F. Arndt and F. W. Gingrich; 2d ed., rev. and augmented by F. W. Gingrich and F. W. Danker; Chicago: University of Chicago, 1979).

148. Fitzmyer seems to have forgotten his own lucid words: "Thus, with the imagery of the sword piercing Mary, Simeon hints at the difficulty she will have in learning that obedience to the word of God will transcend even family ties. Recall how Mary will be depicted in Luke 8:21 and 11:27-28," *Luke I-IX*, 430.

149. Fitzmyer, *Luke X-XXIV*, 926.

150. Mercurio, 122.

151. Bridcut, 367.

152. This is precisely how Chrysostom understands the passage: "The answer was not that of one rejecting his mother, but of One who would show that her having borne Him would have availed her nothing, had she not been very good and faithful. Now if, setting aside the excellence of her soul, it profited Mary nothing that the Christ was born of her, much less will it be able to avail us to have a father or a brother, or a child of virtuous and noble disposition, if we ourselves be far removed from his virtue," *Homily* XXI, 3.

153. Moloney, 28.

154. *MNT*, 284.

155. Cf. Moloney (29) who sees much significance in the presence of Mary in this passage: "As they await the gift from on high, 'the mother of Jesus' is with them. Why does Luke single out this 'woman,' the 'mother of Jesus' in such a way? It appears to me that we have in Acts 1:14 the first indication of an intuition of the earliest Church.... The 'woman' and the 'mother of Jesus' (Jn 2:1-11) becomes the 'mother of the disciple' and the 'mother of the Church' (19:25-27)."

156. Gaventa: "she does not figure in the emerging church of Jerusalem and beyond" (73).

157. Others are recognized in this way, including John the Baptist (1:5; 11:16; 19:3-4).

158. Raymond Brown, "More Polemic than Instructive: R. Laurentin on the Infancy Narratives," *Marianum* 47 (1985): 188-207.

159. René Laurentin, *Queen of Heaven* (London: Burns, Oates and Washbourne, 1956), 12.

160. Ibid.

161. Gaventa, 73.

162. Mary as *epitomized* disciple is different than the oft-proffered Mary as *model* disciple. The latter is seen as a deliberate symbol on the part of Luke, whereas the former is simply a recording of true events. The latter will be dealt with in detail in our next chapter.

VI. Marian Symbolism in Luke

1. There are others as well, including Mary as a symbol of David; cf. Richard D. Nelson, "David: A Model for Mary in Luke?," *Biblical Theological Bulletin* 18/4 (Oct. 1998): 138-142. These suggested symbols need not detain us. Such symbolism is on the fringe and does not seem to have merited special consideration from other scholars. We will therefore forego discussion of it here.

2. R. E. Brown, "The Annunciation to Mary," 250.

3. Lonsdale, 141.

4. Senior, 95.

5. Bearsley, 478.

6. Bearsley, 480. Bearsley denies the contradiction by making a distinction between Mary's role as mother of God as an ontological priority and Mary's discipleship as an epistemological priority. The former has priority as the cause of her discipleship while the latter has priority as a way to view the former. But if all this is true, then his initial premise (viz., that Mary's discipleship is of more value to Jesus than her motherhood) is indeed contradicted. Did Jesus need to see Mary's discipleship before he could conclude that she was his mother? And if he was aware that her status as "mother of God" was an ontological priority, how could he have indicated (as he most certainly did) that her discipleship was more important? At the end of the day, Bearsley's thesis has unsuccessfully attempted to reconcile the biblical text with Roman Catholic dogma. The fact that he has gone to such lengths to reconcile the two says more about the obvious tension between them than it does about the proper understanding of the biblical texts.

7. Senior, 95-96.

8. Brown, "Mary in the New Testament," 377.

9. *MNT*, 162-63.

10. So Kugelman, 66-67.

11. McHugh, 38-39.

12. He uses χαίρειν in Acts 15:23 and 23:26 as a greeting in a letter.

13. Tambasco, 32.

14. Ibid.

15. *MNT*, 128.
16. Ibid., 131.
17. Ibid., 132. So also Tambasco, 32.
18. McHugh, 45.
19. Ibid., 46.
20. Ibid., 46-47.
21. Though, oddly enough, McHugh later contends that Luke 1:31 "is a virtual citation of the Greek text of Is 7:14"! (Ibid., 54).
22. Ibid., 37.
23. Ibid., 47, 50.
24. Tambasco, 32. Proponents of this view include McHugh, Laurentin, Burrows, and Flanagan.
25. Kugelman, 78.
26. McHugh, 57-58.
27. Ibid., 63.
28. Ibid., 62.
29. Ibid. Cf. also Kugelman, 82.
30. *MNT*, 133.
31. McHugh, 62.
32. Ibid.
33. Ibid.
34. This is true even of Roman Catholic scholars, including Tambasco (32) and those on the *MNT* taskforce.
35. McHugh, 62.
36. Interestingly enough, the third-century father, Hippolytus (Bishop of Rome), saw Jesus as the Ark of the Covenant:

> At that time, then, the Savior appeared and showed His own body to the world, (born) of the Virgin, who was the "ark overlaid with pure gold," with the Word within and the Holy Spirit without; so that the truth is demonstrated, and the "ark" made manifest. From the birth of Christ, then, we must reckon the 500 years that remain to make up the 6000, and thus the end shall be. And that the Savior appeared in the world, bearing the imperishable ark, His own body (*Commentary on Daniel* 2.6).

The phrase "who was the 'ark overlaid with pure gold' finds its antecedent in "the Savior" and not in "the virgin" as is evident from the final sentence which identifies the "ark" as Jesus' body. The first instance of the ark as a term for Mary seems to have come from another document, the author of which is unknown: "For the holy Virgin is in truth an ark, wrought with gold both within and without, that has received the whole treasury of the sanctuary," *First Homily on the Annunciation of the Holy Virgin Mary*. On this, the editors of Eerdman's 28-volume set of the Early Church Fathers note: "it was produced after Nicaea, and probably after Ephesus.... The titles of these Homilies are the work of much later editors; and interpolations probably occur frequently, by the same hands."

37. Leah's prior humility stems from the fact that she is unloved by Jacob, while Mary's is due to her humble means as a newly betrothed Jewish girl.

38. So Tambasco, 33.

39. McHugh, 76-77.

40. Tambasco, 31.

41. McHugh's suggestion seems driven more by his desire to see a Mary/Israel parallelism than by true similarities in the texts. The parallelism suggested by all the other views takes into account a woman of humble circumstances who overcomes that circumstance by conceiving a child that the Lord gives her. Mal 3:12, on the other hand, is a promise to Israel of future exaltation if she obeys. The context of the promise is even more devastating to McHugh's view, for Israel is not cast in a favorable light in this passage. Instead she is guilty of "robbing God" (vv. 8-12) and blasphemy (vv. 13-14). At the end of the day the only real similarity between this passage and Luke's text is the use of the word "blessed" in each.

42. Neal Flanagan, "Mary of Nazareth," 160.

43. Reese, 31. See also Wansbrough ("Mother and Disciple," 127), "In Matthew's stories,…Mary's responses and motives do not feature. It is Joseph…whose response is important."

44. Wansbrough, "Mother and Disciple," 127.

45. Lonsdale, 140.

46. Most notable of the exceptions, the *MNT* taskforce which includes R. E. Brown and J. A. Fitzmyer.

VII. Mary in the Gospel of John (Part One)

1. Laurentin ("Pluralism") also finds an allusion to the virgin birth in John 1:13, though he is virtually alone in this. Adopting the variant reading ὅς (singular) rather than οἵ (plural), he sees the thrice repeated negative ("born not of blood, nor of the will of the flesh, *nor of the will of man*") as a reference not to believers in general, but to the incarnate Word in particular. He concludes that even if the text does refer to the new birth of believers, that birth is "modelled on the virginal conception" (86), and that regardless of which reading one adopts, the triple negative "would be incomprehensible if it were not *in some way* connected with the visible and tangible birth of the incarnate Word" (87; italics mine). While these statements are true in a general sense, it must be noted that to accept the truth of these vague statements does not entail accepting Laurentin's thesis that there is an allusion to the virgin birth in this passage. In any case, our burden in this discussion is on Mary's role in the New Testament church, not the virgin birth. As we stated in an earlier chapter, since the virgin birth is common ground between Evangelicals and Roman Catholics, it is not an issue we will deal with here.

2. Hartdegen, "The Marian Significance of Cana," *Marian Studies* 11 (1960): 87-88.

3. So Boismard, Brunet, Maeso, Zahn, and Van den Bussche.

4. So Braun, Gächter, Brown, and Deiss. Reese holds that Mary's statement "They have no wine" is intended to discourage Jesus and his companions from joining the wedding feast. By his appearance, Jesus "has create a minor crisis," and Mary "will save the host from embarrassment by getting Jesus to leave" (38). But there is no evidence to support this thesis as Carson (*John*, 169) has noted.

5. So Migliorini.

6. So Ceroke and Galot.

7. It implies "a delicate request of Christ to manifest His divine power... without any restriction of His complete freedom of action," Hartdegen, 88.

8. Eamon Carroll, "The New Testament Charisms of the Blessed Virgin Mary," *One in Christ* 22/2 (1986): 356-364.

9. Joseph A. Grassi, "The Role of Jesus' Mother in John's Gospel: A Reappraisal," *CBQ* 48/1 (1986): 79.

10. Hartdegen, 88.

11. Carson, *John*, 169.

12. Ibid.

13. Ibid., 170.

14. Reese, 39.

15. McHugh, 394.

16. "His mother then demanded a miracle of Him; but He, about to perform divine works, so far did not recognize a human womb; saying in effect, 'That in me which works a miracle was not born of thee, thou gavest not birth to my divine nature; but because my weakness was born of thee, I will recognize thee at the time when that same weakness shall hang upon the cross.' This, indeed, is the meaning of 'Mine hour is not yet come'," *Tract. in Ioannem* VIII.9. See also *Tractate* CXIX.1: "At that time, therefore, when about to engage in divine acts [at Cana], He repelled, as one unknown, her who was the mother, not of His divinity, but of His [human] infirmity."

17. "And so this was a reason why He rebuked her on that occasion, saying, 'Woman, what have I to do with you?' instructing her for the future not to do the like," *Homilies on John* 21.

18. McHugh, 365.

19. *Against Heresies* 3.16,7.

20. *Dialogue II.*

21. *Epist. 41.* See also Irenaeus, *Against Heresies* 3, 16.7.

22. It must be noted here that Hos 13:8 [13:9] is a parallel in thought only, not in the exact Greek phrase used. Hos 13:8 [13:9] has τί αὐτῷ ἔτι καὶ εἰδώλοις ἐγὼ ἐταπείνωσα αὐτόν; whereas John 2:4 has τί ἐμοὶ καὶ σοί.

23. So J. Cortés, *New Testament Abstracts*, III (1958-59), 247. This rendering is fraught with difficulties: (1) contra the proposed rendering, there *was* a change—since this was Jesus' *first* miracle (v 11), he could not have granted this kind of request before; (2) Mary gives no indication that she detected

a change in relationship, so what need would there be for Jesus to ask "what has changed between us?"; (3) this rendering does not account for the fact that in *every other instance*, this Greek construction is a reproof. If it is argued that this cannot be a denial of Mary's request since Jesus *does* eventually grant it, it must also be pointed out that Jesus denies requests elsewhere, only to grant them immediately thereafter (Matt 15:22-28; John 7:3-10).

24. So M. Lagrange and R. Schnackenburg, quoted in Carson, *John*, 171.
25. Hartdegen, 89.
26. Wansbrough, "Mother and Disciple," 128.
27. Ibid., 89-90.
28. Carson, *John*, 170.
29. Hartdegen, 90.
30. Hartdegen, 90.
31. Ibid. Hartdegen appeals to Luke 2:49—"Didn't you know I had to be in my Father's house?"—as an example of where Jesus means "to inform and to teach" rather than reprove. We have already dealt with this passage elsewhere to show why Hartdegen's reading is deficient.
32. McHugh, 364.
33. Ibid., 394.
34. Reese, 39.
35. Reese, 40.
36. As Barrett notes, this phrase "is abrupt and draws a sharp line between Jesus and his mother," 191. See also R. Schnackenburg, *The Gospel According to St. John* (vol. 1; New York: Seabury Press, 1980), who says, "It is impossible to deny that Jesus holds himself aloof from his mother (and her request) to some extent," and goes on to translate the phrase as "leave me in peace!" (328).
37. Bearsley, 485.
38. Ibid.
39. Carson, *John*, 171.
40. Ibid.
41. So Barnabas Lindars, *The Gospel of John* (London: Oliphants, 1972), 129.
42. Wansbrough, "Mother and Disciple," 128.
43. So Lindars, following the *NEB*, which renders it as "mother" (129). See also Carson's survey of views, *John*, 170.
44. So Brown, *John I-XII*, 99.
45. Hartdegen, 91-92.
46. Ibid., 93.
47. See also the discussion of the phrase "What to me and to you?"
48. *MNT*, 188.
49. Cf. Matt 15:21 and Luke 13:12.
50. *MNT*, 189.
51. Six of these occur in John's gospel, five of which are uttered by Jesus. Obviously, if Jesus is addressing other woman by this title we cannot see special significance for its use with Mary without engaging in even more special pleading with regard to Mary.

52. Reese, 39.

53. See the discussion in Carson, *John*, 111-114.

54. The more likely connection with John 1:1 is 17:5 rather than 2:4; see Carson, *John*, 111.

55. Wansbrough, "Mother and Disciple," 128.

56. *MNT*, 188.

57. Carson, *John*, 170.

58. In the case of John 20:15-16, Jesus first calls Mary Magdalene "woman" (v. 15); then "Mary" (v. 16). The first address ("woman") seems to be said with the intent of preventing Mary from recognizing him immediately (cf. Luke 24:16; "they were kept from recognizing him"), and to give the impression that she is speaking with a stranger (viz., the gardener). The second address ("Mary") is clearly intended to close the distance and reestablish the intimacy that Mary once enjoyed with Jesus.

59. So Leon Morris, *The Gospel According to John* (NICNT; Grand Rapids: Eerdmans, 1971), who notes that the use of the term *woman* "probably indicates that there is a new relationship between them as He enters on His public ministry" (180).

60. Bearsley, 485. Hence, B. F. Westcott (*The Gospel According to St. John*; Grand Rapids: Eerdmans, 1958) misses the real point when he says of the word *woman*: "there is not the least tinge of reproof or severity in the term" (36). Perhaps not in the term inherently; but when taken in context with the accompanying phrase ("why are you bothering me?"), combined with the fact that the use of the word *woman* is unattested in regard to one's mother, a different picture emerges.

61. So Reese, 39.

62. So Carson, *John*, 171. Hartdegen, 94-95, is an example of one who takes this as an indicative statement, but sees "hour" as referring to something other than the events surrounding Jesus' death.

63. Bearsley, 485.

64. Ibid.

65. Ibid., 486.

66. So Hartdegen, 95.

67. Carson, *John*, 171. So also Brown, *John I-XII*, who notes that any other view of Jesus' *hour* "runs against the rest of the Johannine use of the term and is refuted by the reiteration [later]…that Jesus' time or hour had not yet come" (100).

68. Brown, *John I-XII*, points to these two passages in particular as the pattern of John's usage for οὔπω that "should serve to convince that the phrase is negative [in John 2:4]" (99).

69. See Svendsen, *The Table of the Lord*, 99-129 passim. So also Brown, *John I-XII*, 104-105.

70. See Carson, *John*, 172-73. Contra Hartdegen (95), who thinks that "hour" cannot here refer to the events surrounding Christ's death since (1) there is nothing in the context to indicate this, and (2) "such a reply would have

been unintelligible to His Mother by whom it was intended to be understood," Ibid. He opts instead to see "hour" in this passage as referring to "the time of beginning to manifest His glory through the messianic power of miracles," Ibid. But Hartdegen's first objection is wrong (as we have just shown), and his second objection is just as much a point against his own view as it is against ours. We are told by John that this is Jesus' *first* miracle (2:11), and Mary could not have been expected to understand something she had never seen Jesus do before.

71. *MNT*, 192.
72. Bearsley, 501.
73. Hartdegen, 100, italics mine.
74. Grassi, 79.
75. 2 Macc 15:11-16; Rev 5:8.
76. Grassi, 80.
77. Carson, *John*, 169.
78. Perkins, 113.
79. Lonsdale, 142. So also Brown, *John I-XII*, who writes: "it must be honestly noted that the evangelist does nothing to stress the power of Mary's intercession at Cana" (103).
80. Reese, 39. Brown, *John I-XII*, mentions the possible allusion, but does not press the point as does Reese (100).
81. Reese, 41.
82. Bearsley, 486.
83. Ibid., 487.
84. McHugh, 393-94.
85. Hartdegen, 88.
86. Notice Jesus' seemingly disjointed response to Nicodemus' affirmation that he is from God: "I tell you the truth, no one can see the kingdom of God unless he is born again" (John 3:1-3).
87. Grassi, 78. Italics in original.
88. Carson, *John*, 173.
89. Moloney (33) notes a similar pattern between John 2:1-11 and 4:46-54. There is a stated problem (vv. 3, 46), then a request (vv. 3, 47), followed by a mild rebuke from Jesus (vv. 4, 48), a reaction (vv. 5, 50), and then a consequence (vv. 6-11, 51-53). Both scenes are followed by a parallel commentary from John (v. 11, 54). In spite of this parallel, and in an attempt to rescue Mary from such a strong rebuke, Moloney points out what he sees as three crucial differences between the two passages: (1) Mary is the first person to come to faith; (2) Whereas the royal official merely acts upon his faith and returns to his home to find his son well, Mary verbally communicates her faith by giving directions to the banquet servants; and (3) Mary is associated with Jesus' "hour," and appears again only when that "hour" has come (John 19:25-27).(35-37). But these differences can be considered "crucial" only if we first agree with Moloney's tacit suggestion that they are *significant* differences. In the first place, Mary is *not* the first to come to

faith in John's gospel, John the Baptist is (1:19-34); and he is followed chronologically in faith by Andrew (1:40), Simon Peter (1:42), Philip (1:43), and Nathanael (1:45-50). Second, why Moloney's second difference should somehow negate the pattern is unclear. Of course there will be *some* differences among the accounts in the pattern, but that should not deter us from gleaning the elements held in common. Third, the significance of Mary being "associated with Jesus' hour" is hotly debated among scholars. It is not wise to use a disputed point to show a difference in a common pattern.

90. Bearsley, 484.
91. *MNT*, 193.
92. Tambasco, 29.
93. Hartdegen, 98.
94. Wansbrough, "Mother and Disciple," 128.
95. Carson, *John*, 173.
96. Brown, "Mary in the New Testament," 377.
97. Brown, *John I-XII*, 107.
98. Ibid., "There can be no doubt that Revelation is giving the Christian enactment of the drama foreshadowed in Gen iii 15 where enmity is placed between the serpent and *the woman*" (italics in original). In fact, there is a great deal of doubt, not necessarily over the allusion to Gen 3:15, but over the identity of the "woman" as Mary, even in a secondary sense. See the discussion on this in a later chapter.
99. Brown, *John I-XII*, 107-108.
100. To our relief, Brown makes a distinction between Mary as a symbol and "a later Mariology which will attach importance to the person of Mary herself" (*John I-XII*, 109).
101. Bearsley, 483-84.
102. Lonsdale, 142.
103. Ibid.
104. This view must be held tentatively. There is much evidence in John's gospel that, in John's view, Mary is not to be seen as a disciple at all until she shows up at the foot of the cross; and specifically in regard to John 2:12 she is listed as distinct from the disciples, *MNT*, 194.

VII. Mary in the Gospel of John (Part Two)

1. Bearsley, 501.
2. Hartdegen, 102.
3. Neal Flanagan, "The Mother of the Lord: An Ecumenical Presentation," *Marianum* 37 (1975): 259-60.
4. Tambasco, 43.
5. Grassi, 72.
6. *Catechism*, Art. 964.
7. Tambasco, 30.

8. Paul Gächter, *Maria im Erdenleben* (Innsbruck, 1953), 203-205, cited in Ceroke, "Mary's Maternal Role," 127, n. 16.

9. (1) The title on the cross (vv. 19-22), bound by *inclusio*; (2) the division of Jesus' garments (vv. 23-24), bound by *inclusio*; (3) the words of Jesus to Mary and John (vv. 25-27), no *inclusio*; (4) the thirst of Jesus (vv. 28-30), bound by *inclusio*; and (5) the lancing of Jesus' side (vv. 31-37), no *inclusio*.

10. Ceroke, "Mary's Maternal Role," 140.

11. Ibid., 140-42.

12. Ibid., 145, 147.

13. Ibid., 145. Cf. 149, "In this theological tradition [of conflict between Jesus and Satan] it would be simply incredible that similar reflection would not have expended itself upon the Mother of Jesus."

14. Ibid., 148.

15. Ibid., 147.

16. Flanagan, "Mary of Nazareth," 164.

17. *Inclusio* is usually defined by an introduction to a subject, a temporary leaving of that subject in favor of an aside, and then a return to that subject at the conclusion to the pericope. The alleged episodes proposed by Ceroke in this passage can only with difficulty qualify as true *inclusios* since there is no real temporary leaving of the subject in favor of an aside in any of them.

18. Laurentin, "Pluralism," 89-90.

19. This is acknowledged even by Ceroke, "Mary's Maternal Role," 123. Cf. also Lindars, who notes that, on its face, Jesus is fulfilling the fifth commandment, as well as his comment about it (Mark 7:9-13), 579.

20. Bridcut, 368.

21. McKenzie, 8.

22. Ceroke, "Mary's Maternal Role," 126.

23. Ibid., 124. Augustine states: "He commends His mother to the care of the disciple; commends His mother, as about to die before her, and to rise again before her death. The man commends her a human being to man's care," *Tractate* 8, 9. See also *Tractate* 120, 3: "Ought we not the rather so to take the words, 'From that hour the disciple took her unto his own,' that everything necessary for her was entrusted to his care? He received her, therefore,...to his own dutiful services, the discharge of which, by a special dispensation, was entrusted to himself." Chrysostom states it this way: "When He Himself was now departing, He committed her to the disciple to take care of. For since it was likely that, being His mother, she would grieve, and require protection, He with reason entrusted her to the beloved," *Homily* 85, 3.

24. Brown, *John XIII-XXI*, 923. Brown notes that the *spiritual motherhood of Mary* interpretation does not appears in the history of interpretation until around the 9th century in the Eastern church with George of Nicomedia, and even later (11th century) in the Western church with Gregory VII (ibid., 925). This is not to say that the interpretation of Mary *symbolizing*

the church cannot be found before this time; only that Mary's spiritual motherhood cannot. Brown explains:

> First, we do not pretend that the interpretation that sees Mary…as the Church is the predominate exegesis of the 4th century or even of subsequent centuries. Second, this symbolic interpretation of Mary's role is quite distinct from the theory that Mary as an individual becomes mother of all Christians.

Brown concludes that the attempt by most Roman Catholic exegetes to see in this passage Mary's spiritual motherhood "goes considerably beyond any provable intention on the evangelist," ibid., 925.

25. Perkins, 114.
26. *MNT*, 210.
27. D. Unger, "The Meaning of John 19,26-27 in the Light of Papal Documents," *Marianum* 21(1959): 186-221 passim.
28. *MNT*, 216.
29. Most scholars agree that by this time Joseph was dead. Some Catholic exegetes adduce from this passage evidence that Mary had no other children. It is unthinkable, it is argued, that Jesus would have entrusted his mother to the care of John if she had other sons who could take care of her. But as the *MNT* taskforce points out, this argument ignores the fact that the "brothers of Jesus" are already described by John (7:1-10) as hostile unbelievers (*MNT*, 211 n. 465). See also Svendsen, *Evangelical Answers: A Critique of Current Roman Catholic Apologists* (Lindenhurst, NY: Reformation Press, 1999), 142.
30. Ben-Chorin, 16, italics his.
31. Cf. 1 Tim 5:1-16 (esp. vv 3 & 8); Rom 16:2, 13; Phlm 2, among others.
32. It was not until later that they became believers; see Gal 1:19; 1 Cor 9:5.
33. Ceroke, "Mary's Maternal Role," 133.
34. Carson, "Matthew," 468, italics mine.
35. "Jesus could have been motivated only by the intent to console His Mother in her suffering," Ceroke, "Mary's Maternal Role," 135-36. This, of course, does not exclude other concerns for Mary's physical welfare (such as material sustenance); only that the latter is not the primary concern.
36. Ceroke rejects the idea that John's intent is to provide material support to Mary based on the fact that according to Acts 2:44; 4:32 the post-resurrection community held all things in common ("Mary's Maternal Role," 133). However, while Ceroke is no doubt correct that John's main intent is not to provide material sustenance, his understanding of the "common purse" in the early church is deficient. The common purse seems instead to have been a temporary solution to the problem of supporting thousands of Jews who had traveled far from home for Pentecost (Acts 2:5), were converted (Acts 2:41), and now needed to know more about their new faith before heading home. Such a situation would dictate that the local Christians support these new converts for the duration of their stay.
37. Ibid. 129.

38. Ibid., 131.
39. Grassi, 72.
40. Flanagan, "The Mother of the Lord," 261.
41. Lindars, 579.
42. Lonsdale, 143. It is significant that Lonsdale is a Jesuit priest.
43. *MNT*, 212.
44. Ibid., 288. So also H. Ridderbos, *The Gospel of John* (ETr. John Vriend; Grand Rapids: Eerdmans, 1991), 612-15.
45. Bridcut, "Our Lord's Relationship with His Mother," 369.
46. Ibid., 370.
47. *On Our Lord's Sermon on the Mount*, Book 1, 15.
48. Brown, "Mary in the New Testament," 377, emphasis mine.
49. Bridcut, 368-69.
50. Ceroke, "Mary's Maternal Role," 137-38.
51. Perkins, 118.
52. Ibid.
53. Carson, *John*, 279-80.
54. See *MNT*, 192.
55. This includes his suffering, death, resurrection, ascension, and even the banquet setting in his kingdom.
56. Ceroke, "Mary's Maternal Role," 125-26.
57. Ibid., 148.

IX. Mary in Revelation 12

1. *MNT*, 225.
2. McHugh, 406.
3. Ibid. We will examine the patristic evidence for this later in this chapter.
4. Ibid., 406-407.
5. McHugh, 406.
6. *MNT*, 227.
7. J. Ramsey Michaels, *Revelation*, (IVP New Testament Commentary Series; ed. Grant Osborne; Downers Grove, IL: IVP, 1997), 148.
8. According to Robert H. Mounce, *The Book of Revelation* (NICNT; ed. F. F. Bruce; Grand Rapids: Eerdmans, 1977), the moon under her feet symbolizes dominion and the crown of stars symbolizes royalty (236).
9. Robert L. Thomas, *Revelation 8–22: An Exegetical Commentary* (Chicago: Moody Press, 1995), suggests that the actual location of the vision is the abode of God, but that the vision itself portrays events on earth (119), as though displayed on a video screen. Other scholars, such as G. R. Beasley-Murray, *The Book of Revelation* (NCB. London: Oliphants, 1974), hold a similar view.
10. G. B. Caird, *A Commentary on the Revelation of St. John the Divine* (ed. H. Chadwick; London: Adam and Charles Black, 1966), 149.
11. The stars "should probably be understood simply as a figure to represent the

dragon's power and not as a reference to Satan's victory over some of the angels," A. Johnson, "Revelation," *Expositor's Bible Commentary*, vol. 12 (ed. F. Gaebelein; Grand Rapids: Zondervan, 1981), 515. The stars that are cast down are more likely a reference to the saints that are persecuted, as in Dan 8:10, 24, rather than to fallen angels (ibid.).

12. Satan intends to defeat Christ by his death; cf. Caird, *Revelation*, 149.

13. Beasley-Murray, 192.

14. A. Johnson, "Revelation," 512.

15. Ibid. Even if there is an allusion here to the pagan myth, it need not alarm us—as though we must conclude that John is relying solely on this story and not the actual vision he claims to have received from God. There are many pagan stories that are similar to—and that predate—the Christian message, and this does not imply that the Christian story is imagined. For instance, the belief in a "god" who died and rose again and provided eternal life to individual adherents was quite common in the Greek *mystery* religions of the centuries just prior to the birth of Christ; see John B. Harrison et al, *A Short History of Western Civilization*, 6th ed. (New York: Alfred A. Knopf, 1985), 76, 98. This does not thereby suggest that the Christian story is myth. Neither does the similarity between the Revelation and the mythology of the surrounding society imply that John's vision is imagined.

16. See Johnson, "Revelation," 513 (cf. 1QH E.3:9-10); G. K. Beale, *The Book of Revelation: A Commentary of the Greek Text* (NIGTC; ed. I. Howard Marshall & D. A. Hagner; Grand Rapids: Eerdmans, 1999), 637-38 (cf. 1QH 1:7-12); and J. Massyngberde Ford, *Revelation* (AB; ed. W. F. Albright and D. W. Freedman; Garden City, NY: Doubleday, 1975), 204-205. The parallels include: (1) both portray the suffering of the community in terms of a woman giving birth, (2) in both the woman = Zion/Israel, (3) both women deliver a male child who is the Messiah, and (4) the enemy of the community (viz., the unrighteous community) is also a portrayed as a woman (cf. the unrighteous "woman" in Rev 17). Ford thinks both Revelation 12 and 1Q3 refer to Genesis 3.

17. Beale, 625. So also, Ford, 196; Beasley-Murray, 197; and Robert W. Wall, *Revelation* (NIBC; ed. W. W. Gasque; Peabody, MA: Hendrickson, 1991), 159. The main part of the text reads: "Levi laid hold of the sun, and Judah seized the moon," paralleling the "woman clothed with the sun, with the moon under her feet."

18. For which see Johnson, "Revelation," 512-13.

19. So Beale, 625; Thomas, 118-119.

20. Wall, 159; Beale, 626. According to Beale, this crown "connotes the saints' share in Christ's kingship and the reward that the true people of God throughout the ages receive for their victory over opposition to their faith, over, that is, persecution, temptations to compromise, and deception" (ibid., 627); cf. Rev 2:10; 3:11; 4:4, 10; and 14:14.

21. Johnson, "Revelation," 513.

22. Ibid.

23. Thomas, 117-118.

24. Michaels, 150.

25. Cf. also Isa 21:3; 26:17-18; 54:1, 7-8; 61:7-8; Jer 4:31; 13:21; 22:23; Hos 13:13; Mic 4:10; 5:2-3.

26. Or, as the *MNT* taskforce puts it, the troubled times that inaugurate the messianic age (230).

27. Beale, 637.

28. Ford, 198. Also, Mounce, who describes these birth pangs as Israel's pre-messianic agony of expectation (237).

29. Beale, 625.

30. So Ibid., 625; so also Wall, 159.

31. So Ford, 195; Beasley-Murray, 197; A. Feuillet, "The Messiah and His Mother According to Apocalypse XII," in *Johannine Studies* (Staten Island, NY: Alba House, 1965), 276; Wall, 159, "the faithful people of God."

32. Moltmann, "Editorial," xiv.

33. So Caird, *Revelation*, 149; Mounce, 236; Johnson, "Revelation," 514.

34. So Wall, who notes that whether Israel in general is in mind, a religious subgroup in Israel, or eschatological Israel "remains debated," 159. The *MNT* taskforce suggests that: "the woman is a personification of Israel, the people of God of the OT, and that the Christian adaptation of the symbolism involves having the woman, after the birth of the messianic child, become the Church, the people of God of the NT" (232).

35. Thomas, 120.

36. Ibid., who nevertheless agrees with most scholars that the "birth pangs" refer to the sufferings of Israel in preparation for the Messiah (ibid).

37. It is not our purpose here to take up the discussion between the dispensationalist and non-dispensationalist view points.

38. This does not militate against Thomas' overall view, since accepting that the woman who gives birth is the "faithful community" of Israel does not lead us inevitably to reject the distinction between Israel and the church.

39. See, e.g., 4 Ezra 6:25; 7:28; 12:34; 13:24-25, 48; 2 Bar 29:4; 40:2; 1 Enoch 83:8.

40. Michaels, 153.

41. Ibid.

42. Ford, 200.

43. Beale, 639.

44. Ibid., 639. So also, Mounce, 238; and Wall, 161.

45. Mounce, 239.

46. Thomas, 126. The dragon is expelled from heaven; cf. John 12:27-31 where Satan is expelled when Jesus is glorified.

47. So Beale, 639.

48. Caird, *Revelation*, 149. So also McHugh, 411. McHugh does so inconsistently, for earlier he attaches significance to the fact that in the symbolism the woman cannot be a community, "for in the Old Testament, the

community gives birth to the community, but only an individual woman gives birth to the person of the Messiah" (407).

49. Feuillet, 258.
50. Ibid., 262.
51. Ibid., 263.
52. Ibid.
53. Cf. Mounce, 239 n. 14.
54. Contra P. E. Hughes, *The Book of Revelation: A Commentary* (Leicester, ENG: IVP, 1990), 135.
55. Feuillet, 258.
56. So Wall, 161.
57. Laurentin, "Pluralism," 90.
58. Bearsley, 491.
59. Ibid., 492.
60. Tambasco, 45.
61. Brown, *John I-XII*, 107-109. Hughes, who is a Protestant, also identifies the *woman* as Mary (though only in a secondary sense), but then gives us no explanation for this identification (136-37). However, we find later that Hughes is forced to abandon this view when he gets to v. 6 of this passage; there he sees the *woman* as the church and not Mary (137, 141).
62. Brown, *John I–XII*, 107.
63. Ibid., 108.
64. Ibid.
65. Ibid.
66. Ibid.
67. Ibid., 108-109.
68. See the discussion on this in our previous chapter.
69. Brown, *John I-XII*, 108.
70. Feuillet, 285.
71. Ibid., 286.
72. Ibid., 286-88.
73. McHugh, 407.
74. Feuillet, 278-79.
75. Ibid., 279.
76. Ibid., 279.
77. Beasley-Murray, 198.
78. McHugh, 419.
79. Caird, *Revelation*, 149.
80. Contra Feuillet who identifies the woman in the desert as the church (280) and then adds:

> Thus, after having given Christ to men, the people of God of the old Covenant has become the Christian Church.... We should not be surprised at the distinction made here between the group as such (the woman) and the members of the group (the offspring). This same kind of distinction occurs in the prophetic

texts between the spouse of Jahweh, or the ideal Jerusalem, and the Israelites, taken as her children (280-81).

This seems to be the view of Mounce as well (236, 247). Yet this does not take into account that while the dragon *cannot* harm the woman, he *can* and *does* harm her offspring; nor that while the 144,000 are "sealed" from harm, the "saints" become the object of the beast's wrath.

81. So Beasley-Murray, 205; so also Feuillet, 279; Mounce, 245.

82. Beale, 629.

83. "In an apocalyptic Jewish context the 'woman' represents the heavenly embodiment of Israel," Perkins, 115.

84. *MNT*, 230. The fact that Joseph counts eleven stars whereas John has twelve should not cause us concern. Joseph could not have made himself one of the stars in his dream, for the dream was intended to show that he was exalted higher than the stars as well as the sun and moon. John's vision, on the other hand, must have twelve in order to correspond to all twelve tribes of Israel.

85. So Wall, 159.

86. Wansbrough, "Mother and Disciple," 125.

87. Nissiotis, 35.

88. Laurentin, "Pluralism," 90.

89. Feuillet writes: "The marian interpretation of [this] chapter is *virtually unanimous,* among ancient as well as among contemporary authors" (283). Yet he footnotes this very sentence with the following statement: "Most of the fathers, both eastern and western, seem to have favored the collective interpretation [i.e., the people of God], rather than the marian, in Apoc. XII" (ibid., n. 66). How Feuillet can at once assert that the Marian interpretation of this text is "virtually unanimous" among ancient writers, *and* that most of the fathers preferred the collective *rather* than the Marian interpretation, is quite baffling. Feuillet is likewise wrong about contemporary scholarship, the majority of which rejects the Marian interpretation as the primary intent of the Revelation, if not altogether.

90. B. Le Frois, *The Woman Clothed with the Sun (Ap. 12): Individual or Collective?* Rome: Orbis catholicus, 1954. See esp. chapter one.

91. Hippolytus, *Treatise on the Christ and Antichrist* 61.

92. Victorinus, *Commentary on the Apocalypse of the Blessed John.*

93. Methodius, *Discourse* 8,5. Methodius' inclusion of the "prophets," "Jerusalem," and "Mount Zion" suggests that he should be categorized among those who hold that the woman is the people of both covenants. Le Frois mistakenly places him in his category (1); namely, the New Covenant church to the exclusion of the people of God in the Old Covenant (2).

94. Methodius, *Discourse* 8,7.

95. Probably written either by Gennadius of Marseilles (5th cent.) or Caesarius of Arles (6th cent.), Le Frois, 25.

96. Of the fathers who hold to the *people of God* view over against a Marian interpretation, eight are canonized as saints in the Roman Catholic church—

Hippolytus, Victorin, Methodius, Jerome, Augustine, Gregory, Paterius, and Bede.

97. Oecumenius, *Commentary on the Apocalypse*, cited in Le Frois, 45. Oecumenius betrays Gnostic tendencies when he continues his explanation: "With reason does the vision picture her in heaven and not on earth, for she is pure in soul and body…having nothing in common with earth and its evil" (ibid.).

98. Le Frois, 49-50.

99. Ibid., 50.

100. Andrew of Caesarea, *In Apoc.*, cited in Le Frois, 41.

101. Le Frois, 41.

102. Methodius, *Discourse* 8,5.

103. Ibid. 8,7.

104. P. Schaff, *The Ante-Nicene Fathers*, vol. 6 (electronic version).

105. Epiphanius, *Panarion* 78, 11, 3-4.

106. Le Frois, 42.

107. It is admitted here that in all his insistence that "Scripture is silent," Epiphanius may merely be referring to the *assumption* of Mary, not so much whether Mary is the woman of Revelation 12. It is possible to hold to the latter without holding to the former.

108. *Hymus de Nativitate Domini* 17 (12) 1, cited in Le Frois, 43.

109. The assertion here that Mary was "granted rebirth" by the son to whom she gave birth indicates that our author could not have subscribed to the notion of Mary's immaculate conception, since the latter teaches that Mary was sinless and needed no rebirth.

110. *Hymus de Nativitate Domini* 16 (11) 11, cited in ibid.

111. Le Frois, 43.

112. Exod 19:4; Ruth 2:12; Ps 17:8, 36:7, 57:1, 61:4, 63:7, 91:4; Isa 40:31; Matt 23:37; Luke 13:34.

113. Le Frois, 43.

114. "Here, the resemblance is less noticeable," Le Frois, 43.

115. Ibid., 50-51.

116. Ibid., 51.

117. Quodvultdeus, *De Symbolo* 3; cited in Le Frois, 52.

118. One example is Irenaeus' assertion in *Against Heresies* 2.22 that Christ must have been over fifty years old when he died, and takes pains to tell us that this is the "tradition" of all the elders and apostles. Would Le Frois wish to indict Polycarp with this belief as well, since Irenaeus' was the disciple of Polycarp, who in turn was the disciple of the Apostle John?

119. *MNT*, 236.

120. Feuillet, 285. So also *MNT*, 235.

121. *MNT*, 237 n. 514. The immaculate conception also implies a painless delivery since on this view Mary was exempted from original sin and its attendant consequences, including pain in childbearing (Gen 3:16).

122. *MNT*, 235 n. 512.

123. Ibid.

124. Lonsdale, 143.

125. Ibid., 143.

126. McHugh, 429.

127. Ibid., 430.

128. Lonsdale, 143.

Conclusion—Toward a New Testament Mariology

1. Brown, "Mary in the New Testament," 378.

2. I use the example of the Trinity because this doctrine is presented by many Catholic apologists as an example of how doctrines develop over time. This is then held out as the same operating principle as is used to justify the Catholic Marian doctrines. The NT speaks of three distinct entities, all of which are called "God." The Word is not only said to be "with" God, distinguishing him from God (the Father), but is also said to be God in his very essence (John 1:1-2). The Holy Spirit is not only ascribed personal attributes (John 14:26; 16:7-15), but is also called God (Acts 5:4-5). Yet the biblical writers also insist there is only one God (Rom 3:30; 1 Cor 8:6; Eph 4:6). Viewed in this light, it would be difficult to conclude anything other than the Christian doctrine of the Trinity.

3. Flanagan ("The Mother of the Lord") goes so far as to parallel Mary with Jesus in reference to "self-emptying." Just as Jesus "emptied himself" in the *kenosis* of Phil 2:5-11, so also Mary had to undergo her own *kenosis*: "Mary's kenosis was a giving up, a separation from her son in the sense that his apostolic life, his ministry…[which] would be neither controlled nor inspired by his human family" (257-59).

4. Wansbrough, "Mother and Disciple," 129.

5. J. A. F. Gregg, *The Primitive Faith and Roman Catholic Developments* (Dublin, 1928), 23.

6. Mercurio, 104.

7. Wansbrough, "Mother and Disciple," 125.

8. Lonsdale, 136-37.

9. Robert Humenay, "The Place of Mary in Luke: A Look at Modern Biblical Criticism," *American Ecclesiastical Review* 168/5 (May 1974): 302.

10. Bearsley, 503.

11. "It is a remarkable fact that everywhere Mary appears during the course of Jesus' ministry, Jesus is at pains to establish distance between them," Carson, *John*, 171.

12. Bearsley, 503.

13. What would then prevent us from "reflecting" on, say, the fact that man is made in the image of God; and extrapolating from that the Mormon notion of progressive deification, in which man actually aspires to become God?

14. Kugelman, 75.

15. This in spite of the fact that Ceroke ("Mary's Maternal Role") insists the opposite; namely that according to Pius XII's *Divino afflante Spiritu*, "the supreme rule of interpretation is to discover and define what the sacred writer intended to express" (123).

Appendix C

1. See the discussion in James R. White, *Mary—Another Redeemer?* (Minneapolis: Bethany House, 1998), 117-135 passim.
2. See Patrick Madrid, *Any Friend of God's is a Friend of Mine* (San Diego: Basilica Press, 1996), 41-50 passim.
3. Even if this is not yet a dogma of Rome, it is nevertheless a widely accepted teaching (cf. the *Catechism of the Catholic Church*, Art. 969).
4. Senior, 95.
5. Ibid., 107. The phrase "Lord" is indeed a royal title, but there is nothing to suggest that "mother of my Lord" carries with it a majestic connotation.
6. Tambasco, 40.
7. Ibid., 39.
8. Svendsen, *Evangelical Answers*, 128-130.
9. One must forgive phrases such as "some of Jesus" and "non-God part." No disrespect is intended; the author is simply making use of the language of logic.
10. Augustine, *Tract. in Ioannem* CXIX, 1.
11. Ibid., VII, 9.
12. Ibid., VIII, 9.
13. Gregory, *Epist.* 41.

Index of General Subjects

Index of Biblical and Ancient Sources

1. OLD TESTAMENT